# PUBLIC OPINION

Fifth Edition

# PUBLIC OPINION

Fifth Edition

**BERNARD HENNESSY**
California State University, Hayward

With the Assistance of
Erna Hennessy

**Brooks/Cole Publishing Company**
Monterey, California

Brooks/Cole Publishing Company
A Division of Wadsworth, Inc.

Printed in the United States of America

10   9   8   7   6   5   4

**Library of Congress Cataloging in Publication Data**

Hennessy, Bernard C.
    Public opinion.

    Includes index.
    1. Public opinion.    I. Title.
HM261.H4  1985        303.3'8            84-20073
ISBN 0-534-04920-6

*Sponsoring Editor:* Marie Kent
*Editorial Assistant:* Amy Mayfield
*Production Editor:* Ellen Brownstein
*Manuscript Editor:* Barbara Salazar
*Permissions Editor:* Carline Haga
*Interior Design:* Brenn Lea Pearson
*Cover Design:* Koney Eng
*Cover Art: Stump Speaking* by George Caleb Bingham. Courtesy of Boatmen's Bancshares, Inc., St. Louis, Missouri
*Art Coordinator:* Michèle Judge
*Interior Illustration:* Art by Ayxa
*Typesetting:* Instant Type, Monterey, California
*Printing and Binding:* Malloy Lithographing, Inc., Ann Arbor, Michigan

To Kimberly and Sean
and everybody's children

# NOT
# A
# PREFACE

# Students:
# Please Read This First

You've been reading textbooks since you were five or six. That means you've had fifteen or sixteen years' experience with textbooks, on the average. Some of you—late bloomers, returnees to college, and starters at midlife or even later— have been exposed to textbooks for thirty or forty years or more.

But the chances are that no textbook author has ever told you what a textbook is. You know it's not a novel or a collection of essays or a book of poems— although obviously there can be textbooks about novels and essays and poems. It isn't a biography, and it's not an instruction manual.

No, it's not an instruction manual, although some textbook companies put out things called manuals to be used with textbooks, often containing problems, laboratory experiments, test questions, and miscellaneous study hints or exercises.

A textbook is a description, an exposition, and an elucidation of contemporary knowledge about some intellectual discipline or field of applied science, designed to aid a learner's understanding of that discipline or field. Thus in some sense a textbook is always *An Introduction to* . . . , because it assumes little or no specialized understanding on the part of its readers.

But the *level* of a textbook must be appropriate both to the sophistication and the narrowness or breadth of the discipline or subdiscipline it deals with. By *sophistication* we mean, for example, the difference between a seventh-grade text titled *Human Health* and a first-year medical student's text titled *Human Anatomy*. The medical student's *Human Anatomy* has great breadth; a text called *Lung Pathology* is very narrow.

Enough of generalizations. This book is moderately sophisticated. You need to be a good reader and a pretty good thinker to get the most out of it. We do our best to write clearly, but some of the concepts are not easy to grasp, nor is some of the discussion that involves several variables. (Anything that changes in its number or meaning over time or from place to place is a variable.) And we must use some terms without defining them and make some assumptions without fully explaining them because, of course, if we had to start from scratch with each concept and assumption, the book would be several times longer than it is, and a hell of a lot duller.

To be comfortable with this textbook you need to have pretty well mastered the material presented in introductory college-level courses in American government and sociology. The material in this book has come from many disciplines. The basic ones are political science and sociology, but we have borrowed a good deal of social psychology and a smattering of biology, anthropology, and economics.

Public opinion is, of course, about publics and opinions—(defined in Chapter 1). The making and remaking of opinions is a general process of human life, not one associated only with publics or necessarily with governments and politics. Nevertheless, we think a public opinion text should be frankly political, and it should put opinion making and opinion change in a political context. Therefore it has to deal with politics and with what we call the opinion-policy process.

You need to *study* this book, not just read it. You need to think through it, returning to the most analytical passages several times. When you finish studying this book, you should be able to understand what kinds of attitudes and opinions are relevant to American political life, how they are formed and re-formed in adults, how these opinions of individuals interact with those of other people in campaigns and elections and in the making of laws and other decisions in our political lives.

We want to encourage you and your instructor to do some fieldwork during the semester or quarter if you possibly can. Design a research project—out in the *real world*, please, not on campus. Draw a sample of persons to interview, go out and get their responses, and analyze the data. The research doesn't have to be superscientific, but follow the best procedure you can. Chapters 5 and 6 offer some help, and you can find more detailed advice in any standard textbook on survey research. We find, and others do too, that students who engage in survey research while studying public opinion almost invariably develop a strong appreciation for the variety of public opinion, for the difficulty of its measurement and analysis, and for the recognition of the linkages between opinions and public policy.

Finally, a comment on one stylistic feature of this text. We are concerned about sexism in the English language. We want to help overcome those social and cultural traits that impoverish all of us by discriminating against half of us. Our language habits are among the worst of our sexist cultural patterns; they insidiously suggest that the male pronouns are the proper and normal ones and the female pronouns are to be used only in secondary and deviant cases. A person is always *he* unless we are pointing to a particular *she*.

To observe the pervasiveness of such language and its implied inequity, however, is only to recognize the problem. The remedy, after so many hundreds of years, is neither obvious nor easy. Shall we use circumlocutions for such words as *mankind,* and say "the two-legged animal"? Shall we create awkward neologisms? Chairperson? Spokesperson? Shall we use indirection, plural forms, and the passive voice to get rid of the generic *hes* and *hims* that convention has long approved? We have tried all these stratagems and have found them all unsatisfactory.

So in this book we adopt another device—which is also unsatisfactory. But it has the advantage over the other devices of being noticeable, even jarring. We simply assume an equality of the sexes in talking about generic and exemplary persons. Sometimes the political leader is referred to as *he* and sometimes as *she*. Sometimes the party activist is in her district and sometimes in his district. We think it might be useful if we who are the temporary custodians of the English language developed new sexless nouns and pronouns. We hope our unorthodoxy in this book will both draw attention to the subtle sexism of our prose and hurry its disappearance.

# Acknowledgments

Anything that deserves to reappear should be improved in its parts without being made into a different whole. If a textbook, like a play, bears repeating, it must be because its audience found it to be tolerably true or instructive or amusing. Since many books are not true or instructive or amusing enough to be tolerable, a favorable judgment about a text would alone caution its author against many changes. Another edition is a chance to make better that which is only good enough. Thus, though we seldom change a text basically, we do amend, shape, qualify, and touch up our creature here and there. We take out a phrase or a paragraph that seems to have missed the point (or that hit it once but misses it now since much of social science, at least, consists of moving points) or add to those matters that are new, or old and in need of more words.

In the social sciences we also update. *Update* is a word much loved by publishers. It means two things. First, updating means substituting recent examples for examples that happened longer ago. Such an operation is often a bit of a fraud—as though to exemplify creation we should use Disneyland instead of God's first six days. Second, it means reviewing and incorporating research and learning achieved since the earlier edition; the principal argument for updating a social science text lies in the need to report what is currently being thought and written in the discipline. This is more than the mere substitution of 1985 for 1975 data, or of one politician for another. It is a search through thousands of pages of hardly dry journals and monographs for those publications that ask new questions or (more rarely) supply new answers. It is a sifting and a sorting owed to readers by the writer of texts, and it constitutes the main justification for the textbook as a species of the literary world. A textbook is not so much show and tell as it is reshow and retell.

We hope that this edition will be such a re-vision. We have tried to *see again* the concepts and the raw stuff of the study of public opinion and to report in a way that is tolerably true, and if not amusing, at least instructive.

We are grateful to the following readers for thinking through with us the inadequacies of the Fourth Edition, and we hope this new edition reflects their help: Charles Andrain, San Diego State University; Penelope Canan, University of Denver; James Gregg, California State University, Chico; and Simon Perry, Marshall University.

Thanks to Bill Hicks and Ellen Brownstein of Brooks/Cole. Special thanks to Barbara Salazar, who has to be the best copy editor in the world.

*Bernard Hennessy*

# CONTENTS

## Chapter 12
## Economics, Politics, and Opinions in the United States     204

## PART FOUR
## Dynamics of Public Opinion     223

## Chapter 13
## Communication and Opinion     225

## Chapter 14
## Primary Groups, Personal Influence, and Public Opinion     232

**Chapter 20**
**Opinion Change and Policy Change**                                      342

**Name Index**                                                            355
**Subject Index**                                                         361

# PUBLIC OPINION AND DEMOCRACY

The two chapters that follow deal with the meanings of public opinion. Chapter 1 reviews the conventional ways in which social scientists use the term *public opinion* and distinguishes that concept from values, beliefs, attitudes, and from *private* opinion.

The definitional elements of public opinion—there are five of them—are discussed at some length. There is necessarily some imprecision in all social science concepts, but good communication requires that the meanings of terms be set forth as explicitly as possible. A definitional chapter may not be the most entertaining way to start a book, but so be it: entertainment is not our business.

Chapter 2 is an essay on the place of public opinion in modern democracies. The scope of that chapter is broad enough to apply, generally, to all democracies. But the context and the examples are from our American experience, and this chapter, like this book as a whole, focuses on the United States in the mid-1980s.

## Chapter 1

# The Meaning of
# Public Opinion

Many terms used by students of human behavior have no precise meanings that are universally agreed upon. *Character, personality, urbanization, liberty, order, justice*—these are only a few of the terms that social scientists use, often with more confidence than is warranted, day in and day out. The chemist knows that water is $H_2O$ with, at worst, a percentage of measurable impurity; but the political analyst can never be sure just what constitutes an "independent voter."

Experts use several key concepts and terms for studying how and what people think, and how what they think affects what they do. The most important of these terms are *beliefs, values, attitudes,* and *opinions.*

We start with the concept *belief.* Milton Rokeach's definition seems most useful:

> A belief is any simple proposition, conscious or unconscious, inferred from what a person says or does, capable of being preceded by the phrase "I believe that . . . " The content of a belief may describe the object of belief as true or false, correct or incorrect; evaluate it as good or bad; or advocate a certain course of action or a certain state of existence as desirable or undesirable. The first kind of belief may be called a *descriptive* or *existential* belief . . . ; the second kind of belief may by called an *evaluative* belief . . . ; the third kind may be called a *prescriptive* or *exhortatory* belief.[1]

Of each individual's thousands of beliefs, most are descriptive or pragmatic. They deal with what is, or what is conceived as possible: I believe that . . . the sun

---

1. Milton Rokeach, *Beliefs, Attitudes, and Values* (San Francisco: Jossey-Bass, 1968), p. 113; italics in original.

rises in the east; . . . manufacturing could be done in space stations. A pragmatic belief is an assertion of appropriateness for the achievement of some objective: I believe that . . . I can save enough money from a summer job to pay my tuition for the following year; . . . this flip-top can does not need an opener.

Belief systems are networks of beliefs that are related to one another because of their mutual perceived relevance to a larger belief or to a value (*value* is defined below).

Belief systems may be quite simple, consisting of only a few beliefs. They may be complex, involving hundreds, perhaps thousands of beliefs. They may be narrow in scope, dealing with a phenomenon felt by the believer to be unimportant. They may be broad in scope, covering a most abstract or broadly inclusive value. The religious belief system of peasants in many less developed countries may be quite simple yet very broad, consisting of resignation, unexamined faith, and acceptance of the didactic instruction of priest or mullah. The scientific belief system of a subatomic physicist may be very narrow yet exceedingly complex.

In all cases, conceptually, belief systems are held together ("constrained") by some organizing principle. The organizing principle or principles do not need to be logical, though logic is often one element in a belief system. The structuring principle(s) may be faith, habit, convenience, or even instinct.

The long academic debate about the political belief systems of elites (leaders) and of masses (ordinary people) is precisely about the complexity, scope, and logic of those belief systems. It is generally accepted that American political elites have more complex, broader, and more logically constrained political beliefs than do nonelites.[2]

A *value* is a special kind of belief. It is, says Rokeach, an enduring belief in a preferred end-state or mode of conduct. Preferred end-states—such as happiness, peace, salvation, self-fulfillment—are "terminal" values. Preferred modes of conduct—honesty, cleanliness, loyalty, truth-seeking, and so on—are "instrumental" values.

Individuals have few values and very many beliefs. Values are basic beliefs about what should be; that is, they have "normative" meaning. They are always statements of goodness and badness. They are the most important evaluative

2. The literature is vast. Representative pieces include Philip E. Converse, "The Nature of Belief Systems in Mass Publics," in *Ideology and Discontent,* ed. David Apter (New York: Free Press, 1965), pp. 206–261; John H. Kessel, "Cognitive Dimensions and Political Activity," *Public Opinion Quarterly* 29 (1965): 377–389; Steven R. Brown, "Consistency and the Persistence of Ideology," *Public Opinion Quarterly* 34 (1970): 60–68; Norman Nie and James Rabjohn, "Revisiting Mass Belief Systems Revisited; or, Doing Research is Like Watching a Tennis Match," *American Journal of Political Science* 23 (1979): 139–175; Joel D. Aberbach et. al., *Bureaucrats and Politicians in Western Democracies* (Cambridge: Harvard University Press, 1981), pp. 30–33, 116–119; and Jerry Perkins, "Ideology in the South: Meaning and Bases among Masses and Elites," in *Contemporary Southern Political Attitudes and Behavior: Studies and Essays,* eds. Lawrence W. Moreland et. al., (New York: Praeger, 1982), pp. 6–23.

beliefs. It is obvious that many beliefs, even trivial ones, may be evaluative—such as Rokeach's example, "I believe that ice cream is good"—but the concept *value* is reserved for the important, guiding, evaluative beliefs.[3]

Values are culturally prescribed. An individual ensconced in a culture that justifies "holy wars" may believe that killing one's enemy is a value. Cruelty may be a value: in the eighteenth century the Iroquois Indians placed great importance on torturing their captives before killing them, and expected to be likewise tortured and killed if they were captured.

Values may be absolute to the value holder. But it appears that most individuals subscribe to a number of values simultaneously, and thus there is a high probability that values will conflict and therefore be absolute. Conflicting values, if not perceived as such, require no adjustment by individuals. When values are perceived to be conflicting, they may not be adjusted—the individual enduring any resulting psychological discomfort—or one or more of the conflicting values may be amended or abandoned as necessary to end the perceived conflict. These matters are considered in greater detail in Chapter 18.

An *attitude* is a normative and/or pragmatic preference with regard to objects. It consists of clusters of beliefs and is therefore one form of belief system. In Rokeach's words, "An attitude is a relatively enduring organization of beliefs around an object or situation predisposing one to respond in some preferential manner."[4]

All writers on the subject agree that attitudes are (a) predispositions to respond and/or to react, (b) organized, (c) results of experience, and (d) directive of behavior. Predispositions are states of psychological or neurophysical readiness. They are organized because thay are based on patterned beliefs, consciously or unconsciously held. They have their origin in what one has experienced or been taught (to be taught something is an experience, of course). And in the presence of appropriate stimuli they lead to action unless other attitudes or inhibitory forces intervene.

An *opinion* is a normative and/or pragmatic judgment about an object. Opinions are more specific than attitudes. Opinions are usually consistent with the attitude or attitudes to which they are related in the perception of the opinion holder. Opinions refer to single objects, or to a set of objects taken singularly, whereas attitudes are more generalized and diffused with respect to their objects. I have attitudes about designer clothes generally; I have an opinion about this or that pair of jeans. Attitudes, remember, are predispositions to respond; opinions are responses.

Beliefs, values, attitudes, and opinions may be summarized as follows:

*Beliefs:* anything that the individual thinks is, might be, or ought to be.

---

3. Rokeach, *Beliefs, Attitudes, and Values,* p. 160.
4. Ibid., p. 112.

*Values:* the most important beliefs, both end beliefs and means
   beliefs.
*Attitudes:* tendencies to respond to objects in predisposed ways.
*Opinions:* judgments about objects.

The following example illustrates how they are related:

A. Value: Government is legitimate only if it is consented to by the governed.
B. Beliefs relevant to value:
   1. Government leaders should be elected.
   2. Short terms in office are better than long terms.
   3. The initiative is a useful device for giving or withholding consent of
      governments.
   4. The Swiss government is legitimate.
   5. Proper elections:
      a. Allow any group to offer candidates.
      b. Give all candidates freedom to campaign.
      c. Permit all adult citizens to vote.
   6. The South African government is not legitimate.
   (Obviously there are many more—hundreds, perhaps thousands—of potentially
   relevant beliefs.)
C. Attitudes relevant to value:
   1. In opportunities for political participation, citizens are to be preferred over
      noncitizen residents.
   2. Executives chosen indirectly are not so fully legitimate as those chosen
      directly.
   (Again, it is obvious that there are other possible relevant attitudes, but not
   nearly so many as the number of possible relevant beliefs.)
D. Opinions relevant to value and attitudes:
   1. The British should not let noncitizens vote in their elections.
   2. It was OK for some American states in the nineteenth century to give the
      vote to immigrants who had declared their intention to become American
      citizens (those who had "taken out their first papers").
   3. The U.S. Electoral College ought to be abolished.
   4. The British prime minister has less legitimacy than the French president.

## 1.1 PUBLIC OPINION

Jean Jacques Rousseau (1712–1778) is sometimes said to have been the first
political thinker to make an extended analysis of public opinion. He dealt with
the relations between governmental policy and the opinions of individuals, and
with the problems of majority rule and representation in a democracy. He clearly
understood that opinions have their origins not in physical nature or in supernat-

ural causes, but in social relationships. More important, he knew that all governments rest fundamentally on opinion rather than on law or coercion.

> Along with these three kinds of law [constitutional, civil, and criminal] goes a fourth, most important of all, which is not graven on tablets of marble or brass, but on the hearts of the citizens. This forms the real constitution of the State, takes on every day new powers, when other laws decay or die out, restores them or takes their place, keeps a people in the ways in which it was meant to go, and insensibly replaces authority by the force of habit. I am speaking of morality, of custom, and above all of public opinion; a power unknown to political thinkers, on which, nonetheless, success in everything else depends.[5]

Rousseau understood, too, that in trying to bring about social change no government dares to be very far ahead of popular opinion, but that over time governments may drastically shape public opinion, so that "all peoples become in the long run what the government makes them: warriors, citizens,... or merely populace and rabble, when it chooses to make them so."[6]

Some of Rousseau's comments on majority rule, when divorced from his mystical and contradictory discussions of the "general will," are remarkably modern. On the use of ordinary and extraordinary majorities, for example, he says:

> First, the more grave and important the questions discussed, the nearer should the opinion that is to prevail approach unanimity. Secondly, the more the matter in hand calls for speed, the smaller the prescribed difference in the numbers of votes may be allowed to become: where an instant decision has to be reached, a majority of one vote should be enough. The first of these two rules seems more in harmony with the laws, and the second with practical affairs. In any case, it is the combination of them that gives the best proportions for determining the majority necessary.[7]

Despite some significant contributions to an understanding of public opinion, it would be too much to say that Rousseau was in any sense the father of modern public opinion. His analysis was not systematic; and, as Hans Speier has remarked, "even Rousseau, who put public opinion in its modern place, demanding that law should spring from the general will, still spoke of opinion also in the traditional, predemocratic way."[8]

---

5. Jean Jacques Rousseau, "The Social Contract," in *The Social Contract and the Discourses,* trans. G. D. H. Cole (New York: Dutton, 1913), pp. 44–45.

6. Rousseau, "A Discourse on Political Economy," in *Social Contract,* p. 243.

7. Rousseau, "Social Contract," p.89.

8. Hans Speier, "Historical Development of Public Opinion," *American Journal of Sociology* 55 (1950): 378.

As a social and political phenomenon, public opinion was of little concern to the holders of power before the ideological revolution of the eighteenth century. It was quite clear that the effect of the egalitarian and majoritarian ideas of Locke, Rousseau, Condorcet, Jefferson, and the other thinkers of the period 1650–1800 was to widen the base of political power. Before this period it did not matter much what the public thought—the public had no way of making its opinions either known or effective in determining policy. But the emphasis on political equality and individualism, coupled with the perhaps more important technological and economic changes of the eighteenth century, meant that a growing part of the hitherto voiceless public would be able to influence governmental policy; and when the public begins to influence policy, it becomes important what the public thinks. "Three hundred years ago," wrote William MacKinnon in 1828, "the requisites for public opinion could not be said to exist in any community. They might [be], and no doubt were, possessed by some individuals; but those were not sufficiently numerous to make them general."[9] By MacKinnon's time the term *public opinion* had gained a fairly wide usage among educated people.

James Madison, a few years earlier, wrote that public opinion, as he put it, is the "real sovereign" in every free country, not because leaders can know or follow every majority, but because mass opinions set limits beyond which responsible policy makers cannot go. Madison quickly saw also that a loose, centrist political party could pull together—could "aggregate"—opinions and thus provide a main instrument for keeping leaders within limits acceptable to the masses.[10]

The modern study of public opinion probably dates from A. Lawrence Lowell's *Public Opinion and Popular Government,* published in 1913, and Walter Lippmann's *Public Opinion,* published in 1922. Writers of the 1920s and the 1930s, building on the newly organized concepts and materials of the psychologists, psychiatrists, and sociologists, developed a great many theories and hypotheses, thousands of pages of data, and a good deal of conceptual advancement—attended, perhaps inevitably, by some confusion. One thing is certain: everyone got into the act. Public opinion courses are taught in American universities by political scientists, sociologists, social psychologists, and journalists.

But do these people agree on what public opinion is? They do not.

How one defines public opinion depends partly on what one thinks of it. In 1820 the British statesman Sir Robert Peel thought poorly of, as he put it, "that great compound of folly, weakness, prejudice, wrong feeling, right feeling, obstinacy, and newspaper paragraphs, which is called public opinion." Leonard

---

9. William A. MacKinnon, *On the Rise, Progress, and Present State of Public Opinion in Great Britain and Other Parts of the World* (London, 1828; reprint Shannon: Irish University Press, 1971), p. 333.

10. Edward J. Erler, "The Problem of the Public Good in *The Federalist,*" paper presented at the Western Political Science Association Meeting, Portland, Oreg., March 24, 1979.

W. Doob, in *Public Opinion and Propaganda,* says that "public opinion refers to people's attitudes on an issue when they are members of the same social group."[11] This statement includes most of the factors other definers think important. Another writer, David Truman, declares: "Public opinion . . . consists of the opinions of the aggregate of individuals making up the public under discussion. It does not include all the opinions held by such a set of individuals, but only those relevant to the issue or situation that defines them as a public."[12] Arthur Kornhauser says that "public opinion may best be thought of . . . as the views and feelings current in a specified population at a particular time in regard to any issue of interest to the population."[13]

The following is a tentative definition that draws upon and to some extent synthesizes the definitions of others.

*Public opinion is the complex of preferences expressed by a significant number of persons on an issue of general importance.*

## 1.2 FACTORS IN THE DEFINITION OF PUBLIC OPINION

It may be of some value to examine this definition by looking more carefully at its basic elements—at what might be called the five *factors* of public opinion.

### 1.21 Presence of an issue

There is a virtual consensus among scholars that public opinion gathers around an *issue*.

In common use, *public opinion* often appears to be a generalized term describing something like a collective attitude or a public mood. People often say, for instance, that everyone should respect public opinion, that public opinion is wise, or that public opinion is unwise. Thomas Carlyle maintained that "public opinion is the greatest lie in the world," and Lincoln once said that it "generally has a strong underlying sense of justice." But a moment's thought will convince us that this common way of speaking about public opinion—as if it were an abstract political or social force—implies the presence of an issue or a combina-

---

11. Leonard W. Doob, *Public Opinion and Propaganda* (New York: Holt, Rinehart & Winston, 1948), p. 35.

12. David Truman, *The Governmental Process* (New York: Knopf, 1951), p. 220.

13. Arthur Kornhauser, "Public Opinion and Social Class," *American Journal of Sociology* 55 (1950): 335–336.

tion of issues. Lincoln presumably meant that, over the years, the people, if allowed to express their views on issues of wide concern, will usually choose wisely and justly.

For our purposes, an issue may be defined as a contemporary situation with a likelihood of disagreement. There seems to be no useful purpose in speaking of public opinion on whether people should breathe or trees should grow; an element of controversy must be at least implied. It is also helpful to think of the issue as involving contemporary conflict, to distinguish opinion from law (as codified policy) and custom (as traditional behavior patterns).

## 1.22 The nature of publics

There must be, in the second place, a recognizable group of persons concerned with the issue. This is the *public* of public opinion. The concept of a public that is used here was made popular by John Dewey, principally in his book *The Public and Its Problems.* Dewey maintained that there are many publics, each consisting of individuals who together are affected by a particular action or idea. Thus each issue creates its own public; and each public will normally not consist of the same individuals who make up any other particular public, although every individual will, at any time, be a member of many other publics. For example, a person may be a church member, a bridge player, a bank clerk, a rider of buses, and a member of a little theater group. When an issue concerning bridge players arises, she will join with other bridge players to form the *bridge-playing public;* and the opinion of these people becomes, for this issue, the *public opinion.*

This view of the transient, occasional, and issue-centered public is dramatically illustrated by Marbury Ogle's story of fifty men in a World War II blackout:

> As an example [of the formation of a public], let us suppose that during a London wartime blackout fifty men were lost in the dark and fog of the night. After long wandering, one of them found that he seemed to have stumbled into a blind alley and that his further progress was barred by walls on three sides. He then decided to sit down and wait until the lights came on, or until the dawn appeared. Suppose that one by one, and silently, all fifty wanderers were drawn by an inscrutable providence to the same place and that all of them made the same decision—to await the coming of the dawn. At this point, let us assume, fifty men were all congregated in a small space and each was unaware of the presence of the others. A small crowd had gathered, but we would have been unable to speak in terms of a public, as far as any practical manifestation of behavior was concerned. Each man would behave as if he were alone. Now let us suppose that one of the men struck a match. Those nearest to him then became aware of the fact that they had company, and before long every one in the group would have recognized that fact. From that moment, we might speak in terms of group consciousness; and

consequently, from that moment, we might expect manifestations of public opinion.[14]

We are primarily interested in the issues that are relevant to the theory and practice of government and in the opinions of the publics that form around those issues. But the formation and re-formation of publics and public opinions are by no means limited to political life; they pervade all social behavior.

## 1.23 The complex of preferences in the publics

The third part of the definition of public opinion, *complex of preferences,* refers to the totality of opinions on the issue by members of the public. It includes the idea of the distribution of opinion in its direction and intensity (for or against suggested courses of action related to the issue). But the expression *complex of preferences* means more than mere direction and intensity; it means all the imagined or measured individual opinions held by the relevant public on all the proposals about the issue over which that public has come into existence.

On each issue, the interested public will divide itself into two or more points of view. Not all these points of view will be contradictory or mutually exclusive. The number of views that can be differentiated, however, will be a function of the attitudes and previous experiences of the individuals who make up the public, as well as of the complexity of the issue. A relatively simple issue, of interest only to a small and homogeneous public, will not generate the variety of views produced by more complex issues. The erection of a monument in the city park, if it becomes an issue at all, may produce only two or three points of view, whereas the introduction of a comprehensive master plan and zoning ordinance may produce a dozen or more recognizably different opinions. But in each case the total constellation of views generated on the issue is what we mean by the term *complex of preferences.*

There are, as we know, a number of devices for reducing and making manageable the multitudinous individual opinions that public controversies give rise to. When public policy has to be made (when the issue has to be "acted on" officially), a dichotomous voting situation is structured. Chapter 2 discusses at greater length what happens when citizens are called upon to be for or against a specific proposition or person. But it should be noted that that is a decision-making technique and a way of aggregating agreement and disagreement, not a matter of defining public opinion. Analytically, public opinion should be thought of as all points of view entertained by members of the public with regard to the pertinent issue.

The disposition of the people who "don't know" on any issue presents a difficult problem. It seems reasonable to believe that the "don't knows" consist of

14. Marbury Bladen Ogle, Jr., *Public Opinion and Political Dynamics* (Boston; Houghton Mifflin, 1950), p. 43. Reprinted by permission of Houghton Mifflin Company.

two kinds of people: (a) those who have no opinion because they don't care about the issue, and (b) those who do care but have suspended judgment. Theoretically, the "don't cares" might be excluded from the complex of views at any given moment; politically, however, it is important to consider them as people who might become "do cares" and thereby change the balance in the complex of views. Those who care but have suspended judgment may be thought of simply as representing one view in the complex.

## 1.24 The expression of opinion

The fourth important factor in the definition of public opinion is the *expression* of the various views that cluster around an issue. Words, spoken or printed, are the most common form of expression of opinion, but at times gestures—a clenched fist, a stiff-arm salute, even a gasp from the crowd—will suffice to express opinion.

There is no agreement among the authorities that public opinion must be defined in such a way that expression is required. Doob, for instance, speaks of both "internal" and "latent" public opinion. When the attitudes that people possess in regard to a certain issue "are not expressed," he says, "reference can be made to *internal public opinion*."[15] Supposedly, three factors determine whether these internal opinions become external opinions: (a) the motivational strength of the attitudes involved, (b) the rules of the social group involved (in a police state, for example, attitudes hostile to the state will not become externalized), and (c) the limits of the available media of communication.

One difficulty with Doob's concept of internal public opinion is that it is not clearly enough distinguished from attitude. Another difficulty, and a more serious one, is simply that an internal opinion is not public. There can be no sense of identification among individuals (the *sine qua non* of a public) who have not made known in some way their common interest, no matter how strongly they feel that interest internally.

Doob's other variety of "unexpressed public opinion," what he calls "latent" opinion, refers to "attitudes of people regarding an issue when those attitudes have not yet been crystallized or when they are not being evoked or are not affecting behavior."[16] Latent opinion is what might be called *potential* public opinion.

It may be said that the term *latent public opinion* is important for describing a situation in which a considerable number of individuals hold attitudes or general predispositions that may eventually crystallize into opinions around a given issue. Since political decision makers are interested in future as well as present

---

15. Doob, *Public Opinion,* p. 39; italics in original.

16. Ibid., p. 40. On "images" and opinions, see Dan O. Nimmo, *Popular Images of Politics* (Englewood Cliffs, N.J.: Prentice-Hall, 1974).

states of public opinion (see pp. 103–105 below on the prospective postures of politicians), it is useful to recognize the idea of *latent* public opinion. For those who want to create or change opinions, the patterns of predispositions that are thought to exist in publics are a matter of importance. Generally, it seems appropriate in defining public opinion only to recognize that potentialities for future states of expressed opinion (that is, "latent public opinion") may be a concern of study. For public opinion at any given moment of measurement, expression is necessary.

## 1.25 Number of persons involved

The last factor in the definition of public opinion is the *size* of the public that is interested in the issue. In our definition, the question of numbers is conveniently and deliberately hedged by the phrase "a significant number of persons," with the intention of excluding those minor issues and minor expressions of individuals that are essentially private in nature. For example, we are not really concerned with the distribution of opinion among Mary Jones's friends about the color of Mary's hair. If riots start on campus over the color of Mary's hair, the number of persons, and the issue itself, may become significant; but normally, small groups of persons concerned with essentially personal, trivial, or private matters cannot develop what may properly be called public opinion.

We want to make three points concerning the phrase "a significant number of persons." First, our conception of the size of the public does not require that a majority of the persons affected by the issue hold opinions on that issue. In May 1983 a *Los Angeles Times* poll found that 25 percent of its sample had not "heard enough about" Nicaragua to have an opinion on whether that country was friendly or unfriendly to the United States.[17] Undoubtedly, all Americans are part of the public on the issue of U.S.–Nicaraguan relations, since all are affected by the costs and dangers involved in our Central American relations. Those who had no knowledge of the situation were part of the conceptual public whether they knew it or not; however, since they had no opinion, they were not part of the *public opinion* on the question.

Second, "a significant number of persons" does not require that a majority preference be discernible among those who do have opinions on the issue. Later we shall consider in greater detail the majority–minority problem with regard to opinion holding and the distributions of opinions among members of publics. Here it is necessary only to remind you that clear majority opinions are probably rare; until a poll or a vote is taken, the opinions on far-reaching issues are probably so numerous and varied that a majority preference does not exist. In the very act of polling or voting, however, the preferences must inevitably be structured so that a majority may be (though it doesn't have to be) evoked.

17. "Opinion Roundup," *Public Opinion* 6 (August/September 1983): 21.

Third, effectiveness or probable effectiveness on policy is more important than mere raw numbers when we consider what "a significant number of persons" is. We want to know to what extent the various views held by members of the interested public are effective in either creating or changing preferences of those already members of the public or in attracting nonmembers into the public. In short, does the complex of preferences on the issue have any effect, or is it capable of having an effect, on the opinions or behavior of those who are not members of that public or of members who do not yet have opinions? Since the political analyst is primarily interested in the effect of opinion on political decisions, this problem is usually posed in terms of the influence of public opinion on the making of policy.

Allport believes that the degree of the effectiveness of the opinion is the most important element for analysis and that effectiveness is a function not only of numbers but of the intensity of feelings and of "the *strenuousness of the effort* which individuals will make toward the common objective."[18] He thus agrees (as have all the others who have considered the importance of numbers) with A. Lawrence Lowell, who said, "Individual views are always to some extent weighed as well as counted."[19]

We may say, then, that "significant number of persons" means, in each case, a different and perhaps unascertainable number; the presumption is simply that this number is capable of producing some effect—an effect that is as much a result of the intensity of opinion and the organization of effort as it is of the sheer size of the public.

## 1.3 SUMMARY

In this chapter public opinion has been defined as the complex of preferences expressed by a significant number of persons on an issue of general importance. Each of the five main elements in this definition is important to an understanding of public opinion and to an understanding of how public opinion is differentiated from mores, social custom, or habit and from private interests of no general concern to the larger groups in the society. An *issue* is a matter with a possibility of disagreement that is of some general concern to the community, not just to individuals. The *public* consists of those affected by or aware of the issue. There is no general public as such; there are many publics, each created by an issue in which it is interested. The ideas, feelings, and points of view of the members of

---

18.  Floyd H. Allport, "Toward a Science of Public Opinion," *Public Opinion Quarterly* 1 (1937): 60, Allport would use potential effectiveness as one of the main criteria in selecting issues and publics for study. It is difficult to object to his suggestion. See also W. Kendall and G. Carey, "The Intensity Problem and Democratic Theory," *American Political Science Review* 62 (1968): 5–24.

19.  A. Lawrence Lowell, "Public Opinion and Majority Government," in *Public Opinion and Propaganda,* eds. David Katz et al. (New York: Dryden, 1954), p. 14.

those publics must be expressed; the awareness of the public nature of the issue is itself indicated in part by *expression,* for unexpressed opinions are not identifiable, not measurable, and not public. The *complex of preferences* includes all the expressed points of view that cluster around the issue and are held by the public; the number of such views depends on the psychological factors at work among the individuals in the public and on the complexity of the issue; the resolution of the complex of views into a minority–majority division is a special problem of democratic decision making. The phrase *a significant number of persons* relates to the *size* of the public and means a different number in each case—though not small numbers of people concerned with essentially private matters; *significance* may in part be measured by effectiveness or potential effectiveness, which is a function of intensity and organization and not of sheer numbers alone.

## Chapter 2

# The Opinion-Policy Process and Democracy

Our definition of public opinion is a very modern one. Before democratic ideals and principles became fashionable, public opinion meant something quite different.

Now public opinion means controversy, exchange of conflicting preferences about policy, and a directing force for political elites. The older version of public opinion made it a controversy-*stopping* or -*preventing* force; it was a barrier to debate and dialogue about issues, and it was an instrument for confirming rather than challenging political elites.

Public opinion once meant social pressure to conform. According to Elizabeth Noelle-Neumann, that was the classical seventeenth- and eighteenth-century definition. David Hume and John Locke believed that peer pressure was the most important aspect of public opinion. When they said it was "on opinion only that government [was] founded," they meant that, because people feared to be nonconformist, public opinion legitimized governments and integrated individuals by confirming a consensus about established norms. It also set priorities: "it dictated what problems society [deemed]. . . most urgent." If one wanted to effect social or political change when this older definition of public opinion was in vogue, one had to speak out *against* public opinion and be a nonconformist— "the chance to change or mold public opinion [was] reserved to those who [were] not afraid of being isolated."[1]

The premodern meaning of public opinion has importance today in two contexts. First, public opinion as peer pressure is still an inhibitor of full citizen

---

1. Elizabeth Noelle-Neumann, "The Spiral of Silence: A Theory of Public Opinion," *Journal of Communication* 24 (1974): 43-51; "Turbulences in the Climate of Opinion: Methodological Applications of the Spiral of Silence Theory," *Public Opinion Quarterly* 41 (1977): 143–158; and "Public Opinion and the Classical Tradition: A Reevaluation," *Public Opinion Quarterly* 43 (1979): 143–156, quotations from pp. 154 and 155.

involvement. Expression of minority views is only grudgingly tolerated in many polities, and in some it is tolerated hardly at all. And second, governments have massive resources for creating, strengthening, and guiding pressure to conform. Even the most open and participatory regimes manipulate information, wield symbols of patriotism, and tell outright lies when they believe their "vital interests" are threatened. Under these circumstances there are few indeed who are "not afraid of being isolated."

In later chapters, especially in those dealing with political socialization and governmental relations with the media, we will think again about public opinion as social pressure to conform. In this chapter, however, *public opinion* is used in its modern sense—as controversial exchanges about issues, among the citizens themselves, and between citizens and responsive political elites. This chapter is about the meaning and importance of public opinion for the life of the democratic society. In what sense can it be said—or should it be said—that the people really rule in a democracy? Does the majority principle demand that the opinions of 50 percent plus one of the people on each particular issue be turned into policy? Who *are* the people? What methods are available to make certain that their opinions are properly known? Are sheer numbers enough, or ought one to consider, as many have suggested, quality of opinion as well? These are some of the questions that arise in any consideration of public opinion in a democracy.

We have said that public opinion is the complex of preferences expressed by a significant number of people on an issue of general importance. Note that this definition indicates nothing *directly* about the structure, organization, or processes of any government. One ordinary set of definitions about types of government divides them according to the numbers of persons who exercise political power. Thus the classical philosophers Plato and Aristotle declared that governments in which only one person ruled were monarchies, those in which a few ruled were aristocracies, and those in which many ruled were democracies. The all-powerful king or dictatorial committee may be as responsive to public opinion as the legislature of the purest democracy, but there is a fair presumption that a government controlled by one or few will be less willing to respect public opinion, or less able to measure it, than a government of the many. In practice, nondemocratic governments that are benevolent and successful tend to evolve into democracies; a concern for public opinion has always brought with it a concern for increasing the number of persons who share political power. Likewise, as more persons have gained the right to choose leaders and to become leaders themselves, more attention has been paid to the opinions of interested publics.

Therefore, as a practical matter, democracies are more apt to pay attention and relate themselves to public opinion, and as a consequence to be more responsive to it, than are nondemocratic governments. Although monarchies or aristocracies may sometimes be deliberately responsive to public opinion, attention to public opinion (beyond the minimum level of public acquiescence) is not a necessary part of governments by one or by the few. However, responsiveness to public opinion is an essential ingredient of democratic government.

Our concern in this chapter will be wholly with the relevance and the relationships of democracy and public opinion. This attention is justified because of the theoretical considerations set out in the preceding paragraphs, and because the general focus of this book is on the meaning, importance, and dynamics of public opinion for the political life of our own democracy.

## 2.1 OPINIONS AND POLICY OVERSIMPLIFIED

The *opinion-policy process* is the way in which what people think is related to what government does; no more complicated idea is intended. Simple as this definition is, it contains all of the questions that give rise to all of the thought and talk and violence of all political history.

It appears, at first glance, that the relationship between public opinion and public policy should be a simple one in a democratic society. Democracy is government by the people; what the people think ought to be exactly what the government does.

The obvious model for this view is the small, self-contained, homogeneous community in which public opinion and democratic practice are seen in their simplest form: the New England town. At the town meeting, when more than half of the voters' hands go up, the policy is decided; it might be said that public opinion has declared itself.

But even here the matter is not simple. Suppose the town meeting decides on January 1 (and all voters are present—an unlikely but convenient assumption) to adopt a budget providing $20,000 for snow removal, but that it becomes apparent toward the end of the year that more money must be appropriated or the roads must remain unplowed. What then? A special meeting, or a decision by the town selectmen? If the latter method is followed, the originally well-defined relationship between public opinion and policy is destroyed. The selectmen may indeed decide to follow the same course the people would choose if they were to vote on the matter again—but majority opinion and public policy will then coincide only by chance.

Another problem complicates what appears at first to be ultrasimple. What about the minority? If more than half of the townspeople want to increase the budget by $20,000, what of the views of those who prefer to spend more or less or nothing at all for snow removal? Surely their views should be included in the public opinion that is important to the workings of democracy.

The example of the New England town meeting serves only to indicate that there is no simple relationship between public opinion and democratic practice.[2] The traditional idea of the place of public opinion in a democracy suffers from

---

2. For comments on "the conditions for town-meeting discussions" and their absence today, see Stanley Kelley, Jr., *Professional Public Relations and Political Power* Baltimore: John Hopkins University Press, 1956), pp. 225–232.

several serious faults. It tends to ignore both custom and emotion, it assumes faultless social communication, and it demands what Walter Lippmann called the "omnicompetent citizen." It is probably not applicable, in anything like its ideal form, to a modern industrialized, urbanized, and specialized society.

## 2.2 ESSENTIAL CONDITIONS FOR PUBLIC OPINION IN DEMOCRACIES

All modern writers recognize that certain conditions must exist if popular government is to be successful. One such condition, invariably, is the maintenance of some basic social and political objectives.

### 2.21 Basic agreement on goals and procedures

Earlier writers thought of a society's basic agreement as a common moral and ethical code and a shared conception of the public interest. The traditional point of view is well described by Lippmann. In his classic work on public opinion, he says of Jefferson and others: "In the self-contained community, one could assume, or at least did assume, a homogeneous code of morals. The only place, therefore, for differences of opinion was in the logical application of accepted standards to accepted facts."[3]

Quite probably there was a high measure of value agreement, at least among the franchised, in 1800. Those who did not agree with the moral code could always move on to the frontier. The relatively small, simple agricultural communities of that time probably demonstrated sufficient solidarity of interests and ideals to make such agreement a reasonable precondition for democratic practice. Probably, too, the same degree of homogeneity does not exist today in any of the industrialized societies that describe themselves as democracies.

It may not be entirely necessary for a democracy to have common moral codes or values. Modern writers tend to describe the minimal precondition in terms of procedural consensus and the relative maximization of individual values within agreed-upon institutions.[4] Bernard Berelson has described the necessary homogeneity in these terms:

> Liberal democracy is more than a political system in which individual voters and political institutions operate. For political democracy to survive, other features are required; the intensity of conflict must be limited, the rate of change must be restrained, stability in the social

3. Walter Lippmann, *Public Opinion* (New York: Harcourt, Brace & World, 1922), p.275.

4. See, for example, Robin Williams, Jr., *American Society: A Sociological Interpretation* (New York: Knopf, 1951), pp. 204–205, 209; and Herbert McClosky, "Consensus and Ideology in American Politics," *American Political Science Review* 58 (1964): 376–378.

and economic structure must be maintained, a pluralistic social organization must exist, and a basic consensus must bind together the contending parties.[5]

The nature and extent of the moral and political values and procedures that must be commonly accepted are not clearly understood. James W. Prothro and Charles M. Grigg gathered evidence on the extent of consensus in two American communities. Ninety-five to 98 percent of their respondents agreed on such basic democratic statements as "Public officials should be chosen by majority vote" and "The minority should be free to criticize majority decisions." If agreement to this kind of culturally prescribed abstraction is what is meant by substantive consensus, then the American democracy seems to have it. But when more specific statements were derived from these generalizations, Prothro and Grigg found that "consensus breaks down completely" and that "respondents in both communities are closer to perfect discord than to perfect consensus on over half the statements."[6] They concluded that agreement on democratic principles is unnecessary beyond the most general, superficial, and verbal levels.

Perhaps nothing more is necessary than the symbolic identification of self with nation, and the accompanying feeling that "my country" is based on proper goals and performs justly in an overall sense. These are the sentiments that all opinion surveys since the 1930s have found to be present in the American electorate—and found equally in times of turmoil and in times of relative tranquillity.[7]

Beyond some minimal agreement on values and interests, viable democracy is usually understood to rely on the following institutional and environmental factors: (a) freedom of communication, (b) time for deliberation, and (c) continuing nonpartisan administrative procedures. These factors are critical to democracy. That they be consciously understood and believed in by all the people is unnecessary; that they be understood by those who play influential roles in the opinion-policy process and be acquiesced in by the rest seems vital to the maintenance of a workable democracy.

## 2.22 Freedom of communication

There has always been agreement among democrats, traditional and modern alike, that freedom of communication is one of the basic factors on which democratic discussion and decision making depend. The precise limits of this freedom and the extent to which the individual must be able to speak or write have been debated over the years—and must be debated anew by each generation

---

5. Bernard Berelson et al., *Voting* (Chicago: University of Chicago Press, 1954), p. 313.

6. James W. Prothro and Charles M. Grigg, "Fundamental Principles of Democracy: Basis of Agreement and Disagreement," *Journal of Politics* 22 (1960): 286.

7. See Walter Berns, "The State of the Nation's Morale," and Everett Ladd, "205 and Going Strong," *Public Opinion,* June/July 1981, pp. 2–6 and 7–12, and relevant poll data on pp. 22–35.

of democrats. But there has never been any doubt that on public matters each person must be allowed to think and say anything that does not deny to others a like freedom. On this principle no further generalization is either necessary or possible. Its application, in any community that aspires to democracy, is a matter of specific historical and social conditions and cannot be pursued here.

## 2.23 Time for deliberation

That there must be sufficient time for the public in a democracy to consider all of the relevant facts in the detail demanded by the occasion is another procedural principle that follows inescapably from the premise that the people shall in some way cooperate in making policy. In Jefferson's day there was time for deliberation in solving public problems; this factor may no longer be taken for granted. The probability is that modern technology has placed democracy at a serious disadvantage in its struggle for survival against antidemocratic ideas and powers. Technology is not all on one side. But, on balance, it appears that radio and television can only shorten to some limited extent the time that democracies require for careful discussion of public policy.

## 2.24 Continuing nonpartisan procedures

Neither Thomas Paine nor any of his friends in the formative period of democracy ever used the rather stuffy phrase "continuing nonpartisan procedures." But they thought about this requirement for democratic practice, and they described it as the necessity for good faith and the willingness to carry out as well as to revise majority decision. The essence of this factor is that there must be known and accepted ways of changing policies and changing majorities. It is, of course, related to the ideas of freedom of communication and time for deliberation, but it is more than either. It is the notion that the government must have power to govern, although the power is limited and temporary, and the devices must exist for changing the government and the policy in nonrevolutionary ways. This factor was no less necessary (although it was simpler) in 1800 than it is today. Fortunately, in democracies that have a relatively long history of nonviolent party rivalry and some agreement about bureaucratic impartiality, it appears to be a matter of procedural consensus confirmed in usage. For new democracies, achieving this requirement is always problematic.

## 2.3 PUBLIC OPINION AND PLURALIST DEMOCRACY

Social pluralism is the idea that societies consist of many groups with which individuals identify and to which they give some loyalty. A society is the largest group to which individuals may be said to belong. In clarifying the terms *society* and *social structures,* Charles Andrain says:

> [S]ociety is the most inclusive general concrete structure in the sense
> that a society contains all the other concrete structures—government,
> family, business firm, chamber of commerce, union, church, political
> party, and so forth. As an inclusive membership unit composed of a
> collection of groups and individuals, a society has general common
> concerns. It also maintains a relatively high degree of self-sufficiency
> vis-a-vis other societies.[8]

Government, in the modern world, is the most important social structure, and
the one that can claim superiority over all others within the territory of a society.

A pluralistic society is one that has many identifiable groups, each command-
ing the attention and loyalty of some of that society's members. As a basis for
thinking about the opinion-policy process in America, we need to review briefly
the main elements of the pluralist society.

## 2.31 The fundamental importance of groups

Many early liberal and democratic writers seemed to think that groups were
often oppressive and got in the way of personal development and self-
government. In writing about government and politics, therefore, they tended to
ignore or to disparage group relationships. But the notion that individuals act
singly and separately in their political relations is not now and never was
consistent with the reality of human life. On the contrary, the basic fact with
which all social analysis starts—especially analysis of those modern political
societies that are our major concern here—is the mutual interaction and influences of individuals and groups.

We may categorize the groups in our society in accordance with five basic
types: (a) kinship, (b) economic, (c) moralistic-ritualistic, (d) artistic-
recreational, and (e) political.

Kinship groups, determined by blood or marriage ties of an immediate or
extensive nature, are the principal identifiable groups in traditional societies.
Even in modern societies these groups may be the most important, although they
are relatively less stable and less permanent than in simple societies. Insofar as
kinship groups remain the basic transmitter of social norms and traditions and
continue to be the chief socializers of children, they have first place among the
groups in which individuals share values and expectations.

---

8. Charles F. Andrain, *Political Life and Social Change: An Introduction to Political Science,* 2nd
ed. (Belmont, Calif.: Duxbury Press, 1976), p. 8. For a more abstract and general discussion of the
meaning of *society* and a classical distinction between that term and *community,* see Ferdinand
Tönnies, *Community and Society,* trans. and ed. Charles P. Loomis (New York: Harper Torch-
books, 1963). Tönnies described community as interpersonal relationships that are natural, organic,
private, face to face, personal, and intuitively felt rather than reasoned about, and society as
consisting of interpersonal relationships that are created, mechanical, public, mediated by agents and
groups rather than face to face, impersonal, and reasoned about rather than intuitively felt. See also
the useful introduction to that volume, pp. 12–29, where Tönnies' analysis is compared with
analogous concepts by twentieth-century sociologists.

Economic groups, in the sense in which we know them in modern society, are largely a result of the specialization of labor and the complex patterns of an exchange economy. However, *slaves, freemen, workers,* and *warriors* are group distinctions, partly economic in origin, known to the most ancient societies. Occupational and craft groups were important in Western Europe at least as far back as the Middle Ages. In modern democratic society, it cannot be said that economic factors determine political factors or even that there is an unfailing relationship between economic and political factors. But there are undoubtedly opinion tendencies in each income and occupation group, and these tendencies are subject to reinforcement by the organization of political pressure groups.

Moralistic-ritualistic groups (churches, secret societies, lodges, for example) exist for the confirmation and encouragement of transcendental ends. The need for an ultramaterialistic sense of purpose is so strong in most individuals, and the likelihood of achieving it by private means is so improbable, that moralistic-ritualistic groups appear to be a necessary part of any society. They provide a ritual certainty as an antidote to the insecurity of human life. Equally important in the Western world, they introduce an area of cooperation into a society ordinarily competitive; here (at least in theory) idealism does not have to be tempered with prudence, materialism is devalued, and no stigma is attached to lack of success in competition.

Artistic-recreational groups fill the need for creativeness, beauty, physical exercise, and camaraderie, but are distinguished from the moralistic-ritualistic groups by being relatively less concerned (perhaps unconcerned) with ethical, spiritual, or philosophical issues. Garden clubs, athletic associations, singing groups, and drinking organizations are examples that come to mind.

Groups that are overtly political in whole or in part include political parties (partisan organizations interested in obtaining government offices) and pressure groups (partisan or nonpartisan organizations interested in promoting issues). Political parties will normally not be included in any of the first four categories, but a pressure group may be—in fact, probably will be—one of those groups, participating in the opinion-policy process only specifically and perhaps periodically.

Although this typology of groups in modern society may be conceptually useful here, it is not meant to be definitive. In the study of group organization and function, much more sophisticated classification has been and will be produced. The important point for this discussion is that public opinion is filtered, colored, and transformed in countless ways by individual and group subjectivization of fact and other opinion.

## 2.32 Public opinion, the group struggle, and public policy

Gross measurements of public opinion are interesting and important, but they are not controlling factors in the determination of particular policy issues. All the pertinent studies indicate that generalized public opinion, in the manner of

Gallup's national polls, is not a matter of the highest priority in legislative decision making.[9] Whether administrators make more use than legislators of this kind of public opinion is still an open question; the indications are that administrators, too, are heavily influenced by specialized clientele, other officials, and pressure groups.

Gallup-type surveys between elections are important insofar as they help legislators and administrators recognize and delineate the gross limits and patterns of their political environment. Such reports are keys to the general tenor of public interest, apathy, support, or disaffection in, for example, the overall record of an incumbent, the suitability of candidates, or the fitness of political parties. These feelings of individuals, when measured and collected, might better be called public attitudes than opinions, for they are principally matters of taste, habit, and a pattern of predispositions associated with family, social, and economic factors.[10]

The public opinion that counts in the policy making is a complex of views, group and individual, that should perhaps be called public opinions or the opinions shared by members of publics. These opinions play upon decision makers in a variety of ways and in a medley of voices to influence the declared policy, which is "the equilibrium reached in the group struggle at any given moment."[11] The decision makers—principally legislators and administrators, but frequently the courts also—have a large measure of flexibility, as "countervailing powers" may be played off against one another. In the same way, the citizens, organized into pressure groups, are able to take advantage of the rivalries among competing leadership groups.

## 2.33 A model of the opinion-policy process in modern democracy

With the immediately foregoing discussion in mind, it may be possible to summarize the way the opinion-policy process operates in the pluralist United States.

John Manley agrees that political pluralism is "the dominant theory or para-

---

9. See Robert King and Martin Schnitzer, "Contemporary Use of Private Political Polling," *Public Opinion Quarterly* 32 (1968): 431–436; Eugene Declercq, "The Use of Polling in Congressional Campaigns," *Political Opinion Quarterly* 42 (1978): 247–258; Albert H. Cantril, ed., *Polling on the Issues* (Cabin John, Md.: Seven Locks Press, 1980); and Michael J. O'Neil, "Public Hearings and Public Preferences: The Case of the White House Conference on Families," *Public Opinion Quarterly* 46 (1982): 488–502.

10. Berelson et al., *Voting,* p. 311. On these vague political images and their importance for the political behavior of average Americans, see Dan D. Nimmo, *Popular Images of Politics* (Englewood Cliffs, N.J.: Prentice-Hall, 1974); Dan D. Nimmo and James Coombs, *Subliminal Politics* (Englewood Cliffs, N.J.: Prentice-Hall, 1980); and Charles D. Elder and Roger W. Cobb, *The Political Uses of Symbols* (New York: Longman, 1983).

11. Earl Latham, "The Group Basis of Politics: Notes for a Theory," *American Political Science Review* 46 (1952): 390.

digm of power among American social scientists." The usual definition of pluralism, he says,

> asserts that the American power structure is made up of many competing elites, not just one. Different elites with low elite overlap operate in different issue areas. Political and economic power are by no means evenly distributed among the population,... but most people have some power resources, and no single asset (such as money) confers excessive power....[And] the political system [is] reasonably open to multiple interests if these interests feel strongly enough about an issue to mobilize pressure.[12]

The principal social scientists who have developed the theories of political pluralism are Joseph Schumpeter, Charles Lindblom, and Robert Dahl.[13] They and other political pluralists define democracy as a governmental system in which a large electorate frequently decides upon the general tendencies of governmental action, mainly by choosing, from competing elites, officials to make specific policy. In the intervals between elections the people, individually and through groups, are encouraged to discuss and debate policy and to communicate their opinions freely to policymaking officials and elite rivals.

Within this context—or "paradigm," as Manley calls it—of pluralist theory we can now consider the relationship of public opinion to public policy: the opinion-policy process. That discussion focuses on two major problems of democratic practice: (a) the majority–minority problem and (b) the direct-representative problem.

**2.331 The majority–minority problem.**   The group theory of politics complicates but does not abolish the majoritarian problem in democratic practice. The question of whose interests are to be advanced in the group struggle leads inevitably to the concern for majorities and minorities. We need not go into the philosophical or moral reasons for the majoritarian principle in democratic theory. Rather, the practical reasons for the principle, and some of the operational difficulties, ought to be examined briefly in the model suggested here.[14]

Emil Lederer has pointed out that in a democracy,

> when a decision has to be taken...as in voting for a political party or

---

12. John F. Manley, "Neo-Pluralism: A Class Analysis of Pluralism I and Pluralism II," *American Political Science Review* 77 (1983): 368–369.

13. Joseph Schumpeter, *Capitalism, Socialism, and Democracy* (New York: Harper & Row, 1962); Robert A. Dahl and Charles E. Lindblom, *Politics, Economics, and Welfare* (Chicago: University of Chicago Press, 1976); Charles E. Lindblom, *Politics and Markets* (New York: Basic Books, 1977); Robert A. Dahl, *Polyarchy* (New Haven: Yale University Press, 1971) and *Dilemmas of Pluralist Democracy* (New Haven: Yale University Press, 1982).

14. See Robert A. Dahl, *A Preface to Democratic Theory* (Chicago: University of Chicago Press, 1958), pp. 34–62, for a careful analysis of some operational problems associated with the majoritarian principle; see also his helpful summary note on the literature, p. 36.

for a special measure, this vast complexity that forms opinion must be reduced to a clear-cut issue. The technique of every political or administative body requires the reduction of complicated matters to a "yes" or "no"; majority rule is inevitable whenever unanimity is unattainable.[15]

This collapsing of all relevant viewpoints into a yes-no question, or a series of yes–no questions, is unnecessary during the period of discussion and general consideration within and among the interested publics. But as soon as a decision must be reached at any level, dichotomization is strongly indicated. Mathematically, it is difficult to obtain majority consent for policy when more than two relevant alternatives are presented, and this difficulty increases as the number of alternatives increases. Thus, as a practical matter, a democracy has to make up its mind by means of a series of either–or questions and answers: Shall we adopt plan A or plan B? Or, more typically, shall we adopt plan A, yes or no? This, *at the point of decision,* is the necessary dichotomy out of which majorities are made.

Although public opinion, in its most global sense, is not majority opinion but the whole complex of views on an issue of public importance, there is apparently no way to escape calling the opinion that by a vote-counting process is carried into policy in a democracy *majority opinion.*[16] In the dichotomized situation necessary for making decisions, the less-than-half opinion that remains is, again inescapably, *minority opinion.*

In summary, public opinion means all the views with respect to an issue. Majority opinion refers to those views on the issue when they have been collapsed and compromised, in a yes–no voting situation, into a single view favored by 50 percent plus one of the members of the voting public. As soon as a policy decision is necessary in a democracy, those who decide the policy must produce a majority opinion. This opinion will be produced among the electorate itself in a direct democracy (see Figure 2-1). In a representative democracy the majority opinion is produced in the legislative body (see Figure 2–2).[17]

**2.332 The direct-representative problem.**    Representative democracy interposes a decision-making body between the electorate and the public policy. But

---

15.  Emil Lederer, "Public Opinion," in *Political and Economic Democracy,* eds. Max Ascoli and Fritz Lehmann (New York: Norton, 1937), pp. 284–293, at p. 286. A. Lawrence Lowell also stressed the need for limiting alternatives at the choosing stage. (*Public Opinion in War and Peace,* Cambridge: Harvard University Press, 1923, pp. 127–128, 134–137, 148–150).

16.  Precision requires us to distinguish legislative decision making from election: the choice of one candidate when three or more are running is frequently an expression of what might be called *plurality opinion.*

17.  The model presented in Figures 2–1 and 2–2 is concerned not with the psychology of decision making but only with the way in which expressed individual and group opinions are related to governmental policy. The model itself says nothing about why or how people or groups develop their opinions on public issues.

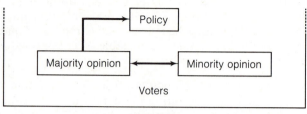

**Figure 2-1.**   *Model of opinion-policy process (on issues)
in a direct democracy*

this addition of the legislative level makes the interaction of public opinion and policy considerably more complex. As in the case of direct democracy, a majority and a minority opinion will be produced on each of the either–or propositions that constitute the last stage of policy making. But in representative democracy, this simple division takes place only in the legislature. Although the complex of views that makes up general public opinion on any issue is capable of being ordered, through compromise, to produce majority and minority opinions, this result is unlikely; and when it does happen, the majority opinion among the public may not be the majority opinion at the legislative level. Thus we need to introduce the idea of *effective opinion*. In direct democracy, and at the legislative level in representative democracy, majority opinion is always effective opinion. But at the level of the general electorate in representative democracy, it is possible (as in Figure 2-2) for a minority coalition of individual and group opinions to become effective opinion. Examples of this case are the long-standing public support (ranging from 60 to 70%) for universal national service, coupled with its persistent defeat in Congress, and the even longer public support for major federal gun control, blocked since 1940 by the "gun lobby" in Washington.

Effective opinion appears to turn on the degree of participation, intensity of effort, and efficiency of organization among the individuals and groups who constitute the involved public on any particular issue. But to make this generalization is only to say that who gets what depends on who supports what points of view, how strongly they feel on the matter, and what methods are available to further their ends. Any more detailed understanding must be pursued in terms of specific issues and in the context of a particular time and place. We may then be able to identify satisfactorily majority, minority, and effective opinion in the given case, but our knowledge of other cases will not be increased. Still, this generalization may offer some understanding of the overall opinion-policy process, and it may also serve as a crude matrix for the investigation of policy decisions on specific issues.

**2.333 Governmental agencies in the opinion-policy process.**   A brief comment may help to clarify a relationship that is not explicitly shown in Figure 2–2. Lines

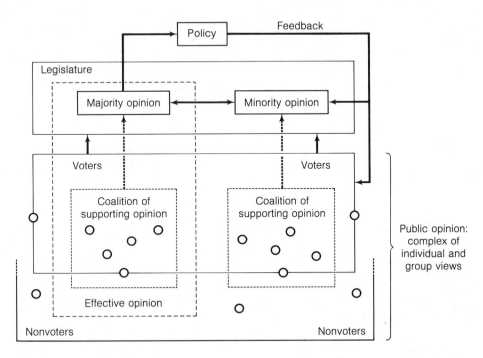

$O$ = political interest group

**Figure 2–2.** *Model of opinion-policy process (on issues) in a representative democracy*

of influences (voting and communications) in this schematic representation run from groups and voters to the legislature. For illustrative purposes this over-simplification seems justified. For a clearer understanding of democracy in action, however, a further point needs to be made—namely, that self-government involves a reciprocal relationship between governmental and nongovernmental networks of groups and individuals.

This enriched view of the opinion-policy process necessitates an understanding that (a) governmental agencies other than legislatures influence (often decisively) policy outcomes, and (b) all such governmental agencies and their individual officials may influence the continuous dialogue through which opinion and policy are shaped.

Governmental officials and agencies—especially executive and administrative but frequently judicial too—are central participants in the opinion-policy process. The definition of problems, the formulation of proposals, even the detailed drafting of legislative bills are increasingly done by bureaucrats in Washington and the capitals of American states. Charles Jones reminds us that the massive "War on Poverty" of Lyndon Johnson's administration was formulated almost entirely by twelve national administrative agencies and the Ford Foundation, "with virtually no consultation with members of Congress," and that "neither the poor nor the blacks had any role in the development of the program which was to affect them."[18]

Administrative officials and agencies may be thought of as elements in the majority and minority coalitions that support legislative voting alignments. In addition to this participation as lobbyists at the legislative level, administrative agencies shape public opinion intentionally through public affairs and information programs and through the effects of experimental and demonstration projects. They influence mass opinion also through the largely unintentional effects of countless bureaucratic decisions in the carrying out of legislative policy and in subtle "feedback" to voluntary associations that tailor their demands and strategies accordingly.

## 2.4 THE LEGISLATOR'S DILEMMA

The obligation of governmental officials to be sensitive to public opinion and in some measure to reflect the views of the citizens is most dramatically posed in the legislator's dilemma: should elected representatives regard it as their duty to vote as they think their constituents want them to or exercise their independent judgment? This dilemma is one that appointed officials share, in slightly lessened degree, with elected officials; but the classic case is framed as a problem in legislative responsibility. "The bald issue," as V.O. Key, Jr., put it, "appears in the contrast between the representative bound by instructions from his constituents and the representative bound by conscience to exercise his best judgment in the interest of the nation."[19] In their interviews with legislators in four states, John Wahlke and his colleagues found that legislators do in fact regard their responsibilities in one or the other of these two quite separate ways. The "delegate" role, according to this study, is adopted by legislators who tend to follow what they take to be the instructions of their constituents, and "they seem to imply that such consultation [with constituents] has a mandatory effect on their behavior." The legislator who adopts the "trustee" role "sees himself as a free agent in that, as a premise of his decisionmaking behavior, he claims to follow what he considers right or just, his convictions and principles, the dictates of his conscience."[20]

Although the dilemma can never be resolved as a matter of principle or "right," it may be helpful to distinguish between the representative's obligations with respect to the basic *values* of his constituents and with respect to the *opinions* of his constituents. *Values* is used here, as elsewhere in this book, to mean long-

18. Charles O. Jones, *An Introduction to the Study of Public Policy,* 3rd ed. (Monterey, Calif.: Brooks/Cole, 1984), p. 98.

19. V. O. Key, Jr., *Public Opinion and American Democracy* (New York: Knopf, 1961) p. 481.

20. John C. Wahlke, Heinz Eulau, William Buchanan, and LeRoy C. Ferguson, *The Legislative System: Explorations in Legislative Behavior* (New York: Wiley, 1962), pp. 272, 276.

term, enduring, basic preferences toward objects; *opinions* are shorter-term and more specific orientations toward objects. To clarify legislators' responsibilities one may say that legislators ought to try to realize the long-term value orientations of their constituents; but on matters of opinion, on which constituents are likely to change their views and on which specialized information  may be available, the legislators' views ought to take primacy over those of their constituents.

This difference between values and opinions seems to be what Edmund Burke had in mind when he wrote his defense of the legislator's freedom of conscience. He says of the legislator's relations with his constituents: "Their wishes ought to have great weight with him; their opinions high respect; their business unremitted attention. It is his duty to sacrifice his repose, his pleasure, his satisfaction, to theirs—and above all, ever, and in all cases, to prefer their interest to his own." Without doing too much violence to Burke's philosophy, one can read "their values" for "their interest" here. "But," Burke goes on, "his unbiased opinion, his mature judgment, his enlightened conscience he ought not to sacrifice to you, to any man, or to any set of men living. . . . Your representative owes you, not his industry only, but his judgment; and he betrays, instead of serving you, if he sacrifices it to your opinion."[21]

## 2.5 THE OPINION-POLICY PROCESS: GOOD OR BAD? A POSTSCRIPT

Is it good or bad that in a representative democracy the opinion-policy process may produce decisions contrary to majority opinion? The answer is, in the end, a matter of individual judgment. It depends on how majoritarian one wants one's democracy to be.

Most of those who made the U.S. Constitution thought the minority decision making inherent in representation was a good thing. The writers of the *Federalist Papers* defended their deliberate effort to block the effectiveness of majority opinion.[22]

But even without deliberate efforts, representative government may frequently make minority opinion into effective opinion. As long as legislators may listen to any one of the numerous, conflicting, and inaccurately measured voices of the people, just so long may they either mistake or ignore the majority coalition of opinion. Whenever policy is made by agents (as distinguished from *plenary*

---

21. Ross J. S. Hoffman and Paul Levack, eds., *Burke's Politics: Selected Writings and Speeches of Edmund Burke on Reform, Revolution, and War* (New York: Knopf, 1949), p. 115.

22. For instance, they declared that equal representation in the Senate would discourage "the propensity of all single and numerous assemblies to yield to the impulse of sudden and violent passions, and to be seduced by factious leaders into intemperate and pernicious resolutions" (*The Federalist*, no. 62).

policy making in a direct democracy), the one-to-one relation of opinion and policy predicated by majoritarian democrats becomes difficult if not impossible to demonstrate.

However, whether it is either theoretically or practically important that minority opinion sometimes becomes effective opinion is doubtful. First, though populist democracy is not achieved and minority coalitions often make public policy, that is not the end of the matter. In the democratic polity nothing is ever settled. All policies are temporary policies. And in the democratic community, as in other kinds of political communities, power makes policy. For the democrat, the issue is not the existence of the power struggle but the political, economic, and social conditions within which the struggle takes place. These conditions and the way they are institutionalized determine whether the policy-making process can be termed democratic in the light of the elements described in this chapter.

Second, majority public opinion may be wrong, in that it may adopt a position incompatible with the future operation of the democratic process. The history of civil liberties in the United States contains many minority defenses of basic democratic rights in the face of widespread, possibly majority opinions that would deny those rights. Persecutions of unpopular people and groups during national crises are too common in American life to justify any easy assumption that public policy invariably ought to be determined by gross public opinion. The witch-hunts that followed both world wars and the systematic discriminations at state and regional levels against racial, religious, and labor groups (blacks, the Jehovah's Witnesses, and union organizers) have all, at certain times and places, threatened procedural and substantive rights indispensable to democracy itself. On the whole, in each of these instances of antidemocratic activity, a minority dedicated to civil liberties has defended and acted to restore democratic practice.

Research of the 1950s and early 1960s indicated that opinion elites and political leaders were more committed to civil liberties than were nonelites. Those findings reinforced the view that a working democratic society was possible even though much intolerance and many antidemocratic attitudes were to be found in the general public. A widely accepted "theory of democratic elitism" asserted that "a democratic system can survive the intolerant attitudes of the masses as long as they are balanced by the tolerant attitudes of the politically active."[23]

Although this "theory of democratic elitism" has been criticized, no one has successfully challenged the central claim that on all verbal measures American social and political elites have greater commitment to democratic norms than nonelites.

Two lines of commentary on democratic elitism should be briefly noted, however. One is that part of the difference in verbal responses about democratic

23. David G. Lawrence, Procedural Norms and Tolerance: A Reassessment," *American Political Science Review* 70 (1976): 82.

norm-holding may be due precisely to the fact that they *are* verbal: elites are educated and articulate; they know what acceptable democratic responses are and have the capacity to phrase them properly. No doubt some of the differences between elites and nonelites are due to these measurement effects. However, the actual behavior of legislative and judicial elites (and probably party leaders as well) shows greater dedication to civil liberties and civil rights than does the behavior of ordinary citizens.

The second point is that elite protections of civil liberties seem to give way when the protection of national interests, as the elites see them, are at stake (for example, acquiescence in the internment of Japanese Americans during World War II) or when mass demands for more restrictive policies (for example, for "law and order") are politically irresistible. To this criticism civil libertarians can only reply that the theory of democratic elitism never suggested perfect and certain respect for democratic norms—only that elites seem *more* sensitive to them than do nonelites.

Reo Christenson summarizes the reasons why minorities who support civil liberties are usually successful but sometimes fail:

> What democracy does need is a substantial stratum of educated persons who do believe in democratic processes and democratic rights and who are *willing* to work for their preservation. This stratum will necessarily be a small percentage of the total population but, because it is concerned, articulate, activist, influential with the mass media, and skilled in pressure politics, it can normally ensure that democratic values are reasonably well respected. The apathy of the average citizen ordinarily enables this stratum to wield influence far out of proportion to its numbers. But whenever the bulk of the population feels threatened from within or without, its security becomes more important to it than those rights of heretics or minorities which seem to constitute or heighten the peril. In these circumstances, no Constitution, no Supreme Court, no democratic elite can withstand a frightened or inflamed populace.[24]

Some contemporary academic and popular writers condemn American democracy because power is not so widely shared as they believe it should be. That complaint is not new. Perhaps, however, it is to be taken more seriously because it is old. Since the beginning of this nation, some people have argued for a much wider distribution of power and much greater participation by ordinary people in decision making.

In the late 1970s and early 1980s even some of the leading pluralist theoreticians lamented the unequal distribution of political power in America. They questioned whether *pluralism* satisfactorily describes group conflict and the way

---

24. Reo M. Christenson, *Heresies Right and Left: Some Political Assumptions Reexamined* (New York: Harper & Row, 1973), pp. 41–42.

policy is made. They also turned their attention to the gap between our ideals of equality and the realities of powerholding in America. Charles Lindblom has even questioned his earlier belief that there is an acknowledged or implied unity of purpose between those who have most power and those who have least power in America. Pluralist thinking takes this supposed unity for granted. Suppose it does not exist, and the state is not a "mutual benefit" institution, but a structure for the suppression of the have-nots by the haves? He also asks whether pluralist approaches may not implicitly admit—even defend—a chronic inequality of power, status, and wealth based on the existence of permanent underclasses and overclasses.[25]

So, in the 1980s, two main antipluralist arguments are put forth. One, based on analyses of social classes, some of which are Marxist in orientation, asserts that pluralist theories serve (intentionally or not) as apologies for domination of ordinary people by economic and political elites. Decision making by compromise and by trade-offs among countervailing groups is said to justify status quo interests and to make stability more important than justice and equality. Poor people and discriminated-against racial and ethnic minorities are especially disadvantaged by pluralist societies because they do not have the resources to compete in the group struggle.

The other antipluralist argument focuses on the lack of community that pluralism implies. In a pluralist democracy group interests are partial, selfish, contrived, and ungenerous. Nowhere in the pluralist version of democracy, critics in this group say, is there a vision of the community as a whole; nowhere is there a generous and spontaneous mode by which the individual can act out a sense of public adventure and thereby gain the highest—that is, a socially admired and acclaimed—personal fulfillment. In the works of these critics the citizen of the ideal democracy appears to be some combination of Aristotle's Athenean citizen and the modern existentialist hero. Politics, says Henry Kariel,

> can be self-fulfilling for the knowledgeable spectator, giving him a more comprehensive perspective not because the ends attained by politics are satisfying but because politics provides a succession of progressively enriching experiences. . . . The criterion for personal action (which is simultaneously the criterion for public action) is therefore wholly pragmatic: *a decision is desirable to the extent that it facilitates comprehension of the greatest diversity of experience.*[26]

25. Charles E. Lindblom, "Another State of Mind," *American Political Science Review* 76 (1982): 9–21. For other commentary on and criticism of group and pluralism theories, see G. David Garson, *Group Theories of Politics* (Beverly Hills, Calif.: Sage, 1978), and William A. Kelso, *American Democratic Theory: Pluralism and Its Critics* (Westport, Conn.: Greenwood Press, 1978).

26. Henry Kariel, *The Promise of Politics* (Englewood Cliffs, N.J.: Prentice-Hall, 1966), pp. 30–31; italics in original. For an attempt to sort out the ingredients and implications of this school of antipluralist thought, see Michael Leiserson, *The End of Politics in America: Experience and Possibilities* (Boston: Little, Brown, 1972), pp. 214–231.

It seems to us that it is important to be clear that *pluralist democracy* refers to a set of political institutions and processes, and not to any particular mix of group benefits. The term describes many individual behaviors, many groups, many issue areas within a political community, the conflicts among those individuals and groups, and the temporary management of those conflicts by majority coalitions in public policies that are always amendable and even reversible. Where policies are made by such processes and institutions, pluralist democracy exists.

Whether the temporary policies thus made are satisfactory to involved individuals and groups is a matter for those individuals and groups to decide. Most social scientists who examine political America find it to be a pluralist democracy. That does not mean that they are necessarily pleased with the distribution of power, dignity, and wealth found in America. They may be, or they may not. A descriptive statement of political conditions and processes is not an endorsement of policies produced at any given time by those conditions and processes. Many people who find that the United States and some other nations meet the criteria of pluralist democracies are nevertheless dissatisfied with the achieved levels of equality, justice, and citizen participation.

We go further. It seems to us that a good case can be made for the proposition that justice, dignity, and self-fulfillment in large and heterogeneous societies are possible only when those societies are pluralist democracies. Simple versions of democracy that rest on notions of ideological or cultural unity can be achieved only by societies that are small and have common cultural values. In large and diverse societies the mutual accommodation of many groups can be achieved only by the civil values of toleration, discussion, and compromise—which means politics, pluralist style. William Carleton was right, we think, when thirty years ago he wrote:

> Democracy is the system of the future because democracy alone is consistent with the pluralistic and multigroup society which industrialism inevitably creates. All other types of government are essentially oligarchic, and oligarchies represent too few groups to satisfy modern pluralistic societies.[27]

---

27. William Carleton, "Is Democracy to Blame? *Virginia Quarterly Review* 33 (1957): 228. For a more recent statement of the strengths of political pluralism, see Nicholas R. Miller, "Pluralism and Social Choice," *American Political Science Review* 77 (1983): 734–747. Michael Walzer argues provocatively for a more equal distribution of social goods within eleven spheres of human values and activity in *Spheres of Justice: A Defense of Pluralism and Equality* (New York: Basic Books, 1983).

## Chapter 3

# The American Voter

This chapter summarizes what we know about the political ideas and actions of Americans in the 1980s. Diplomats, in reporting and updating one another, have a useful phrase, "tour of the horizon," which means a description of the current environment in general terms, with the major facts and concerns highlighted but without much detail. This chapter is a tour of the horizon about American political behavior.

Two preliminary points are necessary. First, the term *political behavior* is a very broad one, referring to political beliefs, attitudes, and opinions (as defined in Chapter 1) as well as to what people *do* in politics. As Chapter 2 has made clear, we hope, voting is the central act of citizens in democracies, and so we focus on the voting act; but all the thoughts and actions related to voting are relevant for this chapter about Americans as political participants.

The second point is that a minority of Americans—those labeled here *political elites*—have much greater interest and knowledge and higher participation levels than do ordinary Americans *(nonelites)*. Let us be as clear as we can about this, too. Political elites are superior to nonelites only in their levels of political interest, knowledge, and power. They are not morally or socially or intellectually superior to nonelites. *Political elites* is not a term of approbation, and *political nonelites* is not one of condemnation. They are general *descriptive* terms; and they are used because the distinction helps us understand differences in individual political behavior, and how those differences provide one of the bases for the way the American political system and its many subsystems work.

## 3.1 THE DEMANDS OF POPULIST DEMOCRATIC IDEALS

Our public school civics texts and our myths about democracy tell us that government is the concern of "all the people" and that we "all participate equally" in working out what is "best for the whole country." Abraham Lincoln's aphorism "government of the people, by the people, and for the people" is the rhetorical summary of this view. These are what we mean by the populist democratic ideals.

We have seen briefly, in Chapter 2, that populist ideals presuppose adult citizens who are individually self-motivated and not dependent on group ties to determine their individual political understanding and policy preferences. This is what Walter Lippmann called the ideal of the "omnicompetent citizen." We have seen, however, that a more realistic view of human behavior recognizes that groups shape and to a very large degree determine our individual behavior. Of course, ideals are not reality. The ideal and the real are each important. Ideals are essential and tell us what we would like to be. The real tells us what we are. They interact at each moment, as the ideal helps us to overcome habit, sloth, and mindlessness and the real helps us to know our limits and to manage our anxieties.

Less abstractly, and to summarize the first point of this section: populist democracy asks each citizen to think and act for herself. But that is not all. Each citizen, acting alone, must be (a) interested in the issues, (b) informed about the issues, (c) motivated by principle rather than narrow self-concern, and (d) capable of choosing rationally from among competing persons and policies. In the next section we shall consider to what extent Americans meet these standards in the 1980s.

## 3.2 CONTEMPORARY PRACTICE AND POPULIST IDEALS

We believe, as an ideal, that each person who has a share of political power should be interested in public issues. Since the earliest days that ideal has been one of the bases for laws and political practices. Both the Athenians and the Romans, at various times, chose officials by lot on the assumption—probably valid in the context of their day—that by and large, citizens were about equal in their interest in and knowledge of public affairs. In contemporary democracy, as one means of justifying universal suffrage and the one-person–one-vote principle, it is still convenient to postulate some minimum level of interest in public affairs for all citizens.

### 3.21 How much political interest do Americans have?

The evidence is undeniable that voters today do not all have an interest in public issues. On the contrary, on many issues the "don't care" group runs as high as the "do care" group. Table 3-1 reveals the proportions of the polled electorate who have claimed to be interested in presidential elections since 1940. There seems to have been a significant increase in interest in 1984, for the first time in 44 years. If this turns out to be real, and not an aberrant measure, then the "don't cares" may

**Table 3-1**   Americans' self-described interest in presidential campaigns, 1940–1984

| Interested in campaign? | 1940 | 1952 | 1956 | 1960 | 1964 | 1968 | 1972 | 1976 | 1980 | 1984 |
|---|---|---|---|---|---|---|---|---|---|---|
| Very much..... | 38% | 37% | 30% | 37% | 38% | 38% | 31% | 37% | 34% | 48% |
| Somewhat ..... | 54 | 34 | 40 | 37 | 37 | 41 | 41 | 42 | 46 | 38 |
| Not much ..... | 8 | 29 | 31 | 25 | 25 | 21 | 27 | 21 | 20 | 14 |

Sources: For 1940, P. F. Lazarsfeld et al., *The People's Choice* (New York: Columbia University Press, 1948), p. 42; for other years, Center for Political Studies, University of Michigan.

be fewer than we have believed, although we must bear in mind that polled individuals probably exaggerate interest to approximate more nearly the democratic ideal.

With respect to the act of voting itself, the patterns since World War II may be quickly summarized: a smaller proportion of Americans vote now than voted forty years ago.

There are two methods of estimating voter turnout. One is to ask a sample of those eligible to vote whether they did or did not vote, and then project the answers to the whole population. The other is to use census data only, first estimating the total number of potential voters on election day, then from official election returns calculating the proportion who actually voted.[1] Not surprisingly, the first method produces higher estimations of voter turnout than the second. Polled citizens exaggerate their participation in elections because they want the questioners to believe them to be good citizens (the general problem of the "good citizen ideal" in opinion measurement is discussed on page 95). The second method tends to overestimate the number of potential voters, thereby *under*estimating the proportions of those who actually vote.

Both estimating methods show declines in voter turnout since 1948; the survey data indicate a slide from 62 percent to 54 percent in the proportions of Americans who voted in presidential elections from 1952 through 1980; census and election-return data indicate the slide in nonpresidential years to be from 42 percent in 1954 to 36 percent in 1982.[2]

Within this overall trend a number of regional variations can be noted. Southern voting turnout has increased. Black voting has increased dramatically nationwide. And, less dramatic but also important, southern white voting is up as the Republican party has become competitive in many southern counties. Critics of American "electoral laziness" say the increase in black voting and in southern white voting is merely from very, very low to very low, and is therefore no cause for rejoicing. A comparison of voter turnout in the United States with that in

---

1. Each of these techniques has serious sources of error. For a good description of the methods and their problems see Walter D. Burnham, "Voter Participation in Presidential Elections, by State, 1824–1968," in Bureau of the Census, *Historical Statistics of the United States, Colonial Times to 1970,* pt. 2 (Washington, D.C.: Government Printing Office, 1975), pp. 1067–1072, and the brief note by Everett C. Ladd, "Setting the Record Straight," *Public Opinion,* December/January 1983, p. 25.

2. *Public Opinion,* December/January 1983, p. 24.

other democracies reveals that Americans are among the lowest participators in elections.

U.S. voter turnout *is* low compared with turnout in other democracies. And it is low compared with those levels of involvement we would like to see in the best of all worlds. There are many cultural, social, and especially institutional reasons why American voter turnout is low; and there is some reason to believe that if the institutional barriers alone were removed, Americans would participate as much as citizens of other democracies.[3] Our record of low and recently declining voter turnout is not necessarily a matter for hand wringing.

Voting is one actual measure of our interest in public affairs. So is self-expressed interest in elections, as reported in Table 3-1. Another measurement of Americans' interest in public affairs is the attention they give to news about issues. Much research has been done on the reading, listening, and viewing habits of Americans. As a people we take in a staggering amount of information each day from the mass media. Most of that information is not political and therefore is no measure of our political interests. Much of it is not even sought after, but comes as a by-product of a search for something else. What we want, in this section, is information about the level of political material that is consciously sought from the media by citizens; that would be a useful index of Americans' interest in public affairs.

Doris Graber provides some evidence on this matter from her recent intensive study of twenty ordinary citizens of Illinois. She had screened out persons scoring lowest on her preliminary interest-in-politics measurements. Her conclusions about conscious search for political information in the media would seem to be applicable to the middle levels of political interest. Most of her panelists had expressed high levels of interest in the 1976 presidential debates. But as she says, "verbal affirmations of great or little interest, by themselves, defy accurate interpretation" and "must be judged by the extent of relevant behavior." On relevant behavior she reports:

> Despite the high interest levels, 7 panelists were dropouts in each presidential debate. Of those who watched, only half managed to pay attention to the entire broadcast. Half of all respondents missed the vice-presidential debate. Two individuals missed all four debates and two others saw only one. Despite professions of high interest, the panelists were not generally motivated to catch up on learning about the debates through other sources. Only 6 reported that they tried to watch a rebroadcast of the events or to read about them in the print media.[4]

We have seen (Table 3-1) that 34 percent of Americans said they were "very

---

3. See David Glass et al., "Voter Turnout: An International Comparison," *Public Opinion,* December/January 1984, pp. 49–55.

4. Doris A. Graber, *Processing the News: How People Tame the Information Tide* (New York: Longman, 1984), p. 119.

interested" and 46 percent said they were "somewhat interested" in the 1980 presidential campaign. Of that same sample, 37 percent said they watched TV news every day and 42 percent said that when they watched TV news they paid "a great deal of attention" to it. About one third (34.5%) claimed they used magazines as a source of political information, and 22.8 percent said they used more than two magazines. Seven in ten (70.5%) of the respondents said they used newspapers as a source of political information, with 25.4 percent saying they gave newspapers "a great deal of attention" and another 29.6 percent saying they paid "some attention" to newspaper information.[5] The picture that emerges is of an electorate in which about one-half to two-thirds pay some attention to political news during the six months leading up to a presidential election, with one-quarter to one-third showing enough interest to use several of the mass media for information and opinion about national politics.

## 3.22   How much do Americans know about politics?

It is easy to show that the average American voter or potential voter does not know much about most of the issues or candidates in elections. Probably the most frequently used measure of the knowledgeability of voters is whether or not they know the names of their major officeholders. In recent years, from 50 to 92 percent of the voters in the biennial surveys of the Michigan Center for Political Studies have been able to recognize their U.S. representative from a list of names; about half can recall the name without a list to choose from. About half the voters know who their state governor is, and two-thirds or more can recognize at least one of their U.S. senators. These name-recognition findings apply to voters; nonvoters score much lower, and there is much regional and subcultural variation in these findings.[6]

With respect to how knowledgeable people *think* they are, the National Opinion Research Center discovered in 1979 that in twelve policy areas from 19 to 45 percent of the public thought themselves poorly informed, and 9 to 20 percent thought themselves well informed. The data are in Table 3-2.

---

5. All data in this paragraph are from University of Michigan Center for Political Studies, 1980 National Election Survey, June/July Interviews (N = 1,408). For more information and speculation on news sources, see Evans Witt, "Here, There, and Everywhere: Where Americans Get Their News," *Public Opinion,* August/September 1983, pp. 45–48. As a matter of public interest in politics, consider the following: during prime time on July 16, 1984, New York's governor Mario Cuomo made the keynote speech at the Democratic National Convention; according to the Nielsen ratings, about half as many Americans watched as had watched the Miss Universe Contest at the same time one week earlier (Dudley Clendenen, "Political Party on TV: Some News Just Won't Die," *New York Times,* July 18, 1984).

6. A 1980 study in Oregon and Washington found that "two of every three voters in the general election electorate demonstrate the capacity of correctly identifying at least two of the four judicial candidates on the ballot" (Nicholas P. Lovrich, Jr., and Charles H. Sheldon, "Voters in Contested, Nonpartisan Judicial Elections: A Responsible Electorate or a Problematic Public?" *Western Political Quarterly* 36 [1983]: 241–256, at 246.).

**Table 3-2**    How well public claims to be informed on issues

| Issue | Very well informed | Moderately well informed | Poorly informed |
|---|---|---|---|
| Foreign policy.............. | 9% | 54% | 37% |
| Agriculture ................ | 10 | 44 | 45 |
| New scientific issues......... | 10 | 52 | 37 |
| New inventions ............. | 10 | 50 | 39 |
| Economics and business ..... | 14 | 55 | 31 |
| Space exploration........... | 14 | 57 | 29 |
| Women's rights ............. | 17 | 53 | 30 |
| Minority rights ............. | 18 | 53 | 29 |
| Energy policy .............. | 18 | 58 | 23 |
| Food additives ............. | 18 | 63 | 19 |
| Nuclear power plants........ | 18 | 60 | 22 |
| Local schools .............. | 20 | 48 | 32 |

Source: National Opinion Research Center, 1979, in *Public Opinion,* June/July 1981, p. 19.

When asked, most Americans are ready to admit that the public at large does not know enough about some issues to make informed decisions.

> "Do you think the public can understand the issues involved in a nuclear freeze well enough to vote on it, or is the question of a nuclear freeze too complicated for the public to decide?" Too complicated: 63%; public can understand: 37%.[7]

## 3.23 Can Americans make rational, public-regarding choices?

The ideal of the omnicompetent citizen says, remember, that voters must be interested, knowledgeable, rational, and moved by a sense of the public good instead of, or at least in addition to, a concern for their own personal good. In this section we look at the last two traits, rationality and public-regardingness.

The minimum test of rationality is whether or not a person exhibits clinically psychotic behavior, or behavior sufficiently neurotic to diminish good judgment significantly. Estimates by mental health experts indicate that as many as one in ten, to perhaps one in seven, American adults have emotional/mental limitations of that order.

One maximum test of political rationality may be the degree to which a person can order all or most of the political items in her universe according to a set of interrelated values, attitudes, and beliefs. Students of political ideology say this is the case with those who are described as "full ideologues." The classic statement is Philip Converse's:

> We define a [political] belief system as a configuration of ideas and

---

7. CBS/*New York Times* Poll, May 19–23, 1982, in *Public Opinion,* August/September 1982, p. 38.

attitudes in which the elements are bound together by some form of constraint or functional interdependence. In the static case, "constraint" may be taken to mean the success we would have in predicting, given initial knowledge that an individual holds a specified attitude, that he holds certain further ideas and attitudes.[8]

Converse's own estimation of the proportion of 1956 and 1960 voters who had "constrained" (that is, fully consistent) political ideologies was 3.5 percent, to which he added another 12 percent that he called "near ideologues." Scholars who have analyzed data from the 1960s and 1970s have found an increased number of voters who had logically consistent political ideologies,[9] but no one has claimed that more than one in five or at most one in four Americans are able to pass this ideological test of thinking rationally in the political sense. Taking all these estimations together, we may conclude that most American adults, probably two-thirds or more, have the emotional and intellectual capabilities to make rational choices among candidates and ballot measures.

The next question asks whether Americans possess a sufficient measure of the "public-regardingness" that democratic theory requires. In their approach to public policy questions, are Americans motivated by a sense of public interest or by self-interest alone? We don't know for sure. The research, such as seems relevant, reveals a mixed picture.

The conventional view in American political thinking is that persons act in their self-interest. The stoutest defense of our new constitution in 1787–1788, in fact, was that it created the conditions for a government that could turn self-interest into a tolerable polity marked by lawfulness, order, and a sufficient measure of social cooperation. James Madison, in his famous *Federalist* no. 10, argued that self-interest, and especially economic self-interest, was the principal motivating force for individuals in politics, that such self-interest could not be prevented or tamed in a free society, and that effective democratic governance could be achieved only by requiring that power be shared by many groups, each of which could temper the demands of other groups and several of which in concert could veto the demand of any single group. Thus self-interest at the individual level could be made consistent with the public interest at the collective level.

The folklore of twentieth-century American politics repeats the conventional wisdom that it is usual for voters to vote their own interests. Candidates search

---

8. Philip E. Converse, "The Nature of Belief Systems in Mass Publics," in *Ideology and Discontent,* ed. David E. Apter (New York: Free Press, 1964), p. 207.

9. For one comparative measure that reports a doubling of the number of ideologues and near-ideologues between 1956 and 1972, see Arthur H. Miller and Warren E. Miller, "Ideology in the 1972 Election: Myth or Reality—A Rejoinder," *American Political Science Review* 70 (1976): 844. In 1983 Charles D. Elder and Roger W. Cobb found "relatively few who might be described as 'consistent ideologues' in their orientations toward political symbols. Although it is impossible to estimate their number exactly, research on public opinion and popular involvement in politics...suggests that 15 to 20% would be a generous estimate. A more stringent reckoning might reduce their number by half" *The Political Uses of Symbols* [New York: Longman, 1983], p. 62).

for what it is the voters want, and the most material of those wants—jobs, housing, subsidies, "pork barrel" spending in the district—are promised or hinted at during campaigns. Scholarly researchers, too, widely support the view that individuals seek in politics what is in their own interests; the mainstream conclusion is that voters calculate in a rough-and-ready way what is best for them and support the candidates and parties that they similarly calculate to be the most like them.[10]

A careful analysis of a national sample of voters, however, turned up very little evidence of self-interested voting in the congressional elections of 1978. When David Sears and his collaborators examined the importance of self-interest in such specific policy areas as employment, health insurance, forced school busing, and crime, as against what they called "symbolic attitudes" (party label, liberal /conservative ideology, and racial prejudice), they found almost no relation between self-interest and candidate or policy preference but a strong correlation between symbolic attitudes and candidate/policy choice. These researchers suggest three possible reasons for the importance of symbolic politics over self-interest politics. One is that symbolic attitudes are some long-term summary of what the voter perceives his or her self-interest to be (for example, the Democratic party is good for me no matter what it or its candidates stand for at the moment); but neither logic nor research evidence supports this possibility. Another possibility is "that self-interest operates indirectly through perceived shared group interest," and there may be, they think, some evidence for this explanation of self-interest by proxy. Finally, symbolic attitudes may be truly public-regarding. They may express the adult's

> sense of the public good, and are quite deliberately and self-consciously given more weight than private considerations when voters make judgments about public policy. Perhaps political socialization teaches people to weigh most heavily the collective good when they don their "political hats," and to weigh their private good most heavily only when dealing with their personal affairs. To us, this too is plausible.[11]

## 3.3 DOES THE MASS PUBLIC HAVE TO CONSIST OF "OMNICOMPETENT CITIZENS"? ANSWER: NO

How much does the general public *have to know* to provide a citizen base for

10. See Anthony Downs, *An Economic Theory of Democracy* (New York: Harper & Row, 1957), and Morris P. Fiorina, *Retrospective Voting in American National Elections* (New Haven: Yale University Press, 1981).

11. David O. Sears et al., "Self-Interest vs. Symbolic Politics in Policy Attitudes and Presidential Voting," *American Political Science Review* 74 (1980): 670–684, at 681. See also M. Stephen Weatherford, "Economic Voting and the 'Symbolic Politics' Argument: A Reinterpretation and Synthesis," *American Political Science Review* 77 (1983): 158–174.

democracy? That question is as important as the question "How much *does* the public know?" Most people know little about specific policy proposals, even about those that are heavily reported by the media.

But do "most people" have to know about specific policy proposals? The answer must be that they do not. Specific policy knowledge is the domain of political elites—of persons, usually group leaders or people who in some sense have representative roles, whose special interests and training make them participants in policy debates. What "most people" need to have is (a) some understanding of and confidence in the ethical and procedural rules of the political community, (b) an overall commitment to order and the rule-making processes, and (c) the willingness to participate as voters in the principal national and subnational elections. Elections are symbolic rather than substantive for "most people"—which means that the very existence of elections that are free and are perceived to be free is more important for the mass public than are the details of policy choices.

But—and note this well—opportunities to gain knowledge and to become members of policy-discussing political elites must also be real and be perceived to be real by the mass public.

In summary, three sets of attitudes and behaviors characterize nonelites in their political lives. First, they recognize the omnicompetent citizen ideal and, uncomfortable with their implied shortcomings, they are defensive, often exaggerating their good-citizen qualities unless they think such exaggerations will be exposed. Second, they regard politics as important and worthy of their time and attention (even as they give little attention and time to it). And third, they recognize that others—those we here call policy elites, often referred to as "they" by members of the mass public—will deal with the details of public policy in an open adversary context in which many "interests" (though not necessarily their own personal interest, however defined) will be considered and dealt with.

Given these three attitudes/behaviors/roles of nonelites, it is altogether appropriate that different kinds of questions be asked the mass public from those asked of elite policy publics. We want to know what kinds of concerns are on the minds of nonelites, how these concerns are perceived in a general political way, and the directions and broad outlines of the preferred ways of managing the concerns that are perceived as political. Thus such questions as "What are the major public problems of today as you see them?" and "How good a job do you think [the president, Congress, state officials] is/are doing right now?" are often asked. We want to know also, and perhaps even more urgently, how nonelites feel about the workings of our democracy: is/are government (legislature, policy, social workers, etc.) responsive? fair? strong enough? too strong? And we want to know how nonelites perceive the opportunities for them to become members of elite groups: does the "system" help one to get ahead? or are there things in the way that cannot be overcome even with effort?

Finally, to make possible some measure of consistency between the preferred values and directions of nonelites and the actual establishment and maintenance of law, elites need the continuous recording of those values and directions within each of the policy areas. Elites need to know what the "latitude of acceptance" is for realistic public policy—what the "ballpark" is, as the cliché goes.

## 3.4 POLITICAL ELITES: WHO THEY ARE, WHAT THEY THINK AND DO

The American polity, like all past and present political communities we have any records of, is one in which some people have more power than other people. Remember that the word *elite* is, as James Q. Wilson says, "a technical term used by social scientists to describe persons who have a disproportionate amount of some valued social resource—money, schooling, prestige, political power, or whatever."[12] Political elites have more political power (usually more prestige, schooling, and money also) than nonelites do.

Social scientists have never debated whether America is run by political elites. On that question there is unanimity. The debates have been over (a) whether, and if so why, American elites are more open, accessible, and democratic than political elites of other countries, and (b) whether American political elites are unified in their ideals and policy preferences or whether they reflect in their diversity the major social cleavages and factions in our disparate society. We shall not deal with the first question, whether American political elites have been historically and are now different from other nations' political elites. Some clarification of the second is essential to our understanding of opinion differences, representative leadership, and public policy making in the United States.

One group of scholars has argued that a "ruling class" of American leaders, consisting mainly of top corporation officers, high political executives, and ranking military men, effectively controls all important policy decisions and governmental activities in the United States. Some of their analyses are explicitly Marxist, but much of their thinking is based on an even older tradition that stresses how a concentration of economic market power is translatable into political power (especially in America where the political power of an established church and a gentry of old families has never offset raw economic power).

Those who think there is an economic/political ruling class in the United States may be called "pyramidal elitists" because they believe that there is a single apex of power, and that the relatively few persons who are at that apex of power are self-conscious, agreed on policy, and concerted in their political actions. The power structure they see in the United States is represented in Figure 3–1. They

---

12. James Q. Wilson, *American Government: Institutions and Policies,* 2nd ed. (Lexington, Mass.: D. C. Heath, 1983), pp. 111–112.

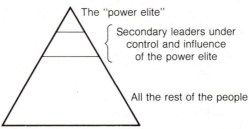

**Figure 3–1.**  *The "pyramidal elite" model of power in the United States*

believe that the members of this unitary power elite are self-conscious; that is, that they know they are in the elite group and know the other members of the elite group—they constitute a network of acquaintances and are in permanent institutional touch with each other. Second, those who believe in the existence of pyramidal elitism in the United States also believe that the members of the power elite are agreed among themselves not only on the values that governments should pursue but on all the principal elements of public policy. Finally, this conception of the American power structure rests on the notion that the members of the power elite work together through Congress, executive/administrative agencies, and the courts to achieve their policy objectives.[13]

The other view of political elitism in the United States believes that there are many political elites, that most members of political elites are specialized within policy areas. There are, these analysts believe, foreign policy elites, education policy elites, economic policy elites, military policy elites, and so on through each policy area. This model of the American power structure may be called "plural elitism" and may be seen as a pyramid with many apexes, as in Figure 3-2.

Plural elitism, like pyramidal elitism, says that the elite few do indeed rule the United States, but that the members of the various policy elites are not for the most part in touch with each other and often do not even know each other. The members of the foreign policy elite, for example, will know who the other foreign policy elitists are and will be in regular institutional touch with them, but they will not know or be part of a network that includes members of the agricultural policy elite or the ecology/conservationist policy elite. Plural elitists also believe, and find in their investigations, that members of the same policy elites are not agreed among themselves on the values or specific governmental policies that ought to be enforced and do not work together; on the contrary, the plural elitists believe the very heart of pluralist democracy in the United States to be the

---

13. The classic works are C. Wright Mills, *The Power Elite* (New York: Oxford University Press, 1956), and G. William Domhof, *Who Rules America?* (Englewood Cliffs, N.J.: Prentice-Hall, 1967). See also two further works by Domhof, *The Higher Circles: Governing Class in America* (New York: Vintage Books, 1970) and *Who Really Rules?* (Santa Monica: Goodyear, 1978).

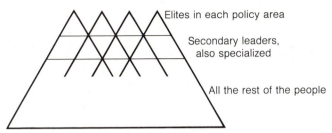

Elites in each policy area

Secondary leaders,
also specialized

All the rest of the people

**Figure 3–2.**    *The "plural elite" model of power in the United States*

conflicts and disagreements within the policy elites, policy area by policy area.[14]

Do American political elitists know one another and constitute a self-conscious network, as pyramidal elitist theory contends, or are there many groups of separately acting elites, as plural elitist theory would have us believe? Those who assert that the United States is ruled by a single, pyramidal elite do indeed find impressive evidence in the world of corporations, finance, and prestigious law firms that there is great overlap of executive officers. Floyd Hunter asked top-ranked business leaders to name the most powerful of their kind and found that "between one hundred and two hundred were consistently chosen as top leaders...of national policy-making stature."[15] Thomas Dye found that 15 percent of a large, diverse sample consisting of 4,325 top corporate officers, 2,705 "public interest" leaders (mass media, education, law, foundations, and civic organizations), and 284 governmental leaders held more than one top position at a time. Though only 15 percent of the individuals were "interlockers" (his term), 32 percent of the top positions were interlocked. He identified a top-top group of thirty-one persons (twenty-nine men and two women) who held six or more top positions concurrently in 1980–1981, and concluded that

> by any criteria whatsoever, these individuals must be judged important figures in America. The fact that our investigation of positional overlap revealed such impressive names lends some face validity to the assertion that interlocking is a source of authority and power in society.[16]

14. For "plural elite" thinking, see Robert Dahl, *Pluralist Democracy in the United States: Conflict and Consent* (Chicago: Rand McNally, 1967); Arnold M. Rose, *The Power Structure* (New York: Oxford University Press, 1967); Kenneth Prewitt and Alan Stone, *The Ruling Elites: Elite Theory, Power, and American Democracy* (New York: Harper & Row, 1973); and Charles E. Lindblom, *Politics and Markets* (New York: Basic Books, 1977).

15. Floyd Hunter, *Top Leadership, U.S.A.* (Chapel Hill: University of North Carolina Press, 1959), p. 176.

16. Thomas R. Dye, *Who's Running America? The Reagan Years,* 3rd ed. (Englewood Cliffs, N.J.: Prentice-Hall, 1983), p. 172.

Dye also points out that members of this small top-top group know each other socially and "come together not only in multiple corporate boardrooms, but also at cultural and civic events, charitable endeavors, foundation meetings, and university trustees and alumni get-togethers."[17] But he also says "it should be remembered that most of the remaining 85 percent of top position-holders were 'specialists.'" And he found that between 1970 and 1980 there had been a modest but "real" decline of interlockers, from 20 to 15 percent.[18]

Do American elites agree with one another about all the basic political values and most of the main policy choices? The pyramidal elitist view says they do; the plural elitist view says they do not. A large study of American leaders in 1976 (N=2,282) and again in 1980 (N=2,502) was designed, in part, to probe this question. Significant differences among perceptions, priority values, and policy choices were found among three groups of elites whom the study authors label as "cold war internationalists," "post–cold war internationalists," and "semi-isolationists."[19] They concluded that the schisms of the Vietnam controversies of 1965–1974 were still evident in their 1980 survey, and that as of 1983

> American leaders are strikingly divided on a broad range of foreign policy questions; there is good reason to believe that dissensus far exceeds that of the period between Pearl Harbor and the mid-1960s...[and] cleavages appear to be at least as strong as those that characterized the United States during the years preceding World War II.[20]

While this study tells us nothing about domestic policy cleavages among American elites, most researchers conclude that consensus has traditionally been greater on foreign policy than on domestic policy.

The last characteristic that differentiates pyramidal elites from plural elites is the degree to which elites interact and cooperate with one another to achieve their common values and to manage the policy conflicts that divide them. This is what analysts call "elite integration." How much of it is there in contemporary American politics?

One study in the 1970s obtained data from 545 leaders who were described as "top position holders" in "key organizations in each [of seven] sector[s]," the sectors being political office, civil service, business, labor unions, news media, voluntary associations, and academic professions. The investigators found thirty-two "cohesive groups" of leaders in the American national network. One

17. Ibid., p. 175.

18. Ibid., p. 176.

19. Ole R. Holsti and James N. Rosenau, *American Leadership in World Affairs: Vietnam and the Breakdown of Consensus* (Boston: Allen & Unwin, 1984). See especially Chapter 4, "A Leadership Divided: Who Are the Cold War Internationalists, Post–Cold War Internationalists, and Semi-Isolationists?" pp. 140–178.

20. Ibid., p. 249.

"large, inclusive social circle" consisted of "227 persons...having numerous connections to other circles and cliques." Of the thirty-one smaller circles and cliques of interactors, twenty-six were specialized in a single policy area, such as ecology, economic policy, or military policy, and five dealt with several policy areas. Their discovery of these widespread patterns of elite integrations evoked this generalization:

> ...linkages between sectors are more evenly distributed than the power elite and ruling class models would lead us to expect, and they are more frequent, especially among the most central persons, than the plural elite model seems to imply.[21]

They conclude that neither the pyramidal elite nor the plural elite view is accurate, though elements of both exist. They say America has a "consensually integrated elite" leadership.

> There is an inclusive network of formal and informal communica-tion, friendship, and influence-wielding among top position holders in all major elite groups.... No single elite group predominates in the network. Instead, interaction among all elite groups is frequent, and it is markedly centralized in and between a relatively small number of persons for all major groups. Because ready access to key decision makers is the structure's *raison d'être*, political-governmental elites bulk large as the targets of elite interaction and as switching points in the interaction network.[22]

This view of "consensually integrated elites" is consistent with Thomas Dye's 1983 conclusion about the nature of political elitism in the United States, illustrated in Figure 3-3.

Finally, from many sources, Figure 3-4 represents the best estimates of the proportions of American adults in five categories of political activity, from most to least active. The term *mobilizable* refers to those who, on the basis of their sustained knowledge and organizational memberships, can be quickly called upon to exert effective influence on specific policy issues.[23] *Attentive* means they are consistently interested in politics, seek out political information, and fre-quently talk politics with friends and acquaintances. Political elites are all those who are fully participant and many of the mobilizable and attentive as well, depending on time, place, and issue.

---

21. John Higley and Gwen Moore, "Elite Integration in the United States and Australia," *American Political Science Review* 75 (1981): 593.

22. Ibid., p.584.

23. On "mobilizable" and "attentive" citizens see James N. Rosenau, *Citizenship between Elections* (New York: Free Press, 1974). See also Kenneth P. Adler, "Polling the Attentive Public," in *Polling and the Democratic Consensus,* ed. L. John Martin, *The Annals* 472 (March 1984:): 143–154.

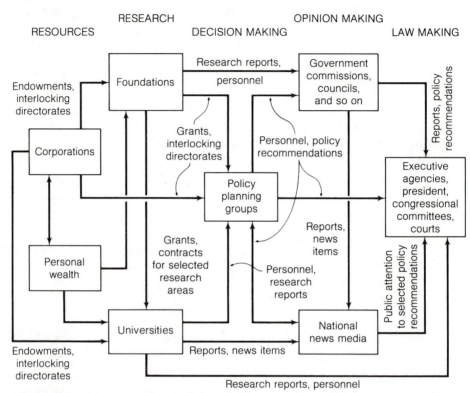

**Figure 3-3.** *The policy process: the view from the top* (Thomas R. Dye, *Who's Running America? The Reagan Years,* 3rd ed., © 1983, p. 240. Reprinted by permission of Prentice-Hall, Inc. Englewood Cliffs, N.J.)

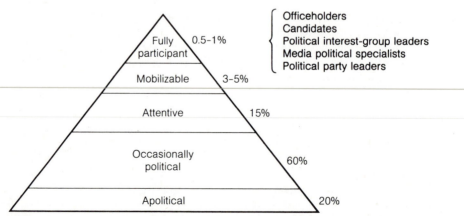

**Figure 3-4.** *Proportions of political actives and inactives among American adults*

# MEASUREMENT

In the 1982 election for governor of California, about 7.75 million people voted. That number represented 69.8 percent of registered voters, or 49.1 percent of the estimated eligible adults. Was that public opinion? Certainly the turnout represented by those figures was in some sense an expression and a measurement of public opinion.

But elections are crude—if important—measures of public opinion. The complexity and subtlety of popular views on public issues, as defined in the preceding chapters, need to be explored and measured in a variety of ways. In Chapter 4, opinion measurement is considered as a natural and commonplace activity of all people, especially political leaders, and as a necessary part of the democratic process. Chapter 5 then describes the objectives and procedures of scientific opinion research.

# Opinion Measurement:
# Prescientific and Informal

The measurement of public opinion is, in its simplest sense, finding out what people think. So defined, it is as old as society; and it developed, without being named, along with the other characteristics that marked the latter stages of the descent of the human race: language, the division of labor, and habits of cooperative work.

The differentiation of social status in even the smallest and simplest societies occurred long before there were any reliable records of precisely how such differentiations developed. For our purposes, it is enough to note that social differentiation was always accompanied by the development of some kind of communication, by *gestures* and *verbalization,* and that it created situations in which it was frequently important for some people to know what certain numbers of the others thought about matters of common interest. One cannot imagine a simple community without also imagining a collection of the more influential men sitting around a fire or flat rock—the "council rocks" of American Indians are still common landmarks in many parts of the United States— discussing things that were important to them all.

Although the societies and the meetings were vastly different, the council of Mesopotamian warriors in 5000 B.C. and the yearly New England town meeting served the same purposes for running society. *Functionally,* these meetings were similar. Each constituted, among other things, a *measurement of opinion.* By the time of the development of New England self-government in the seventeenth and eighteenth centuries, there were other ways of measuring opinion: church meetings, handbills and simple newspapers, officials whose job it was to communicate regularly with the people regarding public matters. But the *meeting* and the *vote,* or the "sense of the meeting," have been fundamental ingredients in the measuring of opinion for thousands of years.

## 4.1 THE POLITICAL IMPORTANCE OF OPINION MEASUREMENT

All communities have some concern for the opinions of the people. The power holders of every society pay some attention to the thinking and desires of the masses. Even before political leadership was distinguishable from religious or tribal-blood leadership this must have been the case to some degree.

Later, when the division of statuses produced kings, no king was ever absolutely absolute. Even when absolutism was a fairly respectable theory, no king could afford to ignore the wishes of the population completely.

We may differentiate between what may be called positive public opinion, on the one hand, and mere acquiescence, on the other. It can be argued that all rulers of all times have needed the acquiescence of the masses but not necessarily the support of positive public opinion. To the extent that the masses were uninterested, unable, or unwilling to think or act with regard to public affairs, positive public opinion was of no consequence. Until fairly recently, as anthropological time goes, the masses had no education, no information from outside their own villages, and no energy left over after obtaining scant physical necessities. They had few or no opinions regarding public matters.

Daniel Lerner found that even today many Third World peasants are unable to conceive of public events outside their own villages. They cannot imagine what the nonpersonal world is like. They are unable to place themselves in the role of another person. When interviewers asked Turkish villagers questions that required them to imagine themselves as head of a government, editor of a paper, or manager of a radio station, they often simply could not respond. Lerner says:

> The strenuousness of such demands upon persons untutored in empathic skills was underlined by the many respondents, in every country, who thought of suicide rather than imagine themselves in these exalted ranks. "My God! How can you say such a thing?" gasped the shepherd, when Tosun put such questions to him.[1]

This lack of opinion among the masses and an inability even to conceive of the holding of opinions on matters relating to large publics were the almost universal condition until well into the modern period of Western history.

Concurrent with these social and economic factors, which prevented any real sense of publicness in the opinions of the masses, was the prevailing doctrine of premodern times that the masses had no business entertaining notions about public matters even if they were capable of doing so. The doctrine of the divine right of priests and kings persuaded rulers and ruled alike that it was not the

---

1. Daniel Lerner, *The Passing of Traditional Society* (New York: Free Press, 1958), p. 70. Lerner's discussion of lack of "empathy" ("the capacity to see oneself in the other fellow's situation") and the consequences of this lack for the modernization of traditional societies is a vital contribution and part of a pioneering book that no student of human behavior should fail to read.

business of the people to think or say anything except those simple thoughts and words that were appropriate to that station in life to which they had been called by an omniscient Providence.

Thus both theoretical and practical elements combined until fairly recently to impede the development of positive public opinion. The mute acquiescence of the masses was mandate enough to legitimate, in this sense, whatever government existed.

Gradually, however, technological changes created some leisure and freed a few persons from the exigencies of mere survival. With the discovery of new land and the rediscovery of old learning there came into existence in the Western world a new set of beliefs about the relationship between the rulers and the ruled.

Niccolò Machiavelli, whom political scientists both claim and deny as patron saint, stands at the bridge between old and new. He recognized that it is useful and preferable to gain the positive support of the people but that the passive toleration of the masses is a necessary minimum for stability. The ruler, he says,

> who has but a few enemies can easily make sure of them without great scandal, but he who has the masses hostile to him can never make sure of them, and the more cruelty he employs the feebler will his authority become; so that his best remedy is to try and secure the good will of the people.[2]

## 4.2 POLITICAL REPRESENTATION AND OPINION MEASUREMENT

When the number of persons whose opinions count is very small, as in primitive societies and in tiny self-governing communities, the opinions of all can be measured. Nonpublic organizations, such as church congregations, social clubs, and economic groups, may also conduct their business by meetings of the whole membership, by mail balloting, or by questionnaires sent to their members. As we shall see, these private *primary groups* constitute an important element in the larger network of public opinion. But restricting our consideration to governmental units, we may say that only the unlimited town meeting and perhaps some special districts of very small power and geography can be based on the idea that the opinions of *all* the voters will be measured. Classical *direct democracy* is nearly gone in America.

Today many New England towns have adopted the "limited town meeting," in which a number of persons are chosen to vote annually on the questions placed before them by the town officials. In these meetings, the opinions of some are assumed to be *representative* of the opinions of all. With the choosing of such persons to decide on the issues in the name of all townspeople, direct democracy,

---

2. Niccolò Machiavelli, *The Discourses* (New York: Random House, Modern Library Edition, 1940), p. 162.

with its one-step measurement of opinion, has been abandoned. In the election of representatives, the opinion of the whole voting population is still asked, but only on the question of which persons are to be chosen to decide for a limited time on the issues before the meeting. Thereafter, on all matters except new elections, public opinion cannot be measured by a simple vote of the whole population, but only by a two-step process, in which the vote of the representative meeting is assumed to *reflect* the opinions of all the people. That this process introduces distortion is certain. But it is equally certain that the public business in all except the smallest communities could not be carried out otherwise.

Size, then, is the factor that limits the direct measurement of opinion. This is not the case when voting for candidates or for referenda is the means for measuring opinions. It is, however, as we shall see, the case with other means for measuring opinion, such as personal interviewing. Assemblies of constituents—such as town meetings or rallies—are simply not effective when more than three or four hundred people are in attendance. The member of Congress or congressional candidate cannot obtain the opinions of all voters (or all who are eligible to vote or all adults or all people) in the district. Some kind of representation device must be introduced. The opinions of *some* of the people are measured, and from these measured opinions deductions are made about the opinions of all.

This two-step process, oversimplified here, is a form of *sampling*. Whether it is good sampling or bad sampling depends most importantly on whether accurate deductions can be made from the measurement of the representative group. Thus it may be said that in a sense there is bad representation and good representation.

The measurement of public opinion is as important in a society as the extent to which the support of the masses is necessary or thought to be necessary, for the legitimating or the operation of government. Briefly, the importance of public opinion (and therefore of the measurement of public opinion) depends on the degree of democracy in the society. Insofar as there are theories that say the people have a right to influence their governments, so far is public opinion important.

As a practical matter, political leaders are selective in their assessments of public opinion. They try first to measure the opinions of people who have the greatest influence on their own future and the future of those policies they most strongly support or oppose. The legislator looks first to the opinions of the most influential people of the district.

Which persons and groups are important to officials depends not only on the officeholders' individual beliefs and preferences but also on the notions of political representation that find acceptance in the political theory of the time. Since the sixteenth century, according to Samuel Beer, four rather distinct views of representation have marked British politics. The "old Whig" theory had it that Parliament represented the whole people. Edmund Burke believed in this theory; he said in his famous "Speech to the People of Bristol" that although he represented the people of that town, he also represented all other similar towns (a maritime "interest") and indeed all the people of England. Such a belief disposed him to think relatively little of the judgment of his constituents on the issues of the day. He had small interest in measuring opinions in the streets of Bristol.

The old Whig view of representation gave way gradually, but never entirely, to what Samuel Beer calls the "liberal" theory of representation. In this theory, the predominant view was that each member of Parliament represented not particular groups of people or historical "interests" but the great middle class. A member's independent opinion on the issues of the day was as good as any other member's, and collectively the opinions of the whole Parliament were, almost by definition, those of the dominant Victorian middle class. Holding such a theory of representation, members of Parliament needed to spend little or no time in calculating the opinions of the public upon whose favor they depended. In practice, they thought as did the voters in the "shopkeeper democracy" of the time, and in theory they were under no obligation to discover any differences that might have existed between their opinions and those of their constituents.[3]

Following the Representation of the People Act of 1867, however, a new pattern of voting called forth a new theory of representation. Beer calls this the "radical" theory and says that popular majoritarianism lay at the bottom of it. The tendency was for members of Parliament to be reduced to the status of mere delegates, registering the interests of those groups (agriculture, business associations, labor unions) that supported their election. Thus the emphasis shifted to devices for expressing and measuring public opinion; and the views of various elements or publics were most readily expressed by means of political-action organizations (pressure groups) and political parties. All three of the great British parties of the present century were formed in the years from 1867 to 1910. The development of the radical theory of representation thus depended heavily on organizations that reflected or claimed to reflect public opinion.

The last theory of representation that Beer identified in modern British thought is the "collectivist" theory. It might better be called the "theory of party government," since its main theme is that the political party in power, as a coalition of social groups, represents the whole nation. Party opinion, as formed in the party organization and its constituent groups, is the opinion that counts. The individual is not wholly lost in this process, however, because of opportunity to participate in forming both group and party opinion. Individuals also participate basically, at each general election, by choosing between the parties; but opinion is not *directly* of much consequence to representatives.

The importance to us of Beer's excellent summary of British theories of representation is that the public opinion that is measured is, politically, the opinion that is influential; and the importance ascribed to popular influence is apt to vary from time to time and from place to place. Although the Gallup organization may sometimes measure opinion that is merely interesting or

---

3. This discussion of British theories of representation is from Samuel Beer, "The Representation of Interests in British Government: Historical Background," *American Political Science Review* 51, no.3 (1957): 613–650, and from the first three chapters of Beer's excellent book *British Politics in the Collectivist Age* (New York: Knopf, 1966).

curious, the politician in every time and place attempts to measure the opinion that makes a difference to the theory and practice of government.

## 4.3 THE SIMPLE INGREDIENTS OF EVERYDAY OPINION MEASUREMENT

The measurement of opinion and attitudes is not a recent triumph of computers and statistical manipulation. It is an old enterprise and one in which tried and often very satisfactory devices are still used alongside our latest electronic marvels.

Whether opinion sampling is good or bad, it always involves *asking, listening, and reading.* Politicians ask each other, "What do you hear?" The candidate, the market researcher, and just about every other active person listen constantly and interpret what they hear, consciously or unconsciously, into a measurement of opinion.

The opinion measurer, whether politician or plain citizen, can pick up many clues to the opinions of others just by listening. One need not necessarily ask in order to hear answers. The lounger on the street corner, without asking, picks up information that may be used to measure opinion. The wartime spy may measure public morale without ever asking the feelings of the home-front worker. The British opinion-measuring group Mass Observation attempted to systematize the study of public opinion through nondirective techniques. Mass Observation agents made judgments about public opinion from clues that arose "naturally" in social life—overheard conversations in buses and pubs, attention to certain articles or columns in newspapers, changes in hair and clothing styles.

American social scientists have shown increasing interest in what the authors of one book call "unobtrusive measures" of attitudes and opinions. The full title of their book, *Unobtrusive Measures: Nonreactive Research in the Social Sciences,* identifies it as a summary of research techniques that do not depend on direct responses from those whose opinions and attitudes are being investigated.[4]

Despite the usefulness of indirect measurements, asking and listening are usually interrelated parts of efforts to understand public opinion. The politician questions friends and acquaintances and attempts to create a picture of public opinion on the basis of their responses. The pollster asks respondents broad or narrow questions in as much detail as is necessary.

Much measurement of opinion is done by reading. The candidate reads the district newspapers. The editor of one paper reads other papers. The entrepre-

---

4. Eugene J. Webb, Donald T. Campbell, Richard D. Schwartz, and Lee Sechrest, *Unobtrusive Measures: Nonreactive Research in the Social Sciences* (Chicago: Rand McNally, 1966). Another useful survey for students interested in indirect opinion-measuring techniques is Karl Weick, "Systematic Observational Methods," in *Handbook of Social Psychology,* eds. Gardner Lindzey and E. Aronson, 3rd ed. (Reading, Mass.: Addison-Wesley, 1968), 2:357-451.

neur, looking for a new location for a store, reads the business news, specialized suburban papers, and the public records of new subdivisions and home construction. All these people are sampling public opinion by reading. To be sure, their information and the conclusions they draw from it may be seriously distorted, for they are probably reading an unrepresentative sample of an unrepresentative sample. Since newspapers are not representative of all the opinions held by all the people, they are inevitably distorted. Since the sample of newspapers read by the candidate, the editor, or the entrepreneur is in turn unrepresentative of all newspapers, another distortion occurs. Of the more than 1,700 daily newspapers and 8,000 weekly newspapers in the United States, few individuals can read more than four or five. By using a well-organized staff and a cadre of home correspondents, a member of Congress can perhaps get reports or clippings from all the papers in the district. But the editor and entrepreneur probably cannot so adequately organize their reading samples, and they may seriously mismeasure the public opinion, or public opinions, of concern to them.

Nonetheless, the distortion in most reading samples is readily compensated for in everyday situations. Each of us evaluates almost automatically the representativeness and validity, for our purposes, of the reading samples we employ in measuring the segment of public opinion that is important to us. The person in business distrusts the optimism of the *Paradise Valley Shoppers' News* for the market potential of the new Paradise Valley subdivision. More reliable is the county registrar of deeds' report that 80 percent more residence lots were sold in Paradise Valley than in any other subdivision in the county. In the measurement of opinion, we evaluate all the factors involved in our reading samples and weigh them with all the other factors that go into making judgments.

The endless measuring of opinion is a process that we all share, for opinion measuring is inevitable in every social situation. Most of it is of little general consequence. Whether a person accurately measures the opinions of others in private situations that involve only relationships with them is of no political importance. Nor do we especially care whether an individual accurately measures the opinions of neighbors toward a plan to paint the house purple, although in some circumstances such a plan may become a genuine public issue. But we do care whether the mayor gets a good picture of the citizens' opinions of proposals or of a fundamental change in the structure of city government.

## 4.4 "EAR TO THE GROUND": POLITICIANS MEASURE OPINION

We have said that all opinion measurement involves some combination of reading, asking, listening, and thinking. The person who is interested in public questions—whether government official, party activist, pressure-group leader, or League of Women Voters independent—will use all of these methods in assessing the views of publics. To the holders of political power, keeping an "ear to the ground" meant, before the advent of scientific polls, collecting printed and spoken opinions and discounting them according to the supposed reliability of those who enunciated them.

Politicians avidly read newspaper stories and other expressions of opinion. They read specialized publications, such as the newsletters of organizations that operate in the area or that take political stands. They read their mail carefully and always answer it, with greater or lesser attention, depending on who wrote the letter and how it is written. They see people and talk with people. They ask and they listen. In short, in measurement of opinion, politicians conduct informal interviews.

Politicians probably spend half or more of their talking time, except when they are on a planned sidewalk hunt for opinions (or for votes), in conversation with other politicians. Although families and nonpolitical friends tend to get scant attention—the *virus politicus* is a consuming malady that allows little private life—politicians often talk to casual contacts and constituents. The American cabdriver is legendary as an informant for politicians—probably with good reason, since cabdrivers overhear and participate in many conversations with mobile and influential "opinion leaders" in our society.

In contact with ordinary people and voters, an important consideration is the kind of job the politician holds and the place in which she holds it. A local executive or legislator (a mayor or city councillor, a county clerk or supervisor) will have a clear advantage over a nonlocal in gauging, through casual interviews and observations, opinion that is significant. The representative from the 10th Congressional District of Virginia who lives in a suburb just across the Potomac from Washington can go home every night. But only two or three members of Congress share this advantage. The rest necessarily live separated for months from constituents whose opinions they would like to judge personally day in and day out; some, who live in the East and Northeast, may go home almost every weekend; others, from western states, may get home only a few times during the session.

Geography, then, is one factor. But the type of job is also important. Local officeholders whose jobs take them constantly into the public are probably better able to maintain themselves in office through reelection than are those who are more isolated from their public. Other things being equal (they rarely are), a mayor is less likely to misjudge opinion than is a city clerk; a councillor who is also a vice-mayor, and who therefore attends more citywide functions than fellow councillors, is less likely to misjudge opinion or to fail of reelection than are the other members of the council. In summary, a variety and number of contacts of the *informal-interviewing type* are helpful to the politician with an "ear to the ground."

But the politician doesn't have to initiate all the contacts—even all the verbal and interviewing contacts. Officeholders and candidates are constantly seen in person or telephoned by constituents who seek favors, redress of wrongs, and advice. Some of these people represent organized groups—pressure groups—but many are just ordinary people with ordinary gripes.

"There's a hole in the street out in front of my house. Can't you do something about it?" City and county officials hear this kind of complaint all the time. It is a contact. It is an interview. It is also a measurement of opinion.

If people from all over the district are calling their councillors about holes in the street, then they know the streets are in pretty bad shape (a thing they might be expected to know without such calls) and there's a certain amount of feeling among the public that something should be done about it.

Reading, listening, asking, and talking—these are ways the politician has always kept an "ear to the ground." Door-to-door canvassing is not new in politics. The good precinct captain has done it for years—not scientifically, using the mathematical laws of probability, but with keen practical judgment and knowledge of the area, producing assessments accurate enough for most purposes. There are many stories of ward and precinct politicians who can predict the vote in their areas within one or two percentage points. This feat is not surprising in areas that are small and intensively "worked."

An early attempt to assess the ability of party politicians to predict elections was made by Claude E. Robinson in 1932. He collected two types of data from the presidential election campaign of 1928. First, he gathered Republican estimates by county from three states. He compared these forecasts with the actual election returns and calculated the "plurality error" (the difference between the *estimated* plurality and the *actual* plurality) for each county. He found that plurality errors ranged from 0.1 to 52 percent and that the average plurality error by county was 13 percent for two of the states and 14 percent for the third.[5] Second, from a number of political leaders and newspapermen he compiled a list of estimates by state and political party. In "trustworthy" estimates of Democrats in eight states, the median plurality error in 1928 was 18 percent; Republican estimates in sixteen states showed much better predictive validity, having a median plurality error of only 7 percent.[6]

The differences between their predictions and the actual vote are striking testimony to the proposition that politicians tell themselves what they want to hear. Robinson says that politicians, in estimating the future, suffer from the "elation complex." This is a necessary self-delusion, for "men who believe they are whipped are almost sure to be beaten." But it "constitutes the chief weakness in the predictive technique of the politician" because it "opens the door to delusions of grandeur and power, and causes otherwise normal men to see great and sweeping victories where fate holds crushing defeat in store."[7]

---

5. Claude E. Robinson, *Straw Votes: A Study of Political Predicting* (New York: Columbia University Press, 1932), pp. 6–8.

6. Ibid., p. 9.

7. Ibid., p. 10.

Another informal technique is *crowd analysis.* It has only recently been elevated to the level of a "science" and sanctified by disinterested research. One may suppose that since the beginning of political speechmaking (which means since the beginning of politics and the beginning of civilization as well) the speechifiers and their friends have tried to interpret the behavior, size, and attentiveness of crowds and to gauge crowd responses to particular words, phrases, and styles of oratory.

In democracies political actors are compelled to be attentive to the size, composition, and behavior of crowds. The possibilities of manipulating crowds are much reduced in democratic environments, mainly because other messages and stimuli compete with those that emanate from the government. Nonetheless, democratic politicians desire large, enthusiastic crowds, for four reasons. First, they need the support and votes of the individuals in the crowd. Second, they hope for a bandwagon effect; they want to rouse the individuals in the crowd to persuade other voters as well as give their own votes, and they want to make their cause seem popular to those who are not in the crowd. Third, the crowd provides feedback, letting them sense how they are doing. Even if it is not always possible to amend lapses or improve delivery of a speech under way, they can learn from such feedback to revise or ignore less successful appeals (or phrases or figures of speech) and to emphasize in later speeches the more successful elements. Fourth, crowds "create" political events, so the media will cover them more fully and report favorable responses.

The most famous of all American campaign blunders seems to have resulted largely from a failure to assess crowd reaction. In 1884 James G. Blaine was the Republican presidential nominee opposing Democrat Grover Cleveland. On the evening of October 29—only one week before election day—Blaine spoke in New York City to a large group of Protestant ministers and divinity students. He was introduced by the Rev. Dr. Samuel D. Burchard, who said, among other things, that the assembled ministers supported Blaine and would not identify themselves with the Democratic party, "whose antecedents have been rum, Romanism and rebellion."

It was assumed for many years that Blaine did not hear Burchard's remark. In any case, he did not repudiate the remark on the spot—or, indeed, until three days later.

In 1955 a memorandum of U.S. Supreme Court Justice John Marshall Harlan came to light. A few months after the 1884 election, Justice Harlan had had dinner with Blaine and had written:

> The Burchard incident was referred to by Mr. Blaine, and he said that the utterance of the words "Rum, Romanism and Rebellion" stunned and amazed him for the moment and *went through him like a knife;* that in responding to Burchard's address of welcome he made no allusion to those words, for the reason that, at the time, he did not think they were heard except by a few of those present who stood very near to Dr. Burchard, but who did not seem to recognize their mischievous effect; that, at the instant, he determined not to appear

to have heard what Burchard said, as he supposed that more harm would be done by noticing his remarks than by passing them by without observation.[8]

Commenting on Blaine's critical moment of decision, David G. Farrelly says:

What emerges from the Harlan version is an understanding of the momentary predicament that faced Blaine. With a quick decision demanded of him, Blaine reacted promptly to the situation as he discerned it. Of course if there had been a public address system in those days, everyone in the room would have heard Burchard's remark. Then Blaine would still have had a decision to make, but under those circumstances he might very well have repudiated Burchard on the spot. Indeed, speculating editorially two days before the election, the *New York Times* pointed out that Blaine was usually quick enough and that an immediate disclaimer would have been to his benefit.[9]

Here is an example of misjudging crowd feedback. Blaine had been unable to tell that the persons in attendance that night—especially the newspaper reporters—had heard the anti-Catholic remark of his introducer. He misjudged the crowd, mishandled the situation, and lost the election. New York's electoral votes would have put him in the White House, and he lost them by a scant 1,149 popular votes. Had Blaine's minister supporter not uttered this famous epithet or had Blaine repudiated him at once, Blaine would probably not have lost the fewer than 600 votes that could have made him president of the United States. Blaine himself said shortly after his defeat, "As the Lord sent upon us an ass in the shape of a preacher, and a rainstorm, to lessen our vote in New York, I am disposed to feel resigned to the dispensation of defeat, which flowed directly from these agencies."[10]

## 4.5 STRAW POLLS

Claude E. Robinson says that a straw poll is "an unofficial canvass of an electorate to determine the division of popular sentiment on public issues or on candidates for public office."[11] The first known attempts to measure electoral opinion on a mass scale were the straw polls developed by newspapers in the nineteenth century.

In the summer of 1824 the *Harrisburg Pennsylvanian* sent out reporters to

---

8. "'Rum, Romanism, and Rebellion' Resurrected," *Western Political Quarterly* 8, no. 2 (1955): 269; italics in original. Reprinted by permission of the University of Utah, copyright holder.
9. Ibid., p. 269.
10. Ibid., p. 270.
11. Claude E. Robinson, "Straw Votes," *Encyclopedia of the Social Sciences* (1937), 14:417.

check on popular support for the four presidential contenders of that year. On July 24 the paper reported that a "straw vote taken without discrimination of parties" showed Andrew Jackson to be the popular choice over John Quincy Adams, Henry Clay, and William H. Crawford.[12]

Toward the end of the nineteenth century, the *New York Herald* became more regular in its forecasts for local and state as well as national elections. During presidential campaigns the *Herald* collected estimates from reporters and political leaders in many parts of the country and predicted the Electoral College votes by state. In 1908 that paper began a collaborative effort with Cincinnati, Chicago, and St. Louis papers. The most ambitious straw poll of the nineteenth century seems to have been the 1896 effort of the Chicago *Record,* said to have been politically independent. It mailed postcard ballots to all 328,000 registered voters in Chicago and to one voter in eight in twelve midwestern states. Historian Richard Jensen reports that *The Record* "predicted McKinley would win 57.94 percent of the Chicago vote, off by only .04 percent. But outside Chicago, the newspaper's random sampling proved to be a failure."[13]

In straw polling, as commonly conducted, it is almost impossible to ensure that the persons giving their opinions are representative of all the persons whose opinions are presumably being measured. There is no certainty that the microcosm (the *sample*) is like the macrocosm (the *universe*). For instance, straw polls are often conducted through the distribution of ballots in commercial or recreational places; the ballots are marked by those who care to mark them and the results are tabulated by the conductor of the poll.

A number of newspapers sponsor straw polls or more systematic mail surveys every presidential election year. The *New York Daily News* straw poll is perhaps the best known. "Interviewers" for that paper go about the state, into selected areas, door to door or to shopping centers and other places where adult citizens gather; there they ask respondents to mark ballots and put them anonymously into boxes. The *Daily News* conducted straw polls from 1928 to 1980. The average error in the twenty six polls from 1930 to 1966, inclusive, was 5.9 points; in 1980 the error was only 2.1 percent.[14]

Straw votes are frequently obtained by mail. Newspapers and commercial polling organizations use the mails for *one-way* or for *two-way* balloting. In the first case, coupons printed in the paper can be clipped and returned by readers. Thus popular opinion is solicited for all manner of things, from the most valuable baseball player to plans for the international control of atomic energy. The two-way ballot is a ballot or questionnaire mailed out to all or some percentage

---

12. John M. Fenton, *In Your Opinion* (Boston: Little, Brown, 1960), p. 3.

13. Richard Jensen, "Democracy by the Numbers," *Public Opinion,* February/March 1980, p. 55. See also Irving Crespi, "Polls as Journalism," *Public Opinion Quarterly* 44 (1980): 462–476.

14. Charles W. Roll, Jr., "Straws in the Wind: The Record of the Daily News Poll," *Public Opinion Quarterly* 32 (1966): 251–260; Republican National Committee, "Public Opinion Report," November 13, 1980 (mimeo).

of the persons whose opinions are sought. Newspapers, magazines, or membership organizations may attempt in this way to measure support for policies or candidates.

Other newspapers sponsor "opinion polls" by printing a question about public policy, along with a telephone number readers may call (or two numbers, one for "yes" and one for "no," through which the "votes" are electronically recorded). A few days later the "poll results" are printed. The *San Francisco Chronicle,* sponsor of such a feature, candidly says, "the *Chronicle* Poll is not a scientific survey, but it does give a lively and timely sampling of current opinion on topics of impelling interest." In 1982 Barry Orton reviewed this renewed interest in straw votes and predicted that "despite the earnest wishes of some pollsters, pseudo-polls are not going to vanish from the public arena. On the contrary, we can expect to see many more uses of the basic forms outlined here, as well as further development of the electronic variations."[15]

The best-known straw poll of this century was that conducted by the *Literary Digest* magazine from 1916 to 1936. During the presidential contest between Charles Evans Hughes and Woodrow Wilson in 1916, the *Digest* asked its readers simply to send information about popular sentiment; it also took a poll among its subscribers in the five key states of Illinois, Indiana, New Jersey, New York, and Ohio. In 1920 the *Digest* mailed 11 million ballot cards to test public reaction to possible presidential candidates; this was, in a sense, an unofficial presidential primary. In the fall of 1924 the magazine mailed 16.5 million ballots to owners of telephones and automobiles in the United States, asking their choice between the presidential candidates of that year. In the presidential poll of 1928, more than 18 million ballots were mailed. The *Literary Digest* also conducted three nationwide polls on prohibition, in 1922, 1930, and 1932.

Although the *Digest* polls were widely quoted and commented on by other magazines and newspapers, the chief reason for their establishment and growth seems to have been their advertising and subscription-getting value. With each ballot card a subscription blank was mailed to the prospective straw voter. Robinson reports that "as a result of the 1930 postcard poll on prohibition, which was mailed to 20,000,000 people throughout the nation, the *Literary Digest...* was able to say, 'Almost overnight we have advanced circulation tremendously.'"[16]

The *Literary Digest* flourished during the 1920s and early 1930s. It predicted the elections of 1924, 1928, and 1932 accurately, and official referenda in ten states indicate that polls on the prohibition amendment caught the trend in favor of repeal between 1926 and 1932.

But in 1936, after its gigantic blunder of predicting an Electoral College majority for the Republican nominee, Alfred M. Landon, the *Literary Digest*

---

15. Barry Orton, "Phony Polls: The Pollster's Nemesis," *Public Opinion,* June/July 1982, p. 60.
16. Robinson, *Straw Votes,* p. 51.

went out of the polling business forever. Soon thereafter, in 1938, it went out of *all* business forever.

What had happened? The short answer is that the errors inherent from the first in the *Digest's* polling procedure were compounded and exaggerated in 1936. Poll cards, as we have noted, were mailed to persons whose names were obtained from telephone books and automobile registration lists. Two factors were operating in 1936 to produce from this sample a Republican response that was wholly unrepresentative of Republican strength among voters at large. The first factor has been much discussed: in the serious economic depression of the early and mid-1930s, telephones and automobiles tended to be concentrated in middle- and high-income households. Thus the more well-to-do were polled by the *Literary Digest;* but the support of these people for the Republican Landon was overwhelmed in the election by the large numbers of the less well-off, not included in the poll, who voted heavily for Democrat Franklin Roosevelt.

Another factor operated in 1936 to swell the Landon column in the *Digest* poll and mislead its editors. As in all mail polls, those who felt strongly on the matter returned the cards in greater numbers. Thus the heavy return from enthusiastic Landon supporters—which probably, in the context of the campaign, meant rabid Roosevelt opponents—was not balanced by enthusiastic Roosevelt supporters, comparatively few of whom were polled. This imbalance, caused by the distribution system, was aggravated by the more apparent error of sampling mainly the middle and upper classes. In sum, the *Literary Digest* came a cropper because of a serious *sampling error,* plus the failure to assess and discount the heavy return from voters with unrepresentative political motivations.

Had the *Literary Digest* editors cared, and had they read Robinson's book *Straw Votes,* they might have made adjustments to prevent or at least minimize the 1936 debacle. Robinson pointed out in 1932 that the *Digest* had consistently overpredicted the Republican votes in 1924 and 1928:

> From this consistent overestimation of the Republican vote arises the hypothesis that the "tel-auto" population (owners of telephones and automobiles) which forms the *Literary Digest* "electorate" is more Republican than the voting population at large; hence, under the *Digest* sampling methodology, overprediction for this party can be expected from year to year, and the predictive error shown by one poll can be used to correct the bias of the succeeding poll.[17]

Using this predictive-error method of adjusting the *Literary Digest* poll results to compensate for the Republican overprediction, Robinson established a "corrected" *Digest* prediction for 1928 of 6 percent average plurality error by states. He found this adjusted prediction to be better than any nationwide poll in that year except that of the Hearst newspapers, which had a 5 percent average

---

17. Ibid., p. 72; parentheses in original.

plurality error.[18] Robinson also pointed out that the *Literary Digest* could hardly have been expected to change its polling methods—since, as a business, its success depended on subscriptions from the auto and telephone owners who were polled—but that it might have adopted techniques of adjustment in analyzing its returns.

## 4.6 INFORMAL OPINION MEASUREMENT TODAY

Although there has been no improvement in techniques of *informal* opinion measurement since 1936, political tacticians, journalists, and other observers still give close attention to political phenomena and still rely with great pride and no little skill on "horseback" evaluation of opinion. What has happened since 1936—and it is a most significant development for opinion measurement, as we shall see in Chapter 5—has been the combination of field interviewing of people with probability mathematics in the creation of a whole new science of survey research.

The political application of survey research and especially the use of polls by officeholders and candidates are now thoroughly accepted in American life. But it should not be thought that informal, everyday, and intuitive measurement of opinions has disappeared from politics. Candidates and managers have to make multiple measurements, attending to signs and clues of all kinds, judging as they go what actions are likely to be productive or unproductive for them. In their world, scientific polling has now, in the 1980s, become a fact of life. But the details, the doubts, the confidences, and the existential "feel" of politicians for their political milieu still inform the creation, the interpretation, and the use of scientific polling.

---

18. Ibid., p. 67. In an imaginative use of 1924–1936 *Literary Digest* poll data, W. Phillips Shively demonstrated the "sudden" party realignment along economic status lines in 1936: "A Reinterpretation of the New Deal Alignment," *Public Opinion Quarterly,* 35 (1971–72): 621–624.

## Chapter 5

# Survey Research:
# What It Is
# and How to Do It

On October 31, 1960, Republican vice-presidential candidate Henry Cabot Lodge told a campaign audience in Paterson, New Jersey, that public opinion polls were "passing fads." "In the future," Mr. Lodge is reported to have said, "people are going to look back on these polls as one of the hallucinations which the American people have been subjected to.... I don't think the polls are here to stay."[1]

In every presidential campaign since 1960 some candidates have criticized opinion polling as being unscientific, biased, unreliable, or fraudulently used. Governor George Romney of Michigan, far behind in the 1968 polls, said: "Experts have been wrong before. I'm reaching the people and the people are responding"[2]—but withdrew from the race a few days after making that statement. In 1972 George McGovern's supporters and the candidate himself characterized poll releases during the campaign as "propaganda that the Democratic Party can't win," "another wrong and inaccurate piece of information," and, on the day before the election, with regard to the last poll, "It's nuts."[3]

In September 1984, with the polls showing him 15 to 20 percentage points behind President Reagan, Democratic presidential candidate Walter Mondale was quoted as saying "only half in jest, 'you can stuff those polls'."[4]

On October 11, 1984, Democratic Vice-Presidential candidate Geraldine Ferraro said, in a nationwide TV debate, "Let me say that I'm not a believer in polls." Of course she "believed in polls." What she was implying was that she didn't want

---

1. *Washington Post and Times Herald,* November 1, 1960.

2. *New York Times,* February 25, 1968.

3. Robert H. Blank, "Published Opinion Polls and the Conduct of the 1972 Presidential Campaign," paper delivered at Western Political Science Association Meeting, San Diego, April 7, 1973, p. 3.

4. Sara Fritz and Jack Nelson, "He's 'Hit His Stride,' Aides Say of Mondale," *Los Angeles Times,* September 15, 1984.

her supporters or potential supporters to lessen their campaign activities because the polls were not in her favor at that point in the campaign.

The antipoll comments of practicing politicians invariably come from those who are running behind. We assume, therefore, that much of their criticism is self-serving and is best understood as part of the campaign rhetoric and the charges and countercharges of electioneering. Candidates who attack opinion polls because the polls show them to have less support than their opponents tend to focus on the motivations and integrity of the pollsters as well as on the accuracy of the polls. A possible exception was President Harry Truman, who in 1948 said the pollsters were wrong when they forecast his defeat. As it happened, Truman *was* elected. But the election was close, and it was a number of relatively small errors by overconfident—and to some extent careless—pollsters that accounted for the failure to predict Truman's victory.

If the polls had not been here to stay, they would have disappeared after the 1948 surprise, just as the *Literary Digest* and its poll went out of existence after its 1936 surprise. The truth is that public opinion polling, as conducted by trained and careful personnel, has established its usefulness, its accuracy, and its permanence.

## 5.1 THE EMERGENCE OF SCIENTIFIC POLLING

Modern public opinion polling has origins in journalistic straw votes, as we have seen; in *market research;* in *psychological testing;* and in the application of the *mathematical laws of probability and sampling* to human behavior.

The earliest market research reported by private enterprise was that of N.W. Ayer & Son in 1879. For a manufacturer of threshing machines, the Ayer company assembled crop statistics throughout the country and gathered information about the circulation and advertising rates of newspapers in appropriate areas. Generally, however, the market research business did not grow quickly in the forty years after 1879. Albert B. Blankenship says that some manufacturers and advertising agencies had research staffs before World War I, but that "no real impetus in this movement occurred until after the war."[5]

Before the 1920s, producers made items as they saw fit (or were able) and offered them for barter or sale where they could and as they were. In the transition to a consumer economy, however, they found that new technology and new transportation opened the possibility of creating, so to speak, mass products fashioned to mass desires. For instance, in the early years of this century, a unit of the Quaker Oats Company, which had milled oats for porridge since 1856, found that cereal grains could be "shot from guns," renamed, repackaged, and sold at a higher rate of trade if the market could be puffed up like the product.

---

5. Albert B. Blankenship, *Consumer and Opinion Research* (New York: Harper & Row, 1943), p. 5.

Thus new technology in manufacturing was important for the growth of market research. But even more important was the development of new packaging and merchandising methods. Market research discovered that a more attractive package may lead to bigger sales. Cigarette companies do a great deal of market research, and it is said that the American Tobacco Company changed from a green package in World War II not because "Lucky Strike green has gone to war," as it patriotically proclaimed, but because it found that a white package was more attractive to women smokers.

Much of the market research activity of the 1920s and 1930s depended on a minimum level of psychological and sociological knowledge. Meaningful market research—beyond the mere collection of economic and demographic facts—could not have emerged before there was at least some understanding of human attitudes, motivation, conditioning through repeated stimuli, and the creation and reinforcement of habit.

Finally, in addition to substantive psychological knowledge, some understanding of testing devices and techniques was necessary before attitude and opinion measurement could claim to be scientific. Most important is the application of the mathematical laws of probability. The Swiss mathematician Jean Bernoulli first described the science of probability in 1713, but only fairly recently has this knowledge been used for measurement in business and in the social sciences.

The basic proposition of probability is that, given chance conditions and a finite number of elements, single elements or combinations thereof recur in an infinite series with predictable regularity and frequency. For example, a single die has six sides and on any given throw is as apt to come up on one side as on any other (assuming that it is perfectly balanced); thus there is an equal probability (designated 1/6) for each side to appear. The combinations of spots on the tops of two thrown dice can total from 2 to 12, but the possibility that some combinations will consist of identical numbers of spots means, for instance, that 7 is more likely to appear than 2. The reason is that only one combination gives a sum of 2 (1 on each die) and one a sum of 12 (6 on each die), whereas there are two combinations each for 3 and 11 (for 3, 1 on the first die and 2 on the second, or 2 on the first die and 1 on the second), three combinations each for 4 and 10, four combinations each for 5 and 9, five combinations each for 6 and 8, and six combinations for 7. Thus in thirty-six throws of a pair of dice you might expect to get 2 or 12 once each, 3 and 11 twice each, 4 and 10 three times each, 5 and 9 four times each, 6 and 8 five times each, and 7 six times. You will not get such a distribution, of course, because on each of the thirty-six throws the same number of combinations is separately possible no matter what combination comes up any other time. This is the meaning of the statement that individual cases can never be predicted by the laws of probabilities—only the distribution of aggregate (collected) cases can be predicted. (But in opinion sampling this is precisely what we want to do: predict the range and distribution of aggregate cases.) So, if we throw the dice 1,000, 10,000, or 100,000 times, we can be sure that, within some predictable range of error, 2 and 12 will each come up 1/36 of the time, 3 and 11 2/36 of the time, and so forth, with 7 coming up 6/36 (1/6) of the time.

Some sophistication in understanding probability and sampling was necessary before pollsters could hope to measure public opinion reliably by gathering opinions only of selected persons in the public. This sophistication was first achieved in American industry, through its experience with production control and product standardization.

Random, spot inspection and regular $n$th[6] inspection have been used for years in mass-production lines when continuous inspection of each item is competitively unnecessary or economically prohibitive. A manufacturer of hairpins may find it necessary to check the size, strength, coating, and bends of only one out of 100,000 of the products; a maker of vitamin tablets may have to run standardization tests on only one tablet out of every 10,000 produced. In both cases the laws of probability are being used; from inspection of the few, valid inferences, within known margins of error, can be made about the many.

Once there was understanding of the way sampling could be used to predict the uniformity of things with shared characteristics, it was only a step to sampling the characteristic attitudes and opinions that people are assumed to share.

## 5.2 SCIENTIFIC POLLING COMES OF AGE

The American Institute of Public Opinion (AIPO) issued its first release in October 1935. George Gallup, the organization's founder, described the formation and objective of AIPO in these words:

> After a preliminary period of experiment, beginning in 1933, the American Institute of Public Opinion, with the cooperation and support of a number of American newspapers, began a series of week-by-week national polls which have continued to the present day. The Institute's purpose was to perform the function of fact finding in the realm of opinion in the same general way as the Associated Press, the United Press, and the International News Service functioned in the realm of event. This attempt to improve and objectify the reporting of what people think met with warm response and active encouragement from editors throughout the country.[7]

Before the outbreak of World War II, Gallup organized or cooperated with British and French institutes of public opinion. The British Institute has been in

---

6. The letter $n$ is the mathematician's way of saying "the given number." It probably meant, originally, just "number"; now it means the number designating the interval size used. To get a sample of six cards from a bridge deck, one way is to choose every eighth card; eight is the $n$th number.

7. George Gallup and Saul Forbes Rae, *The Pulse of Democracy* (New York: Simon & Schuster, 1940), p. 46. Reprinted by permission of Simon and Schuster, Inc.

continuous existence since 1938. The French Institute was reconstituted after V-E Day, and these two Gallup affiliates have been joined since 1945 by others. The agencies are coordinated through the International Association of Public Opinion Institutes, also a Gallup organization. Other organizations exist abroad outside the Gallup empire; European university and research centers have rapidly increased in number since the mid-1950s, but their development has not significantly influenced the growth of opinion research in America.

Since 1946 the Survey Research Center (SRC) of the University of Michigan has conducted a number of important studies in American political behavior. In each of the presidential elections from 1948 to 1984, and in most of the intervening congressional elections, it has extensively investigated the voting and nonvoting publics. The general character of its political behavior program is described as follows:

> The presidential vote has been the object of extended investigation in a series of national studies in the United States. . . . Since 1952 biennial studies have also paid substantial attention to congressional elections and the juxtaposition of the congressional elections with national presidential politics. The election study series continues to be reported in articles, monographs, and books.[8]

In 1980 the Michigan SRC expanded its election research by starting polling during the early primary-elections period, February to April, and by designing nesting and overlapping samples for the nearly yearlong campaigning.

In 1957 a library of polling data, the Roper Public Opinion Research Center, was established at Williams College in Massachusetts. It has collected sample survey data from American and foreign opinion researchers and made these data available to educational and nonprofit agencies. In 1977 the Roper Center became a joint enterprise of Williams, Yale, and the University of Connecticut, and by 1980 it had data from more than 10,000 surveys from seventy countries housed at Storrs, Connecticut.

## 5.3 SURVEY TECHNIQUES

The objective of public opinion surveys is to obtain responses to uniform questions from a select number of persons (the *sample*) who, according to criteria thought to be relevant, are representative of the whole group of people (the *universe*) about whom one wants information. The sample, then, ought to be either an exact miniature of the universe or constructed so that the ways in which it differs from the universe will lead to valid information about the universe.

In the first instance, suppose the pollster wants to study class feeling about

---

8. *Institute for Social Research: A Report on Recent Activities* (Ann Arbor: University of Michigan, 1968), p. 27.

price controls in a country in which 30 percent of the population are in the lower socioeconomic class, 55 percent are in the middle, and 15 percent are in the upper. If the pollster is limited to 2,000 interviews, it will be necessary to seek out 600 persons in the lower class, 1,100 in the middle, and 300 in the upper class. Assuming that other measures are taken to prevent bias, a sample will be obtained that, on class lines, is as near a small universe as can be. The results from 2,000 interviews can then be directly projected onto the whole universe with reasonable certainty of being accurate.

Suppose, however, that the purpose of the study is to learn about the popular acceptance or rejection of government price controls. The pollster may then reason that the views of the upper class are more significant for policy making—first, because of the direct impact of these views on governmental decisions, and second, because of their influence on the views of the middle and lower classes—and may therefore decide to oversample the upper-class segment. In this way, one deliberately constructs a sample that is not representative of the socioeconomic universe in order to obtain a sample that is more representative of the universe of influence—which, in this case, is more important than mere socioeconomic correspondence between the sample and the universe.

In the construction of a scientific public opinion survey, several distinct steps may be seen:

1. Statement of information desired.
2. Identification of the universe.
3. Determination of sample size and type.
4. Construction of the questionnaire.
5. Recruitment and training of interviewers.
6. Fieldwork.
7. Processing and analysis of data.

These steps are not all of equal magnitude, nor are they equally demanding of the time and energy of the pollster. However, it can be argued that they are of equal importance, since, like the links of a chain, each is vital to all. No matter how precise and sophisticated the theoretical formulation of sample and questionnaire, if there is any breakdown in the steps involving the collection, processing, or analysis of data, the survey fails. In turn, if the right questions are not asked of the right people, perfection in other steps is fruitless.

## 5.4 STATEMENT OF INFORMATION DESIRED

All too frequently, students begin fieldwork in public opinion with only the foggiest notion of what they want to find out. Given the somewhat artificial situation in which such "laboratory practice" occurs, this uncertainty is perhaps not too surprising. But it is surprising that in political polling—and, it is said, in commercial market research—persons who have a real need for survey work are sometimes unable at first to say what they want to discover.

If the candidate is to spend money wisely, the pollster must be told what kinds of information are wanted from what kinds of people in the constituency. For instance, if one wants to know what issues and themes to stress in a campaign, it is of little worth to gather responses about the public image of one's opponent—the question "What is there about Mr. X that you especially like or don't like?" will not evoke responses that can be used as guidelines for a whole campaign. The responses may give valuable hints on how to exploit an opponent's weaknesses, but they will tell nothing about what issues may interest the electorate.

Suppose the mayor or the city manager asks the pollster to find out whether the residents are in favor of slum clearance and urban renewal, and the pollster reports a good response to such questions as "Would you favor the redevelopment of the Old Town section?" Nevertheless, the mayor's proposal may be defeated in the referendum to authorize the project because the pollster did not ask the citizens "Would you support a $200 million bond issue for the redevelopment project?" and because the residents of the Old Town area were not asked whether they would be willing to live elsewhere if necessary. This kind of error can hardly be blamed on the pollster—although, in these exaggerated examples, it is apparent that some of the fault would lie there for failure to help the client define goals.

## 5.5 IDENTIFICATION OF THE UNIVERSE

Whose opinions are to be sampled?

Should a magazine, to gather information about possible ways of increasing its circulation by changing contents, sample its readers or nonreaders? To learn the tastes in styling of potential buyers of Cadillacs, should General Motors choose a sample from below or from above the $30,000-income class? Should it interview only men in the selected income group, as many women as men, or 70 percent women? Should a candidate take as a universe the potential voters in the constituency or only the habitual voters or (for primary elections) only those who are registered in the candidate's party?

The question of whose opinions to measure, like the question of what information is desired, depends on the factors of the individual case. Public opinion surveys are not and never will be substitutes for thinking about social cause and effect, or for decisions based on facts and opinions that are not derived from opinion surveys. The opinion survey is a tool, with clear limits of usefulness and no magic whatever.

## 5.6 SAMPLE SIZE

The number of people to be interviewed in any poll depends in part on the importance the sponsors place on being able to make an accurate prediction and on the money available for conducting the poll.

Public opinion surveys are expensive. You will discover why when you under-take fieldwork; even the best interviewer cannot gather many interviews in a day if she uses the techniques that keep distortion at a minimum.

Ignoring for the moment the fact that cost is a limiting factor, how large should the sample be? It should be *large enough to ensure that the results are within the limits of chance error that satisfy the sponsor.*

## 5.61 The chance sampling error

Here we must refer to the mathematics of probability. If we assume (a) that there is a real but unknown distribution of all possible answers to a question, (b) that our sample is random (every person is just as likely to be chosen as every other person), and (c) that our techniques are capable of obtaining a true opinion from each person, we will be able to tell how representative the responses are. For example, if opinion divides 70 percent yes and 30 percent no on any question in a nationwide sample of only 756 interviews, the chances are 997 to 1,000 that this 70–30 response is not more than 5 percent inaccurate. If the sample is as large as 17,000, the probable error is reduced to less than 1 percent, given the same 70–30 division of yes and no answers. If the indicated division of opinion is 50–50, the sample must consist of 900 interviews to obtain a 997-to-1,000 chance of less than 5 percent error, or more than 22,500 interviews to reduce the error to less than 1 percent. These examples refer only to the *error attributable to size of sample,* the so-called *chance sampling error.* This sort of error is wholly a matter of statistical probability and should not be confused with errors that arise from faulty sample selection or from imperfect interviewing.

## 5.62 Very large samples usually unnecessary

The size of the sample is not the major source of error in most opinion surveys. When errors occur, in almost every case it is not because too few persons were interviewed but because the wrong persons were wrongly interviewed. As early as 1940 George Gallup declared that "both experience and statistical theory point to the conclusion that *no major poll in the history of this country ever went wrong because too few persons were reached.*"[9]

In the first year of the American Institute of Public Opinion, Gallup conducted a number of experiments on the effects of sample size alone. He describes one of these experiments:[10]

> In 1936, a survey of 30,000 ballots asked the question: "Would you like to see the N.R.A. revived?" The first 500 cases showed a "no" vote

9. Gallup and Rae, *Pulse of Democracy,* p. 68; italics in original.
10. Ibid., p. 72.

of 54.9 per cent. The complete sample of 30,000 cases returned a "no" vote of 55.5 per cent. In other words, the addition of 29,500 cases to the first 500 cases in this instance made a difference of 0.6 per cent in the national findings. Here are the figures:

| Number of Cases | | Percentage Voting Against Reviving the N.R.A. |
|---|---|---|
| First | 500 ballots | 54.9 |
| First | 1,000 ballots | 53.9 |
| First | 5,000 ballots | 55.4 |
| First | 10,000 ballots | 55.4 |
| All | 30,000 ballots | 55.5 |

The effective use of relatively small samples is illustrated in the polling of recent presidential elections. In five of the seven presidential elections since 1960, the major nationwide poll forecasts all came within 2 percentage points of the actual vote results (see Table 5–1). To be sure, the prediction record in 1980 was bad. In that election there was no strong voter commitment for either President Jimmy Carter or Governor Ronald Reagan; opinions were extraordinarily volatile, with the lead changing several times during the campaign; and polling done on the Sunday before the election apparently did not catch Democrats who were last-minute deciders for Reagan or last-minute vote-switchers who changed their mind because of developments in the Iranian hostage crisis. It should be clear that the 1980 errors were not attributable to size of samples; there is no reason to believe that larger samples would have increased the accuracy that year.[11] As the 1984 data in Table 5–1 show, the major pollsters' prediction record that year was good. Note that the Gallup sample of 1,970 respondents was as accurate as the much larger sample interviewed by the ABC/*Washington Post*.

A sample of a few thousand—maybe even one thousand—is capable, statistically, of accurately reflecting the opinions of 100 million or more people. Contrary to what may appear to be common sense, very large samples (say, 10,000 to 50,000) are not much more accurate than medium-sized samples (1,500 to 5,000), and the improved results of such large samples are almost never worth their costs.

## 5.7 SAMPLE SELECTION

More important than the size of the sample, beyond some minimum, is the *type* of sample. The early straw pollsters interviewed anyone they happened to meet. The so-called inquiring reporters of many newspapers still talk to people they haphazardly encounter. But serious attempts to measure opinion always involve interviewing people who are in some sense *representative*.

11. See Nelson W. Polsby and Aaron Wildavsky, *Presidential Elections* (New York: Scribners, 1984), p. 156.

**Table 5-1**   Percentage error of forecasts by major polls in presidential elections

| 1960 polls | Sample size | Predictions | | Results | | Percentage error |
|---|---|---|---|---|---|---|
| | | Kennedy | Nixon | Kennedy | Nixon | |
| Gallup............... | 8,000 | 51.00 | 49.00 | 50.1 | 49.9 | 0.90 |
| Roper .............. | 3,000 | 48.94 | 51.06 | 50.1 | 49.9 | 1.16 |
| John Kraft .......... | 2,000 | 51.58 | 48.42 | 50.1 | 49.9 | 1.48 |

| 1964 polls | Sample size | Predictions | | Results | | Percentage error |
|---|---|---|---|---|---|---|
| | | Johnson | Goldwater | Johnson | Goldwater | |
| Gallup.............. | NA | 64.0 | 36.0 | 61.4 | 38.6 | 2.60 |
| Harris .............. | NA | 64.0 | 36.0 | 61.4 | 38.6 | 2.60 |

| 1968 polls | Sample size | Predictions | | | Results | | | Percentage error* |
|---|---|---|---|---|---|---|---|---|
| | | Nixon | Humphrey | Wallace | Nixon | Humphrey | Wallace | |
| Gallup...... | 2,800 | 43.0 | 42.0 | 15.0 | 43.4 | 42.9 | 13.6 | 0.40 |
| Harris ...... | 2,559 | 43.0 | 39.8 | 17.2 | 43.4 | 42.9 | 13.6 | 0.40 |

| 1972 polls | Sample size | Predictions | | Results | | Percentage error |
|---|---|---|---|---|---|---|
| | | Nixon | McGovern | Nixon | McGovern | |
| Gallup (11/6/72)...... | 3,500 | 62 | 38 | 61.8 | 38.2 | 0.2 |
| Harris (11/6/72) ...... | — | 60 | 37 | 61.8 | 38.2 | 1.8 |
| Yankelovich (10/30/72) (New York Times)† | "Approx. 1,500" | 65 | 36 | 61.8 | 38.2 | 3.2 |

| 1976 polls | Sample size | Predictions | | Results | | Percentage error |
|---|---|---|---|---|---|---|
| | | Carter | Ford | Carter | Ford | |
| Gallup............... | 3,500 | 48.0 | 49.0 | 50.0 | 48.3 | 2.0 |
| Harris .............. | — | 49.0 | 48.0 | 50.0 | 48.3 | 1.0 |
| Roper/PBS .......... | 2,000 | 51.0 | 47.0 | 50.0 | 48.3 | 1.0 |
| NBC News ........... | — | 49.0 | 49.0 | 50.0 | 48.3 | 1.0 |

| 1980 polls | Sample size | Predictions‡ | | Results | | Percentage error |
|---|---|---|---|---|---|---|
| | | Carter | Reagan | Carter | Reagan | |
| Gallup............... | 3,500 | 44.0 | 47.0 | 41.6 | 51.7 | 4.7 |
| Harris .............. | — | 41.6 | 46.8 | 41.6 | 51.7 | 4.9 |
| CBS/New York Times | 2,264 | 44.7 | 46.8 | 41.6 | 51.7 | 4.9 |
| NBC/AP ............ | — | 40.0 | 48.0 | 41.6 | 51.7 | 3.7 |

| 1984 polls* | Sample size | Predictions | | Results | | Percentage error |
|---|---|---|---|---|---|---|
| | | Reagan | Mondale | Reagan | Mondale | |
| Gallup ............. | 1,970 | 59.3 | 40.6 | 59.0 | 41.0 | .3 |
| CBS/N. Y. Times .... | 2,075 | 60.9 | 38.9 | 59.0 | 41.0 | 1.6 |
| ABC/Wash. Post ..... | 9,000 | 59.3 | 40.6 | 59.0 | 41.0 | .3 |
| USA Today ......... | 2,219 | 63.0 | 37.0 | 59.0 | 41.0 | 4.0 |

*In 1984 the "undecided" are distributed proportionately between the two candidates.

NA = not available.

*Because of George Wallace's third-party candidacy, the 1968 predictions and poll errors are not clear. Nixon got 43.4% of the national popular vote, and the errors are calculated on that figure.

†The Yandelovich polls are not strictly comparable. They consisted of telephone interviews with potential voters in 16 states important in the electoral college.

‡The Anderson predictions and votes are not given, and "undecided" are distributed proportionately among all three candidates.

Representativeness in a sample is ensured only by *randomness* or by some combination of *stratification and randomness*. Randomness means that each unit of the universe has an equal chance of being drawn into the sample. Stratification is the division of the universe according to criteria that the pollster thinks may be relevant for the matters being investigated.

A hypothetical case shows how randomness and stratification are used. A U.S. senatorial candidate from New Jersey has, let us say, a universe that consists of all registered voters in the state. He could have the name of each voter put in a capsule to be whirled in a cage, then blindly pick out 1,000 names to be interviewed. He would have a pure random sample.

But suppose our candidate also knows that the youngest and the oldest voters are less likely to vote than those in the middle age groups, and that those with incomes under $10,000 are less likely to vote than those with incomes over $10,000. If the candidate is able to obtain the relevant data from the voter registration lists or census, he may want to divide his total universe into sub-groups, or strata, drawing into his sample proportionately more middle-aged registrants and more from the over-$10,000 stratum. He may then be able to obtain the same accuracy with 900 persons in this stratified sample that he would get in the 1,000-person pure random sample. The decision to stratify in some ways rather than other ways is always a human judgment, based on the related-ness of the stratification factors to the information desired.

A candidate assessing his strength and the issues in his constituency may want to know how he is faring among men and women voters and among voters in various age groups, economic brackets, and ethnic or religious groups, and maybe those in various educational or professional groups. If he is running for mayor of a mining town where there are 60 men for every 40 women, it will not do for him to sample homes on weekday afternoons or to be satisfied with a stratification that results in a sample consisting of 60 percent of women.

As we point out later in this book, in the 1980s it is common practice for election pollsters to "segment" their samples—that is, to stratify according to sharp social and demographic criteria—in order to obtain the most pertinent information for campaign strategy. Elections may be won bit by bit, as it were—small increases in support among Italian-Americans, labor union members, women, under 30s, and so on may tip the scale. As Richard Joslyn explains:

> [T]he goal is to communicate with those who are supportive of or undecided about a candidate and to ignore, if possible, those who already have negative feelings. [C]ampaigns must rely on the distri-bution of votes for the candidate previously (if available), or on the distribution of votes in a previous race thought to be similar to the present one, or on information gleaned from a public opinion poll. This is one reason that so-called benchmark polls are so valuable to campaigns and that some campaigns consultants refuse to work without one.[12]

---

12. Richard Joslyn, *Mass Media And Elections* (Reading, Mass.: Addison-Wesley, 1984), p. 60.

Thus it is that pure randomness in choosing samples of voters is becoming less important and the artistic combinations of stratified sample "segments" more important.

In general, pollsters consider their research design and what they want to find out, then ask themselves something like this: "For the ideas we are trying to test or the information we hope to get, what kinds of people do we want to interview?" This, in a homely, overall way, is what we mean by selecting relevant attributes for stratifying the sample.

## 5.71 "Area random" samples

In area random sampling all individual respondents are predetermined by the survey designers. That predetermination is made either through purposive and systematic selection or by a series of random choices.

The first step in creating an area sample is the division of the universe into smaller units called *primary sampling areas.* The selection of primary sampling areas may be the result of judgments relating to the hypotheses or information to be studied. Of the 600 precincts in a city, 20 may be chosen for political, economic, ethnic, or other reasons related to the study. Or the primary sampling units may be chosen by *chance* methods—for example, by taking every thirtieth precinct (*selection by constant intervals*) or by drawing twenty numbers out of a hat (*random selection*). If chance methods are used, all parts of the universe must be covered by the smaller areas (with no overlap) and each of the smaller areas must have as good a chance of being selected as any other.

For samples drawn from a large geographical universe, such as the whole United States, it is often desirable to choose secondary or subsampling areas. Thus the primary sampling areas might be 600 of the more than 3,000 counties in the nation. From these 600 units, 30 secondary sampling areas (cities, parts of cities, and townships) might be drawn. When intermediate area segments of this kind are used, they should be selected, like the primary areas, purposively or by chance.

The next step in obtaining an area random sample is the determination of all the dwelling units within the chosen geographical areas from which the individual respondents are to be selected. Sometimes these units can be determined from public or quasi-public sources—from city or county maps, directories or lists, or the records of utilities or construction companies. Often, however, it is necessary for the field staff (perhaps the interviewers themselves) to locate every dwelling unit in the sampling areas.

Next, a number of occupied dwelling units (ODUs) are chosen, almost always by constant-interval or random selection, from the complete list of such units. Finally, a particular person is designated in each of the chosen dwelling units. All such persons together constitute the sample. Figure 5–1 illustrates the process through which, in area sampling, the respondents are chosen by successive steps from the universe.

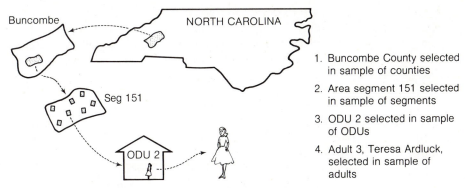

**Figure 5–1.**  *Example of sampling in four stages*

1. Buncombe County selected in sample of counties
2. Area segment 151 selected in sample of segments
3. ODU 2 selected in sample of ODUs
4. Adult 3, Teresa Ardluck, selected in sample of adults

## 5.8 CONSTRUCTION OF THE QUESTIONNAIRE

In this section, think of the questionnaire as meaning, in general, the total of all the questions asked—or, more broadly, the total material used to elicit responses from each person interviewed. Normally the questionnaire consists of one or more printed, mimeographed, or typewritten sheets on which questions are written. But in some surveys, cards, posters, or other display materials are used to clarify or expand the questions or to increase interviewing uniformity and reliability. Such supplementary items are properly thought of as part of the questionnaire.

Questionnaires are so common in our everyday life that their construction may at first seem a task that any reasonably well-educated and honest person could do as effectively as any other. One is tempted to believe that straightforward answers can be evoked by simple, straightforward questions. This is not always the case. Aside from the etymological vagaries of English (and all other languages), each questionnaire constructor and each respondent bring to each question particular and often unusual meanings and nuances. One does not have to be a semanticist to appreciate, after the shortest attempt at question construction, the significance of what Stuart Chase termed "the tyranny of words."

### 5.81 Precision, respondent relevance, and tacit assumptions

Three principles govern the creation of clear, concise questions.[13] The first is precision. Precision has to do with what the question means: What kind of

---

13. This section owes much to Paul Lazarsfeld's article "The Art of Asking Why: Three Principles Underlying the Formulation of Questionnaires," in *Public Opinion and Propaganda,* ed. Daniel Katz, (New York: Dryden, 1954), pp. 675–686. See also Elizabeth Noelle-Neumann, "Wanted: Rules for Wording Structured Questionnaires," *Public Opinion Quarterly* 34 (1970): 191–201.

information do you want to get? What goals do you have? Do you want to describe what you're selling or offering? These queries are related to the kinds of things the interviewer or the person making the schedule (as questionnaires are often called) asks; they are not questions asked of the respondent, except in translated form.

The second principle is that of respondent relevance. The intent of the question constructor here is to make it possible for the respondent to answer meaningfully. The main objective is to relate the wording of the questions to the experience of the respondent or to put each question into a framework that is significant for the respondent.

The principle of respondent relevance does not mean that questions cannot, under some circumstances, be technical or complex; it means only that they should be understandable to the persons asked. We were once interviewers for a University of Wisconsin study of farmers' attitudes toward new farming methods. They were asked about such practices as "side-dressing corn with nitrogenous fertilizers." If you asked a city dweller such a question you would be seriously violating the principle of respondent relevance. You must try to enable the respondent to answer in terms that he understands and that are within his experience.

This principle may be more important for market research than for political surveys, because the latter must make certain assumptions about political opinion holding. We assume that the ordinary person knows something about politics. This is perhaps an unrealistic assumption; most people don't know very much about the kinds of things the political opinion pollster asks them.[14] Nonetheless, for opinion bearing on public policy, no questions at all are possible unless they are put into some kind of political context.

The third principle is that of *tacit assumption*. A most insightful and important observation lies at the base of this principle. "People don't answer what you say," Paul Lazarsfeld says, "but what they think you mean." This simple point needs to be remembered and constantly brought to our attention when we make questions. Lazarsfeld relates the case of the British lady of rank who answered her friend's question "Is anyone staying with you?" with "No," even though the house was full of servants. The lady took the question to mean, "Is anyone of our class, anyone we would think to be *anyone*, staying with you?" This tacit assumption ruled servants out of the answer, because *people respond not to what you literally say but to what they think you mean when you say it*.

---

14. These comments refer, of course, to interviews of members of mass publics. In interviews with members of political or social elites, quite different research designs, schedules, and procedures may be used. (For a review of literature on elite interviewing plus a model undertaking of her own, see Harriet Zuckerman's "Interviewing an Ultra-Elite," *Public Opinion Quarterly* 36 (1972): 159–175.) In general, the survey research recommendations in this section of the book pertain to inexpert, amateur, and ordinary citizens.

## 5.82 Forms of questions

Structurally, three kinds of questions are asked in public opinion studies: *dichotomous, multiple-choice,* and *open-ended.*

The dichotomous question is, like the pawn, both low in rank and vital to the game. *Dichotomous* means, simply, two-sided: yes–no, true–false, plus–minus. Though the limitations of the dichotomous question are clear, it has great importance for all kinds of simple fact and opinion gathering. It is used especially in obtaining biographical or census-type data: "Are you married? Do you own your home? Are you a registered voter? Do you belong to a labor union?"

The multiple-choice question is a type with many subtypes, such as checklists, rank ordering, and matching-answer questions. Sometimes referred to as the "cafeteria" question, it gives the respondent some alternatives beyond the very confining yes–no choice of the dichotomous question. Moreover, it avoids the subjectivity and difficult problems of coding and analysis that open-ended questions give rise to. It is widely used in public opinion research precisely because it is a compromise, structurally, between the other two types.

Open-ended questions are answered in the respondent's words and style. Because the answers are wholly idiosyncratic, they cannot be analyzed with complete precision. However, what is lost in analytical precision is gained in richness and subtlety of response. In the hands of skilled interpreters, enough responses can be categorized to yield analyses that are frequently more penetrating and possibly more valid than the rigid results of dichotomous or multiple-choice questions. Nevertheless, generalizations are hazardous, and outside advice may be a disservice to the investigator who wants to know when to employ open-ended questions; thoughtful judgment is the best guide.

## 5.83 Kinds of information desired

Consistent with the principle of precision, we may explore the kinds of information that questions can elicit. There are four such kinds of information.

First, there are questions that elicit *direct facts*—sometimes called *census-type* questions: "How old are you? Where do you live? Did you vote in the last election?" Normally they can be specific, and there is no reason to make them open-ended; most census-type questions can be dichotomous or cafeteria in form.

Second, there are questions that elicit *direct information*—usually opinions but sometimes facts—on one or more points: "Will you vote in the coming election?" Such questions are normally either dichotomous or checklisted, but open-ended questions may also appear. "Will you vote in the coming election?" deals with intentions and is therefore more subjective than pure census-type questions.

Third, there are questions that elicit *indirect* or *inferential material.* They are usually either dichotomous or multiple-choice, but open-ended questions have been increasingly used.

The kind of question used depends on the kind of information desired. To elicit general opinions rather than specific factual information, dichotomous questions are used less than open-ended questions. At the subjective end of the order, the two-choice dichotomies and the multiple-choice checklists become less useful. A third-order example, then, might be: "Do you feel strongly about the candidates running in this election?"

The fourth kind of question has to do with eliciting *attitudes and material for background and richness in analysis.* You might ask, "How important is politics to you?" or "Please describe your family history of interest and activity in politics." Even some of these questions can be answered yes or no; but at this level of complexity, detail, or psychological depth, where opinions run into attitudes, yes–no questions are not very helpful. Dichotomous questions can be good jumping-off points when you follow them with probing. "Were your parents active in politics?" If yes, "What offices or activities did your father or mother engage in?" Thereafter, you have to spell it out in the respondent's own language—or in yours, if you aren't a very good interviewer.

## 5.84 Wording and phrasing the questions

It is most important that you use words, insofar as possible, in the way your respondent uses them. Once, in talking with a neighbor about the British queen, I said I had no strong feelings about royalty although I was basically a republican. Though my remark must have appeared to be a curious non sequitur, he replied: "I'm a Republican too, although I can't support the most conservative leaders in our party." The mistake was mine; I could hardly have expected him to know that a small-r republican was a person opposed to monarchical government.

Avoid rarely used words. Here is an example from the study, mentioned earlier, of Wisconsin farmers and their acceptance of new farm practices: "Farmers learn about new things in farming in different ways. From which of the following have you got most information about new things in farming?" (followed by sources of information to be ranked). All of these words are common. The question was written by sociologists, who don't always express themselves so simply. They may have wanted to ask about "innovations," which would have been more accurate than "new things," but they wisely resisted that temptation.

There are times when technical words may be used. In the Wisconsin study we were interviewing farmers who knew about nitrogenous side-dressing for corn. Most adult Americans would not know about this technique; but all the interviewed farmers, even those who were not using it, knew what it was. They had heard about it from the county agent or read about it in farm magazines. They could be questioned in such technical terms—barn drier, strip-cropping, alfalfa-brome mixture, 2-4-D weed control—because they could reasonably be expected to be familiar with them. Common sense and judgment about the people you are going to interview will tell you how much technical material you can introduce in the questions.

A third suggestion: The form should be conversational. Don't ask, "For whom do you intend to vote?" Most people don't talk that way. Say, "Who do you intend to vote for?" or "Who do you think you'll vote for?" or "If the elections were held today, which of these candidates do you think you'd vote for?"

It is equally important not to talk down to respondents. There is a stage when the developing interviewer may try to get too folksy. This may not be quite so bad as being stuffy and academic, but it's bad. You have to hit some middle level of language. On the farm, you can't lapse into dialect; when interviewing teenagers, you can't adopt their slang. You will encounter the temptation, especially when talking with people of limited education, to rephrase questions closer to your respondents' language. But if they get the notion that you're talking down to them, rapport is almost sure to be lost. They expect people who have considerably more formal education than they to speak differently, to use different words—not words they don't understand but words they don't ordinarily use.

The fourth suggestion is to try not to ask "loaded" or "leading" questions—questions that tend to predetermine the answers. It is assumed that questions are not intentionally loaded, but they may be inadvertently loaded, to the detriment of valid responses. A poll on the Panama Canal Treaty of 1977 provided a striking example of the importance of question wording. In May a sample of Americans was asked:

> *Do you favor the United States continuing its ownership and control of the Panama Canal, or do you favor turning ownership and control of the Panama Canal over to the Republic of Panama?* Results: Approve Treaty, 8%; Disapprove Treaty, 78%

In August another sample was asked:

> *The proposed new treaty between the U.S. and Panama calls for the U.S. to turn over ownership of the canal to Panama at the end of this century. However, the U.S. will maintain control over the land and installations necessary to operate and defend the canal. Do you approve or disapprove of this proposed new treaty?* Results: Approve Treaty, 39%; Disapprove Treaty, 46%[15]

Burns Roper says the "art" of opinion polling is often neglected in favor of the "science" of opinion polling. An NBC poll, he reports, found 68 percent of Americans favoring the SALT II arms agreement with the Soviet Union, while a Roper poll at the same time showed only 33 percent in favor of SALT II. Question wording seems to have made the difference:

---

15. "Opinion Roundup," *Public Opinion* (March/April 1978): 33. For question construction generally, see an old but very good work, Stanley L. Payne, *The Art of Asking Questions* (Princeton: Princeton University Press, 1951).

[The NBC question] read, "Do you favor or oppose a new agreement between the United States and Russia which would limit nuclear weapons?" Note that it said "*a* new agreement" not "*the proposed*" new agreement." Note too that the word "SALT" never appeared in the question. By contrast, our question told respondents some of the basic provisions of what was identified as "a SALT treaty." It pointed out that there was a lot of "controversy about this proposed treaty" and it then asked, "Do you think the U.S. Senate should vote for this new SALT treaty or against it?" Now it's a bit clearer why the two surveys got a 35-point difference in results. And clearly the answer lies in the art part, not the science part.[16]

## 5.9 PRETESTING

The sample is created and the draft questionnaire is ready. But you can't begin the interviewing quite yet—at least you shouldn't—because you aren't as sure as you can be that you have the best questionnaire possible. To get bad questions out of your schedule you need to do some pretesting.

Go out and use your tentative questionnaire in fifteen or twenty interviews—or as many as you need. Pretesting should be as much like the real thing as possible and should be conducted under circumstances similar to those you anticipate meeting. Pretesting is a very important and necessary step if you are to do a serious and accurate job of interviewing. Some of the polling organizations, especially the academic groups, do a great deal of pretesting. They may go through three or four drafts of the questionnaire, pretesting between each two successive drafts. It is an expensive and time-consuming process but there is no alternative to it, because the people who are involved in the planning of the research or the survey cannot always anticipate the problems that come up. You may think the question is clear, but if you ask five people and get five different interpretations of what it means, you've got a bad question. One of the occupational hazards of field research is that you get immersed in it and begin to take many things for granted. You think that because you know what a question means, everyone else will, too. Such an assumption is a serious mistake and can be avoided only by careful pretesting.

## 5.10 MAIL AND TELEPHONE SURVEYS

Until recently it was an invariable assumption in survey research that the information was to be obtained by face-to-face interviewing. But nowadays there is a great deal of telephone interviewing, and the use of mail questionnaires continues, especially for professional and elite samples.

---

16. Burns W. Roper, "Some Things That Concern Me," *Public Opinion Quarterly* 47 (1983): 304. See also Howard Schuman and Stanley Presser, *Questions and Answers in Attitude Surveys: Experiments in Question Form, Wording, and Context* (New York: Academic Press, 1981).

Sometimes respondents cannot be seen in person. To interview each member of the sample at home might be prohibitively expensive. In some cases, especially when the polling must be done quickly, there may be too few trained interviewers available, or simply not enough hours to see every respondent in the field. A recent and unfortunately growing problem for face-to-face interviewing is the climate of fear and suspicion among Americans. Pollsters report that in many big-city apartment areas it is nearly impossible to reach respondents' front doors. Doormen, locked entrance halls, and refusals through apartment squawk boxes defeat even the most inventive and hardy interviewers. Under such conditions mail or telephone surveys have to be taken.

Mail surveys have two distinct and serious disadvantages. One is that the response to mailed questionnaires is usually much lower than the response to personal interviews. Those who return mail questionnaires (often as few as 10 or 15 percent) are likely to be unrepresentative of the whole universe—but it may be impossible to specify in what ways they differ or how the responses can be "corrected" by weighting.

The second disadvantage of the mail survey is that it does not allow for quality control of the responses. In the face-to-face situation the interviewer knows that the individual respondent alone gave the answers, and that they were not carelessly or flippantly given (a flippant answer is not necessarily an inaccurate answer, but it often is). A good interviewer can usually prevent unresponsive and manifestly careless answers and will discount, perhaps eliminate, the completed questionnaire if it is not possible to control its quality. There is no such remedy in the mail survey.

A review of the literature (and the wisdom of many years as professional sample designer and teacher of sampling techniques) led Leslie Kish to the following conclusions about the response-rate problem of mail surveys of "literate populations":

1.  High responses can be elicited with skillful, brief, simple question-naires.
2.  Three or four mailings will often raise the response to more than 80 or even 90 percent.
3.  Interview follow-ups on a subsample of nonresponses will further raise the response rate.
4.  Low responses to one or even two mailings should not be accepted, because they often contain severe selection biases.[17]

Telephone surveys carry with them many of the problems of mail surveys—

17. Leslie Kish, *Survey Sampling* (New York: Wiley, 1965), pp. 538–539. For good discussions dealing with response-rate problems, see also Arnold S. Kinsky, "Stimulating Responses to Mailed Questionnaires: A Review," *Public Opinion Quarterly* 39 (Spring 1975): 82–101; William J. Crotty, "The Utilization of Mail Questionnaires and the Problems of a Representative Return Rate," *Western Political Quarterly* 19 (March 1966): 44–53; and Jerry Calvert, "The Social and Ideological Bases of Support for Environmental Legislation: An Examination of Public Attitudes and Legislative Action," *Western Political Quarterly* 32 (September 1979): 327–337.

failure to complete the call, high rate of refusals, lack of quality control, danger of interruptions, inattention—and in addition require that the interview schedule be reasonably short. Despite these disadvantages, telephone surveys seem to be more and more frequently used. By 1984 most political polling was being done by telephone, but longer and more intensive survey research by Gallup, Roper, and such academically based agencies as the National Opinion Research Center in Chicago and Michigan's Survey Research Center continued to employ face-to-face interviews.

The best advice, for the kind of survey research most social scientists do, is that personal interviews are much to be preferred over mail or telephone surveys. Nevertheless, the mail may be used when costs would be otherwise prohibitive, and the telephone can supplement both personal interviews and mail questionnaires.[18]

## 5.11 FIELDWORK

Selecting the sample may involve some fieldwork. In area sampling, members of the central staff or of the interviewing staff may have to make a map or a list of all the dwelling units in the smallest sampling area. The fieldwork with which we are concerned consists of those activities in which the respondents are directly involved—from the time of the first interviewer–respondent contact through the interviews themselves to all the efforts to complete the planned number of interviews.

In some studies it is necessary or desirable to make an appointment with each respondent, particularly if the people to be interviewed are prominent—the so-called elite study. Appointments are made either by the directors of the project or by the interviewer. Respondents in nonelite samples are sometimes given notice that they are to be approached for interviews. Pollsters are by no means agreed on the effects of prior notice, however, and the decision in every instance has to be made on the basis of the facts and the expectations of the particular study.

If you send letters or call respondents—the first course is preferable—be careful to give them enough information about your study to make them aware of its general nature but not enough to allow them to prepare for particular questions. You should err, if at all, in the direction of generalization and even vagueness rather than give them an opportunity to gain information or obtain or change opinions about matters included in the questionnaire. There is a serious possibility of introducing bias and distortion into your study, and if a letter

18. See Robert M. Groves and Robert Kahn, *Surveys by Telephone: A National Comparison with Personal Interviews* (New York: Academic Press, 1979); A. Regula Herzog et al., "Interviewing Older Adults: A Comparison of Telephone and Face-To-Face Modalities," *Public Opinion Quarterly* 47 (1983): 405–418; and James H. Frey, *Survey Research by Telephone* (Beverly Hills, Calif.: Sage, 1983).

cannot be sent without the creation of such distortion, you should not send it at all.

If you do send a letter, it should (a) note the scientific and representative character of the sample in which the respondent's name appeared, (b) stress the importance to the study of completing each planned interview, (c) state (if true) that no personal or potentially embarrassing questions will be asked, (d) frankly admit the amount of time being asked of the person, and (e) predict as nearly as possible when the interviewer will call. You probably should give only a general return address and no encouragement to those who receive the letter to call you. If someone calls and says she cannot or does not want to be interviewed, your chances of persuading her otherwise are small; your odds of getting the interview are much greater if such resistance arises on her doorstep, face to face. In any case, don't worry about refusals at this stage—or ever. Refusals are rare in public opinion polling conducted by respectable organizations and reasonably accomplished interviewers. The technique of prior notice, where it can be applied, is one way refusals can be reduced.

Interviews should always take place in surroundings familiar to the respondents. Other persons should not be present. If responses are recorded on the spot (the usual and recommended practice), the interviewer, not the respondent, should do the writing. In trying to prevent irrelevance, the interviewer should steer toward some middle ground—to be felt at the time, not predicted in advance—between resignation to any amount of wandering and courtroom adherence to admissible evidence. Long interviews may be completed at a later time, if necessary, but make it to the end in one sitting if you can; no moment in time is like any other, and the joining of an interview obtained in two halves is more than the mere addition of later to earlier responses. Hurried interviews are almost always unsatisfactory; come back later rather than try for a thirty-minute interview in fifteen minutes. Likewise, common sense warns against distractions during the interview.

## 5.111 "Not at home": Call-backs and substitutions

The results of a public opinion survey can be severely biased or even rendered useless by failure to interview all or nearly all of a sample that is based on the specific assignment of respondents. Those who are not at home the first time the interviewer calls tend to differ in their occupations, work habits, age groupings, and sex from those who are at home. Accordingly, the not-at-homes tend also to differ from the at-homes in their opinions.[19]

Varying your hours of interviewing according to your experience in the area (or your preinterviewing knowledge of the area), asking neighbors when the hoped-for respondent is usually home, or, in the most difficult cases, telephoning

19. See Tom W. Smith "The Hidden 25 Percent: An Analysis of Nonresponse on the 1980 General Social Survey," *Public Opinion Quarterly* 47 (1983): 386–404.

for an appointment—all these tactics should be used in the attempt to reach each person assigned. Considerations of time and money and the urgency with which you need the particular not-at-homes for stratification purposes will determine how much energy should be spent in an attempt to reach the 100-percent-interviewed mark. Make a number of call-backs, marking on your schedule or field notes the time and circumstances of each, before dropping the name. Consistency is important, both among the cases handled by the same interviewer and among all the cases handled by all the interviewers; if you make four call-backs for some not-at-homes, make the same number for the others. When inexperienced interviewers are used—or when many interviewers are used, experienced or not—agree at the outset on the minimum number of call-backs to be made.

When the required call-backs have been made, or when obtaining the particular interview is not worth additional effort, the question of substitution may arise. (In practice, the question of substitution should be raised and settled in the early planning of the study.) Whether substitution is required, encouraged, permitted, or forbidden will depend on the judgment of the study designers. It would be folly to generalize about the wisdom of any substitution policy. Whatever policy is adopted ought to be uniformly followed, especially if substitution is required to conform to some procedural formula (for example, interviewing a person of the same sex in the dwelling unit with the next higher street or building number). In small samples especially, call-back and substitution policies are important, since the introduction of systematic bias by only a few cases can have serious effects on the results.

## 5.12  PROCESSING AND ANALYSIS OF DATA

At the completion of the fieldwork in any public opinion study, *all* material ought to be kept for the use of those who do the analysis and write the reports. Field notes and the scribbled remarks of interviewers sometimes contain facts or hints that are vital to the analysis. Even the maps and procedural materials used by the interviewer may be useful later and should be collected at the end of the fieldwork. The rule of the pack rat is a good one to follow: *save everything.*

The processing of survey data is less easily discussed. The technological possibilities of machine processing have increased so enormously that a small library on the subject—most of it understandable only to experts—could be assembled. Fortunately, no extended treatment of electronic data processing is necessary here.

Several texts and monographs are now available to students of the social sciences, the best of which is probably Kenneth Janda's *Data Processing: Applications to Political Research* (available from Northwestern University Press). It is enough to say that most research, even small class projects, generate information sufficiently complex and detailed to warrant the use of machine analysis. Processing data in this way always involves intermediate tasks—principally the coding of responses and entering data on discs or tapes—into which error may be injected; but these efforts and risks are usually worth taking for the increase in speed and in the variety of analyses that are possible with computer-stored data.[20]

No matter how much quantitative analysis one is able to do with public opinion data, the evidence is hardly ever clean-cut and neatly stacked for or against hypotheses. At this stage in the history of social science, conclusive findings are very rare, and analyses that purport to be conclusive ought to be looked at long and suspiciously.

There is no reason, therefore, to apply only statistical tests to your data or to present only quantitative analyses. Although quantitative and other objective forms of interpretation are supposedly to be preferred in dealing with survey data, it is quite proper to engage in speculation and under certain conditions to apply tests of taste, aesthetics, and value preferences. Scientific method and the rules of fair play require only that all analysis be described in enough detail to avoid misleading others, and that all conclusions, however arrived at, be presented as modestly and as simply as possible.


## 5.13 A CONCLUDING NOTE

Despite remarkable growth in both use and accuracy of public opinion surveys since the mid-1930s, problems remain. For instance, it is not always certain that accuracy is foremost in the minds of those who engage pollsters or determine the conditions under which they work. Both commercial and political results of opinion polling are frequently determined to some extent by the motive for the investigation rather than by its findings. The half-truth is more common than either the whole truth or the whole lie.

But to suggest that motives are unavoidably impure in the use of opinion polling is merely to state a truism of behavior. Polling as a career and as an aid to careers cannot rise above the standards of the other human thoughts and acts to which it is related. For the purposes of this chapter, we have assumed the desire for complete accuracy in opinion measurement. On the purely technical side, we have seen that there are many opportunities for error in the opinion survey and that the means for eliminating errors do not yet exist. We have also seen that the size of the sample is not, generally speaking, a problem in scientific polling. Beyond some fairly small minimum—1,500 or 2,000 for a national sample and perhaps as few as 500 in a smaller universe—the size of the sample does not significantly influence accuracy.

The way the sample is chosen, however, is critical to the accuracy of the survey.

---

20. In addition to Janda's book, Earl R. Babbie's *Survey Research Methods* (Belmont, Calif.: Wadsworth, 1973) contains chapters helpful to undergraduates interested in data analysis. Reanalysis of survey data obtained from repositories is also increasingly possible for graduate students and serious undergraduates; see Herbert H. Hyman, *Secondary Analysis of Sample Surveys: Principles, Procedures, and Potentialities* (New York: Wiley, 1972).

So are the way the questions are constructed and ordered in the questionnaire, the way the interview is carried out in all of its aspects, and the way the responses are subjected to quantitative and qualitative analysis. In all these steps, the artistry of the designer, the interviewer, and the analyst blends with the more mechanical, routine, and uniform elements.

The objective of survey research is to make it possible for more and more aspects of public opinion to be handled mechanically, routinely, and uniformly. In the twenty years between 1933 and 1953, the practitioners of opinion research established their claim, on the basis of this fundamental criterion, to have developed the "scientific measurement of opinion." The fact that the science is by no means complete and probably never will be makes their achievement not less but more exciting.

## Chapter 6

# Opinion Measurement and American Democracy

Public opinion polling is by now an accepted and regular part of political life in America. Survey research has such varied and valuable applications for candidates, policy makers, and administrators that it would be unthinkable to do without it.

To be sure, political polling has its critics, and the arguments of some of the critics will be dealt with in this chapter. The attacks on polling and pollsters are mainly of two kinds. One claims that survey research as applied to politics is so inaccurate that it is worth very little as a measurement of voters' real policy views or candidate preferences. That argument says, in effect, that there are so many sources of error that good judgment would not trust the findings of pollsters.

The other main criticism of political polling says that it is injurious to democracy. It declares that evil and injury to democracy would follow if pollsters did what they claim to do; accurate and reliable polling, these critics assert, would be a disservice to democracy.

The two arguments surely differ and may not be logically consistent. Those who make the dangers-to-democracy argument at least implicitly say polling is accurate, for if the polls were truly such inaccurate measures as the first critics claim, then they presumably would not be used and would not injure democracy. But it might be countered that political polls are both inaccurate and dangerous to democracy precisely because citizens and politicians, not aware of their inaccuracies, place unwarranted faith in them. The two criticisms of polling are not separable in reality, then, and the arguments necessarily overlap.

## 6.1 METHODOLOGY: INACCURACIES

Probably the most common complaint against pollsters is that they do not achieve representative cross sections of the universe whose opinions they aspire to measure. Beyond the questions about the representativeness of samples already dealt with, only two points need to be made.

The first is less general and refers to the measurement of opinions and the prediction of behavior from *subsamples*. Because of the operation of the Electoral College, presidential elections depend on a candidate's getting a plurality of votes in states that together produce a majority of Electoral College votes. A national poll that forecasts a countrywide popular vote for a candidate is therefore no predictor of success in a close race. Ideally candidates need to know how they are doing in each state, or at least in those major states that can produce an Electoral College majority.

Although there is no device analogous to the Electoral College at the state level, on occasion the question of the predictive use of subsamples may arise there. A candidate for governor of Illinois, for example, will want to know how she is doing in Chicago and in suburban Cook County as well as in the state as a whole, because voting patterns in those areas are somewhat more volatile and machine- or media-manipulable than patterns in the rest of the state.

Bear in mind that very small samples are unreliable. Hadley Cantril indicates that 200 is about minimum for any useful sample and that samples of less than 50 are not even worth experimenting with.[1] That is, tolerably trustworthy predictions for major states or for important areas within a state require samples of several hundred potential voters.

Despite this requirement, pollsters have reported results for individual or important states on the basis of national samples during presidential campaigns. If we make the unrealistic assumption that the respondents in a sample of 2,000 are distributed throughout all fifty states according to the population of each state, the prediction for a state of 7 million would have to be based on a sample of 77 interviews, for a state of 3 million on 33 interviews, and Nevada's prediction on the basis of a sample of two voters. This breakdown, of course, is a *reductio ad absurdum,* but it illustrates the impossibility of predicting state votes from subcells of national samples. The importance of the electoral college system to the presidential race, however, makes it imperative to consider state-by-state forecasts. Although many one-state studies are done and much information is traded among pollsters, subsample breakdowns are still made from national samples—despite the clear warnings of a 1944 congressional report: "The size of the samples used for many of the States was not large enough, even if properly drawn, to ensure reliable individual State estimates based solely on polls of the voting population."[2]

---

1. Hadley Cantril et al., *Gauging Public Opinion* (Princeton: Princeton University Press, 1944), pp. 130–131, 150–171, 298. Cantril's samples, between 50 and 100 in size, were all experimental and limited to small geographical areas, and produced rather large errors.

2. *Congressional Record,* p. 15778, (August 22, 1960). Daniel Yankelovich believes that at least 250 interviews are necessary to obtain a 6% sampling error within a state (*Public Opinion Polls: Hearings before the Subcommittee on Library and Memorials of the Committee on House Administration, September 19–21 and October 5, 1972* [Washington, D.C.: Government Printing Office, 1973], p. 247).

The second point about sample size is that techniques are available for creating samples that, within rather small limits, closely resemble the universe from which they are drawn. If not all pollsters use these techniques—and some do not—those who have the responsibility for such surveys and those who use the results are obliged to assess for themselves and their readers what the consequences of their technological imperfections may be. Some polling for commercial purposes, and perhaps even for political purposes, may quite honestly be done with less than the best techniques, when, for reasons of cost or time, no better can be employed. But the procedures and probable errors should always be described when the results are reported.

## 6.11  What does "don't know" mean?

Fairness requires that pollsters describe not only their sample design and actual sample but the analytical assumptions and devices on which their reports or conclusions are based. For instance, the handling of the "don't know" responses has always been a source of disagreement among pollsters and of confusion among the public. The "don't know" dilemma is an unsolved problem about which pollsters ought to be candid.

In preelection polls of the who-do-you-intend-to-vote-for variety, a "don't know" is reported as "undecided." The terms are used interchangeably, but the problem of interpretation does not therefore disappear. Are the "undecideds" truly undecided or just indifferent? If they are indifferent, most of them probably will not vote at all. If those who vote divide between the candidates, the category can be ignored. It is likely, however, that those who are indifferent yet actually vote will choose the candidates favored by their friends, their neighbors, or their socioeconomic class; through the use of such indexes, an intelligent prediction may be made of the distribution of these votes. The ultimate choice of the true undecideds may likewise be predicted by the use of *expected correlations* between individual behavior and socioeconomic factors. But it may be necessary, in addition, to look for idiosyncratic clues in each questionnaire. However the undecideds are handled, pollsters have an obligation to disclose—and readers have a right to know—the process by which the analysis was made.

Yet, the practical difficulties of this kind of reporting are apparent: discussions of assumptions and explanations of procedures tend to be dry, technical, and uninteresting. The requirements of crisp reporting and analytical exactness may be incompatible. Newspaper reporting of public opinion measurement cannot be expected to meet the ideal requisites of social science research, although conscientious journalism might make more use of feature stories and expert critiques in reporting poll data.

Some critics of modern polling point out that the "don't know" categories, besides being inadequately interpreted, are generally underestimated. A number of reasons are advanced to explain this underestimation. It is argued that the structure of the questionnaire and the sociopsychological pressures of the interview situation account for a serious error in measuring "real" opinion. However,

brief and somewhat superficial interviews of the kind done by pollsters—
"superficial" as opposed to the intensive interviews of psychologists and
psychiatrists—*must* be structured to a considerable degree. Questions are often
of the dichotomous or cafeteria sort, and the respondent finds it easy to give
definite rather than "don't know" answers. In most cases, one may do so without
any danger of being exposed by later questions, even when one does not have any
opinion. The use of two-step or other screening questions has been recommended
to filter out the "knows" from the "don't knows."

"Filter" questions or statements are increasingly used in political polling.
"Have you been able to follow the campaign for the governorship this year?" "Do
you happen to know the names of the candidates for United States senator from
this state?" "I'd like to ask you some questions about China, and of course many
people aren't familiar with the details, so on some of these you may not want to
give any opinion." Note the wording here; an effort is made to overcome
embarrassment and the tendency to give socially acceptable answers—it may
even be that the last example (a filter *statement*) gives the respondent too much
encouragement to answer with a "don't know." Filter questions are difficult; the
trick is to evoke what the respondent really knows and thinks.

Studies at the University of Cincinnati's Behavioral Science Laboratory in
1978 revealed how serious the problem of separating the "don't knows" from the
"do knows" is. A fictitious issue, the possible repeal of "the 1975 Public Affairs
Act," was embedded in a series of domestic and foreign policy issues asked of
1,820 persons. A different filter question was used with each of three one-quarter
parts of the sample, and respondents in the fourth quarter were asked, without a
filter question, simply whether they agreed or disagreed with the move to repeal
"the 1975 Public Affairs Act." Only 7.1, 7.4, and 4.5 percent of respondents in the
filter-question groups gave an opinion on this nonissue (that is, 92.6 to 95.5
percent said they didn't know), but 33.2 percent gave an opinion when no filter
question was used. On real issues the use of filter questions increased the number
of "don't knows" by 11.7 percent in the case of private versus governmental
health insurance, and by a whopping 58.7 percent on the question of the resump-
tion of arms aid to Turkey. These researchers concluded that unless filter
questions are used, we may be getting meaningless answers about policies from as
much as one-third of our respondents.[3]

## 6.12  Do they tell the truth?

This brief consideration of the problems of measuring "don't knows" leads to a
related criticism of pollsters. It has been said that respondents will not give

3. George F. Bishop et al., "Pseudo-Opinions on Public Affairs," *Public Opinion Quarterly* 44
(1980): 198–209. See also, by the same authors, "Effects of Filter Questions in Public Opinion
Surveys," *Public Opinion Quarterly* 47 (1983): 528–546.

honest answers to many of the questions asked in opinion surveys. Lindsay Rogers, whose dyspeptic book *The Pollsters* is one of the most celebrated attacks on opinion measurement, wonders whether "public opinion is ever the sum of the answers that people are willing to give to strangers" and quotes the view of the director of Mass Observation that *"public opinion is what you say out loud to anyone.* It is an overt and not necessarily candid part of your private opinion."[4]

Although people will not always tell exactly what they think when asked, it is of no value to leave the matter with such a useless generalization. Whether truth will be obtained seems to depend on (a) what the question is about, (b) who asks the question, and (c) what the respondent thinks will be done with the answer.

Indications are that a considerable number of people incorrectly answer even factual questions for which the truth can be checked in public records. One study of 920 Denver adults, conducted in early 1949, found invalidity in one-seventh to one-fourth of the answers to questions about voting in six earlier elections.[5] In another study, 13 percent of the respondents who said they had voted in the 1948 presidential election actually had not.[6] A more recent investigation—of the 1976 Michigan presidential election sample—found almost the same percentage of untruthful responses: "a total of 15 percent of the study respondents [were] registration misreporters and 14 percent. . .[were] voting misreporters."[7] Similar research in 1978 produced similar results; 55 percent of the national sample that year claimed to have voted, but only 43 percent had actually done so. Over 90 percent of the untruthful responses were given by persons who said they had voted and had not; only about 9 percent said they had not voted but actually had.[8]

The accumulated evidence indicates that distortions and untruths are almost certain to exist in all poll data. Leo Crespi argues that conscious fraud is rare and that distortion is largely a result of respondents' disinterest, fatigue on long schedules, and a desire to appear informed and helpful.[9] It seems hard to believe, however, that fatigue or a desire to be helpful would prompt a respondent to misrepresent pure census-type data such as car and home ownership. There appears to be a hard core of liars on even the most socially neutral questions—a group that is joined by many others as the questions become increasingly

4. Lindsay Rogers, *The Pollsters* (New York: Knopf, 1949), pp. 41–42; italics in original.

5. Hugh J. Parry and Helen M. Crossley, "Validity of Responses to Survey Questions," *Public Opinion Quarterly* 14 (1950): 61–80.

6. In Waukegan, Illinois, 22 of a sample of 204 (10.8%) gave untruthful answers when asked whether they had voted in the 1950 election (Mungo Miller, "The Waukegan Study of Voter Turnout Prediction," *Public Opinion Quarterly* 16 [1952]: 397).

7. Michael W. Traugott and John P. Katosh, "Response Validity in Surveys of Voting Behavior," *Public Opinion Quarterly* 43 (1979): 367.

8. John P. Katosh and Michael W. Traugott, "The Consequences of Validated and Self-Reported Voting Measures," *Public Opinion Quarterly* 45 (1981): 519–535. See also I. A. Lewis and William Schneider, "Is the Public Lying to the Pollsters?" *Public Opinion,* April/May 1982, pp. 42–47.

9. Leo P. Crespi, "The Cheater Problem in Polling," *Public Opinion Quarterly* 9 (1945): 431–445.

ego-related. The importance of distortion has to be estimated and a way to minimize it devised for each case on the basis of its own conditions.

It is equally impossible to generalize about the effects of strangers as interviewers. The implication of Rogers' criticism is that people will tell the truth more readily to their friends than to strangers. The answer to this implication is yes and no. A number of psychological theories suggest (and interviewing experience supports) the notion that some kinds of people are more candid about some things with strangers than with friends. All interviewers have heard truths from respondents who would under no condition tell them to friends or neighbors. And it may be—although it has not been proved or even tested to our knowledge—that opinions on political issues are more freely given to strangers. A case can be made that the impersonal stranger, once established in the respondent's eyes as a reputable fact gatherer, is more likely to be trusted with a confidence than is someone the respondent must see on a day-to-day basis.[10]

An even stronger argument could be made to justify respondents' willingness to confide in strangers. Although the average respondent cannot be expected to appreciate it at the time of the interview, every interviewer realizes that two factors in the polling process tend to separate names from data in the collection and analysis of results. First, there is a thoroughgoing air of anonymity about every opinion study—even, to a considerable extent, elite studies. Often names are not known at all; even when, as in most cases, they are or can be known, poll takers maintain a pervasive indifference toward them. Although there appears to be no discussion of the presumption of anonymity in the literature (perhaps because it is taken for granted by social scientists), it probably results from the fact that the opinion researcher is interested primarily in *collected opinions*—in the aggregate views of categorical and social groups. Emphasis is necessarily on the many, and though each respondent is important in the building of the sample, each alone is, generally speaking, insignificant.

The second factor is simply this: To remember names and to associate particular opinions with particular persons would not be possible for the interviewer or analyst even if she wanted to do so. Names uselessly clutter up the minds of the persons who analyze opinion data. Thus, just as in large-scale statistical work the institutional tendency is to ignore names, so at the personal level the rule of economy prevails. Since names are irrelevant and inconvenient, anonymity is practical as well as ethical.

As polling becomes increasingly common (even vigorous critics expect more rather than less polling) and as the public understanding of opinion measuring

---

10. "A stranger frequently hears important truths at the fireside of his host, which the latter would perhaps conceal from the ear of friendship; he consoles himself with his guest for the silence to which he is restricted, and the shortness of the traveller's stay takes away all fear of his indiscretion" (Alexis de Tocqueville, *Democracy in America* [London: Oxford University Press, 1946], Author's Preface to First Part, p. 17).

improves, the expectation of anonymity on the part of the polled may begin to equal the presumption of anonymity that already exists for the pollster. One need be neither naive nor prophetic to see that when such a condition is reached, it will be necessary to stand Rogers's criticism on its head. Meanwhile, there is no reason to believe that people in general are less honest in interviews with strangers than with friends.

## 6.2 SELF-IMAGE MANAGEMENT AND THE GOOD-CITIZEN IDEAL: A SPECIAL PROBLEM IN OPINION MEASUREMENT

A general phenomenon operates with respect to what respondents will tell pollsters. It is what we call self-image management. Facts or opinions that reflect on a person's self- or social image are apt to be misreported.

Response will be distorted if (a) the respondent believes a truthful answer might reflect adversely on him as a person, (b) he thinks he knows how to avoid such adverse reflection by distortion, and (c) the anticipated possible consequences of the distorton are less threatening than the adverse reflection itself. This rule, applicable in all social intercourse and not merely in survey research, goes far to explain untruth in many settings, from market research in suburban shopping centers to perjury in law courts.

In the usual poll on public issues or political behavior, the model of the good citizen provides contextual clues for self-image management. The good-citizen model says we have a right to expect Mr. or Ms. Good Citizen to be informed, interested, and rational about public issues, and furthermore that Mr. or Ms. Good Citizen has an obligation to demonstrate those characteristics. In many cases the pressure to appear informed, interested, and rational will lead to distorted responses, unless the respondent perceives distortion to be more threatening to his or her self-image than failure to achieve the good-citizen ideal.

The good-citizen ideal is the special problem in survey research on public issues in democracies. In other polities, we assume, and surely in investigations not involving citizen ideals, respondents can allow themselves to be ignorant, uninterested, and irrational if they like. Question: "What do you like about this beer?" Answer: "It's less filling, tastes great." Question: "Should people hug their children today or hug a gorilla in the zoo?" Answer: "I don't know and I don't care."

But there cannot be many Americans who would say that "I don't know and I don't care" is an acceptable answer to a seriously asked question on public policy. We are pervasively *required* to know and care, even as the evidence is overwhelming that we don't *in fact* know much or care much. This contrast between ideal and reality is an enormous burden on both the popular psyche and public opinion measurement.

## 6.3 VALIDITY AND RELIABILITY

*Validity* in polling has to do with whether the respondent's real opinion is discovered. But, strange as it may seem, for some purposes and under some circumstances it does not matter whether real opinion is revealed. Although the psychologist may be concerned with the correspondence between private opinion (what the individual *really* thinks) and public opinion (what he *says* he thinks), the political sociologist is primarily interested in the correspondence between public opinion and related behavior. If a respondent claims to believe in building new schools and votes on the bond referendum accordingly, the political scientist has a rational set of data, even if the respondent is secretly opposed to building new schools. If an individual supports candidate X in preelection polls and votes for candidate X in the election, whether she really prefers candidate X is, for most political analyses, irrelevant. Although the reasons for liking or disliking a policy or a candidate are important for strategic purposes—and tests of logic and relevancy may be necessary for certain kinds of analyses—the first practical test for the political meaning of public opinion is not the ultimate truthfulness of an expressed conviction but the internal consistency of public behavior.

To the political scientist, survey *reliability* is probably more important than validity. Reliability is judged by the reproducibility of a measurement result. A testing technique is said to have high reliability when it consistently measures the same dimensions with similar results. Thus an intelligence test is reliable when it measures the *same dimensions* of the intellects of all children given the test at any single time and when successive measurements of individuals show *consistently similar results*. It is not a valid intelligence test when elements unrelated to intelligence (for example, style of language or other learned cultural factors) are measured along with native intellectual ability. But though it may not be valid, it is reliable if it yields consistent measurement results.

Are public opinion polls, in this sense, reliable? Some evidence is available. In one interesting experiment, the National Opinion Research Center sampled voter intentions in Boulder, Colorado, and on election day had all voters fill out a second ballot immediately after they had cast their official ballots. The preelection poll turned out to be very close on candidate choice (an error of less than 1% in each of two contests) and quite close on two of the three policy questions on the ballot. A rather large error on the third referendum may have been explainable by factors not pertinent to the question of polling reliability.[11]

A revealing analysis of polling reliability disclosed that 24 percent of a California sample misrepresented their voter registration status (most seemed to be lying for purposes of self-image management). But they were so consistently untruthful that for predictive purposes the lack of validity of individual responses would not have reduced the reliability of the whole survey.

---

11. Harry H. Field and Gordon M. Connelly, "Testing Polls in Official Election Booths," *Public Opinion Quarterly* 6 (1942): 610–616.

*'Greased polls'*

While those who lied about registering also lied about voting, their lies so faithfully mirrored the responses of genuine voters that their inclusion in the sample would lead to a "prediction" *in this instance* that was substantially as accurate as one from the more reliable but less numerous group of known registrants.[12]

The 1976 study indicated, however, that "misreporters" were slightly more likely to be Democrats and that "although the differences...are well within sampling error, they do illustrate a distinct partisan difference in the candidate preferences of the misreporters."[13]

Validity, of a kind, and reliability may be measured by the correspondence of preelection polls and election statistics. From the technical point of view, this is a major reason why pollsters like the chance to forecast elections. Elections constitute one of the rare means for checking poll results—perhaps the only regular and systematic test that is not experimentally staged or based on demographic and sociological assumptions. The "givens" in an election are regularized, anticipated, and (aside from a possible bandwagon effect) beyond the influence of the pollster.

The margin of error between the predicted popular vote and the actual vote for a candidate is a rough test of the validity of the prediction for that election. The discrepancies between the predicted and actual results of several elections may be

---

12. Charles G. Bell and William Buchanan, "Reliable and Unreliable Respondents: Party Registration and Prestige Pressure," *Western Political Quarterly* 19 (1966): 43; italics in original.

13. Traugott and Katosh, "Response Validity," p. 366.

taken collectively as a gross measure of poll validity. Similarly, the differences between or among poll forecasts for the same political race constitute a test of reliability. When aggregated, they may give us clues to the general reliability of polls.

The average error in all 245 national, sectional, state, and local election predictions made by the Gallup Poll from 1936 to 1950 was 4 percentage points.[14] Since 1948, however, Gallup and the other major political pollsters have vastly improved their polling techniques and their understanding about political behavior. In six presidential and congressional elections from 1950 through 1960, the Gallup agency averaged an error of *less than 1 percent.*[15] Gallup's error in 1964 was 2.6 percent; in 1968 it was only 0.4 percent; in 1972, 0.2 percent; in 1976, 2.0 percent. In the mercurial 1980 election, confounded by the independent candidacy of John Anderson, all pollsters' predictions were wide: Gallup's error was 4.7 percent. But, as we have seen in Table 5–1, Gallup's 1984 error was a scant .3%.[16]

Despite attempts to check the reliability of polling, one interesting early suggestion has apparently not yet been followed. Many years ago Lucian Warner declared that the "ideal empirical check" of sample survey results would be to interview the whole universe at the same time that the sample was being interviewed. Such a check could be made in a community of 5,000 to 10,000 persons without great cost.

> The original survey should employ the methods currently accepted and should sound opinion on a variety of topics. The 100 percent canvass of the population should be made simultaneously to avoid the possibility of a shift in opinion. A large regiment of workers should be employed that the work might be complete [sic] within a single day.[17]

Although such an experiment would be neither as easy nor as significant as Warner thought, it or some modification of it would seem worthwhile.

## 6.4  INTENSITIES OF OPINION

Critics of opinion measurement often say that polls do not measure the intensities of opinion. The complaint has little merit. Since the beginning of scientific polling, serious practitioners have recognized the importance of measuring what

14. George Gallup, "The Gallup Poll and the 1950 Election," *Public Opinion Quarterly* 15 (1951): 21.

15. Paul Perry, "Election Survey Procedures of the Gallup Poll," *Public Opinion Quarterly* 24 (1960): 531–542; and, by the same author, "Gallup Poll Election Survey Experience, 1950 to 1960," *Public Opinion Quarterly* 26 (1962): 272–279.

16. Despite the general accuracy of the 1984 predictions, some were surprisingly wide of the mark; the last Roper Poll had an error of more than four percent.

17. Lucian Warner, "The Reliability of Public Opinion Surveys," *Public Opinion Quarterly* 3 (1939): 390.

Rogers calls the "loudness of the yeses and noes." On the other hand, and despite the undoubtedly genuine concern with the problems of intensity and the techniques for dealing with them, pollsters have not improved their practice very much since the early days.

When and under what conditions do we care how strongly people hold their opinions? The answer seems to be that intensity is an important dimension whenever and wherever members of the public are actively engaged in efforts to persuade others to change their attitudes and opinions. Intensity, then, is important to the extent that there is a public issue that is expected soon to be settled by election or action of a representative body, when individuals are free to participate according to how strongly they feel, and when intensity therefore has predictive value for estimating the outcome of the settlement.

If, for example, a poll is taken on the same day as the election to which it is related, intensity of opinion is not an important element. In the election each vote is equal to every other vote, no matter how intensely the voters feel about the election—and on election day we may assume it is too late for voters who feel intensely about the election to influence the opinions of voters who do not feel intensely about it. On the other hand, whenever there is an opportunity for persons who feel intensely about an issue to influence the opinions of those who do not feel strongly, the strength of opinions is important for meaningful measurement if any prediction is being attempted.

To deal more satisfactorily with intensity of opinion, it may be helpful to introduce the concept of *distribution* of opinion. On any issue the range of possible opinion is from "strongly favor" to "strongly oppose"; we imagine a continuum of opinions with each person falling on the scale somewhere between these two ends. In practice, question construction results in the grouping of opinions into three positions ("favor," "neutral," "oppose") or five ("strongly favor," "favor," "neutral," "oppose," "strongly oppose"). So arranged (as continua or in scales showing both direction and intensity), opinion distribution may be said to have two basic forms: consensual patterns and conflict patterns.

The late V. O. Key, Jr., described as a "supportive consensus" the situation in which opinion underpins existing policy and practice.[18] A supportive consensus distribution is shown in Figure 6–1.

A "permissive consensus," as shown in Figure 6–2, is one that allows but does not actively support a policy (*policy* here means an official or governmental position on an issue).

Conflict distributions of public opinion may be bimodal or multimodal, but the two most common are those in which opinion is quite sharply polarized, with

18. Key's discussion of the distribution of opinions—both distribution of intensity and geographical distribution of intensity in America—is the best in the literature, and we are indebted to him for many of the ideas and some of the language of this section. See V. O. Key, Jr., *Public Opinion and American Democracy* (New York: Knopf, 1961), chap. 2–5. See also Anne H. Hopkins, "Opinion Publics and Support for Public Policy in the American States," *American Journal of Political Science* 18 (1974): 167–177.

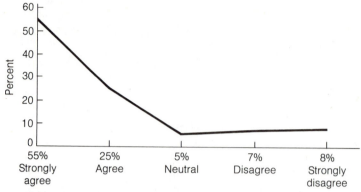

**Figure 6–1.**  *A "supportive consensus" distribution of opinion*

few neutrals, and those in which there are opposing groups with strong feelings but also a relatively large indifferent middle, shown in Figures 6–3 and 6–4.

Do pollsters give sufficient attention to intensity of opinions? Like most persons, pollsters *know* better than they *do*. Louis Harris is no doubt one of the most thoughtful experts in the field and also one of the most candid. He admitted in 1958 that, with regard to election polling, "qualitative dimensions of intensity and firmness of opinions have rarely been systematically analyzed, but may make a real difference in any kind of precise percentage-point result."[19] During a campaign, the journalistic pressures and the pressures from the clamoring players of the game of politics seem to prevent the application of the most refined (usually the most costly and almost always the slowest) research tools. The headlines inevitably make their own conditions when attention is focused on political opinions; qualifications of findings, scales of pluses and minuses, and rows of figures without clear winners and losers do not appeal to the consuming public in periods of political fever. But when political fever gives way to the other fevers recorded by the mass media, who then will pay for Gallup's 900 interviewers, the analysts, and the machine time to consider the intensity with which respondents like or dislike a candidate, or whether a "No" answer is really "I guess not" or "Hell, no"?

## 6.5 POLITICAL POLLING: HOW MUCH, BY WHOM, AND SO WHAT?

Some of the early public opinion pollsters apparently believed that their work would make possible the achievement of the last stage in the evolution of self-government. The ultimate step on the long march to democracy could now

---

19. Louis Harris, "Election Polling and Research," *Public Opinion Quarterly* 21 (1957): 115.

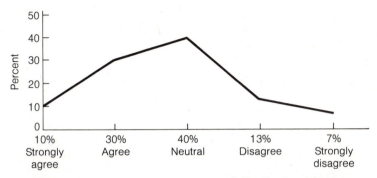

**Figure 6–2.**   *A "permissive consensus" distribution of opinion*

be taken. Democracy, they seemed to say, means that all persons participate in making governmental decisions; decisions are made on the basis of opinions about issues, and polling techniques make it possible for the first time to measure accurately the opinions of large numbers of persons. Therefore, polling makes possible the perfection of democracy. The opinion-policy process in direct democracy presumes that popular opinion is turned directly into governmental policy. When sampling techniques become perfect (or nearly perfect)—or so the argument goes—opinion polls will be equal to referenda. Instead of having all the people make policy, as in a plebiscite, a perfectly representative sampling can do so. Thereupon, legislatures may be reduced to making detailed rules and acting as constituency-service agencies—or, ultimately, abolished. Such a system, while as yet practically unattainable, has a certain superficial appeal in theory.

We may call this kind of direct democracy *opinion-sample majoritarianism,* to distinguish it from the face-to-face majoritarianism of town-meeting democracy. No pollster has ever quite declared that majority opinion, as measured by sample surveys, ought to be translated directly into policy. But some pollsters have implied that opinion-sample majoritarians might be found among them if the necesary opinion-measuring machinery could be created. And proponents of instant national TV referenda (sometimes called "teledemocracy") are occasionally to be found among both journalists and academicians.[20]

At the opposite extreme from direct majoritarians are avowed minoritarians. They believe that policy ought to reflect the views of elite groups who for special reasons of birth, wealth, intellect, or tradition are "fit" to govern the masses. To minoritarians, the opinions of large publics are of no concern except as they may be manipulated by "superior" groups in the struggle to control governmental policy.

Earlier minoritarian theories of government, referred to by the Greeks as

---

20. See Benjamin R. Barber, "Voting Is Not Enough," *Atlantic Monthly,* June 1984, pp. 45–52, and his *Strong Democracy* (Berkeley: University of California Press, 1984).

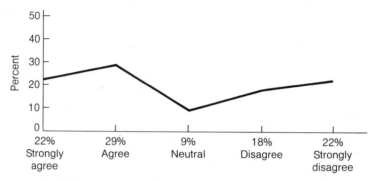

**Figure 6–3.**    *Bimodal conflict distribution of opinion*

monarchy and aristocracy, are no longer viable in the Western world. (Perhaps it is safer to say that such theories are seldom now publicly expressed, for the fascism of 1923–1945 was a form of aristocracy, and one cannot say that it could not happen again, no matter how frightening the prospect.) Nevertheless, the most powerful nondemocratic societies today are governed by explicitly minoritarian systems. The stated objective of the Soviet government and other governments of Marxist ideology is a majoritarian system; but in the early, so-called socialist stages of the system's development, their theory calls for a dictatorship of the few Communist party members over the many nonmembers. It is not just coincidence that the Communists say, at least up to now, that public opinion research in the capitalist state is a stratagem by which the masses are hoodwinked into believing that they have influence and political power.

For our understanding of the meaning of public opinion in democracy, the important spectrum of beliefs on the majority–minority continuum are those that may be described by the term *coalition majoritarianism*. Within a complex and fractionalized governmental framework of federalism and separation of powers, policy is made by temporary and ad hoc coalitions of groups and individuals. There is a presumption—only a presumption, because the reality is immeasurable—that a popular majority (or something near it) is represented by the coalitions that are successful in making policy on particular issues. Under these conditions, the opinion-policy process is much like that described on pages 23–28. When policy is made by coalition majorities in the United States, the coalitions consist not of internally disciplined parties, as is usually the case in continental Europe, but of political individuals and groups (including party groups) with various strengths, goals, and access to the decision-making process.

### 6.51 Public opinion polling and mixed democracy

Believers in the American system of mixed democracy (or coalition majoritarianism) both agree and disagree about the place and the significance of public opinion polling. After fifty years of agitation and controversy, pollsters and

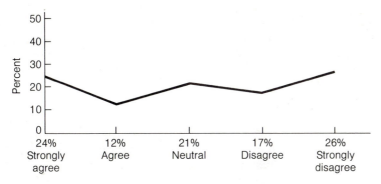

**Figure 6-4.** *Multimodal conflict distribution of opinion*

critics appear to agree that most public opinion polling serves some intelligence function for policy makers—it gives them information that may influence their understanding or beliefs—and that skillful polling may give them certain kinds of information that cannot be obtained in any other way. Beyond this point, however, views tend to conflict. On three matters especially pollsters and critics disagree.

**6.511 Should all opinions be known?** This basic question is one on which some students of democracy differ from the pollsters. The latter say that all views should be known because, even if simple notions of plebiscite majoritarianism are not accepted, policy makers ought to understand as thoroughly as possible what popular thinking happens to be on each issue.

Some writers have suggested that this view of the importance of polling is too simple. W. E. Binkley took issue quite early with pollsters' contention that their reports constituted an important contribution to democratic practice. Our democracy, Binkley seems to say, does not operate on the basis of some simple national majority; and pollsters' projection of poll results into gross national figures is misleading because it presumes a kind of democracy that we do not have:

> It is to be doubted whether the American people want national issues decided on the basis of national referenda which opinion polls suggest. . . . A feasible national policy rather represents the net result of the concurrences and balances of the dominant interests of the sections, states, and congressional districts. . . . Perhaps our opinion polls might turn their attention more to discovering these concurrences than confining their investigations so much to the pattern of simple national referenda. Thus might they approximate the reality of the process by which national policy is formulated.[21]

21. W. E. Binkley, review of J. Bruner, *Mandate from the People,* in *Public Opinion Quarterly* 8 (1944): 428–429.

Another critic argues that the activities of pollsters—especially their reporting of findings—and the way their findings are accepted (interpreted) by newspaper-reading Americans constitute a "disservice to democracy." The essence of democracy, according to John C. Ranney, lies in an endless discussion of issues and policies. Dynamic, ever-changing, and always open dialogue among individuals and groups is, as we have seen, the heart of the opinion-policy process. To Ranney, the danger in public opinion polls is that the participants in this critical dialogue may take the polls to be more important than they are.[22] To the degree that poll results are assumed to be the last and, in a sense, authoritative word on any public issue, the opinion-policy process becomes slowed, rigid, and inoperative—and to that extent democracy has been ill served.

There is little evidence, however, to indicate that poll reports have significantly slowed the opinion-policy process. So many elections are determined within the 6 percent range that pollsters allow themselves for error, and so many issues depend on unpollable factors in the opinion-policy process, that participants in the dialogue have found that poll results cannot be the sole or even the major determinant of their behavior. If the pollsters could claim 100 percent accuracy or near it, their pronouncements might have the outcome Ranney fears. But as long as their admitted margin of error is greater than the margin that usually determines the important elections, the political controversy on which democracy depends is unlikely to be stopped or even appreciably slowed.

Although this speculative danger does not seem to be imminent, Ranney at least implies that perfect measurement of public opinion would be a disservice, because cross-sectional readings of the opinion of the moment would be substituted for an understanding of the opinion-policy process as a dynamic, never-ending phenomenon. Despite the way pollsters used to talk, no one believes that other factors should be excluded from policy making. Above all else, policy makers have to be forward-looking. They must think about tomorrow. Aside from the possibility that opinion may be wrong, nothing is more certain than that opinion will change. Decisions must be made on many grounds, involving many facts, judgments, and plain old hunches. In one profound sense, what the people think today is not so important to political actors as what the people will think tomorrow, especially if tomorrow happens to be election day. The politician who takes the momentary measurement of opinion—however accurate—as the sole criterion for decision making is not only unfit for public office in a democracy but, from the point of view of a political career, an ignoramus. If the perfect measurement of opinion had the effect of making large numbers of policy makers follow public opinion slavishly, democracy would indeed suffer a disservice. It is hard to believe, however, that even perfect measurement would induce any

---

22. John C. Ranney, "Do the Polls Serve Democracy?" *Public Opinion Quarterly* 10 (1946): 349–360. See also Michael Malbin, "Teledemocracy and Its Discontents," *Public Opinion,* June/July 1982, pp. 58–59.

number of political actors to be so simpleminded in their understanding of the opinion-policy process.

What if the belief in or fact of perfect measurement encourages the *electorate* to reduce the amount of testing, weighing, and discussion of public policy? In this event, we could again agree with Ranney that the polls would be doing a disservice to democracy. But it seems no more probable that knowing what people think today will determine what people will think tomorrow than that it will determine what decision makers decide today. The political nonelites are, after all, influenced by public officials and other opinion leaders, just as the reverse is true. The opinion-policy process is a two-way street, and as long as significant numbers of the public recognize the complex nature of this interplay there is little danger that the political dialogue will be slowed or ended. The leaders of interest groups will continue to attempt to influence opinion no matter how accurately it is measured. Some individuals and groups seem, in fact, to be more vigorous when they suspect they are in the minority. Those who enjoy majority support know that when the count is taken again their happy position may be reversed or weakened unless they continue to promote the democratic dialogue. It seems safe to assert that the dangers Ranney envisioned forty years ago are now no more likely to materialize than the early pollsters' vastly more simple notion that polling heralded the last and perfect stage of democracy.

**6.512 Democracy and the accuracy of polling.**   We have considered some criticisms of the methodology and the practical accuracy or inaccuracy of modern public opinion polling. Now we turn to the importance of polling accuracy to the political life of a democracy.

The controversy over how to calculate percentage error is an old one. Pollsters figure their error as a percentage of the 100 percent sample. Many critics contend that the error percentage is obtained by dividing the difference between the predicted and actual vote by the predicted vote. Thus, although Gallup claimed that he missed the 1948 Truman vote by 5.4 percent—he predicted 44.5 and President Truman received 49.9—Lindsay Rogers and others assert that the error is over 12 percent (5.4 divided by 44.5)

This debate may have some interest for partisan maneuvering and forensic effects. For our purposes, it is a quibble we may ignore. The pollsters' calculation recommends itself because it involves simpler and more apparent arithmetic.

The possible misleading effect of name familiarity is a more significant matter for polling in a democracy. The argument is simply that respondents often give preference early in the campaign to potential candidates merely because they know who these individuals are. Senator Albert Gore suggested that a poll in which this effect is pronounced misleads the public as well as the potential or actual candidates.

Pollster Elmo Roper candidly said that early poll results are "certainly much more a reflection of familiarity with names than anything else—until after the campaign itself has started."

In a sense, I share some of Senator Gore's misgivings, particularly about the effect of the polls on *nominations*. I have been dismayed to find many convention delegates exhibiting an obsessive and exclusive interest in finding a winner, dismayed at the weight given to preconvention polls which are in my opinion little more than a name-familiarity game, but which are often accepted as gospel evidence of the ability to win in November.[23]

The complaint that name familiarity has an unfortunate effect on the nomination process should be related to the criticism, considered earlier, that pollsters do not give adequate attention to the views of influential political decision makers. The relationship is something like this: Early "trial heats" clearly reflect the fact that some names are more widely known among the voters or are temporarily more in the news, and such celebrities receive higher poll ratings. Party activists and other political leaders, however, are well aware of the name-familiarity effect and discount it, appreciating that the campaign later can give visibility to a less well-known candidate and thus improve her poll ratings.

In the Democratic presidential nomination races in 1976 and 1984 the early trial heats showed low support for little-known candidates. But in each of those years, after the party caucuses in Iowa and the New Hampshire primary, a trailing candidate "broke out of the pack," as the saying goes, and the names of Jimmy Carter and Gary Hart became very familiar to voters. That such notoriety, spurred by sudden media attention, was based on the votes of a few people in two of our smaller states may be a problem, but if so it is a problem of another sort, not related to opinion polling or its effects.

**6.513 The bandwagon effect of preelection polls.**    The third complaint of many political critics relates to the alleged "bandwagon effect." It is said that undecided and apolitical voters tend to support an apparent victor simply because he is an apparent victor. Presumably people like to back a winner.

There is little evidence that a bandwagon effect occurs. In the first place, the logic of the argument is not persuasive. People like to back a winner in matters to which they attach importance. But the bandwagon argument supposes that the voter is indifferent to the outcome. If the voter is indifferent, however, he will not care who wins or whom he votes for—nor will he, at the moment of voting, have any memory of poll predictions; on the other hand, if he favors candidate A, he is unlikely to vote for B simply because a poll has predicted B's election.

Beyond this argument, which is something of a definitional quibble, it is not at all clear that public faith in pollsters is high enough, despite the good showings of the 1960s and 1970s, to warrant wide adoption of a bandwagon psychology. Roper's comment on a possible bandwagon effect merits attention:

---

23. Elmo Roper, "Polls and Sampling," *Saturday Review* 43 (October 8, 1960): 58; italics in original.

> I don't think there is much evidence that the polls directly influence the voters' preferences. If there were a "bandwagon effect," it seems to me that polls would always underpredict the margin of victory, since the whole theory of bandwagon is that more and more people jump on it, and there just has to be a week between the last poll and election day. As a matter of fact, surveys have overpredicted the margin of the winner at least as much as they have underpredicted it.[24]

Additional inferences about possible bandwagon effects—or possible "underdog" effects, which postulate that people will shift support to a candidate who is said to be behind in the race—come from predictions broadcast early on presidential election days and from experimental studies. Since the 1960s the major national TV networks have been predicting the presidential winner on the basis of sampling in eastern and midwestern states (this practice and the concerns raised by it are discussed more fully below). Predicted winners are known to some proportion of voters in western states before they cast their ballots, and if a general bandwagon or underdog effect exists it could be detected in the behavior of those voters. The most careful studies have found no bandwagon or underdog reactions from westerners who voted after the TV networks had projected a winner.[25]

Likewise, experimental studies do not find systematic bandwagon or underdog effects in responses to public opinion polls.[26]

## 6.52 Significance and insignificance in polling

Pollsters ask many questions of little or no political importance. Questions about entertainment-world celebrities are only rarely of genuine public interest. But the critics who object to such questions fail to appreciate that the mass media that support the largest pollsters have commercial interests to satisfy as well as public responsibilities to discharge. As long as human-interest stories are sought by the consumers of mass media, the opinion column, whether it is the local "inquiring reporter" or the national Gallup Poll, will have a certain fascination as casual reading to fill coffee breaks and commuting rides with information that is welcome precisely because it is of no importance.

Jargonized questions, like the questions of no importance to political life, are also easy targets of the antipollsters. Jargon questions are perhaps more deplorable than trivial questions. They may encourage the plain-folks brand of anti-

---

24. *Congressional Record,* p. 2204 (February 11, 1960).

25. See Sam Tuchman and Thomas E. Coffin, "The Influence Of Election Night Television Broadcasts in a Close Election," *Public Opinion Quarterly* 35 (1971): 315–326, and their citations.

26. See Robert Navazio, "An Experimental Approach to Bandwagon Research," *Public Opinion Quarterly* 41 (1977): 217–225, and Stephen J. Ceci and Edward L. Kain, "Jumping on the Bandwagon with the Underdog: The Impact of Attitude Polls on Polling Behavior," *Public Opinion Quarterly* 46 (1982): 228–242.

intellectualism that sees stuffily worded poll questions as the products of "eggheads" who are as removed from the world of real language as they are from the world of real people. But jargon and academese on any subject may have this unfortunate effect, and it is unfair to single out pollsters from all the other abusers of language.

Two related but more subtle points bear on the matter of what is asked of whom. As we saw in Chapters 2 and 3, it is the unanimous judgment of the most thoughtful students of democracy that the people as a whole are not able to give specific policy direction. At the same time, the maintenance of popular government demands that the broad objectives and processes toward which and through which power is directed be approved by the masses. One might say, for example, that it is necessary for the American people in general to approve the large-scale, continuous U.S. involvement in European economic and military life that began in 1947, but it is both unnecessary and naive to expect large numbers of Americans to understand the operation of the European Common Market or the structure and powers of the North Atlantic Treaty Organization.

Despite the repeated demonstration that a high level of public knowledge and thinking is neither necessary nor expectable (however much it is to be desired), pollsters often ask questions that are inappropriate to all except a small percentage of the citizens of any society. Consider the following: "As you know, it has been discovered that 2,000 to 3,000 Russian combat troops are now stationed in Cuba. In response to the presence of Russian combat troops in Cuba, do you favor or oppose the United States. . .threatening to take military action against Cuba if the Russian troops are not taken out of Cuba?"[27] Besides asserting for a fact what was quite unclear at the time—that is, whether the Russians in Cuba *were* combat troops—this item implies that average Americans ought to be able to advise on the delicate tactics of diplomacy.

Some questions are just dumb. They may require no detailed and expert information from the public, but they are mischievous irrelevancies that betray the pollster's ignorance of politics in a democracy. One such question, asked by AIPO in 1981 and 1982: "When a large business concern, a foundation, or a university needs a new president, the usual practice is to appoint a search committee to seek out the best candidates. Do you think that search committees should be used by the Republican and Democratic parties to find the best possible candidates and then let party members choose the one they prefer?" Thirty-nine percent of those polled in 1981 and 54 percent of those polled in November 1982 said the parties should use search committees to find their presidential candidates![28]

Burns Roper summarized the problems, as he sees them, of the way polling is used and reported by political journalists. He says that among the "effects of journalism on polling" are the following:

27. ABC News/Louis Harris Poll, September 26–October 1, 1979, reported in "Opinion Roundup," *Public Opinion* 3 (February/March 1980): 25.

28. *Gallup Report,* February 1983, p. 9.

Source: Drawing by Chas. Addams; © 1982 The New Yorker Magazine, Inc.

*"Would you say Attila is doing an excellent job, a good job,
a fair job, or a poor job?"*

1. At first journalists saw polls as competitive and threatening, "so that polls did not achieve the visibility that they now have and that they deserved back in the thirties, forties, and fifties."
2. Now that the "media converts" have taken uncritically to polling and gotten into the business themselves they have:
   a. established bright junior reporters as their survey experts after "a two- or six-week course on polling techniques";
   b. "overstressed sampling error and understressed the other more important and considerably greater sources of error" (especially question wording);
   c. created a serious conflict-of-interest situation in which they push their own polls rather than report various and possibly more balanced findings of several polls; and because of deadlines they demand speedy, simplistic, and often distorting procedures of their poll employees.
3. On the positive side, "the media embrace of polls has also created a broad awareness and acceptance of polling which it would not have otherwise."[29]

---

29. Burns W. Roper, "The Media and the Polls: A Boxscore," *Public Opinion* 3 (February/March 1980): 46–48. The most conscientious pollsters are aware, as Roper is, of the danger that stress on chance sampling error will lead to a greater public confidence in polls than is warranted. The Field Institute's releases on its California Poll make this disclaimer: "Sampling error is not the only criterion, and we caution against citing only the sampling error figure alone as the measure of a survey's accuracy, since to do so tends to create an impression of a greater degree of precision than has in fact been achieved."

Since 1968 the Standards Committee of the American Association for Public Opinion Research (AAPOR) has recommended that pollsters include in any news release essentials of the survey methodology and inform their private clients *in detail* of the elements of the research design. Their "minimal disclosure" standards for news releases are worth listing in full:

1.  Identity of *who sponsored* the survey.
2.  The exact *wording* of questions asked.
3.  A *definition of the population* actually sampled.
4.  *Size of sample.* For mail surveys, this should include both the number of questionnaires mailed out and the number returned.
5.  An indication of what allowance should be made for *sampling error.*
6.  *Which results are based on parts of the sample* rather than on the total sample. (For example: likely voters only, those aware of an event, those who answered other questions in a certain way.)
7.  *Whether interviewing was done personally,* by telephone, mail, or on street corners.
8.  *Timing* of the interviewing in relation to relevant events.[30]

Robert Blank examined all presidential poll releases carried in the *New York Times* and the *Washington Post* from September 1 to November 6, 1972. He applied to them the AAPOR standards of minimal disclosure with the following results, by percentages of the sixty-one stories based on polls: sponsorship was revealed in 18 percent; exact wording was given in 30 percent; 21 percent gave information about the population sampled; sample size was specified in 85 percent; in only 8 percent was the sampling error given; 62 percent indicated which data were based on parts of the sample; 61 percent reported *how* the interviewing was done; and 61 percent revealed *when* the interviewing was done.[31]

A similar analysis was done on 116 articles reporting polls in three newspapers—*Atlanta Constitution, Chicago Tribune,* and *Los Angeles Times*—from 1972 through 1979. Sample size and sponsorship were found to have been most often reported: 85 and 82 percent of the time, respectively. Sampling error was least reported, only 16 percent of the time. Interestingly, AAPOR standards were more often met in election polls than in other polls, and telephone interviews with editors of the three papers revealed "that election polls are handled more conscientiously because they are more important than other polls." This investigation also discovered that the methodological standards more often

---

30. "Standards for Reporting Public Opinion Polls," release of the American Association for Public Opinion Research, September 27, 1968 (mimeo).

31. Robert H. Blank, "Published Opinion Polls and the Conduct of the 1972 Presidential Campaign," paper delivered at Western Political Science Association Meeting, San Diego, April 7, 1973.

appear in print if they are included in the body of the releases put out by the polling agency rather than in trailing appendixes.[32]

Sampling error seems to be specified more frequently in the 1980s than it was in the 1970s, and it appears that the AAPOR's minimal disclosure standards are gradually being more fully met, but that many poll results are still given without sufficient information to permit full evaluation of them.


## 6.6 TRENDS AND NEW DEPARTURES IN POLITICAL POLLING

Recent developments in survey techniques and electronic data processing have led to innovative campaign and opinion measurement devices. In 1972 a data-processing firm collected the names of 1.5 million Democratic and independent voters in Ohio and arranged them geographically by education, union member-ship, religion, homeownership, age, and income level. The Ohio Democratic party, which paid $250,000 for the service, could then make specialized appeals to subgroups of potential supporters.[33]

By the mid-1980s the "tracking and targeting" of voters had become very sophisticated. Large-scale computers were first used in 1960 when social scien-tists from M.I.T., Yale, and Columbia analyzed probable public opinion on various strategies that the presidential candidate might follow. Data from 66 surveys, representing a total of more than 130,000 interviews with the public from 1952 to 1959, were fed into the machines. On the basis of these data, it was possible to make forecasts of future electoral behavior. Columnist Roscoe Drummond called this computer project a "people predictor," able to "forecast public reaction to alternative possibilities in a way that makes public opinion sampling seem as slow and outdated as a horse and buggy."[34] Drummond's comment was misleading. The Simulmatics Project was simply the projection of opinion trends from a time series of samples. But it was the first combination of many surveys to help analysts understand trends in opinions about elections.

H. L. Nieburg explains the modern computer-assisted analysis of poll data as "the ability to target and track demographically with rapidity and precision the views and behaviors of people collectively and individually."

> Tracking refers to collecting feedback rapidly in order to measure the moment-to-moment impact of an ongoing campaign. Targeting re-

---

32. M. Mark Miller and Robert Hurd, "Conformity to AAPOR Standards in Newspaper Reporting of Public Opinion Polls," *Public Opinion Quarterly* 46 (1982): 243–249, quotation at 247.

33. Warren Weaver, "Company, Collecting Data on Voters, Combines Tradition and Technology," *New York Times,* October 2, 1972.

34. *New York Herald Tribune,* December 19, 1960.

fers to breaking down the public into its constituent audiences in today's segmented market place, so that campaign strategy and media locations can be most effectively tailored to reach the intended targets. Both tracking and targeting make possible continuous and sensitive monitoring of communications, so that strategy and tactics can be fine-tuned responsively to the opportunities and importunities of events.[35]

The organizations of major candidates now routinely track groups of potential voters, design appeals to targeted groups, and reach them through mailings, associational networks, cable TV, and even home computers. At a conference in late 1982, some political consultants suggested that the American electorate might become divided and embittered if ever more narrow appeals were made to "left-handed Lithuanians, Irish homosexuals and pro-abortion dentists," but others thought messages aimed at targeted groups would enrich the already vital pluralism of American life. All expected the use of narrow appeals to increase.[36]

In 1976 there was a new development in election survey research; nationwide "exit polling" was introduced that year. Voters leaving the voting places were asked how they had voted and why. In that way the public quickly learned what voters thought of candidates and issues. Exit polling was used very extensively in 1980 by the major media opinion researchers and by the presidential candidates' own pollsters. In the long presidential nomination process, exit polling during early primaries, such as those in New Hampshire, Florida, and Massachusetts, allows candidates to revise their strategies and to selectively highlight issues that seem to be favoring them. Further, exit polling facilitates rapid and detailed analysis of the vote. On November 4, 1980, the *New York Times*/CBS News exit poll interviewed "more than 10,000 voters leaving polling booths across the nation," providing reporter Adam Clymer with forty column-inches of statistics about the Reagan–Carter split by partisanship, sex, socioeconomic status, region, race, union membership, and rural–urban residence.[37]

Mark Levy's evaluation of four major 1980 exit polls in three primaries—New Hampshire, Florida, and California—and in the general election found them "to have been conducted with a degree of meticulousness which compares favorably to the highest standards of commercial and academic research." In the three primaries ABC News's prediction error ranged from 0.6 to 5.8 percent, and in the general election it was only 0.2 percent. Levy believes that exit polls are "an efficient and constantly improving technique—a method for gathering data which has enormously enhanced the practice of election reporting."[38]

35. H. L. Nieburg, *Public Opinion: Tracking and Targeting* (New York: Praeger, 1984), p. 39. See also Gary A. Mauser, *Political Marketing* (New York: Praeger, 1983).

36. Adam Clymer, "Problems Foreseen in Campaign Technology," *New York Times,* December 22, 1982.

37. Adam Clymer, "Behind Carter's Poor Showing," *San Francisco Chronicle,* November 5, 1980.

38. Mark R. Levy, "The Methodology and Performance of Election Day Polls," *Public Opinion Quarterly* 47 (1983): 66, 67.

Whatever the merits of exit polling, another problem with election reporting has been festering since 1964. In that year the TV networks began to sample votes in a few "bellwether" or swing precincts and to predict winners, in some instances even before the polls closed.

In the critical California Republican primary of June 1964, the Columbia Broadcasting System, using what is called "voter profile analysis,"predicted Senator Barry Goldwater's victory on the basis of just 42 of the more than 32,000 precincts in the state, The premature computer reporting of election results could be most serious in national elections. Midwestern and western congressmen were concerned by "the serious possibilities for unduly influencing election results by telling the country how the vast cities and populous states of the East have made their decisions before millions of Americans farther west have exercised their solemn duty of voting for the candidates of their choice.[39] Some members of Congress thought a simple congressional resolution would suffice to persuade the networks to exercise self-restraint in the announcement of computer-proclaimed victories. One senator proposed a bill to outlaw the broadcasting of both *returns and predictions* until all polls had closed in the United States. Other senators moved to establish a uniform closing for federal elections—one version would close the polls at 11:00 P.M. in the eastern time zone and at 5:00 P.M. in the Bering time zone (the zone of the Aleutian Islands, off the coast of Alaska).

The experience of elections from 1968 through 1976 reduced but did not eliminate anxieties about the possible effects of election-day forecasts and pre-dictions on turnout and voting behavior in western states. Several studies indi-cated that early returns and computer predictions did influence western voters, but the findings were unclear and contradictory in part.

The problem of premature TV victory announcements resurfaced in 1980. On election night NBC proclaimed Ronald Reagan the winner at 8:15 EST, while there were still 2 hours and 45 minutes for voting in California and nearly 5 hours before the polls closed in Hawaii. Even more upsetting for western Democratic candidates and party activists was President Carter's concession speech at 9:45 EST, an hour and a quarter before the Far West voting was over. William Switzer of Corvallis, Oregon, was quoted as saying: "Something is terribly wrong with this democracy if the networks can call the election and a president can concede before millions of Americans vote." In California the Secretary of State announced that she would "seek federal legislation to require that all voting places from coast to coast open and close at the same hours," and she later estimated, on the basis of a Field Institute poll, that 401,000 Californians refrained from voting because of the TV projection and President Carter's concession.[40]

Research at Michigan's Center for Political Studies concluded that TV

---

39. Tuchman and Coffin, "Influence of Election Night Television Broadcasts," pp. 325–326.

40. James A. Finefrock, "How Early Concession Hurt Demos in West," *San Francisco Examiner,* November 5, 1980; John Balzar, "Demos Hurt by Early TV Vote Report," *San Francisco Chronicle,* March 11, 1981.

election-day coverage, early predictions, and President Carter's concession reduced overall turnout by 6 to 12 percent in 1980.[41] A later critique of that research and the report of another study that incorporated Michigan data asserted that these actions by the networks and the president probably reduced western voting by only 0.2 percent.[42]

In 1984 all three networks were once again caught between the pressure to be first to "call" the election and the annoyance of western voters and politicians. They all agreed not to make predictions of a winner in an individual state before the polls in that state had closed. But since President Reagan won in all the eastern states and in all the midwestern states except Minnesota, the electoral-vote winner was known by 5:30 Pacific Standard Time—once again, two and one-half hours before the polls closed in California. Predictably, the local affiliates in the western states were inundated by calls from irate citizens and distressed local candidates. By prearrangement, all three networks and their affiliates urged their viewers to vote if they had not already done so, pointing out that many state and local races could yet be won or lost in the states where the polls were still open. But those urgings seem not to have assuaged the real or imagined hurts of western citizens. And thus the 20-year dilemma continues: How to reconcile the predictions of winners with the western voters' feelings that they have been ignored, or been cheated out of their part in choosing the American President.[43]

The trend is clearly toward more and more political polling. In 1980, after CBS researchers counted the state and regional efforts devoted to political polling, it was reported that they "had unearthed 147 polls, 43 of which [had] been established since 1978," but "fewer than half of them used methods that could be considered reliable."[44]

Of *private* political polling and pollsters there seem to be more every year. It has been estimated that "ten thousand or more" New York State residents were polled in 1982 by private candidate-hired researchers.[45] Bruce Altschuler lists the major uses of private political polls:

> (1) Deciding whether to run; (2) Image—discovering the strengths and weaknesses of the candidate and his opponent; (3) Issues— discovering which issues are most important to the voters; (4) Key subgroup breakdowns; (5) Resource allocation; (6) When to leak, which raises ethical questions as well as the practical problems of the

41. John E. Jackson, "Election Night Reporting and Voter Turnout," *American Journal of Political Science* 27 (1983): 626.

42. Laurily Epstein and Gerald Strom, "Survey Research and Election Night Projections," *Public Opinion,* February/March 1984, p. 49.

43. TV's Early Projections Again Rile Many in West, "*San Francisco Examiner,* November 7, 1984.

44. E. J. Dionne, Jr., "1980 Brings More Pollsters than Ever," *New York Times,* February 16, 1980.

45. Frank Lynn, "Pollsters in New York Questioning Thousands," *New York Times,* August 19, 1982.

effects of leaked polls on fund raising, the morale of staff and supporters, and press.[46]

In the face of such wide use of polls and of such doubts about their quality, it
has been suggested that governmental agencies be established—perhaps in con-
junction with state universities or private academic centers—to (a) collect the
results of opinion research pertinent to electoral behavior and public policy; (b)
arrange, summarize, and in some cases translate these results into usable forms
for political and governmental leaders; and (c) actively disseminate these materials to those for whom they are produced.

Such services can be regarded as devices to extend the information already
offered by many state governments to their citizens and political decision makers. When referenda are to be held, a number of states require the distribution of
information pamphlets that typically describe the ballot items and present
arguments by those who support and oppose the measures. Likewise, legislators
in many states are given research facilities and aids to help them in deliberations
and decisions. Publicly supported opinion- and attitude-measuring agencies
might be justified in the way that such research facilities have been. A combination of both public and private opinion survey agencies, it seems, would serve the
interests of democracy better than either kind alone.[47]

---

46. Bruce E. Altschuler, *Keeping a Finger on the Public Pulse: Private Polling and Presidential
Elections* (Westport, Conn.: Greenwood Press, 1982), p. 9.
47. Many of the matters dealt with in this chapter are analyzed and appraised in *Polls and the News
Media: A Symposium,* ed. Albert E. Gollin, whole issue, *Public Opinion Quarterly* 44 (Winter 1980).

# THE ENVIRONMENT OF OPINION

The first six chapters dealt with public opinion as an intangible but important ingredient of self-governing polities. We suggested a definition, examined the component parts of public opinion, discussed problems of measurement, and explored the interactions of opinion measurement and democratic practice.

The scope and objectives of the six chapters that follow are quite different. We shall consider the reasons why opinions tend to develop in recognizable and, within limits, predictable patterns.

Social scientists, journalists, and other students of human behavior are normally concerned with differences of opinion. Sociologists may be interested in why and to what extent the opinions of city dwellers are not like those of suburbanites, or why immigrants think differently from second- or third-generation Americans; political scientists may be interested in why and to what extent Republicans and Democrats hold different views; economists are concerned with differences between buyer and seller or manufacturer and distributor. Our mass media (insofar as they have direct social impact), our research and teaching postures at the college level, and our public policy-forming processes concern themselves with disagreements. We focus our attention, quite properly, on the conflicts of opinion in society, for it is only through vigorous but regulated conflict of opinion that vitality is maintained and adaptive change is possible.

At the same time, each person does share a large number of opinions with all other persons—although the conditions that determine the vast amount of agreement in the human community, and in all the subcommunities from nation to family, are seldom considered. Social scientists—and other people too, when they think about opinions—realize that most people agree with most other people about most things. Stated so flatly, this may sound like an irresponsible assertion or an unimportant truism. It is neither. Rather, it is a profoundly important simplicity.

Thus, though our attention is drawn primarily to opinion conflict and disagreement, it is well to notice the existence and importance of the massive substratum of agreement within any society. The great bulk of facts and opinions that are shared and unquestioned by almost every person in every society makes possible and supports the smaller and visible contention that is our major concern in the analysis of public policy and social change.

The body of opinion agreement, which may be called consensus (although that term is subject to abuse and ambiguity), has a crucial function as the guarantor of social stability. It also has significance for the individual.

The plain truth is that most opinions are not determined by an effort of personal reason or will. What we are, what we know, and what we believe are determined in very large degree by conditions we never made and influences we have scant power to change—despite the fact that the range of theoretically possible opinions is almost infinite.

Most people know, for instance, that the world is a globe. Therefore, it is impossible for them to believe that anyone could reach the sun by traveling east in the morning. Yet a few thousand years ago, perhaps even a few hundred years ago, most people could and did believe that. Some primitive people no doubt still believe that the world is flat; and along with their acceptance of that opinion goes the impossibility of accepting thousands of other beliefs related to modern astronomy, geography, and physics. The flatness or globularity of the earth is not now an issue around which public opinion can cluster.

Another way of stating this elementary but important point is that many opinions are both cumulative and exclusive. Almost every opinion (or knowledge of fact—which for the moment is not distinguished from opinion) makes possible additional opinions at the same time that it denies the possibility of still other opinions. If I believe that an object is 100 cubic feet in area, I know that it will not fit in a space of 10 cubic feet but will fit in a space of 200 cubic feet. If I think that candidate A is a completely honest man, I cannot believe my neighbor's report that he has been bribed, or that he knowingly lied during the campaign, or that he is capable of crime in office; but I can easily hold any number of opinions about him consistent with my pivotal belief in his integrity. If I accept the fundamental tenets of religion, I can as easily believe all its ancillary and supplementary doctrines; but any belief in contrary religious dogma is most unlikely.

We should be careful here. It is obvious that individuals can simultaneously hold opinions that are contradictory and even mutually exclusive, just as social groups can contain individuals whose views are different from and even incompatible with the opinions of other group members. The point is only that there are powerful influences that produce (a) vast amounts of agreement in human opinion, (b) clustering of opinions among cultural groups, and (c) certain patterns of inclusive and exclusive opinions within the individual.

In the chapters that follow we suggest a way of thinking about the influences and factors that produce both the uniformities and the differences in opinion holding. We are concerned with the physical growth and limitations of the individual and with the world of mind, with the cultural and social influences that create the environment in which opinions form, and with some of the dynamics of the opinion-forming process.

## Chapter 7

# Opinion Formation: Approaches and a Model

For our purposes, *opinions are expressed points of view about matters that are controversial or susceptible to controversy.* Public opinions are distinguished from private opinions on the basis of how many people are affected by the issue in controversy.

At this point, we are dealing with opinions, both public and private, and we are asking the simple question: What is the process by which we come to have any particular opinion at any particular time, and what are the factors that influence this process?

## 7.1 VARIOUS APPROACHES TO THE STUDY OF OPINION HOLDING

We can approach opinion holding in a number of ways. The simplest and most congenial to the intellectual traditions of the West is the *rationalist* approach. Human reason, the rationalist would say, determines opinions. The human animal is the thinking animal. By the exercise of reason we are able to establish both fact and opinion.

Opinions may be deduced from *facts* (that is, from observed physical reality) and from *laws*. We hold different opinions, the rationalist declares, because we do not all understand the facts and the laws equally well. If we thoroughly comprehended the laws (facts of the physical world are manifestations of the laws) and acted in accordance with them, human reason would be the perfect instrument for the social organization of the perfect world.

It would be inappropriate here to attempt a summary of the history of rationalism in the Western world—inappropriate, presumptuous, and, fortunately, unnecessary. The rationalist tradition, however, has been dominant throughout most of our history since Plato. Even today it is probably as respectable among intellectuals as any other tradition; and no doubt it is widely accepted among the literate public. Christianity (especially Catholicism) has contributed greatly to the dominance of rationalism in Western thought. Theoretical and applied science, too, has appeared to most observers to strengthen the belief that the physical world, at least, is tidily organized in accordance with unchangeable laws that have only to be discovered by human reason.

It may be that the physical world *is* controlled and determined by laws that, in time, will all be discovered by scientific inquiry. Many rationalists, however, are more totalitarian in their claims for reason as authority. Some argue that divine law, though unknowable in its entirety, is the great source and encompasser of the moral law, the civil law, and all lesser laws. These rationalists hold that both faith and reason are means for knowing truth.

Rationalist thought in America is influenced less by the scholastic rationalism of the Catholic thinkers than by the Protestant and humanistic rationalism of continental European philosophers of the seventeenth and eighteenth centuries. René Descartes and Rousseau, especially, made significant contributions to the belief that "true knowledge is obtained by the use of certain absolute principles given with the mind and constituting reason."[1] For Descartes (whose influence in the natural sciences has been especially strong), these "absolute principles" were mathematically formulated. For Rousseau, they were the "natural rights" of all people (which largely explains his influence in Western political thought).

What has philosophical rationalism to do with the study of opinion holding? Simply this: those who accept any of the various subtypes of systematic rationalism are inclined to think that people arrive at their opinions through the exercise of their powers of reason and that the truth or falsity of opinions consists in their correspondence with some ideal truths or nonhuman laws.[2]

Later we shall return to the discussion of the place of reason and deliberation in opinion holding and opinion change. Meanwhile, the course of honesty is to admit that we do not think human reason is the only or even the principal determinant of human opinions. There is, as we shall try to show, an important place for reason and intellectual calculation in what is for us a helpful theory of opinion holding, but no one can make wholly rational decisions on every issue, and most people find it impossible to do so on any issue at all. We have seen, in

---

1. Hugh Miller, *An Historical Introduction to Modern Philosophy* (New York; Macmillan, 1947), p. 268.

2. For a brief modern statement of the traditional (that is, eighteenth-century) rationalist view, which underlies much of American political theory, see *Religion and American Society: A Statement of Principles* (Santa Barbara, Calif.: Center for the Study of Democratic Institutions, 1961). For example, the American political "consensus . . . represents the product of human reason reflecting on experience"; it is possible because "men who are agreed on general principles are more likely to reach rational decisions. . . . The men who argue for consensus are ultimately dependent on their belief that there *are* truths, not merely of a scientific but of a rational, philosophic, and political kind, which are the product of human reflection, are accessible to all, and are 'objective'" (pp. 56, 58); italics in original.

Chapters 2 and 3, that recognition of the large, nonreasoning elements in political life has necessitated the reformulation of democratic theory. Opinion holding and decision making, closely allied in the opinion-policy process, are both largely nonrational. Every analysis that overlooks the pervasiveness of nonreason and assumes the consistent and thorough use of reason is bound to raise more questions than it settles.

Psychologists, especially Freudian psychologists, offer another approach to the study of opinion holding. Psychoanalysis (the school of psychotherapy founded by Sigmund Freud) provides a basis for a number of fairly specific propositions about, and some would say a nearly complete explanation of, attitude and opinion holding. Oversimplified, the Freudian view is that experiences in infancy and early childhood determine the personality structure and attitude patterns of the adult. These patterns in turn limit and shape not only self-image but social outlook and views on political issues. Private and public opinions emerge, therefore, as a limited and usually distorted part of what is possible for the human mind to believe.

Probably the most ambitious attempt by Freudians to explain political opinion holding is the research done for and following the study of the authoritarian personality. A large amount of fairly systematic interview data was collected during the years 1944–1947 by a team of psychologists and other behavioral scientists. From the basic studies came a number of works, of which the most substantively important was *The Authoritarian Personality*.[3]

The authors of *The Authoritarian Personality* attempted to link the attitudes and opinions of individuals with the personality characteristics formed by their respondents' individual life histories. Personality to these authors is "an agency through which sociological influences upon ideology are mediated." Our opinions are, in large part, a result of the way we perceive and "internalize" social events and ideas.

Sociological analysis offers a different approach to the study of opinion holding, one that relies heavily on the idea that opinions are shaped by the cultural traditions, social institutions, and group norms of the society of which an individual is a part.

A great deal of evidence indicates that most people take their opinions ready-made from the stock of acceptable views nearest at hand and tailor them only slightly to bring them up to date as other fashions come along. This evidence has accumulated from the studies of three disciplines that are not neatly distinct in their theoretical or professional foundations: social anthropology, sociology, and social psychology. Since W. I. Thomas's monumental work *The Polish Peasant in Europe and America* (1918), the study of what has come to be called "personality in culture" has illuminated many aspects of the relationship between

3. T. W. Adorno, Else Frenkel-Brunswik, D. J. Levinson, and R. N. Sanford, *The Authoritarian Personality* (New York: Harper, 1950).

the thought and behavior of individuals, on the one side, and, on the other, the cultural requirements or expectations that bear upon the individual in relations with others. Anthropologists have found that the patterns and individual acts of behavior are almost unbelievably varied. So much diversity, in fact, has been discovered in the rules (permissions and prohibitions) of societies that very few practices are considered to be universal.

But cultural compulsions are not the only social forces that shape opinions. Large-scale social organization further narrows the effective choices individuals may make. Interests of class, caste, and secondary-group memberships (national citizenship, religious identifications, professional affiliations) invariably reduce the alternative opinions that affected individuals hold on various issues. What would a landlord's opinion be on rent-control law, for instance, or how would a Jew view an avowedly anti-Semitic political party? It is important to remember, of course, that secondary-group identifications, or any social or cultural factors, do not *determine* opinions. Some landlords support rent-control laws, and there have been Jews who favored anti-Semitic parties. We are concerned here with influence and probabilities. Influence is always more or less, and should be distinguished from causation. We are dealing with the likelihood, not the certainty, that the sociological environment will be related to individual opinion in some way that is not simply a matter of chance. The large-group factors, such as class, nationality, occupation, religion, and education patterns, have traditionally been the bailiwick of sociologists. We look to them for an understanding of how these factors bear on opinion holding.

But small-group factors are important too. Most of the evidence indicates that they are more important than large-group factors. The study of the relationships of small numbers of people has produced the integrative discipline of social psychology. Psychologists, who began with the study of the individual as individual, have enlarged their province, while some sociologists have focused more closely on the person. The two areas of study have joined, rather uneasily, in social psychology. And social psychology, more than any other discipline or combination of disciplines, has greatly added to our understanding of the why and how of opinion holding. Probably the most important contributions of social psychologists have been made through the study of small-group relationships and through an improved understanding of role perception. These contributions will be considered in more detail later. For the moment it is necessary to point out only that our opinions are strongly influenced both by the network of friends and acquaintances whom we see often, or who are important to us, and by our "images" of who we are and of what opinions are appropriate for who we are.

There is one other specialized way to study opinion holding. Of all the approaches, this is the least satisfactory and the most subject to intellectual attack in the Western world. It is the *theory* (sometimes called the *philosophy*) of *economic determinism.*

Despite the fact that economic determination is now regarded by non-Marxist thinkers as not very useful in explaining or predicting human thought and behavior, it is nevertheless an important concept in our time, because (a) large numbers of Western nonintellectuals *do* subscribe in considerable degree to this theory, (b) the "official" doctrines of all Communist societies require their approved thinkers to espouse it, and (c) economic factors clearly do influence the formation and maintenance of individual opinions.

Let's take the last point first. A few paragraphs back we suggested that the large social category of "landlords" could be expected to oppose rent control, and that their shared characteristic (their being landlords) was related to this opinion. It is likely, however, that the influential factors are not social but economic. The implication that the social factor is related to opinion holding is probably spurious. The major influence in landlords' opposition to rent control is no doubt as economic as it is simple—rent control would reduce their incomes.

Although many opinions are influenced by economic factors, the relationship is seldom pure. Noneconomic factors are almost always present and usually more important. Nonetheless, two forms of economic determinism are much admired today. One, popular in the Western world and of great significance in the United States, is the result of the theories of Manchester economics and free-enterprise capitalism. Now held in its extreme form by only a relatively small number of Americans (but in less extreme form subscribed to—at least at the verbal and sloganized levels—by millions), this view maintains that costs and prices of goods and services are properly determined by the unregulated exchange of goods and services between buyer and seller. That this kind of economic order "determines" noneconomic elements of human life is evident in the morality associated with it (the "good" person is a frugal, sober, hard-working lover of individualism); in the political theory and practice it implies (a government of minimum powers, protecting property and freedom of contract); and in the social organization to which it tends (inequality of wealth and sharp class distinctions).

The other brand of economic determinism is the Marxist. To oversimplify again, this theory holds that all social relationships at any given time result from the dominant forms of production. Thus, in a slave economy, society is shaped by the economic relationships between slave and owner; in a feudal system, by the relation between serf and landowner; and under capitalism, by the economic relations between capitalist and worker. Like all simplistic theories—especially, perhaps, those that demand or suggest clear courses of action—this view has superficial appeal; and it has just enough historical substance so that, in the hands of such a powerful thinker and writer as Karl Marx, it could become the ideological vehicle for vast revolutionary forces in the past hundred years. But wide acceptance does not make a theory true—although it does make it important. The importance of the Marxist version of economic determinism is, internationally, that the opinions of Communist officials and thinkers are heavily influenced by it. Although economic determinism in its traditional Marxist sense is not widely believed in the West (and so is not now the most useful perspective

for the understanding of political opinions), economic factors do play an important and on occasion decisive part in shaping opinions on issues. Any study of
opinion holding must recognize this fact and deal with it satisfactorily.

## 7.2 NEEDED: A SYNTHESIS OF APPROACHES TO OPINION HOLDING

What is needed is a way of combining the relevant theories and evidence on
physical growth, psychic development, sociological influence, economic factors,
and reason: an *organism-in-the-environment* approach. Nothing less will do. No
single-factor explanation can suffice.

Now, it is easy to say that such a prescription is needed. Social scientists, singly
and in convention, remind each other that the factors with which they deal are
manifold and cannot be reduced to what Gordon Allport calls the "simple and
sovereign remedy." But on the other side is the equally simple fact that some
generalization is essential. Common sense tells us that we cannot mark, measure,
and explain every influence that may have played on every opinion. When we are
dealing with a single opinion of a single individual, it is often easy to isolate a
number of prior opinions or experiences that are related to, have influenced, or
perhaps even "caused" the opinion in question. Other opinions and experiences
of this person are considered irrelevant to the explanation of the opinion being
examined—although, in the present state of knowledge, no one could *prove* that
other opinions and experiences were irrelevant. Still, considerable agreement can
be obtained among analysts of the opinions of individuals, and libraries are full
of books and theses explaining "the influence of X on Y," and "–istic thought as
reflected in Lilen's novels."

It is difficult to explain single or related opinions of single individuals. It is
more difficult to generalize about the origins and formation of opinions.
Although the exegesis of single opinions or of the opinions of single individuals
may proceed in terms of simple fact and real experience, the discussion of
opinion formation in general must be based on projections of samples of real
experiences, judgments, and, to a considerable extent, an accumulation of
tentative conclusions, any one of which is open to question. Careful study
reveals, for example, that Mr. Oblah's opinions about the Democratic party
result from his early home life with rabidly Republican parents, his experiences
as an adult in a city controlled by an Irish Catholic Democratic "boss," his
distrust of Catholics in political office generally, his regular exposure to five
strongly Republican newspapers and magazines, and probably a number of
other specifically identifiable influences. But to provide a framework for the
analysis of opinion formation generally—or a theory, as it were, of the dynamics
of opinion formation—we have to observe such influences at work in many single
individuals and generalize from them to arrive at an idea of the types of influence

that all or most individuals are subject to. We may then suppose that these types of influence are factors of greater or lesser importance in the formation, maintenance, and change of all human opinion.

In short, we employ the scientific method of observation, generalization, hypothesis formation, and testing. Our great problem, the one that makes the scientific study of human behavior so vastly more difficult than the study of the nonhuman environment, is that we have (a) more factors ("variables," in technical language) to contend with and (b) less opportunity to control these factors. Nevertheless, common sense—in addition to experience with scientific techniques—tells us that in ordinary life we are generally successful in applying a theory of human behavior and a theory about opinions to everyday happenings. Scientific method is systematic common sense. Day by day, observing regularities in human behavior, we come, quite properly, to expect regularities in our own thought and action and in the behavior of others. We respond in similar ways to similar situations because the tendency to conserve our energies leads us into repetitious responses (habits), which do not have to be thought through each time they are made. It is therefore necessary for the individual to develop habitual responses to avoid the wasted effort of repeated analysis of the same data. Awaking in the morning, we engage in a number of routine tasks; we do not stop to consider arguments for and against each action on that particular morning because, quite simply, it is easier not to. We have learned that it is generally less wasteful of energy and time to wash our face each morning than to make a careful examination of the reasons why we should or should not wash our face on any particular morning. Habits free our attention for dealing with situations that are less common and therefore less successfully routinized.

Besides this psychological importance of habits, there is a vital social reason why routinization of behavior is essential. To live together at all, human beings must be able to predict with reasonable certainty the daily behavior of others. To achieve even the simplest objective, we must each day be able to depend on a regular pattern of behavior by hundreds of other people. The network of habitual, interdependent human behavior is the primary sociopsychological condition of society.

Although this statement is as simple and as obvious as it is profound, like other obvious and profound facts it deserves attention. All social stability arises from the predictable network of repeated responses to repeated situations of fact. The stability of opinion and its predictability of response depend equally on habitual responses to repeated situations. Therefore, not only can we count on regular and generally peaceful social interaction among large numbers of people, but—and more important for our purposes here—we need not consider all the factors that *may* have influenced the opinions of any given individual or group. If we know enough about the physical, cultural, social, and intellectual history of the individual or group, we can be reasonably sure that many opinions will not be held by the individual or group, and that other opinions are apt to be held with greater or lesser frequency and intensity.

To sum up this major point: there are important practical limits to the range of opinions (and attitudes) held by single human beings and by social groups. These limits are determined by (a) the habit principle, which minimizes individual exertion and makes social interaction possible, and (b) physical, cultural, and social factors that make some opinions probable and some opinions improbable.

One more important point about the study of public opinion: in considering how opinions form and change, we operate on two levels of analysis. On one level we deal with group and statistical probabilities, in which the mathematical language of sampling, percentages, and tests of significance may be employed. Prediction on this level is always a matter of estimating how groups of individuals will divide in their opinions. On the other level we deal with the individual who forms and expresses opinions. It is necessary in the discussion of public opinion to move smoothly and often from one level to the other. It is important, but not always easy, to make clear which level we are on at a given point. Sometimes we need to view opinion phenomena from the perspective of the individual; sometimes our attention must be given to mass regularities or irregularities. In this chapter we shall focus primarily on the individual and on the various approaches ("conceptual frameworks") to the study of why persons hold the opinions they do.

## 7.3 THE FUNNEL OF CAUSALITY: A FRAMEWORK FOR THINKING ABOUT OPINION FORMATION

It may be helpful to analyze opinion formation and opinion holding in terms of what has been called the *funnel of causality*. The term was introduced to social science by Angus Campbell and his colleagues. In *The American Voter* they used the concept of the funnel of causality as a device for visualizing a chain of events and decisions that lead to a specific political act. Although these authors were concerned with voting behavior, the analogy of the funnel may be applied to opinion formation. (For our purposes here, the casting of a presidential vote and the events that lead to it may be thought of as an example of the formation of an opinion.)

Campbell and his collaborators are properly cautious about the social psychology of decision making. "The notion of a funnel," they warn, "is intended merely as a metaphor that we find helpful up to a certain point, [but] like all physical analogies for complex and intangible processes, it becomes more misleading than clarifying if pressed too far." They describe their model, thus qualified, as follows:

> The axis of the funnel represents a time dimension. Events are conceived to follow each other in a converging sequence of causal chains, moving from the mouth to the stem of the funnel. The funnel shape is a logical product of the explanatory task chosen. Most of the complex events in the funnel occur as a result of multiple prior causes.

> Each such event is, in its turn, responsible for multiple effects as well, but our focus of interest narrows as we approach the dependent behavior. We progressively eliminate those effects that do not continue to have relevance for the political act. Since we are forced to take all partial causes as relevant at any juncture, relevant effects are therefore many fewer in number than relevant causes. The result is a convergence effect.[4]

The Campbell version of the funnel of causality does not attempt to set a fixed point, represented by the large end of the funnel, as the moment for the beginning of analysis. It is useful to think of the starting point as that set of relevant historical events as far back in time as seems appropriate to the case under consideration. The large rim of the funnel merely represents opinions, attitudes, beliefs, and predispositions held by the subject at the time chosen by the investigator. The funnel concept lends itself to the analysis of past, present, or future opinion formation.

Thus, if we are interested in the analysis of Theodore Roosevelt's opinion of civil service reform we might choose his campaign for a seat in the New York State legislature in 1881 as the moment for the start of the analysis and end with his becoming president on William McKinley's death. Or we might (as Campbell and his collaborator did) use the funnel as a framework for thinking about and organizing the analysis of a voter's decision in a current presidential campaign— in which case the relevant beginning point (as represented by the large end of the funnel) might be those attitudes held by the person who, having just reached voting age, is casting a ballot for the first time. Or, in the design of a study of future opinion change, present attitudes and events are represented by the large rim of the funnel, and the analysis may be either a projection of predicted interaction and attitude change in the future or an empirical investigation of real events and interactions over the lifetime of the study. Though the concept of the funnel (illustrated in Figure 7–1) involves observation and data gathering through a time dimension, its application is therefore not limited to completed events. We can use it to study past, present, or anticipated (future) opinion change.

Edward Dreyer and Walter Rosenbaum have elaborated upon the Campbell funnel of causality and made it more generally useful for the study of opinion formation. They recognize that

> events that shape an individual's political attitudes cannot be neatly classified as "cause" or "effect" nor do they always follow each other in a tidy sequence. . . . Nevertheless, orderly and logical study of the forces affecting political opinion and behavior is possible because the closer one approaches a given political act or attitude, the fewer are

---

4. Angus Campbell, Philip E. Converse, Warren E. Miller, and Donald E. Stokes, *The American Voter* (New York: Wiley, 1960), p. 24. Reprinted by permission of John Wiley & Sons, Inc.

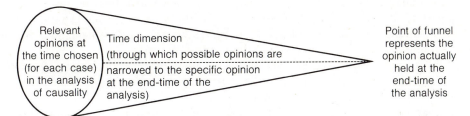

**Figure 7-1.**  *Funnel of opinion causality*

the variables affecting it. Conversely, as one moves backward in time, more variables can be seen entering into the behavior or attitudes being studied. . . .

[The] funnel of causality also suggests a method for describing how the variables affect an individual at a given moment in time. First, the researcher may decide what factors at any given time in the life of an individual are *relevant* or *irrelevant* to his study. The deliberate . . . distinction between relevant and irrelevant variables serves as a reminder that few researchers attempt to study all the forces affecting political behavior. Second, at any point in time a person's subjective political world contains influences that are either *personal* or *external*. Personal conditions are events or influences within the individual's perceptual field; that is, conditions of which he is aware. External conditions are objective events or states about which the individual is unaware but which, if they become known to him, may influence either his behavior, his opinions, or both. Finally, at any point in time an individual sees aspects of his environment as *political* and other aspects of it as *apolitical*. A subjective determination of whether or not an event is political is likely to have important political consequences for a person. . . .

These three sets of concepts are important because they remind us of certain conditions which must be met before an event can influence opinions or behavior. They also warn us against regarding behavior of the moment as isolated events. Moreover, they add to our understanding of the funnel of causality, which is a theoretical description of what may be termed an individual's field of political perception. Before any event or condition can influence a person's political opinions or behavior, it has to be seen by that person as relevant, personal, and political.[5]

The sloping sides of the funnel of opinion causality represent the limits of the

---

5. Edward C. Dreyer and Walter A. Rosenbaum, *Political Opinion and Electoral Behavior* (Belmont, Calif.: Wadsworth, 1966), pp. 9–10. We are indebted to Professors Dreyer and Rosenbaum for clarification of our thinking on the usefulness of the funnel concept. The quotations are reprinted with their permission and that of the Wadsworth Publishing Company.

individual's field of political perception. Elements that influence opinion are concepts, beliefs, events, and other opinions that relate in some personal and political way to the issue. Figure 7–2 represents the way influencing factors combine or are rejected in the opinion-forming process.

As an example of the process illustrated in Figure 7–2, let us say that the opinion (decision) under analysis is the partisan choice of an eighteen-year-old at the time of her registration for voting. Let B represent the influence of her family (father and mother are both Republicans); let C represent the influence of her closest friend, with whom she joins at time 2 (at the age of seventeen) a Young Republican group; let A represent the influence of friends who, also at time 2 (which, let us say, is a presidential campaign), join the Young Democrats; and let D represent what our subject takes to be the prevailing pro-Republican influence among the upper management of the accounting firm where she gets a summer job just two months (at time 3) before registering as a Republican.

Dreyer and Rosenbaum make the following summary argument for use of the funnel concept:

> This model, while an inexact and abstract representation of the real world, provides us with some broad guidelines. First it reminds us that in studying opinion and behavior, we are studying not a thing but a process. Our subject has movement, direction, fluctuation through time. Second, although the model does not state how specific variables (such as social class) affect specific political behavior (e.g., voting, or contributing money to political campaigns), it does give us a picture of the range of forces affecting political behavior and suggests how we are to relate them to each other. Third, our model reminds us, by diagrammatically rendering individual responses, that we must approach the study of political opinion and behavior with a sensitivity to the complexity of personal and social forces behind each individual opinion or political act.[6]

As a framework for thinking about opinion formation, the funnel of causality has been employed by social psychologists, sociologists, and political scientists.[7] But it is important to bear in mind that the "funnel" will not demonstrate causality, nor is it a model in any scientific sense. It is a metaphor whose characteristics remind us of the choosing, combining, including, and excluding processes that over time produce opinions from a narrowing field. It is a figure that may help our understanding. More than that cannot be claimed for it.

---

6. Ibid., p. 11.

7. See, in addition to Dreyer and Rosenbaum, Maxwell E. McCombs and Donald L. Shaw, "The Agenda-Setting Function of Mass Media," *Public Opinion Quarterly* 36 (1972): 176–187; Richard G. Niemi and Herbert F. Weisberg, *Controversies in Voting Behavior*, 2nd ed. (Washington: Congressional Quarterly Press, 1984); David B. Hill and Norman R. Luttbeg, *Trends in American Electoral Behavior*, 2nd ed. (Itasca, Ill.: F. E. Peacock, 1983); and H. L. Nieburg, *Public Opinion: Tracking and Targeting* (New York: Praeger, 1984).

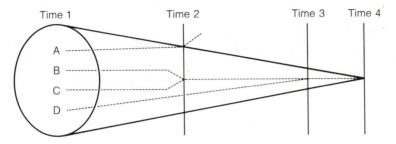

B and C are influencing factors that combine at Time 2

A is an influencing factor that becomes irrelevant at Time 2
as a consequence of the combination of the B and C influences

D is an influencing factor that bears on the opinion at Time
3 late in the development of the opinion and just before
its expression at Time 4

**Figure 7-2.**    *Influence combination in the funnel of causality*

It seems reasonable to suspect that each person carries around in her head, so to speak, the raw materials for opinion formation on those issues of which she is aware. The way influencing variables are related to the end opinion is probably not given any conscious attention in most cases. On many issues the average person never has to formulate an opinion at all. Most Americans may know some things about U.S. immigration policy, but they will probably have no occasion to articulate anything that could be described as an opinion on the subject. Most Americans are never asked what they think about quota systems in the immigration laws, oaths of disclaimer that prospective immigrants have to take, or the provisions for naturalization or denaturalization of immigrants.

The point is that we are in danger of unrealistic thinking and of abusing our metaphor if we believe that a ready-made and well-structured funnel of causality can be extracted from every person on every issue. However, when individuals have in fact formulated opinions, or when they are asked to give an opinion in conversation or writing, we can infer a funnel of causality from what we know about their other opinions and experiences. It should be clear, of course, that our knowledge of the funnel of causality will always be incomplete. There will always be some influencing factors that are not capable of being taken into account. But this is merely to restate, in a particular context, an earlier point about the almost infinite number of variables that enter into the analysis of human thought and behavior.

In the chapters that follow we shall be paying attention to influencing variables that seem to be most significant for the formation of public opinion. These variables include *social relationships,* especially relationships with primary and secondary groups; *economic consideration;* the *mass media* and other elements of the communication network; *intellectual calculation;* and *whimsy.*

The opinion-forming process in any specific case may be slow or rapid or suspended at any point. The limiting and influencing factors—the totality of facts, experiences, and judgments that are part of the making of an opinion— may occur in an almost endless number of combinations with various intensities and various results. There are, we know, powerful influences for sameness of opinion, just as there are powerful influences for diversity. In some cases, a single influence or a few reinforcing influences may overwhelm all others, narrowing the choices rapidly to a strongly held point of view. The funnel to represent such an opinion-forming process will then be short and squat:

In other cases, the influences may be weak, or strong but contradictory, and the ultimate choice difficult and long in being arrived at; the funnel is deep and gradually sloping:

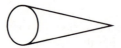

Finally, the process may be suspended for lack of information, or for a lack of resolution of strong but conflicting influences; in this case, we say our mind is not made up:

# Chapter 8

# Opinion Holding
# and Individuals

The opinions any individual holds are the products of that person's unique experiences within an environment shared with others. At birth the individual's uniqueness is wholly, or almost wholly, a physical matter, determined by genes and chromosomes and a body chemistry that, in its essentials, still evades scientific exposure. But from the first breath, and at an increasing rate during growth, the individual's endowments are modified by the effects of social life.

There is much talk about "native ability." Some of it arises from arguments about heredity versus environment—one of the endless debates in academic circles. We know little about the outer limits of intellectual ability, but we do know that physical or chemical impairments prevent some persons from understanding abstractions, concepts, and sometimes even facts beyond a certain level of complexity. We assume, therefore, that all persons have limits (if unmeasured) to their ability to understand and learn. Although an indication of the boundaries of the mind may be obtained from physical examinations and from electrical, chemical, and performance tests, our knowledge of the full potential of the human mind is hardly beyond the point where general medicine was in the early seventeenth century, when William Harvey discovered the principle of the circulation of blood.

Each person's capacity for opinion holding is no doubt limited, then, by physical factors of an ultimately biological or chemical or electrical nature. This is not a matter of much concern for normal persons, because other limiting or influencing factors shape their opinions well within the range of what is physically possible. Other processes and needs, experienced by all persons—but particular to each individual in their manifestations—provide limiting and influencing factors of more significance to attitude and opinion study.

In this chapter we shall consider opinion holding as it relates to the basic potentialities of the human equipment; to the development of intelligence and personality; to feeling, perception, cognition, and reasoning; and to the satisfaction of psychological needs. Our survey will help provide a background for considering the political significance of opinion holding.

## 8.1 OPINION-HOLDING CAPABILITY:
## THE PSYCHOBIOLOGICAL PROCESSES

In the prenatal period, a fetal organism develops a self-system that, with decreasing aid from its mother as birth approaches, integrates all of its physical parts and biochemical processes. During this time of rapid cell growth and differentiation, tissue damage can result from disease, bruises, or lack of nutriments (including oxygen), which may permanently impair the organism's abilities and set impassable limits to the capacity for thought. Most individuals, fortunately, suffer no identifiable neurophysiological limits before (or after) birth, and the full and still unexplored range of human intellect is possible for them.

One of the key (and unanswered) questions of behavioral scientists—as well as of medical scientists and philosophers—concerns the separation of mind and body. Can clear distinctions be made between mental and physical parts and processes? Or, if there are no *observable* ways to differentiate mind from body, are there *qualities* of mind (reason, sympathy, love, pride, despair) that may be taken as symptomatic of real, if unobserved, differences between mind and body? Rivers of ink have been drained in speculation about this central question. No purpose could be served by an extended discussion of it here; suffice it to say that we have seen no evidence that the mind is empirically differentiable from the body. Something is known about the electrochemistry of perception, and it does not indicate the separateness of a "mind." But what is known is still very little, and in the future, "mind" may be physiologically distinguishable from body. For now, it need only be said that "mind" in the first sense, as something separate from body, cannot be proved.

The concept of mind may be used to describe a collection of qualities of which some are *normative* (that is, they have aspects of "goodness" and "badness") and all are nonphysical. If we want to, we may employ the word *mind* to mean those particular capacities of reasoning and feeling by which we manipulate our environment and enter into social relationships. These qualities cannot—at least, not yet—be explained on physical grounds alone; they distinguish humans from all other known forms of life and may, as a collective shorthand, be called *mind*—or even *soul*.

Now, although it may be perfectly satisfactory to use the word *mind* in this latter sense for the qualities, processes, and behavior that cannot be physically identified as some kind of energy, we prefer to use as consistently as possible the term *psychological processes* to refer to instincts, drives, perception, cognition, reasoning, and feeling. These and their subprocesses and parts can be divided when appropriate into the *neurophysiological* and the *nonphysiological*.

There is good authority for abandoning earlier (and still common) notions about the differences between mind and body. It is not too great an exaggeration to say that all psychologists have done so. The great and never-to-be-forgotten contribution of Sigmund Freud was that he made us conscious of the *unconscious*. As long as psychology was the study of reason and of the other "mental faculties" (as emotion and sense perception were quaintly called), it was possible to think of mind as separate from body, although having its locus within the organism. But when Freud made his early discoveries of unconscious suppression of feelings and their relation to (indeed, causing of) physical disability—when the evidence indicated that the unknown elements in the mind could have pathological effects on the body—then it was no longer possible to believe in the tidy separability of mind and body.[1] Since these discoveries of the 1890s, the idea of unconscious psychological processes has been verified repeatedly and unmistakably by physicians and neurophysiologists as well as by experimental psychologists and psychotherapists.

Such evidence renders the earlier, more or less complete separation of mind and body indefensible today. Freudian psychology first challenged the body–mind dichotomy in the 1890s; non-Freudian psychologists have been nearly unanimous in their acceptance of the importance of the unconscious. Moreover, the non-Freudians have been, in general, more concerned about the relationships between the psychological processes called perception, cognition, and reasoning, on the one hand, and our knowledge of the electrochemistry of the body, on the other. Working with the neurophysiologists, the psychologists who may be grouped roughly as behaviorists have begun to understand the way the human psyche receives, records, and analyzes sense data. One celebrated neurophysiologist implies that mind may be wholly explained by body when more is known about the incredibly complex operations of the brain and nervous system:

> Is it likely that physiology will ever throw any real light upon the relationship between the brain and the mind? I believe that, working in conjunction with psychology, it will. I can only guess where present advances seem to be leading us. Think of a pattern. An atom is a pattern of electrons, a molecule is a pattern of atoms. There are patterns of patterns of patterns, and so on indefinitely. The most complicated patterns we know are in the brain. Not only are there twelve thousand million nerve cells out of which the patterns can be made, but nervous patterns exist in time, like melody, as well as in space. If you look at a tapestry through a magnifying glass, you will see the individual threads but not the pattern: if you stand away from it you will see the pattern but not the threads. My guess is that in the

1. It is important to note that controversy has never been acute over the idea of the unconscious. The storm blown up by Freud, both among nineteenth-century puritans and among twentieth-century psychologists, was over the source of the unconscious processes that were the cause of neurosis and psychosis. Freud's troubles—the term is used to mean controversy, not necessarily error—were over sex rather than the idea of the unconscious. See Lancelot Law Whyte, *The Unconscious before Freud* (Garden City, N.Y.: Doubleday, 1962).

nervous system we are looking at the threads while with the mind we perceive the patterns, and that one day we may discover how the patterns are made out of the threads.[2]

The nervous system is, broadly speaking, the apparatus through which and by which psychological processes take place. Psychological processes depend on the nervous system, but they are not (at least not yet) wholly explainable by the nervous system.

Although the nature of psychological processes is not fully understood, certain definitional agreements and experimental findings can help us to distinguish one from another. Most psychologists distinguish perception from thinking and feeling; many distinguish those three processes from a fourth, cognition. We may think of these processes as four (there may be more) kinds of psychological operations, all using common elements of the nervous system (that is, having electrochemical bases) but having characteristic modes of operation that differentiate them according to their dynamics and their end products.

One widely held view maintains that psychology as a scientific study has to do with those elements and processes that are intermediary between stimuli outside of the organism and observable physical responses of the organism to the stimuli. In this formulation, known as *stimulus–response* (or S–R) theory, perception is part of the total process that produces response after stimulation is applied to the human organism. Other possible psychological subprocesses are cognition, feeling, and reasoning. As the following diagram indicates and the brief discussion explains, perception and cognition are necessary to all psychological activity. The individual who is even in the slightest influenced by or aware of a stimulus receives and holds in some way the impact of the stimulus. Feeling and reasoning are not necessary parts of every stimulus–response situation, although most conscious and voluntary responses of individuals to a single stimulus or to fields of stimuli are presumably in some degree influenced by reason or emotion or both.

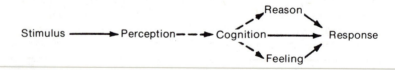

2. W. Russel Brain, *Mind, Perception, and Science* (Oxford: Blackwell, 1951), p. 30. Reprinted by permission of Blackwell Scientific Publications Ltd. This testimony of the mid-twentieth century is only slightly more guarded than the prophecy made by the Goncourt brothers a century earlier (1853): "Every day, science swallows a piece of God. Probably the time will come when our thought processes will be explained in scientific terms as we now explain thunder" (quoted in John Nef, *Civilization, Industrial Society, and Love* [Santa Barbara: Center for the Study of Democratic Institutions, August 1961], p. 11). In the mid-1980s a small number of political scientists, psychologists, and biologists, organized as the Association for Politics and the Life Sciences, were reporting their research at professional panels under such titles as "Neurobiology and Political Behavior" and "Reproduction, Sociobiology, and Politics" (program of Annual Meeting, American Political Science Association, Washington, D.C., 1984).

Perception, cognition, reason, and feeling are sometimes called psychological variables intervening between stimulus and response. There are, of course, other ways of conceptualizing the field of psychology, but the S–R formulation is presented here both because it is widely accepted by psychologists and because its basic elements are easily understood and used by other social scientists.[3]

*Perception* may be defined as the way the organism takes account of a stimulus. *Cognition* is the way the organism gives meaning to the stimulus. *Reason* is the process by which the stimulus is related to other stimuli at the conceptual level of psychological activity. *Feeling* is the emotional connotation produced by the stimulus, either alone or in combination with other stimuli at the cognitive or conceptual level.

Consider the operation of these psychological processes in the legendary farmer who was going home from market with a chicken, a fox, and a bag of grain. He rounded a turn in the road and perceived a river—that is, the light energy in his visual field created in his brain some electrochemical action that he had learned to recognize as a river. But he also recognized that the river was high—that is, the stimulus was classified as well as perceived, and cognition occurred as a concept (a high river) that took on meaning to the farmer.[4] At that point the farmer had a problem and needed to use reason. (Consider for a moment why George Humphrey, among others, has defined thinking as "what occurs in experience when an organism, human or animal, meets, recognizes, and solves a problem."[5] Other persons believe that there are several kinds of thinking, only one of which—reasoning—is problem solving.)[6]

But to return to the farmer. How to get the chicken, the fox, and the grain safely across the river? Rather than being able to carry them all at once across the shallow ford as he had expected to do, he would have to carry only one at a time. If he took the fox first, the chicken would eat the grain before he got back. If he took the grain first, the fox would eat the chicken before he returned. If he took the chicken first, the fox and grain would be safe, but on the second trip he would have to leave either the fox or the grain with the chicken while he returned for the remaining item.

Being a clever farmer, as we all know, he associated the stimuli and concepts of the situation in such a way that he solved the problem by the use of reason. No feeling (emotion) was involved, apparently; but if he had disliked chickens

---

3. See Seymour M. Berger and William W. Lambert, "Stimulus–Response Theory in Contemporary Social Psychology," in *Handbook of Social Psychology,* ed. Gardner Lindzey (Reading, Mass.: Addison-Wesley, 1968), 1:81–178.

4. Some psychologists would say that perception need not be distinguished from cognition; but the farmer, in this case, saw immediately a river with meaning: a high river. This is a family quarrel, which we may leave to the psychologists. Nonpsychologists usually find it helpful to distinguish the processes.

5. George Humphrey, *Thinking* (New York: Wiley, 1951), p. 311; see also Humphrey's footnote, pp. 311–312.

6. See Robert Thomson, *The Psychology of Thinking* (Baltimore: Penguin, 1959), pp. 13–16, 25–27.

because they wakened him in the morning, he might have let feeling interfere with reason and allowed the fox to eat the chicken.

In some cases, only perception intervenes between stimulus and response. The child draws her finger away from the hot stove without experiencing cognition, reason, or emotion. But most behavior, beyond the simplest reaction to intense pain or pleasure, is related to the more complex psychological variables between stimulus and response. Apparently these psychological processes are seldom if ever separate in time from each other. Perception, cognition, reason, and feeling go on simultaneously, and much of what are called thinking, dreaming, imagining, fancying, studying, and the like are combinations of perceptive, cognitive, rational, and affective elements.

From the perspective of the individual, opinions are products of (a) personal experience, as shaped by stimulations; (b) the meanings attached to these stimulations (their relation to classifications and abstractions); (c) the application of these meaningful stimulations to problem-solving situations; and (d) the pattern of emotional charges associated with the stimulations and their related classifications and abstractions. The opinions of interest to us—views on matters of some significance to the small or large community—by definition refer to public problems and problem solving. Reasoning is therefore almost always in order, although it is not always evident in the expression of opinion.

Emotion alone may result in a person's opinion about certain issues, as when all matters of policy are reduced to a slogan like "My country [or family, political party, or religion], right or wrong." But generally, an opinion that is significant for the study of public opinion is created in the individual by some more or less complex interaction of cognition, reason, and feeling.

## 8.2 SATISFACTION AND FIT IN OPINION HOLDING

If the last few pages have demonstrated nothing else, they have shown how little we know about the details of either the biophysical or the psychological processes of opinion formation and change. We know more, however, about the relations between opinions and the observable elements of personality and behavior. Some of what we know or surmise about these matters will be reviewed in later chapters dealing with the effects of communication messages on individuals. Here we will only touch on two points related to the integration of an individual's opinions with his total personality, self-image, and effectiveness in small- and large-group situations.

The first point is that opinions must be at least to some degree consistent with observable reality. In large and common matters, a person's opinions must reflect a reasonably accurate understanding (or at least perception) of objective fact. One may believe quite honestly that no slums exist in city A; but if by every criteria by which slums are measured it is clear that they *do* exist, one has been unable to achieve a good "fit" between objective fact and subjective opinion. When such a fit is only mildly incongruous, the inconsistency is usually attributed to the person's indifference or to bad judgment; a notoriously poor fit may indicate psychosis.

We must be careful, of course, not to overemphasize the need for opinions to square with fact. It is a matter of everyday observation that prejudice, personal interest, and opinions received uncritically as political (or religious or economic) ideology seem to produce an extraordinary capacity for ignoring the most elementary facts.

The second point is that opinions must be, in some general and overall sense, comfortable to the individual. This consideration is partly a matter of the correspondence the opinions bear to observable and measurable reality—most persons in reasonably good mental health will not be comfortable with opinions that contradict what they see and experience in the world about them. But it is more than a matter of mere fit with unambiguous experience, because most opinions worthy of being included in our definition of public opinion are about issues that cannot be resolved by reference to objective fact alone. In these cases, facts and experience are *not* unambiguous; they are subject to various and indeed often quite contrary interpretations. The opinions of publics cluster around matters about which honest people, honestly viewing the evidence, honestly disagree.

Consequently, except in extreme cases, opinions cannot be judged solely on their congruence with facts. The "facts" that give rise to public issues, and therefore to public opinion, are not obvious, objective, and palpable. Except when aberrant opinions are accompanied by aberrant behavior, it is hardly a good measure of the worth of an opinion to say that it is not in accord with the facts. Nor is it enough for the opinion holder constantly to test views against the facts. It is important that such testing be done, of course, and that one be aware of the rationalization processes that so often shape facts to opinions. But try as one may, no matter how candid one's self-criticism, the test of fit is not sufficient when—as in all large public controversies—the nature of reality is so imperfectly known.

It is therefore, in a sense, as proper as it is inevitable that what we believe and hold as public opinion is to some important degree shaped by our personal needs and our self-image. Within the range of opinions that may adequately fit the facts—or matters in which judgment, insight, creativity, and other individual traits are the decisive opinion producers—individuals select the views that best suit their personal needs. Certain persons, for example, seem compelled to engage in scapegoating; they seem to need out-group persons or symbols to blame for in-group troubles. It is characteristic of leaders and activists in American radical movements to find "bad guys" at whose doors the problems of the "good guys" can be laid. As the Know-Nothings blamed the Irish and "popery" and the Ku Kluxers blame blacks and Catholics, so John Birch Society members blame Communists and left radicals blame corporate capitalists for all difficulties.

The scapegoat mechanism is only one of several responses that may be shown by persons who display extrapunitive reactions to frustrating situations. Rosenzweig argued that one dimension (or trait) of personality may be measured by reactions to frustrations. He observed that some persons in frustrating situations turned aggressively on others (these he called *extrapunitive*), some turned aggressively on themselves *(intrapunitive),* and some were able to ignore the situation *(impunitive).*[7]

Following Rosenzweig, M. Brewster Smith obtained, through depth interviewing, opinion and personality measurements from 250 American men. He found that "the 'extrapunitive' group were somewhat more likely than the 'intrapunitive' respondents to blame Russia for United States–Soviet disagreements and to support a 'tough' United States policy toward Russia." "This," he says, "is what one would expect if their attitudes were to be consistent with the rest of their personality tendencies."[8]

Other psychologists, following the work of Henry Murray and his collaborators at Harvard, approach the study of human behavior, including opinion formation, through the analysis of the numbers, intensities, and interactions of psychological and physiological *needs.* All persons, basically, have a need for maintaining their lives, for sexual gratification, and for social relationships. To these physiological needs Murray and his associates systematically added a long list of psychobiological needs, which they experimentally measured. They investigated, among other things, the need for affiliation (in their terminology, "need affiliation" or "n-affiliation"), need nurturance, need play, need seclusion, and need understanding: the total personality, in their view, can be thought of as a result of the patterns and dynamic interactions of more than two dozen such needs.[9]

For our purposes, the application of Murray's personality theory is clear: personality needs—their intensities, their hierarchies, and the ways they are met—all undoubtedly influence in some degree the kinds of opinions held by the individual. People believe, in part, what they find psychologically satisfying. What is satisfying is the fulfillment of psychobiological needs. Opinions that tend to fulfill those needs tend to be held and cherished.

The late Abraham Maslow's work, in some ways similar to Murray's earlier theories and investigations, has received wide and deserved attention. Maslow

---

7. S. Rosenzweig, "Types of Reaction to Frustration," *Journal of Abnormal and Social Psychology* 29 (1934): 298–300.

8. M. Brewster Smith, "The Personal Setting of Public Opinion: A Study of Attitudes toward Russia," *Public Opinion Quarterly* 11 (1947): 520.

9. Henry A. Murray et al., *Explorations in Personality* (New York: Oxford University Press, 1938); see especially chap. 3, pp. 142–242.

argues that the human animal has five "levels" of needs, hierarchically ordered from the lowest, (1) physical survival, through (2) safety, (3) affection, and (4) self-esteem to the highest, (5) self-actualization. The normal human tries to achieve each level in order. When the first two are achieved, a person will seek number 3, affection. If that is achieved, behavior is directed toward increasing self-esteem. In Maslow's theories dissatisfaction and striving are present in all individuals except those who have achieved all five of the "needs."[10] Maslow's work is full of suggestive propositions and implications for opinion research and for study of political behavior generally: To what extent are these needs perceived as political by citizens (that is, as being appropriately met through governmental action)? Are the lowest-level needs—that is, survival and safety— so pressing and insistent on the poor that citizenship as civility is effectively denied them? Do persons who are successfully ascending the needs ladder act differently politically from persons descending the needs ladder? Is politics a vehicle that many people, even a very large percentage of the population, might use to achieve the highest needs, self-esteem and self-actualization?

Maslow's ideas have been incorporated in the work of a number of students of public opinion and political behavior. James A. Davies' *Human Nature in Politics,* Jeanne Knutson's *Human Basis of the Polity: A Psychological Study of Political Men,* and Ronald Inglehart's *Silent Revolution: Changing Values and Political Styles among Western Publics*[11] all rely heavily on Maslow and have, in turn, influenced the direction and foci of contemporary research in political psychology. John Sullivan and his colleagues, for instance, have applied Maslow's emphasis on self-esteem to political tolerance in America.[12]

## 8.3 THE RELATION OF INDIVIDUAL OPINION HOLDING TO PUBLIC OPINION AND POLITICAL BEHAVIOR

It may be useful to review the reasons why it is important to concern ourselves in a book on *public* opinion with the psychology of individual opinion holding. Why, for instance, consider both the neuropsychological equipment with which

---

10. Abraham H. Maslow, *Motivation and Personality,* 2nd ed. (New York: Harper & Row, 1970), especially chap. 4, "A Theory of Human Motivation," pp. 35–58.

11. James A. Davies, *Human Nature in Politics* (New York: Wiley, 1963); Jeanne Knutson, *The Human Basis of the Polity: A Psychological Study of Political Men* (Chicago: Atherton-Aldine, 1972); and Ronald Inglehart, *The Silent Revolution: Changing Values and Political Styles among Western Publics* (Princeton: Princeton University Press, 1977).

12. See John L. Sullivan et al., "The Sources of Political Tolerance: A Multivariate Analysis," *American Political Science Review* 75 (1981): 92–106, and, citing Sullivan's unpublished work, John C. Pierce et al., *The Dynamics of American Public Opinion: Patterns and Processes* (Glenview, Ill.: Scott, Foresman, 1982), pp. 203–204. See also Paul Sniderman, *Personality and Democratic Politics* (Berkeley: University of California Press, 1975).

the individual forms and modifies opinion *and* personality factors that appear to be related (perhaps in some causal way) to the kinds of views the individual finds comfortable?

The importance of this chapter lies partly in the obvious fact that publics consist of individuals, and that the views of publics are therefore the collected views of individuals. As we pointed out earlier, sometimes we need to focus on the individual level to understand what seems to be related to what, as opinions form and re-form. So it is interesting to try to analyze what goes on within the individual. It's interesting, but is it necessary?

Political sociologists may ignore the individual as an individual. In fact, most of the modern study of public opinion is done in precisely this fashion. Thus, even the motivational analyses carried out since 1952 by the Survey Research Center (in terms of party identification, issue orientation, and candidate orientation), which have made significant contributions to our understanding of voter behavior in general, are concerned not with individual motivations directly but with aggregate responses. Therefore, the description and study of public opinion does not require attention to the reasons for the opinions of citizens X, Y, and Z. In politics people focus on events and decisions that are overt and can be clearly perceived. Because of the "convergent selectivity" on real events it often appears that motivation is also homogeneous, when in fact the actors may have many different and idiosyncratic understandings and intentions.

Take the important question of political cynicism, mistrust, and alienation.[13] Some early research showed that cynical and mistrustful persons tended to be indifferent to politics or to withdraw from political participation. But further investigation of individuals revealed that while some people did withdraw as their trust diminished, others increased their conventional political activity or switched to more direct and unconventional activity, such as sit-ins, protests, and civil disobedience. In short, to understand the significance of the aggregate statistics on the claimed disaffection of the American electorate, one had to get more information about individual differences.[14]

One might make the case that it is more important to study the individual characteristics of political leaders than those of ordinary members of the mass public, for idiosyncratic and perhaps relatively minor personality quirks of leaders can have political consequences far beyond their clinical significance. There are, of course, the celebrated cases of the madness of George III and Ivan the Terrible and the reputed madness of Adolf Hitler. There are much-criticized

---

13. Some scholars distinguish among the three terms *cynicism, mistrust, and alienation,* and sometimes those distinctions are helpful to understanding. Here the words are used as generally related terms meaning feelings of doubt, skepticism, and lack of confidence that governments have good intentions toward or produce desirable results for those who hold such feelings.

14. See Paul M. Sniderman, *A Question of Loyalty* (Berkeley: University of California Press, 1981), and Phillip H. Pollock III, "The Participatory Consequences of Internal and External Political Efficacy: A Research Note," *Western Political Quarterly* 36 (1983): 400–409.

but still intriguing exploratory works by Alexander and Juliette George on Woodrow Wilson, by Erik Erikson on Martin Luther, and by Alex Gottfried on Boss Anton Cermak of Chicago.[15] Such case studies illustrate the significance of psychological factors on elite opinion and on public policy.

At a lower but still elite level, that of the political activist, it is likewise important to have an understanding of the psychodynamics of opinion forming. The political strategist (and the student of political strategy) must know why individuals find some opinions more appealing than others. Much of the concern with political "images" seems to center on the most imperfectly understood appeals certain candidates have to ordinary voters. These appeals are related, at least in part, to ideal types that voters want candidates to approximate and to basic personality needs that some candidate-policy combinations satisfy better than other candidate-policy combinations. These matters, like so much else in political life, are far from being understood. But there is ample evidence that the investigation of individual opinion holding can contribute to the political scientist's study of public opinion and political behavior.

## 8.4 DOES BEHAVIOR FOLLOW OPINION?

One of the simplest questions that can be put to the analyst of public opinion is one of the most difficult: Does behavior follow opinion? Is there any reason to believe that people act in a manner consistent with their beliefs? Do people vote the way they think? or the way they would like to? or the way they say they are going to?

Before we can answer, we should rephrase this series of questions more systematically and a little more theoretically. Our concern is, really, about the degree of consistency among three pattern variables, those usually designated attitudes, those designated opinions, and those designated behaviors (or, more accurately, overt and measurable behavior). Are those dispositions toward action that we call attitudes consistent with those expressions of views that we call opinion? Are people's attitudes consistent with what they actually do when they have to express attitudes and opinions in social situations?

Most social psychologists seem to accept the notion that there is a close and almost invariable relationship between attitudes and opinions. Attitudes, they say, are tendencies or dispositions, learned rather than inborn, in regard to

---

15. Alexander L. George and Juliette L. George, *Woodrow Wilson and Colonel House* (New York: John Day, 1956); Erik H. Erikson, *Young Man Luther* (New York: Norton, 1958); Alex Gottfried, *Boss Cermak of Chicago* (Seattle: University of Washington Press, 1962). For a somewhat more general psychoanalytical study of radical leaders, see E. Victor Wolfenstein, *The Revolutionary Personality: Lenin, Trotsky, Gandhi* (Princeton: Princeton University Press, 1967). And for even broader commentary on psychocultural studies, see Mostafa Rejai, with Kay Phillips, *Leaders of the Revolution,* Sage Library of Social Research, vol. 73 (Beverly Hills, Calif.: Sage, 1979).

objects, persons, or groups; these tendencies or dispositions are not specific to any particular set of facts or particular policy questions but apply generally to the objects, persons, or groups to which they relate.[16] Opinions may be thought of as sharpened attitudes, specific to certain real objects, persons, or groups. A bigot may have *attitudes* toward blacks or Catholics or Jews in general; but he has *opinions* about the black chairman of the NAACP, about the Catholic mayor, and about the Jewish candidate who wants to replace him. It would be a mistake, of course, to push too far this distinction based on the generality of attitudes and the specificity of opinions. What we have called private opinion may have considerable overlap with attitude. However, if one accepts our working definition of public opinion as necessitating (a) an issue, (b) publics affected by that issue, and (c) an expression of views, then an opinion may be usefully thought of as a sharpened *object-specific* attitude. Nevertheless, some writers prefer to use *attitude* and opinion interchangeably.

The literature of opinion and attitude study almost invariably assumes that, barring lies and views stated under duress, opinion is always consistent with attitude. This is probably an accurate assumption, as far as it goes. But it is subject to the qualification that lies and views stated under duress are quite common in attitude and opinion measurement. Racially bigoted persons often give verbal responses, recorded as opinion, quite different from the bigoted attitudes they hold. There are other examples of social pressure to conform to widely held norms and ideals, as we have seen in the earlier discussion of the good-citizen ideal and self-image management. Recorded opinions are not, in fact, always consistent with attitudes, although in most cases it is conceptually proper and operationally satisfactory to assume that they are.

It is of greater importance to inquire whether attitudes and opinions are *followed* by behavior. Earlier writers seem to have assumed that behavior was consistent with attitude and opinion. But in a classic experiment in the 1930s, Richard La Piere dramatically demonstrated a difference between attitudes and behavior. He traveled nearly 10,000 miles across the United States twice, and extensively on the West Coast, accompanied by a young Chinese couple, husband and wife. They were served in 184 eating places and were accepted at 66 establishments that offered sleeping accommodations. They were turned away at only one place, and even there it was not clear whether they were rejected because two of the three persons were Chinese. Following these travels, La Piere sent questionnaires to all the places he visited; one of the questions was: "Will you accept members of the Chinese race as guests in your establishment?" He received back 128 questionnaires; of those responding, *over 90% of the lodging and eating places that had served the Chinese couple said they would not serve Chinese, and only one respondent said Chinese would definitely be served.*[17]

---

16. For an excellent review of the development and thinking about the concept of attitudes, see Donald Fleming, "Attitude: History of a Concept," *Perspectives in American History* (Cambridge, Mass.: Charles Warren Center for Studies in American History, 1967), 1:287–365.

17. Richard T. La Piere, "Attitudes vs. Actions," *Social Forces* 13 (1934): 233–234.

What does this apparent contradiction mean? One explanation is that a certain set of social and economic pressures acted on the respondents when they were answering an impersonal questionnaire and that another, quite different set acted on them when they were faced with potential lodgers or diners. The written refusal to serve Chinese may have been prompted by prejudices, by social and economic pressure from friends and other members of the business community, or by personal bias. When confronted by prospective paying guests, they were under pressure to respect the ideals of equality and brotherhood and to accept the income from the rooms and meals (it may be significant that the experiment was conducted during the Depression).

In a similar experiment involving statements of what people would do in an interracial situation and actual behavior in such a case, Melvin De Fleur and Frank Westie found that one-third of their college-student subjects "behaved in a manner quite inconsistent with that which might be expected from their verbal attitudes."[18]

After carefully reviewing the research on the relationship between what people say their attitudes are and what they actually do, Alan Wicker says:

> . . . Caution must be exercised to avoid making the claim that a given study or set of studies of verbal attitudes, however well done, is socially significant. Most socially significant questions involve overt behavior, rather than people's feelings, and the assumption that feelings are directly translated into actions has not been demonstrated.[19]

Eugene and Ruth Hartley explain the differences between attitudes and behavior in terms of role orientations:

> The discrepancy in responses seems to indicate that behavior in the presence of other people is defined by role orientations different from those of behavior in the presence of a questionnaire. . . . Since roles are defined in part by relationships and interactions, the roles activated in the two types of situations must patently be different. The role of the respondent is defined and directed in part by the very presence and behavior of the persons who act as stimuli.[20]

Whether the inconsistencies among attitude, expressed opinion, and behavior are due to role orientations or to responses to felt social and economic pressures (there seems to be little real difference in these cases), obviously we do not always

---

18. Melvin L. De Fleur and Frank R. Westie, "Verbal Attitudes and Overt Acts: An Experiment on the Salience of Attitudes," *American Sociological Review* 23 (1958): 673.

19. Alan W. Wicker, "Attitudes vs. Actions: The Relationship of Verbal and Overt Behavioral Responses to Attitude Object," *Journal of Social Issues* 25, no. 4 (1969): 41–78, quotation at 75. A pertinent study is Don W. Brown, "Adolescent Attitudes and Lawful Behavior," *Public Opinion Quarterly* 38 (1974): 98–106.

20. Eugene L. Hartley and Ruth E. Hartley, *Fundamentals of Social Psychology* (New York: Knopf, 1952), p. 549. See also, for a similar analysis, Leo Bogart, "No Opinion, Don't Know, and Maybe No Answer," *Public Opinion Quarterly* 31 (1967): 321–345.

act according to our beliefs. No doubt the amount of dissimulation the healthy personality can tolerate has some limit. We could not always, or even most of the time, behave contrary to our feelings and opinions. We need to feel that, in general, we speak and do as we honestly think and believe. But most people can achieve this basic sense of personality integration and consistency at the same time that they engage in a good deal of conscious and unconscious dissembling. In the first place, attitudes and opinions are not always clear and uncontradictory; conflicting attitudes make room for conflicting behavior. In the second place, the use of little lies, conventional phrases, circumlocutions, and other forms of behavior that are inconsistent with real attitudes and opinions is widely tolerated, even expected.

Inconsistency between opinions and behavior, then, is a common fact of life. I may dislike getting out of bed in the morning to go to work; yet I do it. I may loathe one of my colleagues; yet I act decently and perhaps even pleasantly toward him. I may be bored at a party; yet I laugh and talk and appear to the hostess to be enjoying myself immensely. As Shakespeare says, "One may smile, and smile, and be a villain."

A single principle seems to govern opinion–behavior inconsistencies: behavior will be inconsistent with opinions when, in the judgment of the behaver, the larger context of the situation requires inconsistency. For example, I would prefer not to get out of bed to go to work in the morning, but I prefer even more to keep my job. My second and stronger attitude prevails over my first and weaker attitude, although the behavior remains inconsistent with my first attitude. Likewise, my opinion of my colleague is that he is disagreeable, weak, and dull, but I am also of the opinion that the work relationship frequently requires me to act as though I believed him to be pleasant, strong, and interesting. My behavior is inconsistent with one opinion, completely consistent with the other.

But the matter of opinion–behavior discrepancies is hardly ended by the simple statement that inconsistencies exist when the individual believes that the context requires inconsistency (or, in other words, that larger consistencies require smaller inconsistencies). Then the relevant questions become: What kinds of "larger contexts" require inconsistency, and what kinds allow consistency? What devices (avoidance, lies, rationalization) are used, and under what circumstances, when inconsistency seems to be necessary? What kinds of changes (if any) occur in attitudes and opinions when behavior is inconsistent with them?

## 8.5 OPINION AND BEHAVIOR: CONVERGENCES AND DIVERGENCES

There are several reasons why people may say what they do not believe:

    **1.** They do not know what they believe and feel required to say something.

(We have already considered this matter, in part, under the "don't know" problem in Chapter 6.)

2. They are unable to express what they believe (that is, their ability with language is too limited to permit them to express their opinions accurately).
3. They are unwilling to say what they believe.
4. They feel social pressure to tell a lie, believing the lie to be innocent, or that they will not be exposed. (This matter, too, is discussed in Chapter 6.)

To the extent that persons say what they do not believe, verbal behavior is inconsistent with opinion. Nonverbal behavior may be inconsistent in the same way, because individuals may be unable or unwilling to act in consonance with their opinions.

The survey research question is one that imposes a second step of consistency or inconsistency in the opinion–behavior dilemma. From the point of view of the opinion researcher, the problem is usually more complex even than the relation of thought to action. The researcher is hardly ever in a position to witness the unprompted expression of opinion at the same time as (or in close proximity to) the behavior that is related to the opinion. The measurement task is not ordinarily a matter of observing the spontaneous expression of opinion and its manifestation in behavior (which may then be judged to be consistent or inconsistent). Rather, the usual case is for the measurement to be in terms of what persons say, in response to a question that is not their own and at a time of someone else's choosing, about what they think and do.

There is no doubt a tendency toward consistency in the three elements of the complex involving (a) private opinions, (b) verbal expressions, and (c) overt behavior. John Dollard believes that opinions, when voiced either spontaneously or in answer to queries, are expressions of "anticipatory" or "forecasting" responses—that is, they give clues to what the respondents believe they would do when faced with choices involving the substance of the question. The clearest political illustration is the answer to the question "Which candidate do you favor?" The question implies a behavioral component: in whose behalf do you intend to act (vote)? The opinion poll on candidate preference is only the most obvious example of the argument that voiced opinions are anticipatory responses; most survey answers can be thought of as forecasts of behavior. Questions about political ideology, policy issues, or political actors may be considered questions about what the respondent would *do* if choices were necessary. If one thinks about the problem this way, as Dollard suggests, the question of consistency between opinion and behavior becomes one of how well the individual can predict future behavior at the time the statement about it is made (that is, at the time the opinion is expressed). Dollard makes some useful and unsophisticated generalizations about the psychological and sociological conditions under which opinions and behavior will be consistent:

1. Neurotics will find it difficult to predict their behavior when their own serious conflicts are involved.
2. Persons with poor verbal skills may find it difficult to forecast their own behavior.
3. People who habitually go into effective action after thinking things over can best predict their own actions.
4. The test situation should not be corrupted by extraneous threats or rewards.
5. A man can best predict what he will do in a future situation if he has been in about the same situation before and thus knows what it's all about.
6. A man can predict what he will do in a future situation provided he doesn't have an experience which changes his mind before this situation occurs.
7. A man can better predict what he will do in a future dilemma if he is told exactly what this dilemma will be.[21]

## 8.6 OPINION-BEHAVIOR CONSISTENCY AMONG POLITICAL ELITES

It is sometimes suggested that political life allows, perhaps even demands, a greater amount of dissembling at every level of involvement than do other arenas of human activity. If such is the case, then political elites may be more likely than nonelites to act in a manner inconsistent with their true attitudes and opinions.

The subject is one on which little direct work has been done. There is, to be sure, a large literature on official withholding of information, propaganda, and the manipulation of popular opinion in general by means of lies and half-truths. But there have been few investigations of whether ordinary political leaders in democratic polities are subjected to more than ordinary pressures to behave in ways that contradict their opinions.

There are two traditions here. One is popular, journalistic, and superficial. It says that politicians are, generically, slippery and evasive people who will not "give you a straight answer" and who, when pressured to give their word (that is, a "straight answer"), are likely not to keep it. The other tradition in regard to politicians and opinion–behavior inconsistencies comes from professional politicians themselves and from their research-scholar friends—and may also be

---

21. John Dollard, "Under What Conditions Do Opinions Predict Behavior?" *Public Opinion Quarterly* 12 (1948–49): 628–632. These are what Dollard calls "common-sense statements"; he rephrases them in social science jargon, but without any increase in clarity or specificity—a nice example of the vernacular's superiority over the affected language of the "expert." The extreme sexism of Dollard's language also may suggest what progress has been made since he wrote in the late 1940s. Several of Dollard's "statements" are confirmed and elaborated by Charles R. Tittle and Richard J. Hill, "Attitude Measurement and Prediction of Behavior: An Evaluation of Conditions and Measurement Techniques," *Sociometry* 30 (1967): 199–213.

superficial. It says that political elites in democracies have to guard against inconsistencies more carefully than do nonelites, and be more explicit about their own opinions and their behaviors; "when you give your word you have to keep it."

The summary explanation for and resolution of these two conflicting interpretations probably lie in the special representational role of democratic leaders. The conflicting interpretations arise from democratic political leaders' need to balance their own opinions and behaviors with their perceived need (a) to think and act for their constituents as well and (b) to secure reelection. Figure 8–1 illustrates the field of forces relevant to the consistency or inconsistency of a political leader's opinions and behavior.

Quadrant II of Figure 8–1 is the problematic case. Here the political leader's perception of what her constituency believes and wants may conflict with her own firmly held opinion on the issue. This is the kind of situation that gives rise to "profiles in courage." If she publicly states her own view, then votes as she believes her constituents desire, she will be called cowardly. If she delays, waffles, or obfuscates her own view, she will be said to be weak and lacking in leadership. If she defies her constituency, proclaims her opinion, and votes it, some will admire her integrity, some will call her headstrong and impolitic—and in any case such courage will inevitably reduce her strength in the district and may lead to her defeat. She, and all other political leaders caught in such cross-pressure, need to do some skillful explaining.

"Congressmen," says John Kingdon, "are constantly called upon to explain to constituents why they voted as they did." Sometimes members of Congress vote their personal opinion and construct a justification later. But, "especially if they do not feel intensely about the matter, they often vote so as to avoid the predicament, [and]. . .it can be said that the necessity to explain one's vote has had an impact on the congressman's behavior."[22] This is the case with opinions and behavior in quadrant III of Figure 8–1.

When the political leader has her own view and perceives her constituents to be of various minds, some supporting and some opposing the measure to be acted on, then her skill in explaining will determine how much her opinion–behavior consistency has helped or damaged her reelectability. Such cases, represented by quadrant I of Figure 8–1, are perhaps the most common political leaders' experience. "Explaining" in such cases will involve various messages to various groups, perhaps each emphasizing a different goal and a different argument as the official tries to get most "credit" from groups that share her opinion and to suffer least damage from those opposed. The superficial but popular notion that politicians are wafflers and hypocrites is strengthened by explaining done in these common situations.

---

22. John W. Kingdon, *Congressmen's Voting Decisions* (New York: Harper & Row, 1973), pp. 46–47.

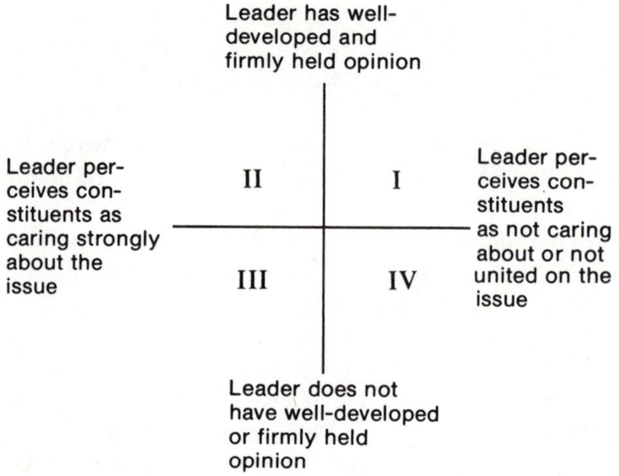

Leader has well-
developed and
firmly held opinion

Leader per-
ceives con-
stituents as
caring strongly
about the
issue

II          I          Leader per-
                      ceives con-
                      stituents
                      as not caring
                      about or not
III        IV          united on the
                      issue

Leader does not
have well-developed
or firmly held
opinion

**Figure 8–1.**  *Matrix for analysis of political leader's opinion–behavior consistency or inconsistency*

Quadrant IV of Figure 8–1 represents the easy cases. This is where, from the point of view of her constituency, the politician has some giveaways. She can engage in logrolling here, building up credit with fellow politicians by behaving as they want her to—by, for instance, giving her vote to a project or bill they and their constituents want—in the expectation, almost always unspoken but understood, that she will get their vote when she needs it and they don't. Here, then, is a common situation that gives rise to the tradition that politicians have to be more consistent in opinions and behavior than ordinary mortals do. Political leaders know the need to explain. And they know that reluctance to take a clear position on something of no great importance to themselves or their constituents makes sense in that it avoids the necessity to explain and the dangers that always lurk in explaining. So political leaders understand the need for waffling rhetoric. But it is also a fast rule of political life that when you give your word, you keep it. Be consistent in what you say you will do and what you do.

In sum, the *appearance* of opinion–behavior inconsistency may be exceptionally great among political elites because explaining, or anticipation of the need to explain, makes politicians seem to be saying different things to different people— as indeed they are—and therefore the degree of fit between their behavior and their opinions is subject to various interpretations.

## Chapter 9

# Culture and
# Opinion Holding

An individual's opinions are limited and conditioned by internal physical and chemical reactions and by unique experiences of development. Though much is known about mental capacity and mental process, debate rages over many key questions, among them the effect of genetic variations on psychophysiological abilities; the nature of the processes by which we perceive, store, and recall sense impressions; the basic psychological and biological drives and needs; and even, indeed, whether mind can properly be distinguished from body.

All these matters are important to the thinking processes, which in turn are basic to the holding of opinions, including public opinions as we have defined them. Nevertheless, there is no reason to believe that these psychophysiological questions must be resolved before we can begin to understand the social and political implications of the uniformities and diversities of opinion. The kinds of problems with which the political scientist and political sociologist deal permit many workable if not provable assumptions. We may assume that individual opinions are shaped by forces that in most cases do not need to be analyzed medically or experimentally. Although a case can be made for the study of politically influential psychopaths[1] and for the significance of personality types in the making or implementing of public policy, the focus of our interest is sociopolitical rather than psychological. Hitler may have been an acute paranoid, but this fact (if it is a fact) is important to us only insofar as it applies to the social environment that could raise him to great power and as it relates to the policies tolerated or supported by the leaders and citizens of Nazi Germany. For our purposes, the key processes are social rather than psychophysiological; they relate to the interactions among people rather than the interactions within individuals.

---

1. For example, see Harold L. Lasswell, *Psychopathology and Politics* (Chicago: University of Chicago Press, 1930).

Most of our attention throughout the remainder of this book will be given to matters that are unmistakably sociopolitical. We are and will be concerned largely with the patterned interpersonal relations that affect the character and distributions of opinions—with how social institutions and group relationships influence agreements and disagreements over public issues.

This chapter is an introduction to and an overview of the theories and concepts of the cultural anthropology of opinion holding, and of the evidence adduced to support those theories. Its intention is to create a background and framework for thinking about the ways collective life molds shared opinions.


## 9.1 THE CONCEPT OF CULTURE

The discovery and elaboration of the concept of culture is one of the few genuine breakthroughs in the social sciences, impossible to overemphasize. The idea of culture is, as John Cuber declares, "fundamental to the understanding of the human being and of groups. Most of the other social science ideas grow out of it or are dependent on it."[2]

Many definitions of culture could be cited. They all agree that it is the whole pattern of learned social values, myths, and traditions, along with the physical products of human labor, created and shared by the members of a society.[3]

*Culture is learned.* Very little of our day-to-day behavior is forced upon us biologically. Though certain bodily functions must of course be performed, the details and rituals of eating, elimination, and sex are subject to cultural requirements (or expectations) and prohibitions (or discouragements). There are, as John Gillin points out, three kinds of evidence that almost all behavior is learned:

> First, we have the investigations on new-born infants, which indicate the extreme paucity of inborn goal-directed activity patterns of any type.... Our second type of evidence consists of various carefully controlled studies of identical twins who have been reared apart from each other and have grown up developing different custom patterns. In these cases, the individuals were identical in inheritance and differed only in the type of experience and training accorded them. If they grew up to exhibit different culture patterns, we can hardly assign the culture to heredity.

---

2. John F. Cuber, *Sociology,* 2nd ed. (New York: Appleton, 1951), p. 65.

3. William R. Catton, Jr., reports that the use of the word *culture (Kultur)* developed rapidly among German scholars in the nineteenth century. In 1871 E. B. Taylor defined culture as "that complex whole which includes knowledge, belief, art, law, morals, custom, and any other capabilities and habits acquired by man as a member of society." But, says Catton, "it was not until the 1920s that the word became firmly established in the sociological vocabulary" "The Development of Sociological Thought," in *Handbook of Modern Sociology,* ed. Robert E. L. Faris (Chicago: Rand McNally, 1964), pp. 943–944. See also Louis Schneider and Charles M. Bonjean, eds., *The Idea of Culture in the Social Sciences* (New York: Cambridge University Press, 1973).

Finally, and perhaps most convincing for anthropological purposes, we have the evidence of the variability of human culture
itself. . . . All qualified experts agree that the species is one, biologically speaking. Yet the cultures practised by diverse groups within the
species vary enormously among themselves. Likewise, there is no
uniformity or regularity in the types of culture to be found within a
single race or other subgroup of the species. . . . When we are
acquainted with the great variety of cultures, it is impossible to
believe that culture is carried in the germ plasm. There are only two
other alternatives: either it descends upon people in some mysterious,
unknown fashion, or it is learned. The first hypothesis has no data to
support it, while the second seems to fit the facts.[4]

It should be clear from the examples Gillin gives, and from the most rudimen-
tary observations everyone can make, that much (probably most) culture is
learned inadvertently. That part which we learn through our conscious imitation
of our cultural teachers, or through the intentional tutelage of those with whom
we associate as infants, children, and adults, is no doubt smaller than that which
we quite literally grow into as we are socialized: basic eating and clothing habits
are not taught in any formal sense, no matter how diligently such minutiae as
spinach eating may be impressed upon the small fry. The boy does not have to be
urged to emulate his father or the girl her mother in the gross behavior that marks
the development of the "little man" or the "young lady." This is not to say, of
course, that the consciously learned subcultural distinctions of social class—and
especially of the acquisition of skills (which is so much a part of the formal
schooling of the child and young adult)—are not important; it is only to say that
the learning of culture in the broadest sense is in a large degree not self-conscious
and intentional.

*Culture is pervasive.* We are figuratively and literally immersed in our culture.
A clue to the total pervasiveness of culture lies in the use of the term *culture* in the
biological sciences. The culture of microorganisms—of bacteria, for example—is
the medium in which they live and thrive. So it is with human organisms. We
could not live without the culture that makes possible not only our social
intercourse but every vital act of our individual existence.

Is this too strong a statement of the pervasiveness and indispensability of
culture? We think not. There is some evidence that the existence and perception
of ideas themselves depend on the most basic ingredient of culture: language. The
argument for this point of view is too complex and lengthy to be set forth here,
but some psycholinguists believe that concepts cannot exist unless they are
expressible in language.[5] And, note well, language is the creature of culture.

---

4. From *The Ways of Men* by John Gillin, p. 191. Copyright, 1948 D. Appleton-Century Company,
Inc. Reprinted by permission of Appleton-Century-Crofts.

5. For an excellent summary discussion of this and other evidence of cultural pervasiveness, see
Clyde Kluckhohn, "Culture and Behavior," in *Handbook of Social Psychology,* ed. Gardner Lindzey
(Reading, Mass.: Addison-Wesley, 1954), 2:921–976, especially 931–940.

But, it may be asked, cannot individuals exist alone without society at all? Are there no Robinson Crusoes? The answer is that there have indeed been Robinson Crusoes. Yet, like the fictional character and the real-life sailor on whom he is based, they took their culture with them. The hut they built, the kind of food they gathered, the clothes they improvised—and even the institution of "Man Friday" slavery—were cultural phenomena washed ashore with them, and without which they would have wandered aimlessly on the beach until death.

One consequence of the pervasiveness of culture is the likelihood that we cannot completely know ourselves, because objectivity in the sense of noninvolvement is impossible. Despite the most exhaustive attempts to "deculturize" themselves, anthropologists have been unable to view alien cultures (or their own) with complete detachment. We do not suggest that cultural anthropologists are unable scientifically to study what they aspire to study, or even that the most able among them are very seriously inconvenienced by their own cultural cages. It is crucial, however, that we recognize and, insofar as we can, guard against the danger of proclaiming as "truth" that which is only a culturally colored observation, measurement, or judgment.

*Culture is patterned.* The elements of culture—the thousands of objects, values, techniques, and behavioral prescriptions—do not exist unrelated to one another. Few if any cultural phenomena are devised or maintained in isolation; rather, they are systematically related. Ruth Benedict's *Patterns of Culture,*[6] one of the most important books to be published in this century, makes this point not only in its title but in all the descriptive and interpretive accounts of the societies she examines. The internal relatedness of cultural traits had been remarked by many anthropologists before Benedict, and some had even noted that the patterns were often unobserved by the culture carriers themselves. Thus Edward Sapir, pioneering in what we now call the field of "personality in culture," observed as early as 1927 that "normal human beings, both in confessedly social behavior and often in supposedly individual behavior, are reacting in accordance with deep-seated cultural patterns...not so much known as felt, not so much capable of conscious description as of naive practice"[7] Sapir's point ties together both the patterning and the pervasiveness of culture.

Note: the statement that cultural elements exist in patterned relationships to one another says nothing about the goodness or badness of the patterns or about

6. Boston: Houghton Mifflin, 1934. Benedict's book is important both because it was a provocative challenge to her fellow social scientists and because, as an early best-seller of the paperback age, it made the culture concept familiar to hundreds of thousands of students in the 1940s and 1950s. It is of interest, at least to political scientists, that some criticisms leveled at Benedict's book by social scientists and others as well were essentially political criticisms. For instance, it was said that she had exaggerated the competitiveness of the Kwakiutl Indians and the cooperativeness of the Zuñi in order to make a disguised attack on free-enterprise capitalism.

7. Edward Sapir, "The Unconscious Patterning of Behavior in Society," in *Selected Writings of Edward Sapir,* ed. David G. Mandelbaum (Berkeley: University of California Press, 1949), p. 548.

the functional or dysfunctional consequences of patterning. All cultures are constantly undergoing the reshaping of their patterns. The dynamic unmaking and remaking of cultural patterns are evident, to some extent, in even the most moribund cultures. In social aggregates experiencing rapid demographic, technological, or ideological change, the repatterning may proceed so swiftly as to defy even the measurement of its change. Only in the years to come will we be able to assess with accuracy the revolutionary cultural changes currently taking place in parts of Asia and Africa. This dynamic process is the meaning of the technologically induced telescoping of historical development stages in all of the societies being modernized: the old cultural ways are being modified or replaced at such a rapid rate that no person, group, or policy is able even to take account of the change, much less guide it into desired forms.

Whether cultural patterns are undergoing revolutionary change, as in modern Africa, or seem static and immobile, as during long centuries in feudal Europe, there is a constant tension in every culture between the factors making for change and the influences for the maintenance of the status quo. Innovation is the great progenitor of change—innovation of ideas and applied technology. On the other side, habit and the convenience of regularity (of the ability to anticipate response) are the great forces underlying the stability of cultural patterns.

The modern era, usually considered to have commenced in the sixteenth or seventeenth century, is characterized everywhere by increased intracultural tensions and by greater change, in general, than any previous historical epoch. While it is impossible to chart or predict the details of these changes within any given culture or any brief time span, a case can be made that in the latter part of the twentieth century two vast secular tendencies in cultural pattern change are under way: intracultural diversity is increasing and intercultural diversity is decreasing.

## 9.2 INCREASING DIVERSITY WITHIN CULTURES

The evidence accumulated by social anthropologists indicates that any given culture has fewer prescriptions and proscriptions than it had fifty, a hundred, or five hundred years ago. The patterns of values and behaviors are less rigid; fewer things "must be done," fewer "cannot be done." The behavior choices for the individual are in most places vastly increased.

One hears a great deal today in the Western world about conformity. It is a bad word for many educators (especially in the humanities and the social sciences), political moralizers, editorial writers, and other preachers, lay and clerical. There is a sense, of course, in which the wide acceptance by adolescents of faddish peer-group styles or activities or the worship by adults of the symbols of money income is unfortunate, stultifying to individual personality, and perhaps harmful to society. But the "conformity" of mid-twentieth-century America must be distinguished from the conformity of twelfth-century Britain or nineteenth-century New Guinea. It is the difference between having choices and not using them and not having choices at all.

Conformity in feudal Europe tended to inhere in the rigid cultural characteristics of fixed obligations owed to and by landholding and ecclesiastical classes. Most of the people (and even to a considerable degree the nobility and higher gentry) were not free to choose their places of residence, occupations, mates, duties to kinfolk and neighbors, or belief–value structures. These were all given them by accident of birth, provided by cultural patterns. The cultural imperatives tended to limit the determination of opinions and behavior. In many cultures, the institution of slavery alone deprived thousands of people of the right to any self-directed opinion or behavior. Serfdom allowed somewhat more self-direction, but still relatively little by modern standards.

Margaret Mead has described the cultural totalitarianism of the Balinese as she observed it in the 1920s. The Bali native did not depend on anything that could be called a public opinion process—even when defined most narrowly as consideration of an issue leading to small-group behavior. The individual was not expected to have an opinion; group and role involvements all so tightly circumscribed thinking that an issue, as we might understand it, could hardly arise. When an unusual matter arose, the facts were unemotionally laid before a leader, whose role it was to determine, within the traditions, what decision should be made.[8]

Modern cultural patterns are much more permissive. In the Western world, and with increasing rapidity in the nonwestern world, the masses are allowed to make, each person individually, all the basic choices denied their ancestors of a thousand years ago.

There are, of course, short-term countercycles in the processes of intracultural diversification. The recent political history of India regarding the erosion of caste barriers and policies on population control illustrates that periods of cultural loosening up may alternate with periods of tightening up. Among nondemocratic polities the Iranian revolution of 1978–1979 was a dramatic demonstration of cultural conformity directed by traditionalistic religious leaders. Such temporary reversals are to be expected in the long-term diversification within cultures, for rapid change is psychologically upsetting to the masses and often profoundly threatening to traditional elites, such as the mullahs of Iran.

Much of the literature on the "mass society" would lead one to believe that in highly developed communities pressures toward conformity are creating increased sameness of cultural patterns. The fear seems to be that mass media, mass living styles, and mass entertainment, tied to the technology of behavior control, will produce a monolithic culture in which individuals are reduced to

---

8. "Public Opinion Mechanisms among Primitive People," *Public Opinion Quarterly* 1 (1937): 5–16.

choiceless automatons. So far, at least, there is little evidence that that is the trend in the United States. In an interesting analysis of changing attitude patterns by age and regionalism, Norval Glenn and J. L. Simmons show that divergencies in Americans' attitudes toward religion, work, international politics, and racial and ethnic minorities seem to be increasing.[9]

The transformation from cultural patterns of compulsion to patterns of permissiveness has been brought about largely by technological and ideological innovation. This statement is by now as trite as it is important; it is enough to observe that modern cultures are without exception more varied and rich in choice for most individuals than were previous cultures. There are still persons in our society for whom cultural choices are not varied and rich enough to satisfy either the promise of the human spirit or the ideals of the good society. For both these objectives, we need to pursue the further enrichment and variation of cultural patterns and to increase the choices available to every individual. But the long trend is clearly in this direction; intracultural diversity is, so far as one can tell, increasing nearly everywhere.

## 9.3  DECREASING DIVERSITY AMONG CULTURES

As intracultural diversity increases, intercultural diversity diminishes, for the same reasons that individual choices increase within cultures—because of technological and ideological innovations. It is an old story that the missionaries who brought the Bible to the South Sea islanders were followed by traders and soldiers who brought radios, wristwatches, K rations, and syphilis. For better or worse, the Papuan's culture became more and more rich and varied, and more and more like that of the West. In small as well as large ways, among subcultures as well as across strikingly different cultures, intracultural variety increases and intercultural diversity is reduced. American quick-frozen foods and supermarkets have been adopted all over Europe; European football, renamed, becomes the American soccer craze.

The possible implications and consequences of these long-run cultural tendencies make for interesting speculation:

**1.**   Within cultures, opinion and behavior become less the direct consequences of the requirements of culture and more a matter of the interplay of the voluntaristic social institutions and more or less free choices of individuals.

**2.**   Law, as the codification of the remaining compulsory elements in the culture, becomes more clearly distinguishable from morals and mores. Govern-

---

9. Norval D. Glenn and J. L. Simmons, "Are Regional Cultural Differences Diminishing?" *Public Opinion Quarterly* 31 (1967): 176–193.

ment, as the agency that possesses officiality and a monopoly of coercive powers, becomes more clearly differentiated from such unofficial, noncoercive power structures as the economic and religious.

3.   Among cultures, the more striking differences tend to disappear.

Probably, as this intercultural uniformity grows, the "hard" facts of various levels of technology, education, and literacy, plus modes of production and urbanization, will have increasingly similar influences on public opinion, culture for culture. As one example, consider the technology of commercial flight. The production and management of jet airplanes is more and more standardized across cultures. Despite fierce national pride, it appears that the supersonic Concorde of England and France cannot prevail against shared international technology, shared international market forces, and even shared international ecological values and attitudes.

Enough intercultural consensus might be forthcoming, in time, to support a genuine world opinion. Thinkers who describe themselves as "functional world federalists" believe that the growing economic interdependence of nations will lead to such a world public opinion and ultimately to a world political union.

One cannot expect the possible salutary effects of diminishing intercultural differences to be either rapid or profound. The roots of international conflict and war have not often been found in cultural diversity: human history reveals more instances of like people fighting one another than of likes fighting unlikes. Still, one hope for the democratization of totalitarian nations (leading, presumably, to a decrease in world tensions) is that a society with high levels of technology is compelled to permit increasing freedom of information and individual choice. In that case, and if there is other evidence that the cultural patterns of nations tend to converge, we may be somewhat more optimistic about the resolution of conflicting opinions and policies.

## 9.4 CULTURE AS A LIMITING AND INFLUENCING FACTOR IN THE FORMATION OF OPINION

Let us sum up the foregoing discussion of culture and recent cultural tendencies in relation to the model of the opinion-forming process. Cultural patterns constitute one of a set of conditions and forces that, figuratively, define the shape and size of the funnel of causality. Cultural prescriptions and proscriptions in a traditional society are a very limiting influence on the opinion-policy process. In the tightly culture-bound society, the possible opinions that may be held on any issue are few. The press of cultural imperatives—the limiting factor—is close upon the individual, and the funnel of causality is small (see Figure 9–1).

In modern societies, the increasing intracultural diversity and the change of many cultural patterns from requirements to influences may be represented as pushing choice farther back into the funnel (Figure 9–2). By contrast with

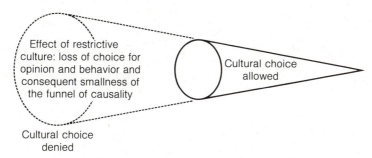

**Figure 9–1.** *Funnel of causality in traditional societies: choice restricted*

primitive patterns, modern cultural patterns *require fewer* opinions, but they *permit* many more. Still, they help to define at some point, along with the other limiting factors, the large end of the funnel of causality.

## 9.5 THE STUDY OF POLITICAL CULTURE

An examination of the sources of public opinion should take note of the cultural patterns related to the processes of governance. For our purposes, the technological state of the society, the institutionalization of large economic and social forms, and the artifacts of the people are important only as they relate to the governmental and the social conflicts that are thought to be properly treatable by public authority. We are more interested in what may be called the *political culture,* namely, those thought and behavior patterns that are especially valued or devalued by the society and that have to do with political leadership and the handling of political conflict.

Sidney Verba defines political culture as "the system of empirical beliefs, expressive symbols, and values which defines the situation in which political action takes place. It provides the subjective orientation to politics."[10] Like many useful social science concepts, the idea of political culture can be applied to any group whose empirical beliefs, expressive symbols, and values seem to differ in some important ways from those of other groups in the environment. So one can speak of Western political culture to designate the secularized, industrial or postindustrial, individualistic political patterns of Europe and North America, or the political cultures of modernizing authoritarian or totalitarian polities. One can speak of *national* political cultures, comparing, say, Spanish and Swedish patterns of empirical beliefs, expressive symbols, and values important for

---

10. Sidney Verba, "Comparative Political Culture," in *Political Culture and Political Development,* eds. Lucian W. Pye and Sidney Verba (Princeton: Princeton University Press, 1965), p. 513.

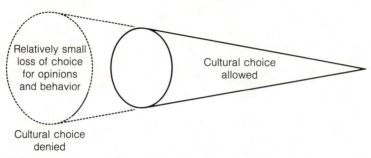

Relatively small
loss of choice
for opinions
and behavior

Cultural choice
allowed

Cultural choice
denied

**Figure 9–2.**   *Funnel of causality in modern societies: choice enlarged*

political action. And by invoking the concept of political subcultures, one can often make useful comparisons within a single country, as Robert Putnam and his colleagues have done in a study of Italian political institutions[11] and as Daniel Elazar and others have done in regard to American politics (see below).

The use of survey research in the empirical study of political culture began in the 1950s. One of the earliest cross-national investigations is reported by Gabriel A. Almond and Sidney Verba in their book *The Civic Culture: Political Attitudes and Democracy in Five Nations.* Noting the rapid decrease of intercultural diversity, Almond and Verba declare that the emerging world culture will be determined in its *social* organization by technology and rationality. But of its *political* orientation only one thing is clear: the mystique of popular participation will be pervasive. Though ordinary people will everywhere be expected to participate, the mode of participation is uncertain:

> The emerging nations are presented with two different models of the modern participatory state, the democratic and the totalitarian. The democratic state offers the ordinary man the opportunity to take part in the political decisionmaking process as an influential citizen; the totalitarian offers him the role of the "participant subject."[12]

The political opinions of average citizens of any country will be heavily influenced by the culture of which they are a part. Interviews with about one thousand persons in each of five countries—the United States, Britain, West Germany, Italy, and Mexico—revealed some striking differences in political culture. Almond and Verba based their comparisons on such criteria as knowledge and awareness of government and politics, political emotion and involve-

11. Robert D. Putnam et al., "Explaining Institutional Success: The Case of Italian Regional Government," *American Political Science Review* 77 (1983): 55–74.

12. Gabriel A. Almond and Sidney Verba, *The Civic Culture: Political Attitudes and Democracy in Five Nations* (Princeton: Princeton University Press, 1963), p. 4. Other useful general works are Walter A. Rosenbaum, *Political Culture* (New York: Praeger, 1975), and Donald J. Devine, *The Political Culture of the United States* (Boston: Little, Brown, 1972).

ment, sense of political obligation and competence, and social attitudes and experiences in other authority contexts.

Since the early research on political culture a great many criticisms have been leveled at the concept itself, at the attempts to evaluate existing polities in terms of their political cultures, and at what has been perceived to be an ethnocentric Anglo-American bias in the idea of the "civic culture." Almond and Verba themselves edited an excellent collection of these criticisms and exchanges in 1980 (*The Civic Culture Revisited*).[13] The usefulness of the concept is widely accepted, however, and it continues to be of central importance for studying the way values get institutionalized in national political systems,[14] for explaining why both popular and elite political behavior varies across national polities,[15] and for understanding how radically and/or quickly sociopolitical change can be brought about by directive governments.[16]

The most systematic exploration of the idea of political culture in America has been done by Daniel Elazar. He believes that three types of political culture have influenced American opinion holding and behavior since colonial times. These three political cultures (or American political subcultures) are:

**1.** *Moralistic.* Beginning with the Puritan settlers of the Plymouth and Massachusetts Bay colonies, "the political order [was] conceived to be a commonwealth—a state in which the whole people have an undivided interest—in which the citizens cooperate in an effort to create and maintain the best government in order to implement certain shared moral principles."[17] The moralistic political culture, still found among the older families and upper social classes in New England, was carried west by preachers, abolitionists, lawyers, land speculators, and farmers. In the nineteenth century renewed political moralism was brought to Wisconsin, Minnesota, and Iowa by stern Lutherans, pietistic sects, and German Social Democrats escaping the European reaction of the 1850s. The progressivism of Wisconsin's Robert La Follette and Nebraska's George Norris in the early 1900s was another cultural outburst of this hardy American moralism, as was the California Progressivism of Hiram Johnson. Elazar's map of American political cultures (Figure 9–3) reveals the geohistorical influence of the moralistic tendencies.

---

13. Boston: Little, Brown.

14. See, for example, Eliezer Ben-Rafael, *The Emergence of Ethnicity: Cultural Groups and Social Conflict* (Westport, Conn.: Greenwood Press, 1982).

15. Henry W. Ehrmann says in his *Politics in France,* 4th ed. (Boston: Little Brown, 1983), that "a discussion of the country's political culture as a major variable determining political behavior has always appeared to be particularly relevant. It also provides the main theme of this book" (p. xiv).

16. Richard R. Fagen, *The Transformation of Political Cluture in Cuba* (Stanford: Stanford University Press, 1969), and Archie Brown and Jack Gray, *Political Culture and Political Change in Communist States* (New York: Holmes & Meier, 1979).

17. Daniel J. Elazar, *Cities of the Prairie: The Metropolitan Frontier and American Politics* (New York: Basic Books, 1970), p. 259.

2. *Traditionalistic.* In contrast to the moralistic culture's emphasis on "doing good" (for God, for self, and for community) is a preindustrial orientation "rooted in an ambivalent attitude toward the marketplace coupled with a paternalistic and elitist conception of the commonwealth." The polity in this culture is recognized and given deference to, but it is not the embodiment of religious or moral values, and it is tolerant of (perhaps even indifferent to) a diversity of routes to salvation or status. The traditionalistic political culture "accepts a substantially hierarchical society as part of the ordered nature of things...and functions to confine real political power to a relatively small and self-perpetuating group drawn from an established elite." The colonial South and states westward have been especially influenced by the traditionalistic political culture, as Figure 9–3 shows.

3. *Individualistic.* In this third American political culture, "the political order is conceived as a marketplace in which the primary public relationships are products of bargaining among individuals and groups acting out of self-interest." In the parts of the United States where the individualistic political culture has been dominant—New York, New Jersey, Pennsylvania, and the trans-Appalachian border states, as shown in Figure 9–3—"government is instituted for strictly utilitarian reasons, to handle those functions demanded by the people it is created to serve"; "politics is just another means by which individuals may improve themselves socially and economically"; and "since the individualistic political culture eschews ideological concerns in its 'businesslike' conception of politics, both politicians and citizens look upon political activity as a specialized one, essentially the province of professionals, of minimum and passing concern to laymen, and with no place for amateurs to play an active role."[18]

While attractive on impressionistic grounds and showing good fit with the common wisdom in regard to political norms in the relevant states and regions, Elazar's political culture types are hard to demonstrate in empirical and contemporary behavioral terms. On Ira Sharkansky's measures, states with traditionalistic cultures "show the least participation and the most restrictive suffrage laws, [while] states with moralistic cultures tend to show contrasting traits of high participation." He concludes that political culture "may be most direct in its effect on popular behavior."[19] On the other hand, when David Lowery and Lee Sigelman tested Elazar's subcultural concepts against popular opinions about

18. Daniel J. Elazar, *American Federalism: A View from the States,* 2nd ed. (New York: Thomas Y. Crowell, 1972), pp. 44–45, 99. Copyright 1972 by Harper and Row, Publishers, Inc. Reprinted by permission.

19. Ira Sharkansky, "The Utility of Elazar's Political Culture," *Polity,* 2 (Fall 1969): 66–83, quotation at 83. Another study found that Elazar's perspectives helped to explain differences among the fifty states in (1) kinds of governmental activity, (2) levels of citizen participation, (3) innovation in public service, (4) local-centralized decision making, and (5) party competition; see Charles A. Johnson, "Political Culture in American States: Elazar's Formulation Examined," *American Journal of Political Science* 20 (August 1976): 491–509.

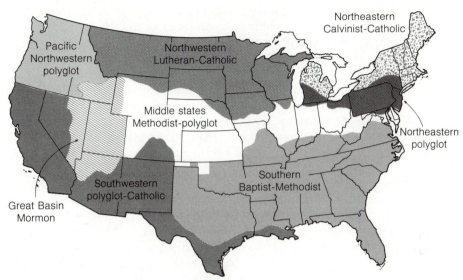

*Based on the flows of the streams as reflected in
the dominant patterns of religious affiliation.

**Figure 9–3.** *American subcultural areas, based on flows of cultural streams as reflected in dominant patterns of religious affiliation* (From *Cities of the Prairie,* by Daniel J. Elazar, p. 195. © 1970 by Daniel J. Elazar. Basic Books, Inc. Publishers, New York)

political efficacy, governmental responsiveness, citizen duties, and self-reliance, they concluded that there was "only weak empirical support for...the linkage between political culture and public choice"; they suggested, contrary to Sharkansky's conclusion, that Elazar's political subcultures may be more applicable to elite behavior than to popular behavior.[20]

Another application of Elazar's political cultures propositions grew out of the 1968 Comparative State Elections Project. Survey responses were available from three states dominated by the moralistic culture and from five states each identified with the traditionalistic and individualistic cultures; it was also possible to analyze mass opinion in six states that had a mix of political cultures. The only consistent support for Elazar's ideas to emerge from that research came in responses relating to notions of civic duty. Apparently values associated with these three cultural orientations are reflected in the various ways in which ordinary Americans view their opportunities, rights, and obligations. Not found, however, were expected patterns of political party organization and leadership, public policies, and bureaucratic orientations. The authors of that study conclude: "Elazar's maps may have been more accurate in the past...[and possibly]

---

20. David Lowery and Lee Sigelman, "Political Culture and State Public Policy: The Missing Link," *Western Political Quarterly* 35 (1983): 376–384, quotation at 382.

the concept of cultural streams is essentially correct but population mobility has caused a decrease in the geographic concentrations of the ethnic and religious groupings which made up those streams."[21] It may be, as these scholars suggest, that the change processes described earlier in this chapter are operating within America: that distinctive geohistorical political values and practices are giving way to a broader and more permissive national mixture; regional "shoulds" and "mustn'ts," though still there, are less demanding in American politics. Other evidence, however, attests to the vitality and perseverance of regional differences in American political subcultures. Although they acknowledge the plausibility of the notion that common national stimuli, transmitted especially by national television, "are breaking down regional political cultures, replacing them with a single national culture," William Claggett and his collaborators find no increase in the nationalization of the partisan vote in America from 1842 to 1970, and conclude that, given the great diversity of regional values and interests, common stimuli may serve "to accomplish the opposite of nationalization, that is, to stimulate dissimilar behavior on the part of geographic units."[22]

Finally, a sextet of studies by Elazar's own students and colleagues from 1972 to 1981 confirms the general usefulness of his American political subcultures for understanding contemporary political behavior.[23]

Whether or not Elazar's formulations become commonly employed in the analysis of comparative U.S. state politics, the concept of "political culture" seems to be helpful for understanding public opinion in America—although it is necessarily complex, protean, and imprecise. Most citizens are influenced heavily by the common traditions, habits, and attitudes of their friends and neighbors with regard to government and politics—and apolitical citizens seem to have few other sources of influence. These common traditions, habits, and attitudes constitute the political culture or subculture. To understand that is to understand a great part of political opinion in the United States.

---

21. Timothy D. Schiltz and R. Lee Rainey, "The Geographic Distribution of Elazar's Political Subcultures among the Mass Population: A Research Note," *Western Political Quarterly* 31 (September 1978): 410–415, quotation at 415.

22. William Claggett et al., "Nationalization of the American Electorate," *American Political Science Review* 78 (1984): 90.

23. John Kincaid, ed., *Political Culture, Public Policy, and the American States* (Philadelphia: Institute for the Study of Human Issues, 1982).

## Chapter 10

# Political Socialization:
# Family, Religion,
# and Opinion Holding

In Chapters 8 and 9 we considered the psychology and what may be called the cultural anthropology of opinion holding. Now we come to the sociology of opinion holding. The question for this chapter is: What are the probable effects of family, religion, and other more or less enduring forms of collective life on the opinions of individuals and groups?

Social institutions create powerful ideological channels and exert significant pressures as individuals form and modify their opinions. But in the relatively democratic community, social institutions alone will not determine or require that the individual hold some opinions rather than others. It should be clear from this statement that we are restricting our consideration to democratic societies. Nothing like a comprehensive survey of the influence of social institutions on opinions is given in this chapter—or in this book—although later and in somewhat different contexts we shall take up in more detail the importance of certain forms of social organization, such as the mass media and governmental agencies.

## 10.1 POLITICAL SOCIALIZATION GENERALLY

*Political socialization* is a concept that has received a good deal of attention in the last thirty-five years. In its largest sense *socialization* refers to the process by which individual human beings learn (and are taught) the ideas and behaviors that enable them to get along with others. Most of the simple and elementary beliefs, attitudes, and behaviors necessary to collective existence are learned early in life, hence the tendency to associate socialization with infancy and childhood. But clearly, socialization consists of marginal changes in attitudes and behavior and in the lifelong filling in of the cognitive maps and affective schemas by which we all live.[1]

Kenneth Langton defines *political socialization* as "the process, mediated through various agencies of society, by which an individual learns politically relevant attitudinal dispositions and behavior patterns." The *agencies* of socialization "include such environmental categories as the family, peer group, school, adult organizations, and the mass media." And the research on political socialization focuses, for example, on the learning of attitudes and behavior related to political legitimacy, the way governmental decisions are or should be made, feelings of confidence or cynicism toward politics, and proper or improper uses of authority. "Thus the concept of political socialization is as broad in its empirical referents as those aspects of social behavior that can be meaningfully related to politics."[2]

Charles Andrain has summarized the research findings on childhood political socialization in America. The main result of early citizenship training is the development of superficial, somewhat stylized, benign, and nonconflictful images of government and politics. The children of Middle America are told and believe that governmental and political decision making is protective, benevolent, and based on moral values. As children grow older, their sources of information become more varied, their understandings become somewhat more complex (though very few teenagers or adults become truly sophisticated about politics), their ability to test reality is increased, and they become less stereotypically supportive and more cynical. As would be expected, children of deprived and harsher subcultures—urban blacks and the Appalachian poor—learn earlier the more adult patterns of political ambivalence and distrust.[3]

## 10.2 INFLUENCE OF THE FAMILY ON OPINIONS

"Blood is thicker than water." "As the twig is bent, so grows the tree." "Like father, like son." With these and many other sayings, the unknown historians of folk wisdom testify to the importance of the family in the shaping of opinion and behavior. One of the ways the rigid cultural patterns of the past bore most heavily on the individual was by the imposition of strict role and status responsibilities on each member of the family. In learning these responsibilities, and the related folklore of the tribe, the children learned to accept the views of their elders as proper and unchallengeable.

1. Edward Zigler and Irvin L. Child, "Socialization," in *Handbook of Social Psychology*, ed. Gardner Lindzey (Reading, Mass.: Addison-Wesley, 1969), 4:450–589.

2. Kenneth P. Langton, *Political Socialization* (New York: Oxford University Press, 1969), p. 5. Students of political socialization will find a most valuable aid in Jack Dennis, *Political Socialization Research: A Bibliography* (Beverly Hills, Calif.: Sage, 1973).

3. Charles F. Andrain, *Children and Civic Awareness: A Study in Political Education* (Columbus, Ohio: Merrill, 1971), especially chap. 4, "The Public Philosophy of Children," pp. 41–55.

In modern America, children do not have to accept uncritically the opinions of their parents. Before they are very old, they are exposed to other views, which are often different from and sometimes incompatible with those of their parents. Nonetheless, they are *likely* to accept their parents' views, for parents' influence is central and pervasive, at least in the first ten or fifteen years of a child's life, whereas their exposure to conflicting views is apt to be fleeting and tangential. Some attitudes and opinions, like most of the individual's personality character-istics, seem to be fixed before the child is ten years old. Modification of family-shaped opinions usually takes place slowly and, in most cases, only under the pressure of strong extrafamilial social influences or of overwhelming evidence of fact or theory. Therefore, within the family there is a high order of agreement on economic, social, and political issues. This agreement is largely a result of three sources of influence.

Consciously and unconsciously, parents indoctrinate their children. What is good and bad, what is right and wrong, what is naughty and nice, what is proper and improper—by direct command and advice, by indirect references, and by the examples they set, parents shape children to their own values and beliefs. This process is an inevitable and necessary part of socialization, of making little humans fit to live in a sort of social close-order drill with other humans, little and big. It gives stability to the culture, predictability in day-to-day social relations, and—not least important—tranquillity to family life.

Children imitate their parents. Like parental indoctrination, childhood imita-tion is both conscious and unconscious. To use the terminology of the sociolo-gist, the ideal role model for the daughter is almost always her mother; for the son, his father. There is some evidence that the influence of the parental model decreases as children grow older, and they find other models among their wider social contacts. But the importance of the parent as a person to be imitated almost never wholly disappears, and it is strongest when the child's opinions and personality are the most malleable.

Members of a family are influenced by the same environmental stimuli. This is the third major cause of the similarity of opinions within the family, although it is apt to be overlooked if we focus too attentively on the interpersonal influence within the family. All members of the family are influenced by the same neigh-bors and neighborhood, by the same friends (who usually share with them such social characteristics as class, religion, and ethnicity), and by the same economic forces that impinge on the area and on the breadwinner's occupation. The family members read the same newspapers, attend to the same TV programs, listen to the same preacher and other local opinion leaders, gather the same gossip, and hear the same stories. Exposed as they are, day in and day out, to identical, similar, and convergent stimuli, no wonder families exhibit a marked uniformity of opinion.

There is evidence of the tenacity of family influence on the political orienta-tions of children, adolescents, and adults. Herbert Hyman reviewed a number of studies of parent–children political attitudes and opinions. His summary of findings supports the common-sense observation that family influence is high (but that there are other important influences) and raises a caution about the psychoanalytic view that children's opinions frequently develop in opposition to or rebellion against their parents' opinions:

> These and other studies establish very clearly a family correspondence in views that are relevant to matters of political orientation. Over a great many such correlations from the different studies, the median value approximates .5. The signs, almost without exception, are *never negative*. The only negative findings bear on the area of war, where we might expect the larger social climate to be powerful, and these are but two correlations out of a total of perhaps one hundred. The import is clear. While influence might conceivably flow from child to parent, what is much more likely is that parents are the agents who transmit politically relevant attitudes to their children. The almost complete absence of negative correlations provides considerable evidence *against* the theory that political attitudes are formed *generally* in terms of rebellion and opposition to parents.[4]

Hyman's view that the family is the principal agent of political socialization has been widely accepted. Yet a number of investigators have concluded that school, teenage peer groups, and work groups may be of equal or greater importance.

In America the family seems to be especially influential in the establishment of the individual's basic political values and orientations. Using data from a national sample of high school seniors, Kenneth Langton and David Karns report that for the development of a sense of political efficacy in teenagers the family has considerably more importance than school or peer group.[5] Political party preference, too, apparently depends more strongly on family than on other socialization agencies. In their study of the 1948 election, Bernard Berelson and his colleagues found that, overall, 75 percent of first voters cast their ballots as their fathers did. Perhaps more interesting is the fact that among adults in families living together, and among those who had made up their minds in October, over 90 percent agreed in their voting intentions.[6] This fact is interesting, yes, but it is hardly surprising either that there should be very high agreement among adults of the same generation or of several generations when they choose to

---

4. Herbert Hyman, *Political Socialization* (New York: Free Press, 1959), p. 72; italics in original; footnotes omitted.

5. "The family accounted for almost four times more movement along the entire efficacy scale than either the peer group or school. In fact it was the only agency that moved students along the whole range of the efficacy scale" (Kenneth P. Langton and David A. Karns, "The Relative Influence of the Family, Peer Group, and School in the Development of Political Efficacy," *Western Political Quarterly* 22 [1969]: 922).

6. Bernard Berelson et al., *Voting* (Chicago: University of Chicago Press, 1954), pp. 89, 92. Factor analysis in a panel study of value climates in ten Illinois high schools indicated that the nuclear family influence explained 68% of the variations in the party preferences of the students. See Martin L. Levin, "Social Climates and Political Socialization," *Public Opinion Quarterly* 24 (1960): 515.

remain together as a family unit and that there should be high (but not quite so high) agreement between parents and children whose ties have loosened.[7]

Families living together are almost certain to show higher agreement of attitudes and opinions than are families living apart. Note that there is no causal implication here; living apart may be the cause or result of differences of opinion, or have no relation to them. The point is merely that, although distance *may* make the heart grow fonder, it is *almost certain* to weaken the influences that produce like opinions among family members and strengthen those that produce unlike opinion.

Though some basic political orientations are evidently strongly shaped by the family, it does not appear to exert greater influence than other socialization agencies on the development of opinions on issues. When R. W. Connell reviewed nearly forty studies of paired parent–child attitudes and opinions on political issues from 1930 to 1968, he found persistent agreement between pairs of parents and children, but the pair correspondence was weak (median value about 0.2, and not the 0.5 correspondence that Hyman reported finding in twelve studies). Connell confirmed that party preference, as mentioned above, is strongly shared by parent–child pairs, but he found that attitudes and opinions on "war and communism, political involvement, prejudice, achievement values, and family roles" are less commonly shared. Connell concluded that

> processes within the family have been largely irrelevant to the forma-
> tion of specific opinions. It appears that older and younger genera-
> tions have developed their opinions in parallel rather than in series,
> by similar experiences in a common way of life.... That children
> may gain from their parents some idea of the range of acceptable
> opinions is quite likely. That specific opinions generally come with
> mother's milk is—for America, 1944–1968—rather decisively
> disproved.[8]

Richard Niemi and his colleagues independently confirm Connell's conclusions. Except for partisanship, young adults (17- to 23-year-olds) do not generally have high levels of agreement with their parents. Youth–parent correlations seldom exceed 0.25 on either broad political orientations (for example, equality in America, private property, importance of national interests and powers) or on specific political controversies (for example, war in Vietnam, abortion, gay rights).[9]

---

7. See also Richard E. Dawson et al., *Political Socialization,* 2nd ed. (Boston: Little Brown, 1977); and Stanley A. Renshon, ed., *Handbook of Political Socialization: Theory and Research* (New York: Free Press, 1977).

8. R. W. Connell, "Political Socialization in the American Family: The Evidence Re-examined," *Public Opinion Quarterly* 36 (1972): 323–333, quotation at 330. On sociological (and psychocultural) explanations, see the excellent article by Joseph Adelson, "The Political Imagination of the Young Adolescent," *Daedalus* 100 (1971): 1013–1050.

9. Richard G. Niemi, R. Danforth Ross, and Joseph Alexander, "The Similarity of Political Values of Parents and College-Age Youths," *Public Opinion Quarterly* 42 (Winter 1978): 503–520.

An ambitious longitudinal study of parent–child pairs adds further support to the conclusion that parents have only modest impact on the political opinions and behavior of their children. Data were available from a national sample of 1,562 high school seniors and their parents. In 1973, 1,179 of those parent–child pairs were reinterviewed so that intergenerational comparisons could be made over time—an unparalleled example of difficult survey research. Findings were on the whole consistent with earlier generalizations about the influence of the family on political opinions and behavior: intergenerational agreement on party identification and presidential candidate choice was high, but it declined in these sample pairs over the eight years covered by the study; agreement on the factors that indicated what was called "psychological involvement in politics" (e.g., interest in public affairs, use of media for political information, and a measure of "cosmopolitanism") was fairly low (bivariate correlation of 0.07 to 0.15); with respect to knowledge of political facts and a sense of political efficacy, parents and children showed a modest level of similarity that was steady over time; what was called "intergenerational concordance" on turnout and campaign activity increased slightly over the eight-year period as the 1965 youths, seventeen and eighteen years old then, became twenty-five- and twenty-six-year-old adults in 1973. Finally, on four public policy issues, agreement was quite high between the 1965 parent–child pairs; eight years later the pairs were more likely to agree on free speech and communists in office, less likely to agree on school integration; the level of their agreement on the issue of school prayers had not changed. The researchers were unwilling to generalize about parent–child agreement over time on public policies, except to say that they believed it clear "that there is no uniform increase in parent–youth agreement levels as young people move out of the 'rebellious' adolescent years."[10]

It is often asserted that the importance of the family has declined in our society as a whole during the course of this century. If so, one would expect other institutions—especially the public and private welfare agencies and voluntary peer-group associations—to become more important in *political* socialization, as in socialization generally. We leave it to others to evaluate such assertions definitively, but draw attention here to some imaginative research of the 1970s that repeated in part the studies of family life in "Middletown" (Muncie, Indiana) during the 1920s. Howard Bahr and his associates obtained data on 1,000 Muncie high school students in 1977 that could be directly compared with similar data on students of 1924. Their findings are important and point both to change and to long-term stability in family relations in one (typical?) middle-sized city:

> Although there is evidence for some continued decline in the central-
> ity of the family, . . . there is no evidence in these data that the genera-

10. M. Kent Jennings and Richard G. Niemi, *Generations and Politics: A Panel Study of Young Adults and Their Parents* (Princeton: Princeton University Press, 1981), p. 95. See especially Chap. 4, "The Dynamics of Family Transmission."

tion gap in 1977 is any wider than it was in 1924.... The continued impact of modernization upon the family ties of Middletown's young people is most apparent upon young women, such that many of the male–female differences apparent in 1924 have now disappeared. Finally, although certain family functions seem to have declined in importance, there is no evidence that there is greater alienation between parents and youth in 1977 than in 1924."[11]

Within families, divergence of opinion comes primarily from cross-pressures that result when stimuli are not shared equally by all members of the family. Perhaps the most important of these pressures are the effects of different levels and types of education within a family. Children *learn* to disagree with their parents; and the disagreements tend to be more profound if this learning involves not just new information but new values and lifestyles—as when the children of newly arrived immigrants go to American schools, or the daughter of the southern hill farmer attends an Ivy League college. Like-mindedness within families is weakened by differences in economic stimuli, as when the son "graduates" from his father's haberdashery to the big department store or when he leaves the farm to become a railroad brakeman. Differences in social status seem to be important, as when the daughter of the shoemaker becomes a physician or the newly rich oil driller joins the country club. Finally, changing family roles tend to create opinion differences, as when a daughter becomes a mother and follows the advice of Dr. Spock rather than that of her mother. Each of these clusters of influence—educational, economic, social status, and role—will be considered separately, albeit briefly, below. Here it is enough to say that they interact with—sometimes reinforcing, sometimes weakening—opinion agreement within families.[12]

## 10.3 RELIGION AND OPINION HOLDING

Although *religious feeling,* however defined, may exist in an individual without the aid or direction of social organization, such idiosyncratic beliefs are so uncommon as to be of little significance in the making and remaking of public opinion. When we talk of the influence of religion in American public life, we mean the influence of religious organizations—churches and synagogues. There may be elements of the individual conscience and of personal ethics that relate

---

11. Howard M. Bahr, "Changes in Family Life in Middletown, 1924–77," *Public Opinion Quarterly* 44 (Spring 1980): 35–52, quotation at 51. Copyright 1980 by Elsevier North Holland, Inc. Reprinted by permission.

12. Environmental pressures may overcome family influence quite early, even on the question of party preference. Norris Johnson reports that in rural Kentucky, among young people whose parents supported the minority party locally, from half to two-thirds had defected to the majority party by the time they were 18 ("Political Climates and Party Choice of High School Youth," *Public Opinion Quarterly* 36 (1972):48–55).

self to cosmos and provide sanction for behavior, but these elements, too, will depend mainly on church doctrine, cultural norms, legal prescriptions, or perhaps on all three.

For this overview of the sociology of opinion holding, it will not be too great a distortion to think of religion in the United States as organized Christianity and Judaism. Our concern is primarily with the patterns and probabilities of influence, in the group and statistical sense, although we shall not overlook the importance of religiously based reinforcement or conflict for the individual opinion holder.

### 10.31 The importance of organized religion in American society

There are many ways of measuring religious influence in a society. The simplest, and by no means the least significant, is to count the number of organized bodies and individual adherents. Recent issues of the *Yearbook of U.S. and Canadian Churches* report that there are more than 250 religious bodies in the United States, with a total of more than 140 million members. Protestant denominations claim a total of about 75 million members, or something over a third of all Americans. The major Protestant groups, in order of size, are Baptist, Methodist, Lutheran, Presbyterian, and Episcopal, but all those except the Baptist showed declining membership in the late 1970s and early 1980s, and the Church of Jesus Christ of Latter-Day Saints (Mormons) had more members than the Episcopal church by 1985. Roman Catholic membership is reported to be about 55 million, or 24 percent of the total population,[13] Jews number something over 6 million, and Eastern Orthodox churches claim more than 3 million members.

Another way of measuring religious influence in American public life is to inquire into individual beliefs and practices. There are ample poll data on Americans' religious views since the late 1930s. A summary of these data shows the following:

1. Between one-third and one-half of adults attend church at least once a week (from a low of 37 percent in 1940 to a high of 49 percent in 1958 to 43 percent in 1979), the 1979 attendance being greater than that in any of ten other selected Christian countries.
2. Catholics, as would be expected for doctrinal reasons, attend church much more regularly than Protestants.

---

13. Catholics count all persons baptized; most Protestant groups base membership figures on persons 13 years of age and older. The relationship between church *membership* and *respondents' proclaimed affiliation* is close for Catholics (membership figures indicate 24% of the total population, interview data indicate 26%) and for Jews (membership figures 3%, interview data 3%) but widely discrepant for Protestants (membership figures 37%, interview data 65%). The explanation seems to be that unchurched people who are unwilling to say they have no religion call themselves Protestants in America. Survey data from *Gallup Opinion Index,* April 1971, p. 70; and "Opinion Roundup," *Public Opinion* (November/December 1978), pp. 32–33.

3. Women attend more regularly than men.
4. There are slight positive correlations between churchgoing and age, education, and family income.
5. Adult Americans are much more likely than adult Europeans to say they believe in God (98 percent of Americans say they do), in life after death (73 percent), in hell (65 percent), and in the devil (60 percent).[14]

Numbers alone are inadequate for assessment of religious influence. For a variety of reasons, Jews (about one-thirtieth of the American people) have greater political and social importance than an equal number of Protestants or Catholics. No doubt the Mormons' political influence is also greater than their mere numbers would indicate. In some policy areas, other Protestant denominations have considerable impact on public opinion and governmental decisions; it is probable, for example, that the Unitarians, Christian Scientists, and Jehovah's Witnesses have each contributed more to the American elaboration of freedom of speech, press, and assembly than have other social groups of equal size.

Until recently social science had neglected the study of the influence of religious organizations on politics. The authors of a recent investigation of religion's influence in Congress say that "in nearly all past studies that have enquired into the identity, activity and motivations of Congress, one area has remained almost entirely unexplored: the area of religion."[15] If the influence of religion and religious doctrine sometimes appears to be inadequately appreciated by academicians, it may be that academicians project their own values and procedures on the world. The person skilled in the use of scientific method (or at least what passes for scientific method in the social sciences) is not apt to be heavily influenced by religious doctrine or by articles of religious faith and so may tend to see the world as uninfluenced by them. Yet, of many possible examples of religion in politics, consider these two, one trivial perhaps, the other at least notorious and possibly significant.

First, for more than twenty-five years members of Congress have assembled once a week for congressional (House) and Senate "prayer breakfasts," where Christian devotion and politicopatriotic themes are rehearsed. An annual presidential prayer breakfast is also held, those in the seventies typically attended by three thousand or more religious and opinion leaders.[16]

Second, the case of school prayers is a striking example of local resistance to and defiance of national policy designed to change religiously based behavior.

---

14. Gallup American and international surveys, reported in *New York Times,* December 22 and 26, 1968; and National Council of Churches poll, reported in *New York Times,* June 20, 1978.

15. Peter L. Benson and Dorothy L. Williams, *Religion on Capitol Hill* (San Francisco: Harper & Row, 1982), p. 1.

16. During the 1980 presidential campaign among three professed Christian activists, Democrat Jimmy Carter, Republican Ronald Reagan, and Independent John Anderson, it was reported that one-quarter of the California electorate regarded themselves as evangelical "born again" Christians; see Mervin D. Field, "California Poll: Politics and 'Born Again' Christians," *San Francisco Chronicle,* August 21, 1980.

Kenneth Dolbeare and Philip Hammond found that in one midwestern state, five years after school prayers had been outlawed by the Supreme Court, there were "no consequences whatsoever for local behavior," that "at least half the class-rooms...engage in some explicitly proscribed religious observance, and that nearly all schools sponsor some form of unconstitutional religious activity."[17] In 1979 the legislature of Massachusetts reauthorized prayers in public schools, with what appeared to be majority support in that state; but after a few days of prayer in Boston, the Massachusetts Supreme Court declared both the law and the practice unconstitutional.[18]

What seems to be happening in the matter of prayers in school is the persis-tence of a majority view that sectarian morality is a proper ingredient of public education. Local and state elites, knowing that prayers are now clearly banned as a principle of constitutional law, nevertheless give in to electoral pressure. Policy makers themselves need not have religious views relevant to this issue. It is enough that they are fearful of taking positions contrary to views held by their constituents.

The presidential election of 1960 was a lesson for political scientists—in addition to being a larger lesson in the patterns and limits of religious influence in the political life of the United States. In 1960 religion *did* make a difference to millions of Americans. Many Catholics seem to have voted for Senator John Kennedy because he was a Catholic; many Protestants seem to have voted against him for the same reason. Though various motivations and influences bearing on voting have not been and cannot be fully explained, the most careful analysis seems to show that Senator Kennedy, had he not been a Catholic, would have been elected by a two-party majority considerably greater than the 50.1 percent he received.[19]

### 10.32 Religious doctrines and political "background values"

Organized religion in America interacts with political opinion in two ways. First, it provides much of what may be called "background values" for individual and group behavior. The cultural values of any society are likely to have their roots in sacred traditions or doctrines, even if they have been highly secularized in the

17. Kenneth M. Dolbeare and Philip E. Hammond, "Local Elites, the Impact of Judicial Decisions, and the Process of Change," paper delivered at the 65th Annual Meeting of the American Political Science Association, 1969, p. 6. For the full story see, by the same authors, *The School Prayer Decision from Court Policy to Local Practice* (Chicago: University of Chicago Press, 1971).

18. Although the Massachusetts law was overturned in March 1980, in August of that same year the Louisiana legislature passed a similar law, and prayer-in-school bills were pending in ten other states; see "Louisiana Law Opens Way for Prayer in Public Schools," *New York Times,* August 30, 1980.

19. Philip E. Converse, Angus Campbell, Warren E. Miller, and Donald E. Stokes, "Stability and Change in 1960: A Reinstating Election," *American Political Science Review* 55 (1961): 269–280.

way they are presented. Second, the doctrines of religious groups have specific applications for many public controversies, such as those over prayer in school and creationism."[20]

General attitudes stressed by American religious groups may be among the causes and reinforcements of *political* tendencies and preferences of our citizens. As Morris Janowitz says, "in the basically secular setting of the contemporary United States, religious and altruistic elements are operative, although they are second-order dimensions."[21] Three basic tendencies of American religious experience help to provide the background values for political behavior: (a) Jewish and Catholic exclusivity, (b) the "Protestant ethic," and (c) religious fundamentalism.

**10.321 Jewish and Catholic exclusivity.**   Both the Jewish and the Catholic faiths have been informed by the same central orientation during much of their histories. Oversimplified: "We are superior to people who have other religious beliefs, and we feel obliged to show our superiority by (1) criticizing their beliefs and (2) shunning their company or (3) converting them to our way." There is some irony in the historic fact that the early Christians rejected the exclusivity of the Jews but soon developed doctrines summed up by the slogan "Anyone who is not with me is against me."

To be "the chosen people" is a heavy burden indeed. For members of a group to believe that their doctrines and rituals have some special godly sanction is unquestionably an effective basis for solidarity. But the in-group cohesion thus gained is paid for in out-group conflict and hatred. And the point here is that religious self-righteousness provides a way of thinking that affects everyday political opinions and actions. The Jewish prohibitions against intermarriage with persons of other faiths; the Catholic dictum, held until very recently, that the Jews collectively were responsible for the death of Christ; the doctrine of "vincible ignorance," suggesting that certain non-Catholics are eternally damned— these are religious supports for American background values that are still strong. The story (perhaps apocryphal) about a papal legate during one of the "heresy wars" illustrates the kind of thinking encouraged by "chosen people" doctrines. A field commander came to the legate with a dilemma: "The heretics and believers look the same. How can we tell them apart?" The legate replied, "Kill them all. God will know His own."

On the other hand, it should also be said that in very recent times and especially since Vatican Council II (1962–1963) called by Pope John XXIII, there has been an important shift in official Catholic perspectives. A Jesuit scholar described this change in the following words:

---

20. See pp. 178–179.

21. Morris Janowitz, *Social Control of the Welfare State* (Chicago: University of Chicago Press, 1976), p. 22.

Had the Council followed the lead of past Catholic tradition in formulating its response to the reality of contemporary pluralism and conflict, it would have proposed a normative model of social structure and political order chosen on the basis of compatibility with Catholic tradition and faith. Such an approach would have repeated past Catholic solutions to the problem of religious pluralism—the proposal of a single ideal religious order in which Catholicism would hold a privileged place. But just as the option of a single normative social-religious system was rejected as the Catholic ideal in the Declaration on Religious Freedom, so also conciliar and post-conciliar Catholic teaching has rejected the ideal of a single, normative model of political and economic order.[22]

If this view turns out to be the new central tendency of Catholic thought, it will, as it trickles down through parish priests to become a norm of the faithful, go far toward ending what John Whyte called the "closed" Catholic political culture of the hundred years before Vatican II.[23] There is hope, then, of long-range movement from Catholic exclusivity to more open, democratic, and even humanistic political perspectives.

**10.322 The Protestant ethic.**    *The Protestant ethic* refers not merely to an attitude toward work or to a personal code of straitlaced morality, though the term is often used to signify both of those things. More accurately, the Protestant ethic is a concentration of attitudinal emphases that may be thought of as a subculture.[24]

The historic ties between Protestantism and capitalism have been described by both Max Weber and R. H. Tawney.[25] Their claims that those two great social movements are related ideologically and attitudinally seem quite persuasive. Although their evidence and arguments cannot be repeated here, it may be noted that, historically, many theories and opinions of the early modern period—the importance of freedom of choice for individuals, the philosophy of salvation through work, the religious and economic colonization of newly discovered lands, and the breakdown of restrictions in regard to money and credit—hastened and reinforced the growth of capitalism and Protestantism alike.

Two caveats are in order. First, the Weber-Tawney argument is historical,

22. David Hollenbach, S. J., "Global Human Rights: An Interpretation of the Contemporary Catholic Understanding," in *Human Rights in the Americas: The Struggle for Consensus,* ed. Alfred Hennelly, S. J., and John Langen, S. J. (Washington, D.C.: Georgetown University Press, 1982), pp. 11–12.

23. John H. Whyte, *Catholics in Western Democracies: A Study in Political Behavior* (New York: St. Martin's Press, 1981), pp. 122–123.

24. See Harmon Zeigler, *The Political World of the High School Teacher* (Eugene, Oreg.: Center for the Advanced Study of Educational Administration, 1966), pp. 8–11; and Ralph Segalman, "The Protestant Ethic and Social Welfare," *Journal of Social Issues* 24 (1968): 125–141, for personality descriptions and correlates of the Protestant ethic.

reflecting Protestantism from the sixteenth century to World War I. It says little explicitly about Protestantism of the late twentieth century. Second, capitalism was initally a form of economic radicalism; although it is no longer radical in the West, it can hardly be described as having been a conservative doctrine during most of the period about which Weber and Tawney wrote.

A powerful background value in American society is *independence*—which seems to mean the ability to make one's way economically and to be free of burdensome social restraints. Americans do not want others to give them either charity or personal advice. Despite the rhetoric of conservative groups (and the occasional laments of high federal officials that there is a turning away from self-reliance), people on welfare are as committed to the work ethic as middle-class people.[26] An underlying impulse toward self-sufficiency was found by Robert Lane in his depth interviews with fifteen working-class men in New Haven. Although they were not very knowledgeable about political issues or about the candidates they voted for, they made little effort to get additional information or help in making up their minds. They appeared to believe that individual citizens could somehow sense, by intuition or some unnamed human virtue, what was right and proper in political matters. Lane calls this stubborn and irrational individualism a belief in "the parthenogenesis [that is, the virgin birth] of knowledge."[27] That American elites share this deep-seated sense of individualism was seen by Karl Lamb as he interviewed 117 politically influential men and women in six cities in 1977. They knew that "their own political influence depends upon relationships with groups and constituencies among the people, although...their values are determined more by the individualist tradition than by their organizational affiliation."[28] Once again, background values. It seems to be not too farfetched to relate such tenacious if naive political individualism to the Protestant ethic. Just as Protestantism itself means, at bottom, rejection of the authority of religious specialists and experts in favor of the view that each Christian has to get a personal truth out of the sacred word, so it gives strength to a powerful background value of self-sufficiency in political attitudes and opinions.

**10.323 Fundamentalism.**    Related to the Protestant ethic, yet different from it, is the third religiously based quality that appears to shape the background values of many Americans. Raymond Wolfinger and his collaborators investigated the

25. Max Weber, *The Protestant Ethic and the Spirit of Capitalism* (New York: Scribner, 1958); and R. H. Tawney, *Religion and the Rise of Capitalism* (New York: Harcourt, Brace & World, 1926).

26. Leonard Goodwin, *Do the Poor Want to Work?—A Social Psychological Study of Work Orientation* (Washington, D.C.: Brookings Institution, 1972).

27. Robert Lane, *Political Ideology: Why the American Common Man Believes What He Does* (New York: Free Press, 1962), pp. 373–377.

28. Karl A. Lamb, *The Guardians: Leadership Values and the American Tradition* (New York: Norton, 1982), p.26.

political attitudes and motivations of several hundred participants in a "Christian Anti-Communism Crusade" in 1962. They found that on most personality and socioeconomic measurements the Christian Crusaders did not differ much from other American adults. They were, in fact, rather better informed than most Americans on public issues and did not seem to be especially authoritarian in their general thinking. What they shared in unusual degree was a quality the researchers labeled *fundamentalism*. People whose "fundamentalist beliefs and intellectual style...are compatible with radical right interpretations of history," they say, may be characterized in the following ways:

1. Belief in the literalness and purity of biblical teachings makes fundamentalists resistant to change.
2. They are affronted by moral relativism, increasingly lenient sexual mores, the decline of parental authority, and other aspects of the secular modern world.
3. The fundamentalist sees "the world as strictly divided into the saved and the damned, the forces of good and the forces of evil."
4. The main danger to the faithful is from the corrosion of faith by invidious doctrines—a danger from within.[29]

The importance of fundamentalism in American politics and in the ways of thinking held by Americans has been recently illustrated by "scientific creationism" controversies in California, Georgia, Iowa, Minnesota, and other states. In those states, books used in the public schools must be chosen from lists of texts approved by state officials. Some fundamentalist persons and groups have argued that grade school science books should give the biblical version of creation equal attention along with evolution as an explanation of the origin of life. In California, though the scientific community was solid for a straightforward statement of evolution that fourth-graders could understand, the Curriculum Commission and its parent State Board of Education endured hundreds of hours of hearings, arguments, and negotiations on behalf of the special-creation point of view. The supporters of the biblical view of creation, apparently the beneficiaries of some sound political advice, argued that both evolution and special-creation points of view should be presented in the texts if their children were to receive the equal protection of the laws. As one reporter put it, "Fundamentalists no longer present themselves as true believers protecting the orthodoxy of eternal truths from heretics but as an oppressed minority whose children are forced to listen to the sermons of antitheism."[30] In Iowa in 1979, a Senate bill

29. Raymond E. Wolfinger et al., "America's Radical Right: Politics and Ideology," in *Ideology and Discontent,* ed. David E. Apter (New York: Free Press, 1964), pp. 281–282. The quote in item 3 is from David Danzig, "The Radical Right and the Rise of the Fundamentalist Minority," *Commentary* 33 (1962): 292.

30. Calvin Trillin, "U. S. Journal: Sacramento, California: A Public Hearing on the Origin of Species," *New Yorker,* January 6, 1973, p. 56.

was introduced that would have mandated equal time for the teaching of "scientific creationism" if evolutionary doctrines were also taught. "Although the 'creationists' insist that their theories are not religious doctrine, and can be defended at least as well by scientific evidence as the theory of evolution propounded by Charles Darwin, the movement appears to draw its strength principally from among the nation's increasing numbers of fundamentalist Christians."[31] In 1982 an Arkansas creationist law was struck down by a U.S. District Court judge, but a 1981 law requiring the "balanced treatment of evolution and 'creationism' in Louisiana's public schools" was still being litigated at the end of 1983.[32] There is some evidence that fundamentalist thinking is more prevalent in the South than it is in the North and West,[33] but it is an important shaper of background values throughout America.

To the extent that religious organizations depend on group acceptance of certain fundamental doctrines that are considered absolute (that is, right, eternal, and incontrovertible), and to the extent that this absolutism becomes a way of thinking about beliefs and behavior, the churches and their members are prone to lose sight of and patience with the relativistic nature of democratic society. It can hardly have been a matter of chance that the part of the Christian world in which democracy has been least successful is precisely that part—Mediterranean Europe and Latin America—in which the most doctrinaire branch of Christianity has had the most power. Nor can it be wholly fortuitous that the most doctrinaire Protestant sects have been strongest in those areas of the American South and Midwest (primarily) where antiblack and anti-Catholic feeling has been the most virulent and accompanied by the most frequent denials of civil rights and civil liberties. Max Lerner nicely sums up the basic and persistent conflict between the spirit of democracy and that of revealed religion:

> Democracy is the policy of individual choices and of majority consent; it can be run effectively only where there is a habituation to hard choices. Those who are certain of the simplicity of revealed truth make the initial choice of submission and do not have to make any subsequent choices; they do not furnish a fertile soil for the democratic seed. Those who expect miracles will not take the risk of dissent. Those who are sure of dogma given to them will not make the arduous effort of winning the slow and gradual victories of an always unfinished society. Finally, those who suffer no conflict within the arena of their own minds will not generate the needed dynamism to transcend the conflict and resolve their conscience.[34]

31. Douglas E. Kneeland, "Evolution Theory Is Challenged in Iowa Schools by 'Creationists,'" *New York Times,* April 25, 1979.

32. "Louisiana Legislature Is Upheld on Creationism," *New York Times,* October 18, 1983.

33. Ted Jellen, "Sources of Political Intolerance: The Case of the American South," in *Contemporary Southern Political Attitudes and Behavior: Studies and Essays,* ed. Laurence W. Moreland, Tod A. Baker, and Robert P. Steed (New York: Praeger, 1982), pp. 76–82, 90.

34. Max Lerner, *America as a Civilization* (New York: Simon & Schuster, 1957), p. 706.

In addition to creating sociopolitical background values, organized religions seem to become more conservative in their economic, social, and welfare doctrines as they become more "successful." Success means a large membership and material wealth, and the fact is that radical groups, almost by definition—except in revolutionary circumstances—have little of either. The historical progression of successful protest movements—and all religious groups have their beginnings in protest—is from a small militant membership out of step with its time to a large, more or less apathetic membership that accepts and is accepted by the dominant social forces of its time. In American political history, this pattern is perhaps best seen in the rise and the taming of the grangers to the Grange, of the One Big Union to the AFL-CIO, and of the woman-suffragists to the League of Women Voters.

It probably cannot be said that by itself the acquisition of wealth is an important factor in the conservatism of church groups. The importance of wealth is sometimes argued—indeed, it will be argued in this book—to explain in part the political opinion of persons associated with big business, and especially with big mass media. But wealth by itself is not a decisive factor in producing conservatism in church doctrine and among church leaders, for at least three reasons: (a) the doctrine of clerical poverty is widely enough held, even among Protestant denominations, so that individual wealth among church leaders offers no temptation to find reason and fairness in the economic status quo; (b) the wealth of church groups tends to be used for reformist ends—charity, teaching, and conversion—which daily remind these groups not only of their own limited resources but of the almost limitless need for reform; and (c) one practical result of church immunity to taxation is that church resources are not reduced, as are those of wealthy individuals and corporations, by government welfare policies.

Although it seems unlikely that wealth alone makes churches conservative, size of membership by itself may have a decided relationship to the organization's social and political opinion structure. It is doubtless not just by chance that the smallest doctrinally identifiable churches in America (to distinguish them from personality-centered, local, or fundamentalist splinter groups) are also the least tolerant of the sociopolitical status quo. The Quakers, Unitarians, Brethren, and Jehovah's Witnesses are all (though in different ways) critical of mass social and political values in modern life; they remain small in numbers. Roman Catholics and members of the larger Protestant denominations seem to be on much better terms with those values. This fact is not surprising, since an organization that is generally supportive of the dominant and majority values of a society will by definition be supportive of the status quo, and will therefore gain many adherents, as long as access is not restricted and personal needs are met by membership. Conformity, in such cases, feeds on conformity, and the status quo is unchallenged.

## 10.33 Survey research on religion and political attitudes

The evidence for the claim that church influence in mid-twentieth-century America is predominantly conservative does not come just from the analysis of doctrine and the official pronouncement of church leadership or policy. Attitude and opinion studies, on the whole, bear out the conservative image of churches and churchgoing. In the three-way breakdown of Protestants, Catholics, and Jews, only Jews are consistently found to express liberal opinions on social and political questions.

Samuel Stouffer and his collaborators analyzed data gathered from 4,939 persons in a nationwide probability sample and from 1,533 community leaders in 123 cities in randomly selected sampling areas. Stouffer was concerned with measuring public toleration for political nonconformity in the context of the real and perceived internal and external Communist threat of 1954. He reported that churchgoers were more intolerant of political nonconformity than were non-churchgoers in the national sample, whether the results were controlled for sex (that is, when the factors of greater churchgoing by women and greater intolerance by women were taken into account), for education, for age, for degree of interest in issues, or for differences in the perceived dangers of internal Communist threat.[35] Twenty-five years later Herbert McClosky and Alida Brill found that churchgoers were still decidedly less supportive of civil liberties than were nonchurchgoers:

> The data . . . clearly confirm that as religiosity increases, support for civil liberties declines. In the CLS study, only 15 percent of the mass public who are deeply religious score high in their support for civil liberties, compared with 55 percent of those who are not religious. Approximately half of those who are high on religiosity, compared with 20 percent who are low, score at the intolerant, antilibertarian end of the civil liberties scale. . . . In the OVS study . . . only 14 percent of the highly religious respondents score high on the civil liberties scale used in that study, while the proportion of nonreligious respondents who are strongly libertarian is 58 percent—a ratio of four to one.[36]

A large sample (4,745) of American Lutherans was interviewed in early 1970. More than 700 items were on the questionnaire, but few tapped political attitudes directly. The sample was said to be representative of American Lutheranism: 98 percent white, 96 percent native-born, they were predominantly Scandinavian or German in background; attended church more than the average American Protestant; were above average in formal education, slightly above average in income, and average in occupational status; were less mobile than the average American; and were concentrated in the Midwest.

---

35. Samuel Stouffer, *Communism, Conformity, and Civil Liberties* (Garden City, N.Y.: Doubleday, 1955), pp. 146, 148, 155, 203, 205.

36. Herbert McClosky and Alida Brill, *Dimensions of Tolerance: What Americans Believe about Civil Liberties* (New York: Russell Sage Foundation, 1983), pp. 406–407. "CLS" is Civil Liberties Survey, a national sample of 1,993 people in 1979–1979; "OVS" is Opinions and Values Survey, a national sample of 938 people in 1976–77.

The political attitudes of these American Lutherans seemed to be consistent with their basic values: a transcendent meaning in life (salvation, forgiveness, a caring God, belief in eternal life), desire for a stable, dependable world, and desire for a controllable world. "Events, programs, ministry, and persons are going to be ranked by most Lutherans in terms of support or threat to these values."[37]

Lutherans expressed a considerable commitment to liberalism and a just society; 80 percent considered the elimination of all racial discrimination to be a goal of Christianity, 97 percent regarded alcoholics and drug addicts as disease victims rather than criminals, and 68 percent said that "every person has a right to adequate housing even if he cannot afford it." On the other hand, 69 percent of the Lutherans interviewed objected to dating by black and whites, 19 percent would not want alcoholics and 38 percent would not want drug addicts in their community, and 77 percent agreed that "poor people would be better off if they took advantage of the opportunities available to them rather than spending so much time protesting." In 1970, 60 percent were in favor of the death penalty.

The picture of the Lutheran faithful that emerged is one of socially conforming, law-abiding, change-resistant, and on the whole nonparticipating citizens. On the Bogardus "social distance scales" they turned out to be apprehensive of persons and groups whose lifestyles they perceived as different: hippies, homosexuals, drug addicts and alcoholics, atheists. Among generally unacceptable groups to Lutherans in 1970 were three that were perceived as political: Communists led the list for unacceptability; Students for a Democratic Society were more acceptable than homosexuals, drug addicts, and hippies; members of the John Birch Society were more acceptable than alcoholics and atheists. Few Lutherans had *ever* contacted a public official on a controversial issue (14%), publicly taken a stand on an issue (11%), publicly supported a political candidate (12%), or circulated a petition (9%). They were about equally divided on the abstract principle of whether their church doctrines "encourage active participation in social reform" (48% agreed, 43% disagreed).

In 1978 the editors of *Public Opinion* combined the data from all NORC General Social Surveys, 1972–1978; this wealth of data allowed them "to speak far more confidently than usual about the characteristics and values of population subgroups." Here are their conclusions from that review of religious groups and sociopolitical values:

> Protestants are most likely to be social conservatives: in a representative question, 49% of Protestants were opposed to premarital sex, compared to 42% of Catholics and only 20% of Jews. Similarly, Protestants were least supportive of civil liberties: only 56% opposed

---

37. Merton P. Strommen et al., *A Study of Generations* (Minneapolis: Augsburg, 1972), p. 95; other data passim.

the removal of a hypothetical atheist book from the library, compared to 65% of Catholics and 87% of Jews.

An irony emerges when we compare religious affiliation and party identification among White Protestants. The religious groups most likely to be Republican—Presbyterians and Episcopalians—are also most likely to be social liberals and pro–civil liberties; conversely, the most heavily Democratic Protestant sect—the Baptists—were most likely to be social conservatives and least supportive of civil liberties.[38]

The Jews are the only religious group that in every study and by every measurement are more liberal than the American norm. Stouffer classified 79 percent of the Jewish males ($N = 76$) and 68 percent of the Jewish females ($N = 82$) as "more tolerant" on his scale, as compared with 31 percent of the whole national sample so classified.[39] In October 1954 the Survey Research Center obtained information about political attitudes and voting patterns of Protestants, Catholics, and Jews. There were no important differences between the Protestant and Catholic responses on U.S. involvement in world affairs or in the need for more domestic social legislation, but the Jewish respondents were significantly more internationalist and supportive of social legislation.[40]

After examining earlier work, and on the basis of his own survey in Jewish wards of Boston, Lawrence Fuchs declared:

> The results of all of these studies show American Jews to be economic liberals—twentieth-century style—almost without regard to differences in class lines within the group, and despite the fact that Jews as a group are now perched near if not on the top of the economic class ladder.
>
> In foreign policy matters, the Jews have been internationalists.[41]

There has been much speculation about the sources of Jewish social and political liberalism. Many commentators have seen it as a result of centuries of Jewish minority consciousness and of Jews' oppression by non-Jewish majorities. Historic underdogs themselves, they tend to take the side of the underdog who needs collective help in material ways (social welfare) and welcomes political and other kinds of change.

---

38. "American Ethnic and Religious Groups: Who They Are, What They Do, What They Believe," *Public Opinion,* November/December 1978, pp. 32–33.

39. Stouffer, *Communism, Conformity, and Civil Liberties,* pp. 143, 151.

40. Angus Campbell and Homer C. Cooper, *Group Differences in Attitudes and Votes: A Study of the 1954 Congressional Election* (Ann Arbor: Survey Research Center, University of Michigan, 1956), pp. 138, 142.

41. Lawrence H. Fuchs, *The Political Behavior of American Jews* (New York: Free Press, 1956), p. 107. Copyright 1956. Reprinted by permission of The Macmillan Company.

It is an interesting and important question whether American Jews are becoming more conservative in the 1980s. Their high social and economic status, the perceptions of some Jews that they are being unfairly treated by "affirmative action" programs that favor other ethnic minorities, and their concern about international policies, especially those that affect the United States' relations with Israel, may be resulting in a rightward trend of Jewish political opinions and actions. A recent review of pertinent research concludes that "the Jewish community appears to be moving to the right with the general drift in America, but it has farther to travel and is doing so at a somewhat slower pace."[42]

## 10.34 Religion and political action

With regard to partisan affiliation, the religious pattern in America has been reasonably clear since the 1930s. Protestants tend to be Republicans,[43] Catholics tend to be Democrats, and Jews are overwhelmingly Democrats. There is a positive association between strength of attachment to religion and strength of attachment to party. That is, Catholics closely identified with their religion vote more Democratic than Catholics not so closely identified with the church, and closely identified Protestants vote more Republican. Conversely, those who are more closely identified with *politics* are influenced less by their religious persuasions. One study found that in the event of political cross-pressure between religion and social class, younger voters are more likely to resolve the conflicts in favor of class.[44]

It may be that the relationships between religion and partisanship are gradually washing out in America. The Berelson study, as we have seen, suggested that economic and social-class influences are more important than religious influences for young men and women. There is scattered impressionistic evidence that Catholics' propensity to be Democrats is not so strong as it has been historically. The 1960 election between Protestant Republican Richard Nixon and Catholic Democrat John Kennedy was the occasion for a temporary display and even exaggeration of the older feeling that the Democrats were the party of "Romanism" and the Republicans were Protestant-controlled. It is unclear just how important religious attitudes and affiliations were for voter choice in 1960. There was undeniably a drift of Republican Catholics to Kennedy and a drift of Democratic Protestants to Nixon. A considerable amount of what appeared to be religiously based switching could probably be attributed either to Catholics

---

42. Abraham H. Miller and Euphemia V. Hall, "Jews, Radicals, and Conservatives: A Review-Essay," *Western Political Quarterly* 37 (1984): 665–677.

43. "Solid evidence of Lutheran preference for the Republican Party is revealed by comparing their voting record in the 1968 presidential election with the actual results. Whereas Nixon had 1% more votes nationally than did Humphrey, Lutherans gave to Nixon 34% more votes than they gave to Humphrey. Regional analysis showed that Nixon outdrew Humphrey in Lutheran support by 27% in Humphrey's home territory (West North Central), and by 43% in New England" (Strommen et al., *Study of Generations*, p. 46).

44. Berelson et al., *Voting*.

coming back to their regular base in the Democratic party after flirting with Eisenhower Republicanism in the 1950s or to Southern Protestants, historically Democratic, moving to the GOP for reasons that had nothing to do with religion.[45] There is also some merit in the suggestion that with the election of a Catholic president in 1960, the importance of religious preference and biases has declined as an influence on aggregate voting behavior.[46] Yet Figure 10–1 reveals no striking changes in the significant relationship between American religions and partisanship in the last three decades.

In the mid-1970s and early 1980s, as we have seen, the more fundamental and evangelistic Protestant groups increased their numbers and political visibility. Surveying American religions in early 1980, the British journal *The Economist* reported that the "mainline Protestant churches" (Episcopal, Presbyterian, United Church of Christ, and the more liberal Methodist groups) were suffering a serious decline in membership. The churches that were growing were

> marked by an insistence on a high commitment from their members, including loyalty and social solidarity. They expect obedience to the commands of a charismatic leadership. They have a missionary zeal, with an eagerness to tell the "good news" of one's salvation to others. They are intolerant of deviance or dissent and are absolutist about beliefs. ("We have the Truth and all others are in error.")[47]

The "born again" sector of American Protestantism grew in political effort and prominence in the late seventies. Such older evangelists as the Reverend Billy Graham continued to be popular, and alongside them arose a merchandising, computer-using organizational brand of religious enthusiasts. The Reverend Jerry Falwell, an electronic church superstar, argued that from a TV pulpit "you can register people to vote, you can explain the issues to them, and you can endorse candidates." Mr. Falwell, an independent Baptist, was said to be raising "$1 million a week through his Old-Time Gospel Hour on 320 television channels."[48] Dinesh D'Souza provides some insight into the political tactics of the Reverend Falwell and his organization, Moral Majority:

> Now, like Billy Graham, Mr. Falwell associates with unbelieving pastors, even with Jews and Mormons and atheists. But, he insists, such alliances are political, not religious. Moral Majority is a political

---

45. Philip E. Converse, "Religion and Politics: The 1960 Election," in *Elections and the Political Order,* ed. Angus Campbell et al., (New York: Wiley, 1966), pp. 96–124.

46. Harry M. Scoble and Leon D. Epstein, "Religion and Wisconsin Voting in 1960," *Journal of Politics* 26 (1964): 396. See also Albert J. Mendenez, *Religion at the Polls* (Philadelphia: Westminster Press, 1977).

47. "America Loves God, or Someone Else of the Same Name," *Economist,* April 5, 1980, p. 17.

48. George Vecsey, "Militant Television Preachers Try to Weld Fundamentalist Christians' Political Power," *New York Times,* January 21, 1980. In April 1980 one of Mr. Falwell's groups, "Moral Majority of Alaska," stacked the district caucuses and "seized control of Alaska's Republican Party" (Wallace Turner, "Group of Evangelical Protestants Takes Over the G.O.P. in Alaska," *New York Times,* June 9, 1980).

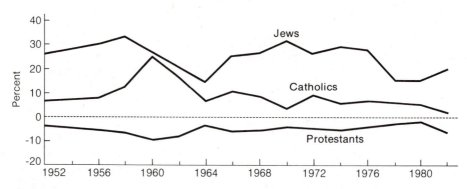

**Figure 10–1.**  *Deviation from the democratic vote norm, by religion, 1952–1982 (From* Public Opinion, *December/January 1983, p. 27.)*

organization, Mr. Falwell says. It is composed of 30 percent Catholics, 20 percent evangelicals and fundamentalists, and the rest a montage of conservative Jews, Mormons, and secular moralists who agree with Moral Majority's four stands: prolife, which means opposition to abortion and euthanasia; promoral, which means fighting pornography and the illegal drug traffic; profamily ("One man for one woman in one lifetime," in Mr. Falwell's words), and pro-American, which means support for a strong national defense, and curiously, support for Israel and Jewish people everywhere.[49]

Although right-wing fundamentalism appears to be ascendant in the 1980s, enjoying, no doubt, one of the highs in the cycles that seem to characterize sociopolitical climates in the United States, some of the attention to the political power of a new fundamentalist right may be an artifact of the campaign postures of born-again presidential candidates in 1976 and 1980 and of the moralizing president elected in 1980. Carol Mueller analyzed data from the NORC General Social Surveys from 1972 to 1980 in search of "evidence for the development over the 1970s of a new consciousness which reflected politicization of a growing moral opposition to three feminist issues: abortion, sexual preference, and women's liberation." All of her findings ran counter to that hypothesis. "It is likely, then," she concluded, "that the political salience of these issues is more dependent on the emphasis they receive from presidential candidates than on general cultural trends regarding approval or disapproval. . . . [50]

49. Dinesh D'Souza, "Jerry Falwell's Renaissance: The Chairman of Moral Majority Is Redefining Both Politics and Fundamentalism," *Policy Review* 27 (Winter 1984): 42.

50. Carol Mueller, "In Search of a Constituency for the 'New Religious Right,'" *Public Opinion Quarterly* 47 (1983): 213, 227. See also Pamela Johnston Conover, "The Mobilization of the New Right: A Test of Various Explanations," *Western Political Quarterly* 36 (1983): 632–649; and Jerome S. Legge, Jr., "The Determinants of Attitudes toward Abortion in the American Electorate," *Western Political Quarterly* 36 (1983): 479–490.

It should be born in mind, despite the media attention to fundamentalists in politics, that religious leadership in the United States shares with the rest of us respect for freedom of speech and the press and for the principles of due process and majority rule. A 1982 poll of 1,112 professors at Protestant and Roman Catholic seminaries found them to be more conservative than the general public on religious and moral questions but more liberal than the general public on many political questions, including nuclear weapons, rates of military spending, environmental policies, and the Equal Rights Amendment. From 52 percent (Lutheran) to 78 percent (Episcopal) rated themselves as liberals and only 25 percent considered themselves politically conservative.[51]

It should also be remembered that the more "establishment" religious groups pursue their special interests steadily and effectively. The unwavering support for Israel since 1947 is not only America's traditional posture toward humanitarian foreign policy and toward self-determination, but also a consequence of concentrated Jewish power in key electoral areas. The power of the "right to life" movement, the principal antiabortion force in the 1970s and 1980s, has been essentially the power of the Roman Catholic hierarchy and its millions of loyal communicants. Likewise, pacifism as a political movement in the United States and our general antimilitary tradition owe much to the leadership of the historic peace churches—and to the Methodists, especially, among the rest of Protestantism.

Though organized religion may become a direct political force on issues of high relevance to central church doctrine, the expectation of church member and the unchurched alike is that the theoretical separation of church and state will have its operational counterpart in a separation of church and politics. Religious influence in political life tends to be indirect, and to be exercised through attitudes and more generalized opinions to which the political issues of the day can be related. This tendency makes religious beliefs (whether generalized precepts or sectarian doctrines) not less important, but more so. In many cases they become the touchstone by which rapid judgments can be made in the absence of facts or rational thought. As a study of religious influence on the 1980 election concludes: "If politics is concerned with the allocation of values. . .then it is hardly avoidable that one of the key sources of values, that is, religion, should sometimes guide political choices."[52]

---

51. Charles Austin, "Poll Finds Conservatism by Seminary Teachers," *New York Times,* June 11, 1982.

52. Arthur H. Miller and Martin P. Wattenberg, "Politics from the Pulpit: Religiosity and the 1980 Elections," *Public Opinion Quarterly* 48 (1984): 316.

## Chapter 11

# Political Socialization:
# Education and
# Opinion Holding

Although the influence of formal education is much investigated, little is known about the ways schools create or recreate opinion. However, though we fail to trace the labyrinth of detail, some large patterns of influence may be observed. After the family, the school is perhaps the most powerful institution of the society in its impact on what is thought by whom on what issues. The average school cannot re-form the opinion network of the average child; this is too certainly determined by the family and environment. But the extraordinary school (there are a few) and the extraordinary teacher (there are many, though never enough) can sometimes re-form the opinions of the average child. What is more important, such schools and teachers, and sometimes even ordinary schools and teachers, can shape the opinions and often the whole life of the above-average child.

In the schools, whether public or private, the creation of opinion leaders begins. This sociopolitical function of the schools has been little remarked—perhaps because it is as obvious as it is significant. In the public schools, the child for the first time is systematically exposed to as great a variety of people and opinion as her school district affords. The narrow world of family, playmates, and parents' church (by which she is deeply marked by the age of six) is supplemented by a routinized but deliberately innovative social institution that not only tolerates but encourages opinion variety. One of the distinguishing and most significant characteristics of the American public school is that here begins the nonvoluntary exposure of the individual to persons with whom she may have little in common except membership in a political community. This exposure constitutes the first direct impact of the polity on the individual. Until children enter school they contact the public (through government) only indirectly; but on the opening day of class, and thereafter for ten, twelve, sixteen, or twenty years, they are obliged to follow some rules, to take note of some differences and similarities, and actively or passively to engage in big and little social controversies. Parents start the socialization process; but at least one important fact about the public schools is that, by virtue of the expanded sociopolitical exposure they afford, they enable the socialization process to take a quantum leap.

Now, it should not be thought that just because the scope of community influence is significantly expanded when the child enters public school, this influence will radically alter or conflict with the values and habits acquired in the family and preschool environment. The schools may in some ways conflict with home conditioning, but the conflicts are usually not many or starkly presented. The hand of the state is on the child for the first time. But it is the gentle hand of a local school board and of local teachers, who have little awareness of their political nature—and who, since they define politics in the traditional but narrow sense of party antagonisms, in fact deny their political nature (which is, perhaps, just as well). The major thrust of the schools is thus, at least in the early years, the reinforcement of family attitudes and family opinions, for although the social heterogeneity of the environment is increased, the child is shielded from its full effect by a curriculum that attends mainly to fact gathering and superficial (if, at this stage, important) social graces. Primarily, he learns numbers and letters and simple words; learns to work with a group, to respect nonfamily authority; learns to behave by rule and time. Moreover, as a developing personality, he is probably intellectually and emotionally unable to absorb the wider implications of the new environment. Thus protection is provided by and from the expanded environment, especially if the family's socioeconomic status is neither extremely high nor extremely low.

American public schools, for many reasons, tend to shape their wards to middle-class patterns. Both underprivileged and overprivileged children experience greater impact from new opinions in the public schools than do the average children of average families. Children of deprived backgrounds have to learn obedience, self-discipline, and sometimes simple cleanliness in the public schools. Wealthy children may have to learn some of the same things, but more often their lesson is one of *toleration*. Children who are culturally and intellectually overprivileged (a small but important group that the public schools are now beginning to recognize) may have the hardest learning of all—to be humble, to be supportive of others, and often to be just plain bored.

## 11.1 SCHOOLS AND INDOCTRINATION IN COMMUNITY VALUES

The schools in any society are major institutions for the conservation of traditional values. One American social anthropologist argues that a public school system cannot, by its very nature, act as a change-producing force. "American classrooms, like educational institutions anywhere, express the values, preoccupations, and fears found in the culture as a whole. School has no choice; it must train the children to fit the culture as it is. School can give training in skills; it cannot teach creativity."[1]

That view is too simple and too pessimistic. There is, of course, a genuine question whether any person or any institution can *teach* creativity. But some conditions are more favorable to creativity than others, and schools and teachers may—even if they seldom do—provide favorable conditions. The old ways—"the culture as it is"—may be challenged daily in American classrooms, even though the overarching purpose of an educational system is admittedly (and necessarily) the shaping of young minds and behavior to acceptable and traditional ways.

It has been argued that historically schools in America have been more important in shaping social and political values than the schools of other countries have been. More of our formal education has been provided by public, tax-supported schools and less by private means (either upper-class or missionary-sectarian). Proportionally more American than European young people have been compelled to attend schools in the nineteenth and twentieth centuries. And, as Charles Merriam noted, other conditions have made it likely that the U.S. school system would be a more influential opinion-forming institution than the European: (a) the influence of the home is weakened by the migratory character of our people and (b) the variety of competing systems of religion weakens the force of any one of them.[2] These characteristics of American society, with their probable effect on the importance of the schools as value-forming institutions, are still significant in the 1980s.

Illustrative of the civic socialization themes of American education were those in the famous McGuffey's *Readers*. Those books, which sold more than 120 million copies between 1837 and 1941, taught self-reliance, hard work, and thrift. According to one analyst, the morality of acquisition was especially emphasized: "There is no trace in McGuffey of virtue for its own sake; on the contrary, virtue *pays*. Those who practice these virtues—honesty, industry, charity, piety, and the like—receive very tangible rewards in return." Furthermore, the readers taught not only the morality of acquisition but the virtues of a simple nationalism and of religiosity ("not so much a doctrine as an attitude").[3]

Thousands of local school boards of the nineteenth century, whether intentionally or not, used the public schools as vehicles for indoctrination in and reinforcement of the dominant middle-class values. The results were no doubt impressive, for during the McGuffey era these books did not compete with other print (or electronic) media for the child's attention or as guides to desired values.

---

1. Jules Henry, *Culture against Man* (New York: Random House, 1963), p. 287.

2. Charles E. Merriam, *Civic Education in the United States* (New York: Scribner, 1934), p.77. For some comments on nationalistic distortions in European and American schools and on UNESCO's efforts to reduce such distortions, see Elton Atwater, Kent Forster, and Jan S. Prybyla, *World Tensions: Conflict and Accommodation* (New York: Appleton, 1967), pp.28–30.

3. D. A. Saunders, "Social Ideas in McGuffey Readers," *Public Opinion Quarterly* 5 (1941): 584.

"McGuffey's social teachings slipped in unnoticed by the child, who absorbed them in the most formative years of life. The printed page itself was more respected in homes where often the only companion volume of the McGuffey *Readers* was the Bible."[4]

The significance of school textbooks as reflections of changes in dominant cultural values over time was measured by Richard De Charms and Gerald Moeller. Themes representing economic and technological achievement increased in number from 1800 to 1900, then decreased until 1950. Themes representing interpersonal affiliation (an index of David Riesman's "other-directed" orientation) generally increased over the 150-year period. And what the authors called "moral teaching" was drastically reduced from high to almost zero over the century and a half.[5]

We wish to emphasize, however, that we are talking about the general values and basic attitudes that the school and the community share in considerable degree. Though the process at the beginning and in the early grades is one of learning and consolidating the most fundamental skills, what is learned as the level of schooling goes up becomes increasingly a filling in of the meanings of values, the relations of these values to the "real" world, and a greater specificity of attitudes and attitude constellations—along with a storehouse of facts and evidential material related (often in very simple ways) to value and attitude. Generally, what we hold in our minds in the way of ideas, things, and persons changes through the educational process and its institutions from fuzzy to less fuzzy. Like the infant's early learning of shapes and colors, the later educational process is one of increasingly subtle differentiation; things and ideas become more clearly distinguished from other things and ideas. Accompanying this differentiation is the more and more subtle ability to reintegrate things and ideas in ways that have wider meaning.

The process of learning, with its attendant fuzziness, only gradually sharpening with age and exposure to stimuli of increasing complexity, is vividly demonstrated by Harold Isaacs in the stream-of-consciousness technique used in his books *Scratches on the Mind* and *Emergent Americans*. The following excerpts catch the residue of moods and attitudes that young adults carry into their world from church and school:

> In our interviews we asked our Crossroaders [college students who participated in an African work-camp project] to scrape their memories for some of these early acquisitions, and here, in their words and phrases, bunched together from the answers of many different indi-

---

4. Ibid., p. 589. Interestingly, *McGuffey's Readers* are still published and "since 1961 they have continued to sell at a rate of some thirty thousand copies a year.... Although controversial they continue to be the desired text of numerous parents who are dissatisfied with modern American education" (John H. Westerhoff III, *McGuffey and His Readers* [Nashville: Abingdon Press, 1978], p. 15).
5. Richard De Charms and Gerald H. Moeller, "Values Expressed in American Children's Readers: 1800–1950," *Journal of Abnormal and Social Psychology* 64 (1962): 136–142.

viduals, is how they located and described what they had seen or heard about Africa in their younger years.

At *church* or in *Sunday school*...

...missionaries,...voodooism in interior Africa; heard about Egypt in Sunday school; about Schweitzer; Sunday school lessons about converting the heathen; Africa a vast jungle,...the primitiveness, illiterate savages, tribal wars, witch doctors; terrible sanitary conditions, people needing medicine and Christianity....

At *school*...

...little or nothing, a little geography, Africa on the world map, the slave trade, some names of countries and rivers, Livingston, Stanley, Rhodes, the Nile, the Sahara, something about the Congo; British and French and Belgian colonies; jungles, tribesmen, primitive people with bones through their noses, head hunters, pygmies, a dark continent full of savages, animals, torrid zones, minerals, huge and unexplored; Bartholomew Diaz going around the Cape, Vasco da Gama; pictures of people carrying rubber trees; life of a boy, happy-go-lucky in the jungle; in high school I heard of Ghana's independence; heard about the apartheid situation in South Africa....[6]

These impressions are not opinions but they are the stuff of which opinions, public and private, are made. It is fuzzy stuff and background stuff, and it moves to the foreground and grows sharp only in the context of a particular time, event, or question. It is all in the funnel of opinion causality, put there by chance and by the deliberate efforts of self and others acting within social institutions and social values. The schools are one such social institution—shaping, suggesting, and influencing the convergence in the funnel—behind every opinion of those individuals whose aggregated views comprise public opinion.

The intellectual and social development of the young, we are suggesting, progresses through a series of environments, psychological processes, and social/institutional influences, some sequential, some concurrent. The general process may be provisionally and inadequately summarized in Figure 11-1. Personality and cultural variables interact in ways discussed earlier, in Chapters 8 and 9. Family and religious influences intermingle with the cultural as the child is gradually, and usually painlessly, introduced to more adult orientations and understandings. The schools mostly reinforce the *orientations,* although some divergent values and norms may be present; the *understandings* are greatly expanded by the impact of school curricula.

---

6. Copyright © 1961 Massachusetts Institute of Technology. Reprinted from *Emergent Americans: A Report on "Crossroads Africa"* (pp. 38–40) by Harold R. Isaacs, by permission of the John Day Company, Inc., publisher.

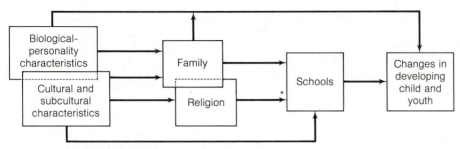

*If the child attends a parochial school, this influence
is strong; if a public school, quite weak.

**Figure 11-1.**  *Institutional and process flow in the development and socialization of American children and youth*

## 11.2  FORMAL POLITICAL SOCIALIZATION IN THE SCHOOLS

Social and political indoctrination, conscious and unconscious, clearly takes place in the public schools. Some such indoctrination in the values of a democratic society is necessary—for "fair play" in school becomes due process in law, and "citizenship" becomes protection of minority rights. Other kinds of values no doubt impede the search for truth which educators everywhere profess to be their goal.

How much of this indoctrination "takes," and how does the school compare in importance with the other agents of political socialization? Herbert Hyman, as we have seen, believes the family is the most important agent. Kenneth Langton says parents and other adults are more influential than age-mates.[7] Robert Hess and Judith Torney suggest that for children of five to thirteen, the schools as a whole (teachers, administrators, and fellow students) have more influence than the family.[8] Lee Sigelman and Jonathan Hantke asked Texas high school seniors and university students to indicate the relative importance of various socialization agents with regard to three kinds of values/attitudes. Their findings suggest that it is unfruitful to debate whether home or school or peers are most important; it seems to depend on the question "Important when, and for what?"

> There is a good deal of *topic specialization* among socialization agents. . . . Home and church, traditional social institutions, have

7. Kenneth P. Langton, "Peer Group and School and the Political Socialization Process," *American Political Science Review* 61 (1967): 751–758.

8. Robert D. Hess and Judith V. Torney, *The Development of Political Attitudes in Children* (Chicago: Aldine, 1967).

their greatest impact on basic values, especially on honesty, and have less influence on political opinions. The media, on the other hand, are particularly influential with respect to political opinions, and markedly less so for social attitudes and basic values....[S]chools appear to have less impact on social attitudes than on basic values or political opinions.[9]

Experimental studies of indoctrination in the schools bear out the common-sense view that pupils can be influenced by one-sided arguments. As early as 1938 H. H. Remmers summarized several experiments on the amount and permanence of induced opinion change. On deliberate attempts to change social and political attitudes, he declared that "a high school teacher is likely to obtain the kinds of attitudes which are consciously set up as educational objectives and striven for as such. And it appears that unless some specific effort is made to change attitudes they are not likely to change." Remmers' investigations were followed about a decade later by a comprehensive series of experiments at Yale. In general, the Yale studies corroborated the findings of the earlier work. Other things being equal, exposure is followed immediately by considerable change in the direction indicated by the content of the message. Over a short period of time, much of the effect of a single exposure wears off, but there remains a net and lasting (in the absence of countering information) change in the expected direction.[10]

Efforts of *schools* to change attitudes are more likely to succeed than are *experimental* efforts to change attitudes. Experiments almost always employ one-shot exposures; schools are able to expose students again and again, under varied conditions, to systematic and reinforcing messages. The evidence is that repeated, confirmatory, and ego-satisfying stimuli can be produced by the schools. Many of the values so inculcated and reinforced will be the modal values of the community in which the school is located. But many will be wider, "cosmopolitan" rather than "local" values, and will suggest or facilitate conflict and social change.

The paradox is this: almost all investigators of formal political socialization efforts in American schools believe that those efforts have considerable impact. Yet attempts to measure that impact often show that it is small or even negligible.

Dean Jaros points out that, on the question of inculcation of political values, the schools could have impact in any one or all of the following ways:

(1) curricular content alone, (2) curricular content mediated by educational quality, (3) teachers' overt expression of their own values in classroom situations, (4) teachers' more casual expression of their own values in less structured, out-of-class situations, and (5) pupil

---

9. Lee Sigelman and Jonathan Hantke, "The Relative Impact of Socialization Agents: An Exploratory Study," unpublished manuscript, 1974.

10. H. H. Remmers, "Propaganda in the Schools—Do the Effects Last?" *Public Opinion Quarterly* 2 (1938): 202, 207.

identification with particular teachers and adoption of values these teachers are perceived to hold.[11]

One supposes that schooling could influence young Americans by (a) shaping their *beliefs, values, and attitudes,* (b) increasing their *knowledge* about government and politics, and (c) motivating or providing opportunities for political *action.* A brief review of the evidence so far indicates that the schools' main effect on beliefs and values seems to be a strengthening and clarifying of political identity (who one is: American, Georgian, Atlantan) and attachment to vague notions of constitutionalism, First Amendment rights, and partisanship. Hyman and some of the earlier researchers implied that schools taught blind patriotism based on primordial and sacred ties. David Easton and Robert Hess report that the "truly formative years of the maturing member of a political system would seem to be the years between the ages of three and thirteen.... By the time children have reached second grade (age 7) most of them have become firmly attached to their political community.... They have learned that they are Americans."[12] Patriotic songs, the pledge of allegiance to the flag, prayers in school (even after their outlawing, as we have seen), and the offhand, probably unconscious comments of patriotic teachers contribute day in and day out to the perpetuation of narrow patriotism in the public schools. In many middle-sized and smaller communities, local patriotic organizations such as the American Legion and the DAR engage in special reinforcing activities in the schools—sponsorship of essay and speech contests with such themes as "Why I Am Proud to Be an American," with prizes awarded at commencement and Class Day.

There is, however, another and contradictory set of values and attitudes fostered in the schools: diversity, toleration, fair play, majority-rule-and-minority-rights. And these are the values that are increasingly called forth over the years of formal schooling as the children (a) become more independent psychologically and socially, (b) gather more knowledge about politics and the bases and structures of authority, and (c) experience conflict both generally and in its political forms. These are the civil values. Responses from fifth- and eighth-grade students in southern California indicate that civil values, more than sacred or primordial values, provide the basis for patriotism and national identity.[13]

American children and youth clearly increase their political *knowledge* as a result of school activity. They learn facts of history and of contemporary events

---

11. Dean Jaros, *Socialization to Politics* (New York: Praeger, 1973), p. 100.

12. David Easton and Robert D. Hess, "The Child's Political World," *Midwest Journal of Political Science* 6 (1962): 236, 238.

13. Charles F. Andrain, *Children and Civic Awareness: A Study in Political Education* (Columbus, Ohio: Merrill, 1971). Andrain asked the children about the basis for "describing Americans," levels of political tolerance, symbols of national identity, and what made them most proud to live in America. By and large, these ten- and thirteen-year-olds seem to base their political feelings and beliefs, and even their sense of national identity, on civil rules, norms, and institutions rather than on the primordial values of blood, language, and soil, or sacred values of eternal texts and doctrine.

and processes. They also learn the opinions of others, and to some extent they learn how to learn about political things. Charles Andrain's careful study of more than 1,300 Southern California fifth- and eighth-graders confirms the common-sense expectation that eighth-graders know much more than fifth-graders about what he calls "the *content* of political knowledge," thus showing "the effect of increased education and cognitive maturity."[14] As one would expect, knowledge depends on IQ and political interest, but even when these variables are held constant, knowledge increases with additional schooling. Other investigations at the high school level indicate that civics courses often do not significantly increase political knowledge for middle-class students, perhaps because those courses are repetitious and uninformative, but they seem to produce more knowledge in disadvantaged youngsters, for whom the factual content is new.[15] In short, schools do teach students some historical and current facts about politics, political institutions, and political issues.

A discouraging report of the late 1970s indicated that, overall, American high school youth did not improve their factual knowledge, their level of interest, or their understanding of or commitment to democratic practice in the seven years between 1969 and 1976. "Knowledge about the structure and function of govern-ment declined from the early to mid-seventies for both 13- and 17-year-olds." "In 1976 approximately three-fifths of the 13-year-olds and four-fifths of the 17-year-olds realized that their civil rights are stated in the U. S. Constitution. These figures represent no change for 13-year-olds and a drop from 1972 performance for 17-year-olds." There were also sharp declines in understanding of local government policy-making processes, from 36 percent (1970) to 26 percent (1976) among 13-year-olds, and from 69 percent (1969) to 47 percent (1976) among 17-year-olds.[16]

John Patrick reviewed the studies of the effects of formal education (from kindergarten through high school) on socialization. His summary:

1.  *Political knowledge.* The impact of traditional public school courses (Civics, Problems of Democracy, American Government, and the like) "has been meager."

2.  *Political thinking.* "Studies of cognitive development and political learning suggest that high school students tend to have the capacity to achieve skills necessary to high-level thinking. . . . Most students fail to achieve these competencies."

3.  *Learning political attitudes.* "Most American adolescents learn very well to be supportive of their political system," but they are often intolerant of "values and conceptions that are very different from their

14. Ibid., p. 76.

15. See Kenneth P. Langton and M. Kent Jennings, "Political Socialization and the High School Civics Curriculum," *American Political Science Review* 62 (1968): 852–867.

16. *Changes in Political Knowledge and Attitudes, 1969–79: Selected Results from the Second National Assessments of Citizenship and Social Studies* (Denver: Education Commission of the States, March 1978), pp. 7, 23, 35.

own" and of dissent from orthodox political views. In short, political education courses do not seem very effective generators of participatory democratic attitudes.[17]

What is the evidence in regard to the third possible way the schools may have a political influence on young Americans? Do they provide motivations and opportunities for political activity?

The short answer seems to be that most schools do not provide much incentive, and few provide real opportunity, for political participation. Edgar Litt's imaginative and often-cited study of three Boston-area schools is instructive: the values and factual content of the civics courses in two lower-class schools were overwhelmingly those appropriate to "subject" and nonparticipatory citizenship roles. Only the upper-class school's content explored controversy in a realistic way and suggested that citizenship included involvement in the political management of conflict.[18] Jack Zewin's research in the early 1980s confirmed Litt's findings that citizenship education that candidly dealt with the clash of values and priorities and with the trade-offs and bargaining of groups was more effective than the rote memorization of precepts and do-good examples that characterize "civics" courses in most schools.[19]

In a provocative article, Richard Merelman argues that American schools do not and cannot teach democratic values. He believes that the order-keeping responsibilities thrust on American public schools impel teachers and administrators to avoid truly democratizing political education. Order keeping seems to demand an authoritarian school environment that is inconsistent with the content and procedures required for the learning of democratic behaviors. "Discussing political values in the classroom invites controversy and division," he says. "As Americans we expect people not only to advance their own political views, but also to challenge the views of others." Yet open discussion also "opens the school to charges of propagandizing."

Merelman also points out that the value-relativism approach, encouraged by democratic processes, "may spread uncontrollably into the teacher's privileged realm of true knowledge, [and the] teacher's self-interest demands that answers to educational questions be construed as either right or wrong." Thus teachers are disposed to teach democratic values as they teach facts of math or science. The problem with this approach is that "teachers who pretend that values are matters of settled fact seem unlikely to imbue such values with passion or conviction. To have the proposition that democracy is a good thing presented as if it were equivalent to the proof that $2 + 2 = 4$ is to remove from the concept of democracy its singular emotional force."

---

17. John J. Patrick, "Political Socialization and Political Education in Schools," in *Handbook of Political Socialization,* ed. Stanley A. Renshon (New York: Free Press, 1977), pp. 199–201.

18. Edgar Litt, "Civic Education, Community Norms, and Political Indoctrination," *American Sociological Review* 28 (1963): 69–75.

19. Jack Zewin, "Future Citizens: Children and Politics," *Teaching Political Science* 10 (Spring 1983): 110–126.

The final irony of the order-keeping climate of American schools is that "bright students soon think their way through the ruse, and conclude that what the school has presented as fact is actually a complex, confusing matter of debate and personal commitment. Therefore, it is to bright students that the school is most disillusioning."[20]

Commenting on Merelman's arguments, Kent Jennings says that democratic values *are* inculcated both directly and indirectly by the schools, and all studies show that the verbal attachment to, or at least statement of, democratic goals and principles increases markedly with formal education. But Jennings and Merelman agree that schools do not teach an understanding of politics or give students practice in political engagement. Politics is the management of conflict, and students are not genuine participants even in the politics of educational policy, except insofar as older students may be voters and except for a handful of students in unusual private colleges. So they agree that, while "democratic values" in the abstract may be discussed and perhaps even learned about (again abstractly), what is not achieved is "any thorough understanding of such concepts, their philosophical underpinnings, the tradeoffs among them, the conditions giving rise to or threatening them, and their translation from belief into action."[21] In short, democratic politics is neither learned about nor practiced.

Higher education does seem to influence sociopolitical values and attitudes generally and contributes to more informed and participant citizenship. In 1969 Kenneth Feldman and Theodore Newcomb published a review of "hundreds" of research reports dealing with the influence of college on students' values, beliefs, and behaviors. These studies indicate, consistently and significantly, that the longer the college experience, the greater the number of respondents whose survey answers tended toward the liberal position and away from the conservative (the liberal position, in the authors' words, "is one which favors change ...[and] is currently based on the desire for political and social equality, full suffrage, civil liberties, labor unions, welfare legislation, and pacifism").[22] These liberal values and attitudes orient social relations generally.

Table 11–1 illustrates the effects of a college education on political ideology. Two inferences may be made from these data. First, college-educated respondents are more sharply polarized than are those who have less formal education: only 18.7 percent of the college-educated claim to be moderates, compared with 24.9–33.3 percent of respondents with other levels of formal schooling. One reason for this polarization is almost certainly that a college education helps people understand the meanings and implications of the terms liberal and conservative and helps them determine their own ideological placement. A

20. Richard M. Merelman, "Democratic Politics and the Culture of American Education," *American Political Science Review* 74 (June 1980): 325, 326, 330. Copyright © 1980 by the American Political Science Association. Reprinted by permission.

21. M. Kent Jennings, "Comment on Richard Merelman's 'Democratic Politics and the Culture of American Education,'" ibid., pp. 333–337, quotation at 336.

22. Kenneth A. Feldman and Theodore M. Newcomb, *The Impact of College on Students,* 2 vols. (San Francisco: Jossey-Bass, 1969), 1:19.

**Table 11-1**   Liberal-conservative self-designation by educational levels, 1980

| Ideology | Level of formal education | | | | | | |
|---|---|---|---|---|---|---|---|
| | Grade school | Some high school | High school | Some college | College | All | N |
| Liberal | 26.1% | 23.6% | 20.5% | 32.6% | 30.9% | 26.2% | 305 |
| Moderate | 28.4 | 29.2 | 33.3 | 24.9 | 18.7 | 27.6 | 321 |
| Conservative | 45.5 | 47.2 | 46.3 | 42.5 | 50.4 | 46.3 | 539 |
| N | 88 | 144 | 430 | 273 | 230 | | 1,165 |

Source: Center for Political Studies, University of Michigan, 1980 National Election Study.

second point to be noted is that half the college-educated described themselves as conservative, yet the academic studies referred to above declared college education to be a liberalizing force. This apparent paradox is probably a result of the tendency for respondents to emphasize economic and social-welfare policies when designating their own placement, while academicians include civil liberties and civil rights policies in their definitions of liberalism. A college education is unquestionably liberalizing with respect to civil liberties and civil rights liberalism, but not necessarily with respect to economic or welfare liberalism.

There is evidence that orientations acquired in educational institutions persist during adult life unless they are countered by regular, reinforcing counterstimuli. Since regular, reinforcing stimuli are not commonplace in our heterogeneous society, the usual tendency seems to be toward long-term stability in liberal orientations acquired in college.

On the other hand, attempts to foster political knowledge and activity by specific college courses or programs of instruction seem not to be very effective. Research at a variety of colleges in the 1950s, 1960s, 1970s, and early 1980s all produced "results that were not encouraging for those who believe the study of political science makes a difference. Cognitive gains were minimal and attitudinal changes almost nonexistent."[23] It appears that a college education does make a difference in the quality of political socialization generally, but individual courses by themselves make no measurable difference.

## 11.3 FORMAL EDUCATION AND POLITICAL OPINION HOLDING AMONG AMERICAN ADULTS

The preceding section summarized what we know about schools as agents of political socialization in America. With regard to specific political attitudes,

23. See Albert Somit et al., "The Effect of the Introductory Political Science Course on Student Attitudes toward Personal Political Participation," *American Political Science Review* 52 (1958): 1129–1132; Charles Garrison, "Political Involvement and Political Science: A Note on the Basic Course as an Agent of Political Socialization," *Social Science Quarterly* 49 (1968): 305–320; and David Caputo and Ilese Houniak, "Assessing the Impact of a Course on Student Attitudes and Knowledge," *News for Teachers of Political Science,* no. 36 (Fall 1982), pp. 1, 17. Quotation is from Jeffrey W. Hahn and Justin J. Green, "Does Studying Political Science Make Any Difference?" *Teaching Political Science* 10 (1983): 178.

opinions, and behaviors, there is evidence that the better educated have more opinions, a greater sense of political efficacy (defined as confidence that they can have some impact on politics and governmental policy), a more accurate sense of the what, where, and why of political events at home and abroad, and higher participation rates.

The better educated have more opinions. The "don't know" and "no opinion" responses to poll questions almost invariably confirm this unsurprising fact, as Table 11-2 indicates. Those with less education may be unwilling or unable to express opinions on foreign issues or complex questions of domestic policy but are as capable as those with more education of answering questions about economic policy that affects them as individuals.

A number of analysts have suggested that people's political behavior is heavily influenced by the degree of confidence they have in the political system of which they are a part. The authors of *The Voter Decides* reported that, "as was expected, education is highly related to the efficacy scale; one half of those respondents who attended college rank high on this scale, as compared with only 15 percent of those who have completed no more than grade school."[24] Later, in *The American Voter*, Angus Campbell and his collaborators pointed out that this sense of political efficacy is in part a function of income and high-status occupation. But the fact that it is "more strongly related to education than to other dimensions of status that may symbolize equal strength in the power structure suggests that education contributes to the attitude in a more direct way."[25] Table 11-3 supports this view.

Is education more or less important than income or occupation as an indicator of political participation? After reviewing much of the earlier literature Robert Lane concluded:

> Perhaps for a simple conventional act such as voting, income is more important, while more complex forms of participation are more dependent upon qualities associated with education. Occupation is hard to grade along a similar, single dimension continuum, but from inspection of the 1952 Survey Research Center data, it is apparent (for what it is worth) that differences among standard occupational classifications are smaller than differences among the educational or income classifications.[26]

A later study confirms Lane's surmise that education is more important than

24. Angus Campbell, Gerald Gurin, and Warren E. Miller, *The Voter Decides* (New York: Harper & Row, 1954), p. 187.

25. Angus Campbell et al., *The American Voter* (New York: Wiley, 1960), p. 280.

26. Robert E. Lane, *Political Life* (New York: Free Press, 1959), p. 222. Copyright 1959. Reprinted by permission of the Macmillan Company. The authors of an early study concluded that "education and SES [socioeconomic status] level seem to have about equal importance in creating and maintaining political interest" (Paul F. Lazarsfeld et al., *The People's Choice* (New York: Columbia University Press, 1944), p. 43.

**Table 11-2** Percent of "no opinion" responses on selected issues, 1973–1983, by level of formal education

|  | College | High school | Grade school |
|---|---|---|---|
| Should wage-price controls be more strict, less strict, or as they are now?<br>(May 1973) | 7 | 7 | 13 |
| Do you approve American planes bombing in Cambodia and Laos?<br>(May 1973) | 6 | 15 | 22 |
| With regard to the Watergate Affair has the mass media provided too much coverage, too little, or about the right amount?<br>(June 1973) | 2 | 6 | 17 |
| Do you favor or oppose choosing presidential candidates by nationwide primary election instead of party conventions as at present?<br>(Dec. 1979) | 5 | 10 | 19 |
| Are nuclear power plants today safe enough, or should their operations be cut back until more strict regulations can be adopted?<br>(Jan. 1980) | 7 | 15 | 30 |
| Are present curbs on the press too strict—or not strict enough?<br>(Jan. 1980) | 8 | 13 | 26 |
| In general, do you feel the United Nations is doing a good job or a poor job in trying to solve the problems it has had to face?<br>(Nov. 1983) | 6 | 15 | 18 |

Source: *Gallup Opinion Index,* dates indicated. On education and "no opinion" responses, see also G. David Faulkenberry and Robert Mason, "Characteristics of Nonopinion and No Opinion Response Groups," *Public Opinion Quarterly* 42 (Winter 1978) 533–543.

**Table 11-3** Trust in government by levels of education, 1958–1978 (percentage difference index)

|  | 1958 | 1964 | 1968 | 1970 | 1972 | 1974 | 1976 | 1978 |
|---|---|---|---|---|---|---|---|---|
| Grade school | 36 | 32 | 8 | −18 | −14 | −40 | −44 | −32 |
| High school | 50 | 48 | 25 | 5 | 1 | −28 | −35 | −37 |
| College | 57 | 40 | 29 | 15 | 12 | −11 | −18 | −28 |

Data from a 5-item Guttman scale. "Percentage difference index" is proportion "most trusting" minus proportion "most critical." Source: Warren E. Miller et al., eds., *American National Election Studies Sourcebook, 1952–1978* (Cambridge: Harvard University Press, 1980), p. 269.

occupation or income as a predictor of more intensive modes of political participation, and more important also for voter turnout. "Education," say Raymond Wolfinger and Steven Rosenstone, "has a very substantial effect on the probability that one will vote. Citizens with a college degree are 38 percent more likely to vote than are people with fewer than five years of schooling. The effect is greatest among those with the least education." They believe that education as a "facilitator" of participation does three things: first, "schooling increases one's capacity for understanding and working with complex, abstract, and intangible subjects such as politics." Second, better-educated adults seem to be "more likely to have a strong sense of citizen duty, to feel moral pressure to participate, and to receive expressive benefits from voting." And third, "schooling imparts experience with a variety of bureaucratic relationships... which helps one overcome the procedural hurdles required first to register and then to vote."[27]

In view of what we know about the correlations of education with information holding, sense of efficacy, and participation in the opinion-policy process, it is tempting to believe that social improvements might be understood and welcomed by the masses if they only knew more. It is part of the liberal mythology that education is a way to get rid of wars, economic dislocations, social injustices, political conflicts, and most of the real and imagined evils attending the human adventure. We have seen enough, even in this brief overview, to conclude that the simplistic notion of education as a panacea for social ills is, like most simplistic notions, a fraud. In the first place, a good deal of what is labeled "education" is no more than public relations—which, as Gabriel Almond points out, will not do:

> It is a great temptation to attribute these differences in political attitudes which are associated with income, occupation, and education to "lack of information" or "areas of ignorance." The policy implications of such an interpretation are clear and simple. Lack of information can be remedied by more information; and "areas of ignorance" can be dispelled by civic-minded campaigns of public education. In actuality, the problem runs a great deal deeper. A discriminating analysis of the evidence suggests that a large sector of the lower-income, poorly educated majority of the population is incapable of assimilating the materials of informational campaigns. Its basic apathy is a consequence of emotional and social conditions. Its intellectual horizon tends to be quite limited, and its analytical skill rudimentary. It will take a great deal more than public relations to remedy such a situation and produce the degree of involvement and activism which is characteristic of the upper-educational and-income groups. Actually, no one has proposed a solution to this basic problem which is not transparently inadequate or obviously Utopian.[28]

It is hard to reach a balanced judgment on the long-run (or even the short-run) effects of education on political opinions and behavior. The voice of pessimism is heard in the Almond quotation above. John Kenneth Galbraith is more hopeful; he argued in 1967 that "a superior and independent education" could provide the individual and social skepticism, and the pluralistic perspectives, to relieve the harsh demands of a superrational industrial system.[29] David Knoke's research suggests that for sociopolitical issues other than race (for example, sex roles,

---

27. Raymond E. Wolfinger and Steven J. Rosenstone, *Who Votes?* (New Haven: Yale University Press, 1980), pp. 34–36.

28. Gabriel A. Almond, *The American People and Foreign Policy* (New York: Praeger, 1960), p. 130. Reprinted by permission of Frederick A. Praeger, Publisher.

29. John Kenneth Galbraith, *The New Industrial State* (New York: New American Library, 1968), pp. 377–385.

defendants' rights, "quality of life" issues), education is the most important independent variable; on racial issues education (after race itself) seems dominant; but for economic questions, occupation and/or income may be more important than education.[30]

Admittedly, we have little evidence that even small numbers of people can be brought suddenly and lastingly into the ways of democratic participation through the influence of formal and institutionalized education. Mass opinions or behavior cannot be changed in any short period of time. Educators can be only slightly in advance of the society they must reflect as they help to recreate it. Change is slow.

Nonetheless, some change does occur, and opinions change more quickly than attitudes and beliefs—especially opinions that are unrelated to personal experiences. Thus in the matter of foreign policy, so critical to the preservation of the evolving welfare democracy in the United States, mass opinions may be decisively altered by bold and imaginative leadership.

Some of the change is due to the fact that education does widen horizons and that in America ever greater numbers of people are obtaining ever greater education. The attentive public is increasing, not just absolutely, as the population grows, but relative to the size of the inattentive.[31] This changing ratio means not only that policy issues may receive more discriminating consideration, but that the pool that produces opinion leaders and decision makers will be correspondingly larger.[32] Talent for creating and leading public opinion is thus being saved and produced.

30. David Knoke, "Stratification and the Dimensions of American Political Orientations," *American Journal of Political Science* 23 (November 1979): 772–791.

31. See James N. Rosenau, *Citizenship between Elections* (New York: Free Press, 1974). William N. Stephens and C. Stephen Long say that from the micro level of the individual, the correlations between education and tolerant, participatory political behavior may be slight, but, viewed "from the vantage point of the political system, the effects appear to be considerable. These 'weak' attitude changes (with greater formal education) add up statistically to the pattern of correlations we have reviewed, and to elections won and lost, mandates given and withheld—to a major tilting of public opinion" "Education and Political Behavior," in *Political Science Annual: An International Review,* ed. James A. Robinson (Indianapolis: Bobbs-Merrill, 1970), 2:25.

32. For a sophisticated and penetrating presentation of a number of the foregoing points, see William A. Gamson and Andre Modigliani, "Knowledge and Foreign Policy Opinions: Some Models for Consideration," *Public Opinion Quarterly* 30 (1966): 187–199.

## Chapter 12

# Economics, Politics, and Opinions in the United States

"Tell me where a man gets his corn pone, and I'll tell you what his 'pinions are." In these words, Mark Twain, no economic determinist of any school, expressed the common observation that opinions arise in large part from economic circumstances.

Opinions can, indeed, be bought and sold like shoes and ships and cabbages— or like votes and other things of political value. More often, however, opinions of individuals are influenced and determined not by market transactions but by less direct and more subtle economic forces. Some opinions serve better than others the immediate or long-range economic needs of each individual. The farmer believes in sales or income taxes rather than property taxes; the small trades-person believes in local regulation of business (if in any regulation of business at all); the southern box and crate manufacturer strongly opposes minimum-wage legislation; and the trade-union leader detests the idea of the open shop. It would be difficult to find any public issue on which all opinions were free from the influence of economic factors. Even simple local ordinances with no specific impact, such as dog-leash laws or rules stating how the streets are to be named and numbered, are apt to provoke economic fears or hopes in homeowners or businesspeople.[1] No doubt some matters of public policy are wholly free of economic factors, but they are surely infrequent and almost never important. In a democracy the public's business, at least in part, is an economic business.

---

1. The businesspeople of New York City's Third Avenue once launched a campaign to change its name to Avenue of the Promenades, to offset the unfavorable image associated with the old elevated tracks (now removed) and the Bowery.

## 12.1 ECONOMIC FACTORS AND THE FUNNEL OF OPINION CAUSALITY

*Economic factors* in this section means the way demands for goods and services are met. It includes all the processes and social forms by and through which physical things and services are identified, created, transferred, and preserved for the satisfaction of human needs and desires. It seems to be, and is, the broadest kind of term. But the definition is meant to *exclude* (a) psychological factors that influence opinion and behavior; (b) social institutions that are primarily religious, recreational, educational, and ideological; and (c) that part of the physical environment that is not exploited in the production of goods and services. Moreover, by *economic factors* we mean not only the goods and services themselves but the relationships among the individuals and groups involved in the creation, transfer, preservation, and consumption of goods and services.

Like most attempts at categorization and definition in the social sciences, this meaning is fuzzy around the edges. It is difficult to know, for example, whether some relationships are primarily religious (the selling of relics and indulgences), recreational (moviegoing by an individual or by the members of a community), or educational (the college degree as a symbol of learning or of earning power) rather than economic. Perhaps in the end it is wisest to speak only of the economic aspects or perspectives of human relations. Moviegoing is largely an economic matter for actors, producers, managers, ushers, and others whose jobs depend on it. For the individual who attends once a week or once a month, its economic impact is slight, probably negligible—although an economic component is present, inasmuch as the admission price could be spent in other ways.

## 12.2 ECONOMICS AND POLITICS IN AMERICAN LIFE

Calvin Coolidge once said, "The business of America is business." Less bluntly, many Americans and foreign visitors have observed that the pursuit of private wealth has marked our society from the beginning. In an insightful chapter of his commentary on the political life of America in the 1830s, Alexis de Tocqueville said, "The desire of acquiring the good things of this world is the prevailing passion of the American people,"[2] and he linked this economic drive to the prominence of the middle class, to a seemingly great restlessness and search for novelty, and to a parallel capacity for religious and political passions.

Others have stressed the relation (often the transferability) of economic power to political power. The interconnections of economic and political power in

2. Alexis de Tocqueville, *Democracy in America,* ed. Henry Steele Commager (London: Oxford University Press, 1946), p. 403.

America have been ably reviewed by Alpheus T. Mason: "Our Founding Fathers inherited from James Harrington's *Oceana* of 1656 the maxim that power always follows property. 'This I believe,' John Adams [said], 'to be as infallible a maxim in politics, as that action and reaction are equal, is in mechanics.'"[3]

Whoever is able to set the terms of the economic order is able in large measure to set the terms of the political order. The organization of economic life in every society is probably the most powerful determinant of political life and, through the mediation of the family or other social institutions, the most persuasive molder of opinion.[4] A strong case could be made for the revealing name by which the study of political science was known in the nineteenth century: political economy.

Nevertheless, the classical liberals of the eighteenth and nineteenth centuries overemphasized the importance of economic forces in individual and collective behavior. Human felicity, domestic tranquillity, and international peace cannot be achieved through the "unseen hand" of private economic enterprise. And, as was earlier pointed out, a major theoretical weakness of Marxism is that it adopts a near identity of economics and politics within a framework of pseudoscientific determinism. The state is much more than, as Marx called it, the "executive committee of the capitalist class."

Some political thinkers of every age have rejected the simple views of Adam Smith and Karl Marx.[5] For the basic fact is that politics is a struggle for wealth *and other forms of power.* According to Machiavelli,

> when men are no longer obliged to fight from necessity, they fight from ambition, which passion is so powerful in the hearts of men that it never leaves them, no matter to what heights they may rise. The reason of this is that nature has created men so that they desire everything, but are unable to attain it; desire being thus always greater than the faculty of acquiring, discontent with what they have and dissatisfaction with themselves result from it. . . . The Roman people were not content with having secured themselves against the

3. Alpheus T. Mason, "Business Organized as Power: The New Imperium in Imperio," *American Political Science Review* 44 (1950): 324.

4. Mason succinctly puts the case for politics over economics in the democratic state: "To escape anarchy, politics must dominate over economics. Official, politically responsible government must insist on monopolizing coercive power, as against any and all private aspirants for such power. It must do this, not because there is special virtue in established authority, or because government is or can be omniscient, but because this is the only way of avoiding chaos, the only way, as Locke's men discovered in his state of nature, to prevent individuals and groups from taking law into their own hands" (ibid., p. 342).

5. Montesquieu, for example, in *The Spirit of the Laws* (1748), bk. XX, "Of Laws in Relation to Commerce Considered in Its Nature and Distinctions." In the nineteenth century, George Cornewall Lewis wrote in *An Essay on the Government of Dependencies* (1841) that dependencies in some cases ought to be kept even if they are a net economic drain on the mother country (Oxford: Clarendon, 1891), p. 212; compare this with Adam Smith's view that dependencies ought to be abandoned if they are not paying propositions (*Wealth of Nations,* bk. V. chap. 3) and with the well-known Marxist view of the nature of capitalist imperialism.

nobles by the creation of the Tribunes, to which they had been driven by necessity. Having obtained this, they soon began to fight from ambition, and wanted to divide with the nobles their honors and possessions, being those things which men value most.[6]

*Honors* and possessions. Not just possessions. Not even possessions and honors—but honors and possessions. Like the American businessman of the nineteenth century, Marx was never able to see that, having to choose between the two, many will consciously prefer honors over possessions. Human beings give up their wealth daily for love, pride, patriotism, safety, comfort, and all kinds of objectives that are mainly noneconomic. Beyond some minimum level of physical comfort, people seek wealth primarily because it is considered a means to nonphysical ends. As Everett Hagen has pointed out in a series of brilliant articles, the psychological and social elements are often much more important than the resource factors in economic growth. Even in the most marginal and primitive economies, for example, some wealth is systematically diverted to nonproductive religious purposes, though it might, given different motivation patterns, go into capital accumulation.[7]

## 12.3 EFFECTS OF ECONOMIC STATUS

Before the introduction of survey-research techniques, the consideration of the economic basis of opinion holding was largely a matter of generalization from scattered testimony or observation, and of hypothetical (and largely unverified) statements derived from theory. Machiavelli had seen that the rulers of Renaissance Italy sought wealth as avidly as they sought power. From these observations came his generalization that "a man will suffer the loss of his father easier than he will suffer the loss of his patrimony." Marx developed a theory that insisted that capitalists, individually and as a class, were driven solely by economic considerations. He could then describe the bourgeoisie as having "pitilessly torn asunder the motley feudal ties that bound man to his natural superiors, and left remaining no other nexus between man and man than naked self-interest, callous 'cash payment' "[8]

Beyond the broadest generalization of political philosophers, what we know about economic influences on opinion holding is almost all of fairly recent origin. When public opinion as we know it began to emerge, and as it became important

---

6. Niccolo Machiavelli, *The Discourses,* Modern Library ed. (New York: Random House, 1940), p. 208.

7. Everett E. Hagen, "Economic Development: Principles and Patterns," *World Politics* 7 (1955): 448–460; "Population and Economic Growth," *American Economic Review* 49 (1959): 310–327; "How Economic Growth Begins: A General Theory Applied to Japan," *Public Opinion Quarterly* 22 (1958): 373–390; and *On the Theory of Social Change* (Homewood, Ill.: Dorsey, 1962).

8. Karl Marx and Frederick Engels, *The Communist Manifesto* (New York: New York Labor News Co., 1945), p. 11.

in the determination of policy, there was at best only a limited knowledge of the distribution of opinions by social class, occupation, and income. What was known was mainly speculation based on "common sense," primitive notions of motivation, and theories of social organization. Much of the speculation was no doubt accurate enough: financiers, moneylenders, and eastern manufacturers were properly alarmed by what they took to be the temper of debtors and inland farmers who voted Jacksonian democracy into states and nation in the 1820s and 1830s. In England the Chartists and Anti–Corn Law Leaguers accurately saw the economic nexus between the views of the landed class and protective tariffs during the same period; the leaders and militants of the early labor movement recognized, generally, the extent to which capitalist views had been written into public policy by 1890.

Nevertheless, "common sense" and theory in the absence of facts led to some very wrong judgments about opinion holding and economic organization. The Marxist view of the pervasiveness and the ever-increasing polarization of class consciousness is an outstanding example of how fact-free theory misleads. Another example is the belief, cherished until World War I by all Socialists, that the brotherhood of class is stronger than the fatherhood of nation. Equally misleading is the "common-sense" notion of classical free enterprise that the motivation of workers is entirely or mainly a matter of money incentives. Although the course of history demonstrated the fallacy of the Socialist views of ever-sharpening class consciousness and of "international solidarity," the belief in the omnipotence of money incentives was not shaken until the coming of social science research in the 1930s.

## 12.4 UNDERLYING PREFERENCE FOR PRIVATE ECONOMIC FORMS: AN ASPECT OF AMERICAN POLITICAL CULTURE

For an understanding of the influence of economic factors on political opinion holding, it may be helpful to adopt, successively, two different levels of analysis. The first perspective, or analytical level, is that of the political culture. We have seen that in every society there are basic collective value preferences and beliefs about authority and power—little-noticed and almost never challenged principles about the distribution of influence and public roles in the society, preferences and beliefs and principles that taken together constitute the political culture.

The American political culture, as we have seen, has always given high place to hard work, thrift, the cherishing of private property, and, on the other side, to a deep-lying suspicion of government enterprise. The emphasis has been on the "right" of individuals to get and keep what they have worked for—or merely to keep and enjoy the profit from what they own whether they have worked for it or not. The strength and pervasiveness of such views mean that owners of private wealth were given *political* preferment in America, whether that ownership was individual or corporate. Near the end of World War II, Gallup asked, "Is your attitude toward owners and managers of business concerns today more favorable or less favorable than it was before the war?" Results: attitude same as before the war, 36 percent; attitude more favorable, 31 percent; attitude less favorable, 19 percent; no indication whether attitude had changed, 14 percent.[9]

In the late 1960s and early 1970s there may have been some decline in the probusiness attitudes of Americans. The president of the Opinion Research Corporation reported in 1972 that "the proportion of the public indicating 'little approval' of business has jumped since 1967 from 46 percent to 60 percent," and that "concerns over ecology, consumerism and the social responsibilities of corporate management have created a skeptical if not hostile atmosphere."[10]

In 1975, 48 percent of Americans had "a great deal" or "quite a lot of" confidence in business; 47 percent had "some, very little, or no" confidence in business. (Comparable percentages for the military were 58 percent and 37 percent, for Congress 40 percent and 57 percent, and for organized labor 38 percent and 58 percent.) When business is considered by size of firm, "large companies" inspire 35 percent high confidence, 61 percent low confidence; "small companies" 57 percent high, 39 percent low.[11] From 1978 through June 1982 respondents in a series of samples were found to have consistently 92 to 95 percent "highly or moderately favorable opinions" of "most small businesses" and 62 to 70 percent highly or moderately favorable opinions of "most large business corporations."[12] Despite changes in the questions asked from 1945 to 1982, it is clear that private enterprise has sustained support in the United States.

Analyses by Seymour Lipset and William Schneider seem to have captured the trends of the last twenty years in regard to the basic probusiness attitudes of Americans. Reviewing the general decline in public confidence in major social institutions, they conclude "that business, labor, and government are all suffering from the same disability: The public believes that, unlike many other institutions, they are motivated primarily by self-interest." The ambivalence of popular attitudes is apparent: "What our political system has in common with our economic system is competitiveness; it is, indeed, competition which most Americans think makes democracy and free enterprise work, but this does not mean that Americans admire the kinds of activities and values inherent in competition." Their conclusion seems accurate: "The American people still believe in the legitimacy and vitality of the 'American system.' What bothers the public. . . is the apparent growth of concentrations of power and the seemingly cynical, self-interested abuse of that power by those at the summits of government, labor,

---

9. Hadley Cantril and Mildred Strunk, *Public Opinion, 1935–1946* (Princeton: Princeton University Press, 1951), p. 341.
10. *New York Times,* February 8, 1972.
11. Gallup, *Opinion Index,* May 30–June 2, 1975.
12. "Opinion Roundup," *Public Opinion,* October/November 1982, 24, citing *Roper Report 82–6.*

and business. . . . There is still an enormous reservoir of trust in the economic and political system."[13]

Advertising, the faithful running dog of American business, is very favorably regarded by the public. Stephen Greyser and Raymond Bauer concluded from studies over eighteen years (1946–1964) that "roughly three quarters of the American public see advertising as an essential economic feature making specific economic contributions, particularly in the form of an improved standard of living." About half of the public over the years said they believed much advertising was false, and 70 to 80 percent believed advertising leads people to buy things they didn't need or couldn't afford, yet a healthy majority said that advertising was getting more truthful and responsible.[14] The same apparent paradoxes and optimism were seen in an August 1983 survey: 88 percent of a national sample said that "advertising was excellent, good or fair, while only 9% said it was poor," 49 percent agreed that "advertising is generally honest and trustworthy" and 44 percent disagreed, and "78% said advertising is accurate, while 18% found it misleading." According to the author of the report, one possible "explanation for this discrepancy. . .is that while the overall perception of honesty is poor, people believe they are selective in their personal use of advertising information."[15]

The evidence seems clear enough. Although the public has large and persistent doubt about the ethics of business, that doubt is rather easily overridden by the powerful cultural tendencies to prefer private forms of economic power.

## 12.5 ECONOMIC INFLUENCES AND ELECTORAL POLITICS

Economic factors are said to influence three aspects of political opinion holding and electoral behavior in the contemporary United States: voter turnout, candidate choice, and preferences on issues. Evidence on the first point is incontrovertible; on the second the evidence is, on balance, supportive; on the third, the findings so far suggest a yes-and-no conclusion.

One of the few certainties in American elections is that voter turnout is higher among those in the higher economic brackets. Table 12–1 illustrates this "law."

With regard to whether voters' preferences for candidates are based on their economic perceptions, the research findings are mixed. There is general agreement that incumbent officeholders are likely to do less well in reelection bids in

---

13. Seymour M. Lipset and William Schneider, "How's Business? What the Public Thinks," *Public Opinion,* July/August 1978, 45, 47. And see the development of these themes by the same authors in *The Confidence Gap: Business, Labor, and Government in the Public Mind* (New York: Free Press, 1983), especially chap. 12, "Is There a Legitimacy Crisis?" pp. 375–412.

14. Stephen A. Greyser and Raymond A. Bauer, "Americans and Advertising: Thirty Years of Public Opinion," *Public Opinion Quarterly* 30 (1966): 73, 74.

15. Nancy Millman, "The Image of Advertising," *Advertising Age* 54 (October 24, 1983): 18.

**Table 12-1** Voter turnout in national elections, 1952–1980, by income percentile.

| Income percentile | 1952 | 1956 | 1960 | 1964 | 1968 | 1972 | 1976 | 1980 |
|---|---|---|---|---|---|---|---|---|
| 95–100% | 95.0 | 89.6 | 94.0 | 87.8 | 92.5 | 90.4 | 91.1 | 86.5 |
| 68–94 | 84.7 | 82.8 | 85.4 | 85.7 | 86.8 | 86.2 | 80.3 | 79.8 |
| 34–67 | 75.8 | 76.2 | 81.2 | 79.0 | 79.3 | 70.5 | 70.9 | 70.8 |
| 17–33 | 68.6 | 65.3 | 70.8 | 72.9 | 66.1 | 62.9 | 65.3 | 68.3 |
| 0–16 | 53.3 | 52.7 | 65.4 | 63.8 | 60.5 | 60.1 | 54.4 | 59.4 |

Source: Warren Miller et al., eds., *American National Election Studies Data Sourcebook, 1952–1978* (Cambridge: Harvard University Press, 1980), 317. For 1980 data, University of Michigan, Center for Political Studies, 1980 Election Survey.

periods of economic downturn. Gerald Kramer says that "economic fluctuations ...are important influences on congressional elections, with economic upturn helping the congressional candidates of the incumbent party, and economic decline benefitting the opposition. In quantitative terms, a 10% decrease in per capita real personal income would cost the incumbent administration 4 or 5 percent of the congressional vote, other things being equal."[16]

Several studies, however, have been unable to demonstrate a connection at the individual level between voters' candidate choices and their perceptions of economic forces. When, for example, Morris Fiorina compared the outcomes of four elections (1962, 1966, 1968, and 1972) with voters' responses on whether their incomes were higher, lower, or the same as they had been the year before the election, he found that the responses had "virtually no relationship to the congressional vote" and a "very weak" one to the presidential vote.[17] Stephen Weatherford, on the other hand, analyzing congressional vote-switching between the 1958 and 1960 elections, discovered a small but statistically significant propensity for working-class citizens to deviate from their expected votes because of economic conditions.[18] Henry Kenski found almost no relationship between inflation and presidential popularity in the Kennedy, Johnson, and Nixon administrations,[19] and Roderick Kiewiet discovered that the inflation issue did not influence the presidential vote from 1956 to 1976, thus supporting Kenski, but that the unemployment issue *did* have a modest impact: the Democratic vote increased among the unemployed.[20]

The best conclusion in respect to candidate choice and voters' economic

16. Gerald H. Kramer, "Short-Term Fluctuations in U.S. Voting Behavior, 1896–1964," *American Political Science Review* 65 (1971): 140–141.

17. Morris P. Fiorina, *Retrospective Voting in American National Elections* (New Haven: Yale University Press, 1981), p. 29.

18. M. Stephen Weatherford, "Economic Conditions and Electoral Outcomes: Class Differences in the Political Response to Recession," *American Journal of Political Science* 22 (1978): 932–933.

19. Henry C. Kenski, "Inflation and Presidential Popularity," *Public Opinion Quarterly* 41 (1977): 86–90.

20. D. Roderick Kiewiet, "Policy-Oriented Voting in Response to Economic Issues," *American Political Science Review* 75 (1981): 448–549.

perspectives is perhaps that "under ordinary circumstances, voters evidently do not make connections between their own personal economic experiences—however vivid, immediate, or otherwise significant—and their political attitudes and preference." [21] In any case, party identification, ideology, and noneconomic "personality" reasons almost always exert much more influence on voters' choices of candidates.

## 12.6 ECONOMIC INFLUENCES ON OPINIONS REGARDING SPECIFIC PUBLIC ISSUES

The concept of political culture is helpful for understanding basic tendencies and preferences of Americans for private forms of wealth and power. But the political culture will not determine or enable us to predict the distribution of opinions of Americans on specific controversial questions.

Any sophistication we now possess in understanding the economic basis of opinion holding has been gained not at the expense of the fundamental proposition that economic factors produce distinctive opinion patterns, but in the elaboration of what kinds of factors tend to be associated with what kinds of opinions and with what significance. A sample of survey results illustrates the contributions to more accurate knowledge made by cross-sectional studies of adult American opinion.

In the following cases, the economic factor is shown to relate to opinion distribution in expected ways:

1. In general, do you approve or disapprove of labor unions? (Gallup, May 1979)

| Occupational segment | Approve | Disapprove | No opinion |
|---|---|---|---|
| National total | 55% | 33% | 12% |
| Professional and business | 48 | 42 | 10 |
| Clerical and sales | 61 | 26 | 13 |
| Manual workers | 62 | 27 | 11 |
| Non–labor force | 51 | 32 | 17 |
| Labor union families only | 77 | 17 | 6 |
| Non-labor-union families | 48 | 38 | 14 |

2. Should Social Security benefits be subject to federal income tax, the same as any other income? (Gallup, December 1982)

| Income | Approve | Disapprove | Don't know |
|---|---|---|---|
| $25,000+ | 22% | 73% | 5% |
| 20,000–24,999 | 16 | 79 | 5 |
| 15,000–19,999 | 21 | 73 | 6 |
| 10,000–14,999 | 16 | 77 | 7 |

---

21. Donald R. Kinder and D. Roderick Kiewiet, "Economic Discontent and Political Behavior: The Role of Personal Grievances and Collective Judgments in Congressional Voting," *American Journal of Political Science* 23 (1979): 522. See also John R. Hibbing and John R. Alford, "The Electoral Impact of Economic Conditions: Who is Held Responsible?" ibid. 25 (1981): 423–439.

| Income | Approve | Disapprove | Don't know |
|--------|---------|------------|------------|
| 5,000–9,999 | 23 | 68 | 9 |
| Under $5,000 | 14 | 67 | 19 |

It is in regard to opinions on issues that have a clear and unambiguous economic impact that economic status turns out to be an influencing factor. This correlation is hardly to be wondered at. What is surprising about question 2 above is that only 14 percent of the poorest approved of something that would be in their interest. But many people—and perhaps especially the poorest and least sophisticated—have trouble sorting out what *is* in their interest (see the discussion in Section 12.7, below).

Distribution of opinions on general questions of policy to aid lower-income Americans shows the effects of economic status, as one would expect.

3.  Do you feel that the government in Washington should see to it that every person has a job and a good standard of living...or do you think the government should just let each person get ahead on his own?[22]

| Income groups | 1956 | 1960 | 1964 | 1968 | 1972 | 1976 | 1978 |
|---------------|------|------|------|------|------|------|------|
| Top (95–100%) | –10 | 14 | –42 | –22 | –45 | –50 | –56 |
| High-middle (68–94%) | 9 | 18 | –30 | –24 | –25 | –32 | –45 |
| Middle (34–67%) | 28 | 39 | –11 | –24 | –15 | –16 | –35 |
| Low-middle (17–33%) | 43 | 45 | – 3 | –12 | 1 | – 1 | –14 |
| Bottom (0–16%) | 59 | 61 | 15 | 8 | 14 | 19 | 0 |

Note: Figures represent "percentage difference index," proportion supporting government intervention minus proportion opposed.

4.  Do you think there should be a government insurance plan which would cover all medical and hospital expenses, or should medical expenses be paid by individuals and through private insurance?

| Income groups | 1956 | 1960 | 1964 | 1968 | 1972 | 1976 | 1978 |
|---------------|------|------|------|------|------|------|------|
| Top (95–100%) | – 5 | 14 | –11 | 5 | –25 | –34 | –40 |
| High-middle (68–94%) | 10 | 16 | 2 | 16 | – 4 | –12 | –12 |
| Middle (34–67%) | 23 | 40 | 25 | 17 | 5 | – 2 | – 1 |
| Low-middle (17–33%) | 43 | 55 | 31 | 38 | 2 | 12 | 9 |
| Bottom (0–16%) | 55 | 84 | 51 | 48 | 26 | 34 | 25 |

Note: Figures represent "percentage difference index," proportion supporting government intervention minus proportion opposed.

## 12.7 ECONOMIC STATUS, LEVELS OF KNOWLEDGE, ISSUE SALIENCE, AND OPINIONS

There are two main reasons why economic factors do not control opinions as

---

22. These data, and those on question 4 below, are from Warren E. Miller et al., eds., *American National Election Studies Data Sourcebook, 1952–1978* (Cambridge: Harvard University Press, 1980), pp. 185, 189.

much as we might expect them to: (a) we often do not know enough about a situation to see clearly where our economic interests lie; (b) the economic aspect of an issue may not be salient for us (that is, we may see it as a social, ethical, religious, or political matter even when it deals with distribution of wealth).

Determining one's own economic interest is not easy. In their excellent study of business attitudes toward tariff policy, Raymond Bauer, Ithiel de Sola Pool, and Lewis Anthony Dexter point out:

> The theory of self-interest as a complete and all-embracing explanation of behavior breaks down when we realize that self-interest is itself a set of mental images and convictions. Whose self-interest does a man see it as his role to serve—his own as a physical individual, that of the corporation for which he works, or that of some other unit? If the corporation is the unit, who does he perceive as constituting the corporation? Over what period of time is he seeking a maximum—the short or the long term? What values does he pursue—solely money, or also respect and other values? The role businessmen played, the communications that impinged upon them, their ideology—all influenced their definitions and perceptions of their self-interest.[23]

Even if self-interest could be adequately defined, the question of alternative ways of maximizing it remains. Self-interest and opportunity are not always equally matched. Bauer, Pool, and Dexter point out that the most important determinant of the messages produced by businessmen on tariff questions was "neither self-interest nor ideology, but the institutional structures which facilitated or blocked the production of messages." Thus behavior and attitudes in regard to what is proper to think and do about the economic aspects of political issues are influenced not by naked self-interest alone, but by considerations of role, access to information, and support or nonsupport of the environment.

Attempts to show the relationships between economic factors and patterns of opinion distribution often reveal the effects of differences in levels of knowledge. The generalization is clear: those of lower economic status often have no knowledge or no opinion (the two may be but are not always the same) and therefore fail to appreciate where their economic advantage lies.

Even those who have a good deal of knowledge and interest in a question, whether or not they are of low economic status, may not be able to sort out their own advantage. The distributions of opinions on issues that are complex, diffuse in their impact, or dependent on many decisions not controllable or predictable by respondents will be quite independent of economic status.

On wage-price controls as they existed in 1973, income level seemed to be unrelated to preference for more strict or less strict controls:

---

23. Raymond A. Bauer, Ithiel de Sola Pool, and Lewis Anthony Dexter, *American Business and Public Policy* (New York: Atherton, 1963), p. 226.

1. Do you think wage-price controls should be made more strict, less strict, or kept about as they are? (Gallup, May 1973)

| Income | More | Less | Same | No opinion |
|---|---|---|---|---|
| $15,000 and over | 54% | 19% | 21% | 6% |
| 10,000–14,999 | 54 | 16 | 24 | 6 |
| 7,000–9,999 | 56 | 16 | 22 | 6 |
| 5,000–6,999 | 54 | 17 | 19 | 10 |
| 3,000–4,999 | 55 | 18 | 18 | 9 |
| Under $3,000 | 48 | 21 | 19 | 11 |

But on the general question of whether wage-price controls should be reapplied in 1980, the poor seemed to be slightly more favorable to controls than the wealthier strata of Americans.

2. Would you favor or oppose having the government bring back wage and price controls? (Gallup, February 1980)

| Income | Favor | Oppose | No opinion |
|---|---|---|---|
| $25,000 and over | 49% | 44% | 7% |
| 20,000–24,999 | 58 | 36 | 6 |
| 15,000–19,999 | 54 | 40 | 6 |
| 10,000–14,999 | 62 | 30 | 8 |
| 5,000–9,999 | 67 | 21 | 12 |
| Under $5,000 | 61 | 25 | 14 |

And on the effects of "Reaganomics" in the early 1980s there seemed to be a good fit between U.S. macroeconomic policy and respondents' understanding of their economic status.

3. In the long run do you feel your economic situation will be better or worse because of the Reagan economic policies? (Gallup, November 1982)

| Income | Better | Worse | Same | Don't know |
|---|---|---|---|---|
| $25,000 and over | 57% | 27% | 12% | 4% |
| 20,000–24,999 | 45 | 32 | 17 | 6 |
| 15,000–19,999 | 44 | 32 | 13 | 11 |
| 10,000–14,999 | 33 | 35 | 19 | 13 |
| 5,000–9,999 | 23 | 44 | 17 | 16 |
| Under $5,000 | 19 | 41 | 20 | 20 |

On foreign policy issues, income seems to be related to isolationism and to a general ideological chauvinism; the poor are less internationalist and less generous with aid to "countries not like us."

1.  This country would be better off if we just stayed home and did not concern ourselves with problems in other parts of the world?[24]

| Income groups | 1956 | 1960 | 1968 | 1972 | 1976 |
|---|---|---|---|---|---|
| Top (95–100%) | 67 | 88 | 80 | 87 | 69 |
| High-middle (68–94%) | 52 | 72 | 74 | 71 | 61 |
| Middle (34–67%) | 40 | 51 | 55 | 62 | 46 |
| Low-middle (17–33%) | 20 | 25 | 41 | 48 | 23 |
| Low (0–16%) | – 8 | 3 | 12 | 29 | 0 |

Note: Figures represent levels on an index of internationalism: the higher the value, the more internationalist.

2.  The United States should give help to foreign countries even if they don't stand for the same things we do.

| Income groups | 1956 | 1960 | 1964 | 1968 | 1972 | 1976 |
|---|---|---|---|---|---|---|
| Top (95–100%) | 36 | 57 | 56 | 39 | 22 | –11 |
| High-middle (68–94%) | 25 | 43 | 42 | 30 | – 2 | –17 |
| Middle (34–67%) | 11 | 24 | 36 | 13 | –13 | –20 |
| Low-middle (17–33%) | 16 | 23 | 29 | 4 | –23 | –22 |
| Low (0–16%) | 13 | 24 | 15 | –16 | –15 | –18 |

Note: Figures represent levels on an index of support for foreign aid: the higher the value, the greater the support.

On the other hand, economic status seems to be unrelated to more remote and complex issues of foreign policy.

1.  In general, is the United Nations organization doing a good job, or a poor job, in trying to solve problems it has had to face? (Gallup, November 1983)

| Income | Good | Poor | No opinion |
|---|---|---|---|
| $40,000 and over | 35% | 57% | 8% |
| 30,000–39,999 | 38 | 53 | 9 |
| 20,000–29,999 | 35 | 58 | 7 |
| 10,000–19,999 | 36 | 49 | 15 |
| Under $10,000 | 38 | 43 | 19 |

2.  Which one of the following should the United States do with respect to Iran if: (a) the hostages are released unharmed . . . or (b) one or more of the hostages is harmed . . . . (Gallup, January 1980)

| Occupation | Do nothing (a) | Do nothing (b) | Punish diplomatically or economically (a) | Punish diplomatically or economically (b) | Use military force (a) | Use military force (b) | Don't know (a) | Don't know (b) |
|---|---|---|---|---|---|---|---|---|
| Professional and business | 22% | 2% | 68% | 55% | 4% | 37% | 6% | 6% |
| Clerical/sales | 17 | — | 68 | 54 | 6 | 36 | 9 | 10 |

24. These data, and those on question 2 below, are from Miller et al., eds., *Election Studies Data Sourcebook*, pp. 235, 243.

| Occupation | Do nothing | | Punish diplomatically or economically | | Use military force | | Don't know | |
|---|---|---|---|---|---|---|---|---|
| Manual | 27 | 3 | 60 | 49 | 7 | 40 | 6 | 8 |
| Non-labor force | 28 | 2 | 55 | 53 | 6 | 29 | 11 | 16 |

Some questions that refer to potential economic policy are so unclear when they are stated as generalizations that they produce no pattern of response by economic class. The uncertain prospects of compulsory mediation in labor disputes produced this distribution of opinion in 1939:

Would you favor a law requiring employers and workers to submit their differences to a federal labor board before a strike could be called? (Gallup, May 1939)

| Economic level | Oppose mediation | Favor mediation |
|---|---|---|
| Upper class | 84% | 16% |
| Middle class | 87 | 13 |
| Lower class | 85 | 15 |

When the question of compulsory mediation can be set in a specific environment, when respondents are alerted to the existence of the issue and have more particular knowledge of the views of those who might mediate, the anticipated differential effect of economic class may be reflected in responses to poll questions. The Labor–Management Act of 1947 (Taft-Hartley) provided for compulsory mediation and a sixty-day "cooling-off period" upon presidential order. As soon as the act was passed, the labor unions began a campaign for its repeal or drastic amendment. In a climate of heightened awareness, the economic-class implications became obvious, and the polls began to show this kind of opinion distribution:

Many businessmen and Republican leaders think that the Taft-Hartley law has worked well and should be kept pretty much as it is. Do you agree or disagree? (Gallup, April 1949)

| Occupational segment | Agree | Disagree | No opinion |
|---|---|---|---|
| National total | 43% | 38% | 19% |
| Union members only | 22 | 66 | 12 |
| Professional and business | 62 | 26 | 12 |
| Farmers | 51 | 27 | 22 |
| White-collar employees | 43 | 39 | 18 |
| Manual workers | 33 | 47 | 20 |

A specific question brings to the surface economically significant opinion patterns that are not apparent in the absence of particular meaning to respondents. In 1939, compulsory mediation was not felt to be of more or less advantage to employers or employees; in 1947, in the midst of a general antilabor swing of the public mood and a swarm of labor-regulation bills before Congress, the class meaning was apparent.

## 12.8 ECONOMIC STATUS AND OPINIONS ABOUT DEMOCRACY

Issues with clear economic implications for various income or occupational groups display opinion distributions consistent with the economic biases of the grouped respondents. It is not at all strange that more than half of the poor in California in 1938 favored a state pension plan for those over fifty and unemployed. What is surprising—and more significant for the study of human motivation—is that *almost half (46%) of the poor did not support the idea.* People do not always vote their own economic interest even when it is plain to see. More than two-thirds of the states have general sales taxes, many of them approved by a majority of low-income voters, whose own interests call for a graduated income tax instead.

However interesting the surprisingly imperfect fit between economic interest and popular opinion on public policy, it is of less importance than whether economic status affects opinions about the values of the democratic order. More simply stated: do economic and economic-class factors relate significantly to a belief in democracy? There are theories that the very rich and the very poor are less attached to democratic views than those with middle incomes. To be sure, these theories rely on criteria of class stratification more complex than income alone but the economic dimension of class is undeniably basic, no matter how it is qualified by other social and psychological variables.

By themselves, economic factors seem to have only a small influence on antidemocratic or prodemocratic opinions and behavior. The very poor may, because of their poverty, have to devote themselves entirely to economic efforts at the expense of all prodemocratic sentiment. The poor person not only may be indifferent to democratic values but may have antidemocratic values—though they will probably stem from factors other than poverty. Lipset has documented the "realization that extremist and intolerant movements in modern society are more likely to be based on the lower classes than on the middle and upper classes."[25] The influences that produce working-class authoritarianism do not seem to be directly economic, but the *by-products,* so to speak, of insufficient material resources. The authoritarian behavior of the lower classes is almost wholly due to social disorganization (for example, lack of family stability), personality deprivations (for example, inordinate punishment, tension, and aggression in childhood), and narrow, rigid attitude sets resulting from lack of education and repeated ego denials. Edward Grabb's analysis confirms the view that intolerance, as one central component of authoritarianism, is indeed higher among the working class than among white-collar/sales, managerial, or professional Americans. He argues, however, that "one need not conclude that greater intolerance is somehow a necessary and immutable fact of workingclass culture.

25. Seymour Martin Lipset, *Political Man: Essays on the Sociology of Democracy* (Garden City, N.Y.: Doubleday, 1960), p. 97.

It appears, instead, that what class differences do exist are largely due to factors such as education and income which are *related to but distinct from* occupational class *per se*."[26] John L. Sullivan and his colleagues say that social status has demonstrable *indirect* effect on intolerance because, as we have noted, "it is one of the major factors influencing personality and political ideology."[27]

Economic factors are evidently related to political activity and inactivity. They have been shown to be significant variables, though often mediated by related noneconomic variables, such as education and group membership. Heinz Eulau and Peter Schneider found evidence for the view that income and other economic factors are not so directly important as education, which "seems particularly relevant in a study of political involvement."[28] A study of local political participation produced the same results; scores on a participation index ranged from 1.64 to 4.75 by income level and from 0.75 to 5.77 by education level.[29] Donald Devine agreed, finding that of demographic variables associated with "attentiveness" (a measure of concern for, knowledge of, and participation in public affairs) the most important was education, with income next, followed by occupation, sex, race, and age.[30]

Income is obviously not the only index of the economic order or of how that order may relate to individual opinion holding or to statistical patterns of opinion holding. Opinion analysis by occupational category is common and often contributes to our understanding. Robert Lane points out that certain occupational groups in the United States are notable for high levels of political activity. Miners and sailors, among whom "contact is close and reinforced by mutual interdependence in the face of danger," seem to have high rates of political participation. Farmers, isolated in their work conditions, have lower rates. Other occupational groups with high propensity for political participation are salespeople, whose verbal skills and many contacts allow them to become communication and organizational links in politics; civil servants, who have an interest in electing their employers; and teachers and lawyers, who have self-defined "civic leader" roles.[31]

Generally, occupation, like income, as a single variable, is less significant than education in the explanation of opinion variation. A widely cited study by Richard Centers, based on a national sample of 1,092 adult males, gathered

26. Edward G. Grabb, "Working-Class Authoritarianism and Tolerance of Outgroups: A Reassessment," *Public Opinion Quarterly* 43 (Spring 1979): 45.

27. John L. Sullivan, George E. Marcus, Stanley Feldman, and James E. Piereson, "The Sources of Political Tolerance: A Multivariate Analysis," *American Political Science Review* 75 (1981): 104.

28. Heinz Eulau and Peter Schneider, "Dimensions of Political Involvement," *Public Opinion Quarterly* 20 (1956): 132.

29. Robert E. Agger and Vincent Ostrom, "Political Participation in a Small Community," in *Political Behavior,* eds. Heinz Eulau et al. (New York: Free Press, 1956), p. 139.

30. Donald J. Devine, *The Attentive Public: Polyarchical Democracy* (Chicago: Rand McNally, 1970), p. 94.

31. Robert E. Lane, *Political Life* (New York: Free Press, 1959), pp. 332–333.

opinions on the role of women in society, the importance of religion, confidence in technology, why some people succeed economically and others do not, sympathies and antipathies toward other occupational classes, and racial and ethnic prejudices. Results were largely what one would suspect from common-sense predictions of occupational class opinions—except that all persons, even those of lowest economic status, seemed to believe that being poor and unsuccessful was basically the fault of the individual. Occupational differences on values related to the maintenance of the democratic society did not appear to be significant in Centers' study; here again education was shown to be more important than occupation.[32]

## 12.9 ECONOMIC INFLUENCE MODIFIED BY PERSONALITY FACTORS AND GROUP MEMBERSHIP

In the funnel of opinion causality, economic factors, as measured by income, occupation, or other indexes, interact constantly with noneconomic factors. Psychological factors related to self-image, world view, and success or failure in the integration of personality and environment are important and have been briefly alluded to in earlier chapters. More specific to the matter of the influence of economic factors on opinion is the way these factors may be mediated by psychological characteristics. As Stanley Feldman says, sometimes people act politically for self-consciously economic motives, and sometimes economic "self-interest plays little or no role in political behavior or in the development of political preferences and attitudes." He says "it depends on how the individual interprets the nature of the problem and where he assigns responsibility."[33]

The effects of economic factors on opinion holding are further mediated and modified by organizations. Commitments to party membership, to group ideology, to role expectations of leaders and followers, and to other aspects of group behavior will often significantly distort the more directly economic influences on opinion holding. Thus wealthy socialists and liberals will support high-spending policies that bear heavily on them as individual taxpayers; or debt-ridden small businesspeople, for the sake of their attachment to free enterprise, will oppose federal aid to their local schools at the cost of continued overtaxation of their suburban tract homes.

Studies of the political opinions of union members and nonunion workers demonstrate the effect of group membership in modifying views presumed to have important economic sources. In research on the 1952 presidential vote, the Survey Research Center found that labor-union members and their families "did

---

32. Richard Centers, "Attitude and Belief in Relation to Occupational Stratification," *Journal of Social Psychology* 27 (1948): 185.

33. Stanley Feldman, "Economic Self-Interest and Political Behavior," *American Journal of Political Science* 26 (1982): 463.

not differ from the rest of the population in the extent of their concern with parties or candidates, [but] they were clearly more likely to be concerned with issues."[34] All studies of the matter indicate that union members vote more uniformly Democratic than do nonmembers. Their political opinions (assuming that expressions of vote intention and actual voting performance reflect opinions) are clearly strengthened by group membership.[35]

After reviewing evidence from three national surveys, Richard Hamilton concludes that among American skilled, semiskilled, and unskilled workers, "the hypothesis that greater wealth leads to greater conservatism is not supported by the data." Social scientists, he says, should treat warily claims "about economic factors as determinants of political behavior." "In lieu of the economic factors it would appear that genuinely sociological factors such as group membership, pressures, and influences should be considered as likely explanatory factors."[36]

Charles Prysby suggests that nineteenth- and early-twentieth-century notions of social class seem less and less pertinent to policy orientations in the 1980s:

> It appears that the distinction between white-collar and blue-collar workers currently does little to explain economic policy orientations. Cleavages between those in the public sector and those in the private sector and between those in the industrial sector and those in the service sector, to mention just the most obvious ones, appear to be more significant. This is particularly true for some of the newly emerging economic issues, such as inflation and pollution. Quite possibly, as the U.S. takes on more of the characteristics of a post-industrial society, these new economic cleavages will further develop and expand.[37]

As a final commentary on why economic factors do not correlate highly with political opinions, consider the fact that political parties in the United States are not ideological parties based on economic class. Tradition, party history, the decentralized structure of government (which results in discrete and overlapping party objectives), and a mobile society that allows (even encourages) an individual to hitch the wagon of political opinions to the star of aspirations rather than to economic state combine to render fatuous any view of a simple correspondence between economic forces and political opinions as reflected in party membership. Whether political parties ought to be more closely based on eco-

---

34. Angus Campbell, Gerald Gurin, and Warren E. Miller, *The Voter Decides* (New York: Harper & Row, 1954), p. 154.

35. Poll data indicate that in the six presidential elections from 1952 through 1972, members of union families consistently voted from 3 to 7% more Democratic than the manual-labor category as a whole (*Gallup Opinion Index*, December 1972, p. 10).

36. Richard F. Hamilton, "Skill Level and Politics," *Public Opinion Quarterly* 29 (1965): 399. See also Robert Alford, "The Role of Social Class in American Voting Behavior," *Western Political Quarterly* 16 (1963): 180–193.

37. Charles L. Prysby, "Mass Policy Orientations on Economic Issues in Post-Industrial America," *Journal of Politics* 41 (May 1979): 563.

nomic class is a question of interest and concern. But the fact that in the United States they are not contradicts Mark Twain's aphorism quoted at the start of this chapter.

There are, of course, some "corn-pone opinions." On some matters, economics presses hard on politics, and political opinions are determined by the appearance or reality of the getting and spending processes. But on most matters of public concern, the relations between the economic and the political are much too subtle to be captured by any determinist prescription and are intricately interwoven with other social and psychological forces.

# DYNAMICS OF PUBLIC OPINION

In the preceding chapters we have been concerned with the nature, the sources, and, in a sense, the ingredients of public opinion. First we dealt with the meaning of public opinion, its measurement, and some problems of the use and abuse of polling in a free society. Next we suggested a model (borrowed from other social scientists) of the opinion-forming process and considered briefly how culture and some of the larger psychological, sociological, and economic forces act as limiting and influencing factors in the shaping and reshaping of opinion. Those forces provide background values and contexts for individual opinions about contemporary issues. Family, schools, religious organizations, and economic status are factors in political socialization, but peer groups and primary groups generally have more immediate impact on political opinions. The influence of the mass media, too, tends to be direct rather than contextual.

We shall focus here on the specialized communication techniques and inter-personal relationships that, in most cases at least, tend to have immediate effects on the creation and redirection of opinion.

We are still dealing with public opinion—with views expressed by significant numbers of persons on issues of general importance—but, for clarity of exposition, we shall have to move back and forth from the aggregate to the individual level. In trying to understand the relationship between voting and opinions, for example, we may suppose that low turnout among poor people (expressed in probabilities and percentages, the language of aggregate data) is related to low sense of political efficacy (which is a measurement of an individual characteristic). In our analysis of the mass media, we shall consider such group phenomena as candidate choice in relation to exposure to opinions on issues in newspapers, to individuals' choice of newspapers, and parts of newspapers they read. We shall examine how and why the individual holds what opinions on public questions, and try to determine in what proportion the various points of view on an issue are shared by the members of the public created by that issue. Our concern may be represented by the following diagram.

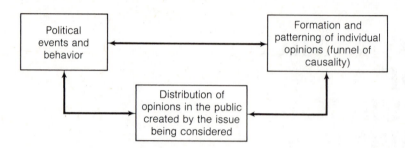

We want to understand political events and behavior. To do so, we need to know something about the politically relevant opinion held by the individual (its cause, intensity, and relation to other opinions) and about the distribution of that opinion in the mass (that is, in the public or publics involved).

Part 4 focuses on the ways face-to-face and mass communication between opinion leaders and opinion followers shape and reshape both individual views and mass distributions.

## Chapter 13

# Communication
# and Opinion

*Communication* is the creation of a social interaction of individuals by the use of expressive signs. It is, says Colin Cherry, the "sharing of elements of behaviors, or modes of life, by the existence of sets of rules and sign usage."[1]

Human communication may be distinguished from animal communication on the basis of its flexibility, its adaptiveness, and its ability to deal with such concepts as space and time. The *coinage* (more technically, the *stimulus*) of communication is the "sign," and signs may be—still in Cherry's terms—languages, codes, or logical sign systems.

Continuing our definition above, we may say that communication is *the meaningful use of signs to establish social relationships.* In most cases, we may narrow our consideration to language as the stimulus (sign), since, except for gestures and symbols, the currency of communication is the spoken or printed word.[2] More than three thousand languages and dialects are spoken in the world today. Many have no written forms—that is, they have no conventional visual symbols that represent the sounds of speech and the ideas those sounds convey—and there are probably only seventy-five to a hundred major languages. But even this number testifies to the flexibility of human invention and the variety of social customs. English is spoken in more places and by more people, as either first or second language, than any other language in the world.

In this book we deal very largely with communication through language and

---

1. Colin Cherry, *On Human Communication,* 3rd ed. (Cambridge,: M.I.T. Press, 1978), p. 6.

2. Of course, such group symbols as national and party flags, songs, salutes, and dances have been frequent and vital sources and shapers of political opinion. Furthermore, the subtleties of body language and other forms of nonverbal communication may have some importance for political opinions; such things are by definition subjective and immeasurable. An interesting and provocative treatment of nonverbal communication is Ashley Montagu and Floyd Matson. *The Human Connection* (New York: McGraw-Hill, 1979).

with the relationship between the small and large communication networks that influence individuals' opinions on issues of public importance.

## 13.1 COMMUNICATION NETWORKS

Communication creates social meaning through mutually understandable signs. The simplest form is that of individual A initiating a sign, which is more or less understandable as A intended it, to individual B. Thus:

$$A \longrightarrow \text{Sign} \longrightarrow B$$

Let us assume that A is a sentry. He becomes aware of B and calls, "Halt." B is then aware of A, and he is aware that he must stop or run the risk of being shot. A simple communication network has been established. The network becomes a conversation when B responds to A's next query, "Who goes there?" by giving his name. A meaningful social relationship exists as a product of communication.

But instead of speaking, perhaps A levels his rifle at B. B recognizes the meaning of A's movement (the sign) and raises his arms. Again a meaningful social relationship has been created through communication. Spoken or written language, though usual in communication, is not essential.

The simplest communication network consists of two individuals exchanging meaningful signs. The primary dyad is not only the simplest but in all probability the most important network for the making and remaking of opinions, public as well as private. Husband–wife, parent–child, friend–friend, employer–employee, coworkers—all these two-person relationships inform the opinions of each of us. The two-person net constitutes (a) a powerful direct influence on individual opinions and (b) the basic structure for more complex communication patterns.

It is now common to distinguish *primary-* from *secondary-group relationships.* Each has its own communication networks, with characteristic and differential effects on public opinion.

### 13.11  Primary groups and primary communication networks

The sociologist Charles H. Cooley was perhaps the first to recognize the basic distinction between primary and secondary human groups. In 1909 he described *primary groups* as "those characterized by intimate face-to-face cooperation and association."[3] George Homans, a latter-day student of small-group behavior, explicitly added the element of *frequent communication* to the definition of the primary group, which, according to him, is "a number of persons who communicate with each other often over a span of time, and who are few enough so that

---

3. Charles H. Cooley, *Social Organization* (New York: Scribner, 1909), p. 23.

each person is able to communicate with all the others, not at second-hand, through other people, but face-to-face."[4]

The common contemporary definition of the primary group is a *collection of persons who interact as individuals and who are distinguishable as individuals from one another.* The *dyad,* or two-person unit, is the simplest such group. Work groups, bridge clubs, school classes, and dozens of other ordinary human aggregates also constitute primary groups. Cooley's requirement that the members communicate face to face need not be taken too literally; it is not necessary that the members of a primary group see each other or be in each other's presence. A conference telephone call produces a primary group—and a primary communication network—though the persons engaged in conversation may be thousands of miles apart and, except for that particular interaction, total strangers. The only essential ingredients of the primary group and of the primary communication network are that the individuals who comprise it be recognizable as individuals and that there be some concerted (probably goal-directed) pattern of activity among them.

Primary groups and the communication networks they establish vary greatly in function, objective, membership, and degree of formality. Some are wholly and permanently apolitical; some are wholly and permanently political; many have some actual or potential political implications activated at various times and in various degrees.[5]

## 13.12 Secondary groups and mass-communication networks

All group relationships in which the members are not recognizable as individuals are *secondary groups.* Categorical groups—all twenty-year-olds, for example, or all left-handed males—are one type of secondary group, normally of little concern for anything but statistical convenience. Our main interest here is what David Truman calls *institutionalized groups,* both primary and secondary. Institutionalized groups—the family, organized religious bodies, corporations, civic and fraternal clubs—show a rather high degree of formality, uniformity, and generality. Those not of the face-to-face variety are what we choose to call secondary groups.[6] In the analysis of public opinion we shall consider categorical, institutional, and associational secondary groups in addition to the primary group.

---

4. George C. Homans, *The Human Group* (New York: Harcourt, Brace & World, 1950), p. 1.

5. See Sidney Verba, *Small Groups and Political Behavior* (Princeton: Princeton University Press, 1961), especially pp. 3–60, for an excellent statement and overview of the importance of primary groups in politics.

6. David B. Truman, *The Governmental Process* (New York: Knopf, 1951), pp. 26–27. Truman's attention is focused on political interest groups and especially on "associations," which he described as groups that grow out of "tangent relations" with institutionalized groups (pp. 33–41).

In the marchland between clear-cut primary and secondary groups are some types of human groups in which individuals may at some times be identifiable as such, with names and significance as persons, but at other times are lost or merged in the collective whole. The *crowd,* the *assemblage,* and the similar but often distinguished *mob* are groups in which the individual, as an individual, may be either visible or submerged in the interaction patterns.

Secondary communication networks can be distinguished from primary communication networks the same way that secondary groups are distinguished from primary groups. Secondary communication networks are mass-communication systems, or simply *mass communication.*

Charles Wright points out that "mass communication is a special kind of communication involving distinctive operating conditions, primary among which are the nature of the audience, of the communication experience, and of the communicator." The audience, he says, is distinguished by its large size, its heterogeneity, and its anonymity; the communication experience is characterized as "public, rapid, and transient"; and the communicator "tends to be, or to operate within, a complex organization that may involve great expense."[7]

The common mass-communication media—the press, radio, television, and movies—meet all the basic requirements of anonymity, publicness, and institutionalization. They are also more or less rapid and transient, although some parts of each may require considerable time for preparation (for example, magazine articles and movies) and may in some instances be designed for semipermanent use (for example, the periodic reissue of old movies). Nevertheless, they are clearly more rapid and transient than such specialized communications as textbooks and scholarly publications, which, at least in theory, have value over an indeterminate span of time.[8]

It will not be profitable for us to try to define every form of communication—especially of such printed communications as pamphlets, newsletters, and memoranda—as mass or nonmass communication. Some may be public, transient, and addressed to a large heterogeneous audience. Polemical pamphlets and "open letters" to public officials probably should be thought of as mass communication; a diagnostic pamphlet issued by a medical society probably should not.

---

7. Charles R. Wright, *Mass Communication: A Sociological Perspective* (New York: Random House, 1959) pp. 13–15.

8. Some scholars define mass communication as all "impersonal transmission regardless of the size of audience...radio, movies, books, newspapers, and magazines are included in this definition, but those involving personal address, the drama, and other face-to-face communications are excluded." See Carl L. Hovland, "Effects of the Mass Media of Communication," in *Handbook of Social Psychology,* eds. Gardner Lindzey and Elliot Aronson, vol 2 (Reading, Mass.: Addison-Wesley, 1954), pp. 1062–1063. Hovland's definition would include textbooks and, apparently, all printed material except that circulating only among known individuals. A play in a book would be mass communication; a play performed would not. The definition has the advantage of being tidy. Its tidiness was apparently insufficient justification for Walter Weiss, who, in the second edition of the *Handbook of Social Psychology,* defined mass media "denotatively" as "the print media of newspapers, magazines and books; the broadcast media of radio and television; and the movies" ("Effects of the Mass Media of Communication," in ibid., 2nd ed., vol. 5 (1969), p. 79.

As in all attempts at categorization, some items are not readily identifiable as mass communication and can be handled only as they appear. Despite the overlap between mass communication and nonmass forms, the general distinction is important conceptually and has been useful in empirical research.

## 13.2 COMMUNICATION AND DIRECT OBSERVATION AS SOURCES OF OPINION

Opinion formation or change is neither necessarily nor always the result of communication. Instinct and unaided learning through individual experience can produce attitudes and views about some matters. But, as we saw in Chapter 7, there can be no opinions worthy of the name without *learning,* and none but the most limited kind of learning can take place without the social relationships that are established only through communication. Thus communication is essential to the formation and re-formation of the kinds of opinions with which we are concerned.

Members of society get almost all their knowledge of public issues through communication. Each person witnesses directly only a tiny part of the facts and opinions that make up what he or she knows and thinks about public matters. We see and hear from others meaningful signs (words and pictures) that help form or change attitudes and opinions. Some of these messages come from family, friends, and others who communicate more or less directly; the rest of the messages are received through impersonal media.

Some research findings suggest that many people use the mass media, especially newspapers and television, as a source of information they think they will need in anticipated conversations. They believe they will need to talk with friends—in primary communications networks, that is—and they use the secondary networks of the mass media to supply conversation material. This linkage of secondary with primary networks appears to be more important for persons of less formal education than for those with higher levels of education.[9] We deal with these matters more thoroughly in Chapter 14.

Communication interacts with personal observation. Although few persons can form or change opinions about public matters without some communication with others, direct observation may supplement, confirm, or disconfirm the meaning of communicated information. Many opinions formed through communication are thus tested by personal experience. Information received from primary or mass-communication networks may have convinced medical students A and B that more extensive public welfare services are desirable in their

---

9. See David Smith, "Mass Media as a Basis for Interaction: An Empirical Study," *Journalism Quarterly* 52 (1975): 44–49; Saadia Greenberg, "Conversations as Units of Analysis in the Study of Personal Influence," ibid., pp. 128–131; and Michael B. MacKuen, "Social Communication and the Mass Policy Agenda," in *More Than News: Media Power in Public Affairs,* eds. Michael B. MacKuen and Steven L. Coombs (Beverly Hills, Calif.: Sage, 1981), pp. 134–136.

community. As doctors, however, A and B may have very different experiences. If A has many indigent and low-income patients, experience will no doubt confirm and strengthen the original opinion. If B's patients are drawn largely from persons who can afford private health services, B's experience will probably disconfirm the earlier view and may lead to a change of opinion.

There are many ways, at both the individual and group levels, to reduce the conflict and dissonance of communication and observation. Alone or in groups we are inclined to see and hear what we want to see and hear; thus communication tends to be identical or at least similar to observation. Nevertheless, the interaction of communicated information and directly perceived information, and especially their reconciliation, is an important part of the dynamics of opinion formation and change.

Most opinions are based on facts or on other opinions, which are not learned at firsthand but are communicated by other individuals. Few opinions are based wholly or perhaps even in part on direct observation. Moreover, those few that *are* based on observation are often made possible by conditions established by prior communications. When people think some events or behaviors are important, or when they are especially sensitive to and watchful for clues that may give meaning to certain events or behavior, we say these events have *attention salience* for them.

What establishes attention salience? One observation may lead to another or still more observations in a chain of observation–salience–new observation–new salience. If Benjamin Franklin's accounts of his own life are to be wholly credited (a matter of controversy among scholars), it was something like this chain that led him from the observation of a kitten's fur to glass-and-wool experiments to the key on the kite and finally to a theory of lightning. The isolated scientist would have no other way to proceed than through ever more well-defined observation-salience-observation cycles. But the progress of science is possible precisely because scientists are not isolated. Communication intervenes, allowing great leaps in the accumulation of information.

So it is also to a large extent with all opinion creation and change. Attention salience is created by communication. We learn sometimes by communication what we should perhaps be learning by observation.[10] Drs. A and B read in the paper that the president has sent to Congress a proposal for expanded health benefits. They then pay special attention to need and inadequacy, or to need and adequacy, as real cases appear in their own practices or in the practices of their fellow physicians. Communication—mass communication in this case—creates for them a salience that leads to direct observation. Or, to take another instance, Catholic politicians have attention salience for the Protestant parents of our

---

10. For some stimulating and even revolutionary propositions about the human capacity to gain and hold knowledge, see Michael Polanyi, *Personal Knowledge: Towards a Post-Critical Philosophy* (Chicago: University of Chicago Press, 1958); and, by the same author, *The Study of Man* (Chicago: University of Chicago Press, 1959).

mythical Mr. Oblah, and their pointed comments are not lost on their son. He subsequently looks for and finds a Catholic party boss in his city. In Oblah's case, primary communication in his family rather than mass communication first triggered his concern. Or, as a final example, the closet academic who becomes a political activist may first become aware of social and political problems through books and scholarly pursuits. What created salience for him or her (books and academic study) was not clearly either primary or mass communication, but some of both.

## Chapter 14

# Primary Groups, Personal Influence, and Public Opinion

Our understanding of the interaction of behavior and opinions has been much extended and clarified by two significant research developments in the past fifty years: small-group studies and scientific sample surveys.

In this chapter we shall consider some of these primary-group studies and try to understand interpersonal influences on opinion within the context of communication networks. Our interest here is in the following variant of the prime question for political analysis: Who, in face-to-face or otherwise close situations, influences whom, how, and with what political consequence? A further question, to which we shall turn at the end of this chapter, deals with the relationships between primary and secondary communication networks—that is, between face-to-face communication and mass communication.

## 14.1 THE CREATION AND MAINTENANCE OF GROUP NORMS

Members of self-conscious groups tend to distinguish themselves from nonmembers. Sometimes human groups are formed on the basis of the physical characteristics of their members (men or women, black or white), place of residence (X community or Y community), age (under thirty, over sixty-five), ancestry (Irish, Italian, *Mayflower*ites), or, probably most often, *shared opinion*. Whatever it is that determines group membership, those who belong have at the outset, or very quickly develop, what Charles Cooley called "we-feeling" and "they-feeling."

Related to we-feeling and whatever common history exists, and often binding the members together in behavior patterns, are the intangible rules for group identification. These are known as *group norms*—values, hierarchies of values, and behavioral expectations, frequently unwritten but by no means unimportant in the achievement of group objectives and the minimizing of intragroup conflict. Even the simplest groups possess norms; they develop in the very act of a group's formation. They are, in a sense, the unacknowledged and informal codification of the interactions that make group consciousness (we-feeling) possible.

One of the earliest systematic investigations of group behavior was conducted in the Hawthorne, Illinois, plant of the Western Electric Company, makers of telephone equipment. A team of social psychologists observed the Western Electric employees under various experimental and nonexperimental working conditions. Of the many studies in this series, the experiment of the Bank Wiring Observation Room best illustrates the way group norms are created—and the difficulty of predicting group norms from wholly rational premises.

The Bank Wiring experiment was designed to test some incentive plans based on the view that workers would work harder for extra pay. The workers whose behavior was being studied had been put together in a special room with an observer whose reputed function was to "keep the records." Under varying conditions of extra-pay incentive—much to the investigator's surprise— production was not significantly changed.

What had happened? Under the circumstances, a special kind of we-feeling had been created among the workers. An informal group had emerged with norms about production output and quotas. This new primary group had developed a very real understanding, only partly verbalized but nonetheless generally accepted. The behavior norms thus created prevented the faster workers from producing more (from being "rate busters") for fear that management would then reduce the piecework rate. Likewise, the norms included the expectation that each person would do her share of the work, and that each member would protect these informal agreements from being learned and dealt with by management.[1]

In the Hawthorne studies, group norms had much greater influence in general on individual behavior and opinions than did the variables of pay and working conditions, which were directly manipulated by the investigators. Other studies have revealed the importance of the group in the establishment and maintenance of rules of right and wrong behavior for members of the group.[2]

## 14.11  Opinion similarity within groups

Depending on the importance of the group to the individuals who comprise it, the group norms will strongly or weakly influence the shared opinions. The

---

1. For the Hawthorne studies, see F. J. Roethlisberger and William J. Dickson, *Management and the Worker* (Cambridge: Harvard University Press, 1939).

2. See, for example, William F. Whyte, *Street Corner Society* (Chicago: University of Chicago Press, 1943); and Henri Tajfel, "Social and Cultural Factors in Perception," in *Handbook of Social Psychology,* eds. Gardner Lindzey and Elliot Aronson, 2nd ed., vol. 3 (Reading, Mass.: Addison-Wesley, 1969), pp. 335–339.

importance of the group to its members is the result of many personal propensities, views, and judgments. Importance can be measured by various tests of cohesion or integration, one frequent element of which is an index of sameness of opinion among the group members.

Much of the study of political behavior depends on the similarities and dissimilarities of opinion and candidate preference within and among groups. In our consideration of the sociology of opinion holding, we discussed the influence of family, religious, and economic groupings. It was not surprising to find clusterings of political opinions significantly related to group membership; indeed, large-scale analysis of public opinion would be nearly impossible if it could not be demonstrated that people who share group membership tend to hold similar political views.

## 14.12 The influence of group norms on "objective" judgments

No one will be surprised that group members have consistent similarities of opinion. It may be of some interest, however, that group members, under certain conditions, tend to agree with one another on judgments that appear to be purely objective—even when such judgments are erroneous.

The social psychologist Muzafer Sherif discovered that perceptions as well as opinions of individuals are influenced by group norms. He was investigating the *autokinetic effect*—the fact that a stationary point of light, viewed through a totally dark box, *appears* to oscillate. He found that reports of the amount of light movement given by individuals in a group setting tended to converge around a group norm. Individuals who first reported greater or lesser movement when alone were inclined after discussion to agree with the median reports.[3]

Solomon Asch, elaborating on Sherif's methods, systematically varied the intensity and division of opinions with the use of "stooges." He found that the "naive" subjects in a large majority of cases yielded to group pressures to converge on the norms established by the "stooge" subjects at the will of the investigator. The "majority effect" attained full strength when three of four subjects agreed; the tendency of a single minority member to yield to the majority position did not change when the majority was increased beyond that point.[4]

## 14.13 Group norms and opinions on public issues

A word of caution is perhaps in order. The pioneering studies of Sherif and Asch, like others carried out in the laboratory, are very dramatic. They illustrate well

---

3. Muzafer Sherif, "Group Influences upon the Formation of Norms and Attitudes," in *Readings in Social Psychology* eds. Eleanor E. Maccoby et al. (New York: Holt, Rinehart & Winston, 1958), pp. 219–232.

4. Solomon E. Asch, "Effects of Group Pressure upon the Modification and Distortion of Judgments," in *Groups, Leadership, and Men,* ed. Harold Guetzkow (Pittsburgh: Carnegie Press, 1951), pp. 177–190.

what is important for our purposes here—namely, the influence of group pressures and expectations on individual opinions. Nevertheless, there is a danger of overestimating these indications of the influence of group norms. Michael Olmsted summarizes the dangers of laboratory experiments as:

**1.** *Generalization from too little information:* "It is evident that these experiments make no claim to have investigated all the possible effects of the group on the individual. . . our knowledge can hardly be said to be very systematic or exhaustive."

**2.** *Transference from unreal to real situations:* "It is . . . important to ask whether behavior observed in the laboratory and that observed in the 'real' world are the same in fact or in name only. . . . The sort of experimentation described above is only in the broadest sense a study of groups at all. These groups—or more accurately, aggregates of subjects—have very little interaction and almost no organization or structure."

**3.** *Temptation to explain all behavior in terms of the influence of groups:* "Third is the danger that 'group norms' become an explanation for everything. Further exploration of group behavior can too easily be smothered by the apparently wise but actually trite explanation that this or that happens because of a group norm."[5]

Bearing in mind the dangers of overgeneralization from too little or insignificant evidence, we can appreciate that the discovery and elaboration of small group/individual relations is one of the most significant developments of modern social science. The influence of small groups on individual members' opinions on public questions does not operate through direct and explicit norms that are essential to the operation and survival of the group and that the individual is constrained to observe. Opinions on public issues are ordinarily not critical to the smooth functioning of primary groups. Many families, work groups, and social clubs include members whose views on public issues differ widely from the average opinion of the group; but there are influences on both the group and the individual whenever even the slightest indication of these opinion differences exist. One important reason for such influences is the fact that individuals respond to what they *believe* to be group norms. Opinions are formed or held in accordance with the *anticipated pressures* from the group. To test this proposition, Ivan Steiner interviewed a national sample and a local (Michigan) sample to discover the respondents' opinions on the economic and political power of big business and the norms they assumed to be held by their closest friends. He concluded "that the perceived primary-group pressures can have considerable effect on attitudes even when there is reason to doubt that group norms and sanctions are operating."[6] Thus it appears that we shape our opinions on some

---

5. Michael S. Olmsted, *The Small Group* (New York: Random House, 1959), p. 76.
6. Ivan D. Steiner, "Primary Group Influences on Public Opinion," *American Sociological Review* 19 (1954): 267.

political or quasi-political matters on the basis of what we think our friends' views are, even when we don't *know* whether our friends have any views at all. This is a special application of what Carl Friedrich calls the "rule of anticipated reaction"; people often behave not on the simple basis of the past but on their expectations of how others will react to what they do.[7]

Whether group norms are known or presumed, it could be argued that the pressure to conform will be greater, not less, in social and political matters than in others. The pressure to conform to the opinions of those around us is strong

> even when there is a clear objective referent for our opinions, but it is more the case with those political and social opinions for which there is no clear and easy test except comparison with the opinions of our fellows. In such testing situations, there is pressure on the individual to change his opinion if it differs from the opinion of others around him. These pressures come both from the individual himself and from the other group members, since the condition of dissonance will be unpleasant to both the deviant and the other group members.[8]

As Sidney Verba surmised in 1961, political opinions may be more vulnerable to group pressures than opinions on matters related to personal experience. On the other hand, as Verba reported in 1965, group pressures on members' political opinions may often be weakened by group norms that inhibit political discourse.[9] For example, the expectation of church members that politics will not be mixed with church matters (a group norm pointed out in Chapter 10) inhibits the kinds of communication that would bring pressure on those church members who have unusual political opinions. Group pressures toward conformity are reduced if there is an understanding (again, the group norm) to ignore nonconformity. In general, then, many group norms will require conformity (for example, the Hawthorne case), but others, such as norms of academic freedom, may specifically protect nonconformity.

## 14.2 GROUP NORMS, AND (AGAIN!) THE CONUNDRUM OF "OPINIONS" AND BEHAVIOR

One important question that needs clarification is: When are group norms important for the *creation* of opinion, the *expression* of opinion, and *behavior*

---

7. Carl J. Friedrich, *Man and His Government: An Empirical Theory of Politics* (New York: McGraw-Hill, 1963), pp. 203–206. The "rule of anticipated reactions" does not reduce the importance of personal or social history, because anticipations of the future reactions of significant others must be based on projections of their reactions to similar events of the past. In order to figure out what they will probably do in the future, we have to know what they have done in like situations in the past.

8. Sidney Verba, *Small Groups and Political Behavior* (Princeton: Princeton University Press, 1961), pp. 23–24. Verba cites Leon Festinger, *A Theory of Cognitive Dissonance* (Stanford: Stanford University Press, 1957).

9. Sidney Verba, "Organizational Membership and Democratic Consensus," *Journal of Politics* 37 (1965): 467–497.

that is related to that opinion? In Sherif's and Asch's experiments with the autokinetic effect, individuals presumably gave their honest opinions about the extent of light movement at first, before group discussion. Then many changed their estimations in expressing opinions after group influence had been brought to bear—presumably in response to what we earlier (in Chapter 6) called self-image management. As H. L. Nieburg says, "the psychic cost of expressing an opinion in confidence and anonymity to an interviewer is thought to be much less than it would be among one's peers. In the real world, psychic cost—that is, the rewards and punishments inflicted in social bargaining (or in anticipation of them)—is an important, if not central, aspect of opinion holding."[10]

In discussion, and in overt behavior that is seen by or may be reported to other members of one's reference group, the norms of the group will influence reported opinion certainly, real opinion probably, and behavior probably. But what about behavior that one thinks will not be known to other members of the reference group? Clandestine activity (disapproved sexual conduct, gambling, use of drugs, and the like) commonly occurs among ordinary people who nevertheless profess in the company of relevant reference groups (spouses, family, neighbors, workmates) that they abhor such behaviors. There is a little Dr. Jekyll and Mr. Hyde in all of us. Something of this sort seems to have happened in the 1982 gubernatorial race in California. Tom Bradley, the black mayor of Los Angeles, a Democrat, was opposing George Deukmejian, the white Republican state attorney-general. Preelection polls showed Bradley running ahead in a state where the Democrats have nearly a two-thirds advantage over the Republicans in two-party registration. Among white voters only, in a state where whites then represented 70 percent of the adult population, the last preelection poll showed Bradley leading by 48 to 43 percent; a secret exit poll on election day showed Deukmejian getting 55 percent of the white vote, with 3.8 percent of Deukmejian voters saying they did not want a black governor. In group discussions or face-to-face interviews very few Americans will admit to racial prejudice, but in the privacy of the voting booth or in a fleeting secret comment on the way out of the voting place, racism may be revealed. In California in 1982, "the net measurable loss to Mr. Bradley because he was black . . . [was] about 96,500 votes, slightly more than the actual Deukmejian plurality of 93,345."[11]

## 14.3 ROLE DIFFERENTIATION IN PRIMARY GROUPS

Not all members of groups perform the same kinds of tasks for the group or behave in identical ways in group interaction. Individuals in groups have various

---

10. H. L. Nieburg, *Public Opinion: Tracking and Targeting* (New York: Praeger, 1984), p. 85.

11. Mervin D. Field "California Poll: The Four Keys to Bradley's Election Defeat," *San Francisco Chronicle,* February 1, 1983; quotation from Tom Wicker, "Dissecting an Election," *New York Times,* February 18, 1983.

roles to play. Although there is considerable disagreement about the nuances and specialized meanings of *role* and *role behavior,* one useful and typical statement defines a social role as "an organized pattern of expectancies that relate to the tasks, demeanors, attitudes, values, and reciprocal relationships to be maintained by persons occupying specific membership positions and fulfilling definable functions in any group." This definition of role emphasizes "expectancies rather than behavior, because the role is defined by what others expect of the person filling it. Behavior refers to actual performance—how a person fills his roles."[12]

There may be *natural roles,* determined by sex and generational differences, as in the obvious examples of the mother and father roles in the primary family group. In formally organized groups, specialized officers may handle *functional roles* (that is, behavior for facilitating the attainment of group purposes), such as presiding over meetings (the president or chairperson), handling group finances (the treasurer), or taking care of group communications (the secretary).

All of these role differentiations are simple, or at least obvious. Less obvious is the fact that role differentiation takes place even in informal groups and may be very important for the determination of opinion. What we think about private or public issues is inevitably influenced by what we believe is appropriate for us to think, depending on who we are and what others expect of us. In discussion and problem-solving groups, in laboratory and real situations, functional-role categories can be identified and differentiated. One team of investigators observed several such roles, including "information seeker" (and "information giver"), "initiator," "energizer," "evaluator-critic," and "harmonizer."[13]

More important to us than kinds of roles is the evidence that social roles influence opinions about political issues. It is a belief among junior corporate executives on the rise that their role requires them to be inactive in politics and without opinions (at least, without *expressed* opinions) on issues of public concern.[14] The clergy will not ordinarily express highly political opinions; and even the pope, whose leadership role for Roman Catholics is broadly defined, speaks infallibly only on matters of faith and morals.

In situations of more highly concentrated politics, social roles heavily influence the nature of opinion creation and exchange. The candidate role carries with it expectations absent from (or even incompatible with) the role expectations of the elected legislator—or, *a fortiori*, the elected judge.

The separation of powers—at least in the United States, where it is institutionally embedded—appears to have strengthened role differentiations associated

---

12. Eugene L. Hartley and Ruth E. Hartley, *Fundamentals of Social Psychology* (New York: Knopf, 1952), p. 486.

13. Kenneth D. Benne and Paul Sheats, "Functional Roles of Group Members," *Journal of Social Issues* 4 (1948): 41–49.

14. Andrew Hacker, *Politics and the Corporation* (New York: Fund for the Republic, 1958), p. 9.

with the functional behavior of legislators, executives, and judges. At news conferences the president often tells his questioners that "it would be inappropriate" (for a person in the presidential role) to comment on this or that topic; and the Supreme Court has developed a whole inventory of "nonjusticiable questions"—that is, matters with which the justices, in their role as judges, will not concern themselves.[15]

At less lofty levels, and throughout the opinion-policy process, role considerations bear on the existence and intensity of public opinion. On questions of public finance, bankers are listened to closely. The views of the "Mothers' Committee of Public School 310" are given special attention on education matters. Almost any older business executive is respected by younger colleagues when public issues are discussed. In all groups (but in primary groups especially), role considerations bear on opinion formation and change. In some group relationships, role may be insignificant, or nearly so, whereas in others it is of central importance.

## 14.4 PERSONAL EXPERIENCE AND PERSONAL INFLUENCE

It is apparent that role is related to experience. The leader has led, the expediter has expedited, and the inside-dopester has acquired inside dope. Conceivably one could fill a role without gaining experience in the practical matters and specialized knowledge associated with that role; role behavior could be irrelevant to role efficacy. In general, however, there should be a fairly close correspondence between influence associated with role and influence associated with experience. In simple societies—and to some extent in those not so simple—the village elder has a large-group social role as patriarch, which is in turn related to his genealogy and his personal experience. His experience supports his role, and his role makes possible an increase in his influence as a leader of opinion.

Role is thus quite obviously related to specialization of labor. Both social role and labor specialization create the presumption of opinion expertise. Plato believed that philosophy, or the study of truth, was a matter of specialization like

---

15. It should not be thought, however, in these examples especially, that role considerations are the sole or even the primary causes of presidential or judicial self-restraint. Frequently such restraint is sheer political strategy, though cast in role-appropriate terms. The president or the Court may find that some situations require less restraint than others; President Truman found no role inhibitions in castigating the Republican-controlled 80th Congress as "do-nothing" and "the worst in history"; and President Nixon repeatedly claimed that the presidential role prohibited his surrender of executive materials to the courts or the Senate investigating committee during the Watergate controversy of 1973 and 1974. Likewise, the Supreme Court justices found it "inappropriate" for them, as judges, to look for unconstitutional legislative motives in a margarine-tax law they agreed with (McCray v. U.S., U.S. 27 [1904]), but quite appropriate in a tax law antithetical to their own economic views (Bailey v. Drexel Furniture Co., 259 U.S. 20 [1922]).

the study of medicine. His antidemocratic bias is in large part traceable to his view that the philosopher-king is the expert in governing, and that this individual's opinion, based on special study and experience, ought to be law.

Plato seems to have assumed that some people have expert training, skills, and competence and others have none. Whatever the case may have been 2,500 years ago in Greece, a more modern view of society would recognize that specializations—and roles and experience based on specializations—are spread very widely. In the nineteenth century, George Cornewall Lewis went beyond the mere fact that specialization of roles and experience means that expert knowledge (and therefore reliable opinion) is unequally divided in society. "In considering the seat of authority," Lewis observed, "it should be borne in mind, on the one hand, that no man is a competent judge on *all* subjects; and, on the other, that every man is a competent judge on *some*."[16]

Some field studies indicate that Lewis was right. Specialized interest and specialized experience create specialized opinion leadership. Among more than 700 women respondents in Decatur, Illinois, Elihu Katz and Paul Lazarsfeld found few "general opinion" leaders—so few, in fact, that those found might have been the products of interviewing errors or dishonest responses.[17] Young single women in the Katz and Lazersfeld study had their opinions sought by other women on matters of clothing style and fashion; married women with large families were sources of marketing advice; in public affairs, the specialized opinion leaders seemed to be those higher in social status and gregariousness (an index of nonneighbor contacts and group membership).

General opinion leaders appear to be rare. In nondemocratic politics they may be accepted as a matter of tradition or trained within a ruling caste or class. But modern democratic practice and the diversification of power in pluralistic societies produce specialized opinion leaders for the most part. Nowadays there are few "men for all seasons." It is significant that a great many of the most knowledgeable and participative members of an elite sample thought themselves quite poorly informed on many of the major issues they were asked about in 1964.[18]

Nevertheless, a paradox must be observed: government, by its nature the supreme and ultimate power grouping of modern society, requires executives who give the appearance of being general opinion leaders. And the institutional aggregation of specialized opinion leadership makes executive generalization more than a mere appearance. Effective staffing provides the political executive

---

16. George Cornewall Lewis, *An Essay on the Influence of Authority in Matters of Opinion* (London: Longmans, Green, 1875), p. 114; italics in original. The work was first published in 1849.

17. Elihu Katz and Paul F. Lazarsfeld, *Personal Influence* (New York: Free Press, 1955), p. 334. However, a reassessment of Katz and Lazarsfeld's material led two scholars to the conclusion that general-opinion leaders existed among the Decatur women. See Alan S. Marcus and Raymond A. Bauer, "Yes: There Are Generalized Opinion Leaders," *Public Opinion Quarterly* 28 (1964): 628–632.

18. James N. Rosenau, *Citizenship between Elections* (New York: Free Press, 1974), pp. 346–349. See also Everett M. Rogers, *Diffusion of Innovations* (New York: Free Press, 1961), pp. 236–237.

with an array of specialization that, through the device of ministerial responsibility, results in the functional equivalent of general opinion leadership. The president may become, in effect, a general opinion leader by pooling the talents of expert assistants, each of whom has quite limited expertise.

## 14.5 PLURALISTIC IGNORANCE

In group situations, people are influenced by what others think, but do they *know* what others think? Ordinary observations and all relevant social science research confirm that people who live and work and interact in any way together profoundly influence each other's beliefs, attitudes, and opinions. It is therefore interesting to ask: How well do we understand what others believe and think?

James Fields and Howard Schuman investigated people's beliefs about the attitudes and opinion of others. Small-group experiments, as we have seen, indicate that in face-to-face situations people are often uncertain and even flatly mistaken about what others actually believe. Fields and Schuman sought information from survey data that might throw further light on such "pluralistic ignorance." They found quite high levels of pluralistic ignorance in regard to racial attitudes; there was a considerably higher degree of tolerance and integrationist sentiment than most people believed: "For Detroit as a whole and for their own neighborhoods a large proportion of respondents misperceive[d] opinion .... "Generalizing, they conclude that

> the dominant pattern, both in magnitude and in pervasiveness, is the
> "looking-glass perception," the belief that others think the same as
> oneself. In the absence of strong counter-forces, a large proportion of
> people feel that the world they live in agrees with their own opinions
> on public issues. Even when an issue becomes a matter of public
> debate—ending the Vietnam war and opposition to legalization of
> abortion are two good examples—partisans on either side claim, in
> all sincerity we suspect, that a majority of the public supports their
> particular view.[19]

Reviewing survey evidence in three consecutive national elections—1968, 1970, and 1972—Hubert O'Gorman discovered very high levels of pluralistic ignorance in regard to racial attitudes. From one-third to one-half of white Americans believed that other white Americans had much more antiblack feeling than was actually the case. Interestingly, black Americans had a more realistic perception of the amount of prosegregationist sentiment among whites.[20] Like Fields and Schuman, O'Gorman believes pluralistic ignorance to be a generalized phenomenon of American public opinion.

19. James M. Fields and Howard Schuman, "Public Beliefs about the Beliefs of the Public," *Public Opinion Quarterly* 40 (Winter 1976–77): 431, 445.
20. Hubert J. O'Gorman, "White and Black Perceptions of Racial Values," *Public Opinion Quarterly* 43 (Spring 1979): 48–59.

Even people who are in the same institutions or associations are often unsure of how other group members think on public issues. The extent to which pluralistic ignorance is found inside organizations appears to depend on the size of the group, the intensiveness of group interaction in the past, the relevance of the issues for group functioning, and the centrality or marginality of the individual whose judgment is under consideration. As would be expected, leaders and centrally located members of small, long-established groups are able to assess very accurately the opinions of the group on issues of salience to it.[21]

## 14.6  PERSONAL INFLUENCE AND MASS MEDIA IN OPINION FORMATION

With the rise of literacy and the mass media—newspapers in the nineteenth century and radio between the two world wars—it was believed that the mass media provided facts and opinions that were directly absorbed without the aid of mediation or translation. The influence of the mass media was thought to be immediate, direct, and more or less equal in its impact. "In short, the media of communication were looked upon as a new kind of unifying force—a simple kind of nervous system—reaching out to every eye and ear, in a society characterized by an amorphous social organization and a paucity of interpersonal relations."[22]

The influence of the mass media is not so simple. Not all persons are equally or randomly exposed to mass media, and people therefore receive different messages. Programming varies from medium to medium and within each medium—another factor accounting for variety in what individuals receive from mass communications. Furthermore, people seem to seek from the mass media information that they believe will be particularly useful for anticipated conversations.[23] Finally, individuals who receive the very same messages find different meanings in them, depending on what they are and are not looking for, the information they already have, and their skill in relating these messages to other messages.

These disturbing complexities led a number of analysts to differentiate individuals (to take them out of the "mass") according to the roles they played in the flow of information and opinions. The authors of *The People's Choice,* first among survey researchers, discovered that some people are, in George Orwell's celebrated phrase, "more equal than others" when it comes to determining the way votes will be cast. Personal influence, they found, was probably more important than formal media in determining voting decisions. Personal influence is apt to

---

21. For a helpful summary of findings, see Harold H. Kelley and John W. Thibaut, "Group Problem Solving," in *Handbook of Social Psychology,* eds. Lindzey and Aronson, 2nd ed., 4:1–101.

22. Katz and Lazarsfeld, *Personal Influence,* p.16.

23. See Charles K. Atkin, "Anticipated Communication and Mass Media Information Seeking," *Public Opinion Quarterly* 36 (1972): 188–199, for evidence on this point and for a review of earlier studies.

reach persons not exposed to media messages. Not only is personal influence more extensive than mass-media political influence, but it also has the following psychological advantages:

**1.** *It is nonpurposive:* "politics gets through, especially to the indifferent...because it comes up unexpectedly as a sideline or marginal topic in a casual conversation."

**2.** *It is flexible when countering resistance:* "can counter and dislodge such resistance...can make use of a large number of cues...can choose the occasion at which to speak...can adapt [the] story to...the other's interests and his ability to understand."

**3.** *It offers immediate reward for compliance:* "When someone yields to a personal influence in making a vote decision, the reward is immediate and personal. This is not the case in yielding to an argument via print or radio [or television]."

**4.** *It allows the individual to put his trust in a known and intimate source:* "The doubtful voter...can trust the judgment and evaluation of the respected people among his associates. Most of them are people with the same status and interests as himself. Their attitudes are more relevant for him than the judgments of an unknown editorial writer."

**5.** *It allows for persuasion without conviction:* "Personal influence, with all its overtones of personal affection and loyalty, can bring to the polls votes that would otherwise not be cast or would be cast for the opposing party just as readily if some other friend had insisted. [It] differs from the formal media by persuading uninterested people to vote in a certain way without giving them a substantive reason for their vote."[24]

It is possible that peers and other personal contacts are more important than the mass media in respect to voting decisions and in helping individuals make up their minds about political issues. Conversations and the real or anticipated reactions of significant others and reference groups may structure the meaning of political events and information. But the citizens of Evanston, Illinois, interviewed by Doris Graber apparently got a much larger proportion of specific new information from the mass media than from conversations with friends. Graber collected 1,568 specific news-information items from her interviews and another 10,121 items from the daily diaries kept by her respondents. Her findings did not support "the conventional wisdom...that interpersonal information transmission is especially effective." Only 4 percent of the total information about news stories came from conversations with friends and acquaintances; 95 percent came from the mass media. Her explanation of this surprising finding was "that most discussion involved information already known to the discussion partners. The

24. Paul F. Lazarsfeld et al., *The People's Choice: How the Voter Makes Up His Mind in a Presidential Campaign,* 2nd ed. (New York: Columbia University Press, 1948), pp. 152–156.

discussion may have added details and may have structured information processing, but it did not provide the bulk of story information." [25] The mass media provide the facts, apparently, while peer and group referents provide much of the meaning attributed to those facts and many of the opinions, which are *interpretations of* and *judgments about* the facts in context.

The power of personal influence to induce *behavior* for what are essentially irrelevant reasons is not found to the same degree in the mass media. Behavior may indeed be induced by the mass media for what are *in fact* irrelevant reasons (as when "Charlie" buys hair oil because he believes the jingle that says girls will therefore like him), but the reasons are *thought* to be relevant. Most of the strength of personal influence lies in the willingness of individuals to think or do things simply because their friends so desire.

A number of researchers have investigated the way influence flows generally in the formation and re-formation of public opinion. In the 1950s and 1960s it was common for communications researchers to talk about the "two-step flow" of information and opinions. The originators of the term said "ideas often flow *from* radio and print *to* opinion leaders and *from* them to the less active sections of the population."[26] By 1961 it could be claimed that "this so-called two-step flow hypothesis has been used in several studies and, with modification, is probably the most popular framework, explicitly or implicitly, utilized in diffusion research."[27]

John P. Robinson's research on influence in the 1968 presidential campaign led him to revise the original two-step flow idea (Figure 14–1).

> The two-step hypothesis did correctly emphasize that *when* interpersonal sources and mass media sources are compared or are in conflict, interpersonal sources wield greater influence. However, that condition of "when" needs to be stressed. More voters in the [1968] study reported being exposed to a newspaper endorsement than to an interpersonal influence attempt.[28]

Certainly individuals get directly from the mass media some material of relevance for their opinions on public matters. A few people ("nondiscussants" in Figure 14–2) rely exclusively on mass-media sources, but most Americans seem to get issue-relevant materials from personal networks and from the media. Collectively, the overall pattern appears to be that of multidimensional networks

25. Doris A. Graber, *Processing the News: How People Tame the Information Tide* (New York: Longman, 1984), pp. 85–86.

26. Lazarsfeld et al., *People's Choice,* p. 151; italics in original.

27. Rogers, *Diffusion of Innovations,* p. 213. For a review of much of the literature on two-step flow research see Everett Rogers and Floyd Shoemaker, *Communication of Innovation* (New York: Free Press, 1971). For a comment on two-step flow theory from the viewpoint of the sociology of knowledge, see Leon Bramson, *The Political Context of Sociology* (Princeton: Princeton University Press, 1961), chap. 5.

28. John P. Robinson, "Interpersonal Influence in Election Campaigns: Two Step-Flow Hypotheses," *Public Opinion Quarterly* 40 (Fall 1976): 315; italics in original.

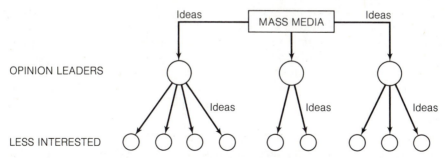

**Figure 14–1.** *Original two-step hypothesis* (From John P. Robinson, "Interpersonal Influence in Election Campaigns: Two Step-Flow Hypotheses," *Public Opinion Quarterly,* Fall 1976. Copyright © 1976 by Elsevier North Holland, Inc. Reprinted by permission.)

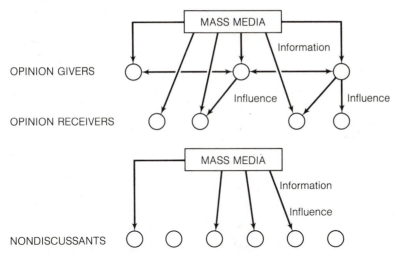

**Figure 14–2.** *Revised step-flow sequences* (From John P. Robinson, "Interpersonal Influence in Election Campaigns: Two Step-Flow Hypotheses," *Public Opinion Quarterly,* Fall 1976. Copyright 1976 by Elsevier North Holland, Inc. Reprinted by permission.)

of opinion giving and opinion taking in which the opinion givers are (a) *many*— although some people's views never seem to be sought and are not accepted if they are volunteered; (b) *specialized*—although "general opinion leaders" may exist in some communities at some social levels; and (c) *effective* (insofar as they are effective) to some considerable degree through informal and unselfconscious techniques of conversation and example-setting.

Much remains to be learned about influence and the transfer of opinions through primary- and small-group communication. It seems probable—

although the evidence is not yet available—that the essentially private matters studied by most sociologists in small-group research (and to a large degree by Katz and Lazarsfeld in their interviews with the women of Decatur) are heavily influenced by the primary-group contacts each person experiences in day-to-day living. Individuals' opinions about public questions seem to be influenced less by peers than by the stratum of people immediately above them, to whom they turn for information and (perhaps more often) conclusions that agree in some general way with (a) their own basic attitudes and (b) the values of the primary groups to which they feel allegiance. As far as public questions are concerned, governmental and group leaders, the managers and producers of the mass media, and others who are visible or powerful in the hierarchies of social institutions (churches, schools) will be more important sources of opinion than friends and acquaintances. The importance of the mass media especially can hardly be exaggerated in their role as "agenda setters." It is to the media and some of their functions that we now turn.

## Chapter 15

# Mass Communication
# and Public Opinion

So far we have considered some of the important factors that shape the opinions of individuals and, through individuals, groups. We have considered the influence of culture (patterns of approved and disapproved thought and behavior) and of large social institutions, such as family, religion, and economic organization. Now we shall deal with the way human communication binds individuals together and makes possible meaningful opinion interaction in a large social context. We will be concerned with *mass communication.*

Charles Wright defines *mass communication* as communication, "directed toward relatively large, heterogeneous, and anonymous audiences; messages are transmitted publicly, often timed to reach most audience members simultaneously, and are transient in character; the communicator tends to be, or to operate within, a complex organization that may involve great expense."[1] Not all of these characteristics are found in all examples of mass communication. And many examples of communication that are neither clearly "mass" nor clearly personal (nor individual, nor private) can be found: political rallies, religious sermons, newsletters, scientific monographs. Nevertheless, the general distinction holds: mass communication is always directed to an anonymous and varied audience; it is public; it is created within and transmitted through complex impersonal channels.

Recent technology, especially cable TV and sophisticated high-speed computers, has made it possible for large audiences to be divided and approached as smaller groups of people with specialized interests. In Chapter 6 we dealt with the

1. Charles R. Wright, *Mass Communications: A Sociological Perspective* (New York: Random House, 1959), pp. 13, 15.

implications of this new technology for political polling. Here it is necessary only to remind ourselves that the audiences of mass communication are not so "mass" and anonymous as they used to be—although the persons who are in the segmented groups, or are members of separate "taste cultures," are still unknown, as persons, and in their interrelations are still essentially different from members of primary groups. As Nieburg says:

> In the past, mass communication was directed at a large undifferen-tiated audience and had only indirect means of feedback. That is no longer true. Today, and increasingly into the future, modern mass communications and polling are moving toward differentiating between special (or targeted) audiences; mass media accomplish this by programming strategies, allowing the general public to differen-tiate themselves as separate audiences for different communications.[2]

Mass communications are made through the mass media.[3] The mass media, in order of importance for public opinion, are the press, television, radio, and movies. By the press we mean, first, newspapers, and second, news and opinion journals. Family magazines, women's magazines, picture magazines, and other periodicals of fiction and entertainment are, of course, part of the American press. No doubt articles in a popular potpourri like *Reader's Digest* have some influence on the underlying predispositions of American voters. For the most part, however, the printed words that matter in American politics appear in the newspapers and in a few weekly or monthly journals such as *Time, Newsweek, U.S. News & World Report, Harper's, Fortune,* and *Atlantic,* and in a few smaller journals such as *Commentary, America, National Review,* and the *New Republic.* In this chapter we shall not concern ourselves much with the part of the press that has only little or indirect impact on controversial opinion related to public policy. But we shall bear in mind that normally apolitical journals sometimes become politicized (as did the publications of the various medical associations in the fight over national health programs) and exert measurable influence on policy making. Sometimes a single book can have political conse-quences by illuminating a policy matter and affecting the opinions that count. In 1963 Rachel Carson's *Silent Spring* warned of the dangers of the indiscriminate use of herbicides and insecticides, and in 1965 Ralph Nader's *Unsafe at Any Speed* surely influenced the auto-safety legislation and administrative orders of 1967.

---

2. H. L. Nieburg, *Public Opinion: Tracking and Targeting* (New York: Praeger, 1984), p. 16.

3. *Media* is the plural of *medium*—and it is one of those Latin plurals not yet naturalized into American English, probably because pedants give it continued visitor's status by writing footnotes about it. A "mass medium" really ought to be a "mass medium of communication," since a "medium" is "that by or through which anything is accomplished" (Webster); but the whole phrase "mass medium" (or "media") has come to mean that by or through which mass communications are accomplished.

## 15.1 MAJOR INFLUENCES OF THE MASS MEDIA ON PUBLIC OPINION

One element of American political folklore is the belief that the mass media, especially the newspapers, have great influence over the course of elections, legislation, and executive decisions. This "common knowledge" is especially cherished by defeated candidates and reformist groups, who take some comfort in identifying scapegoats for the failures of their causes. But winners and status quo organizations also subscribe to the view that the mass media can move political mountains.

There are some valid reasons why the mass media are felt to be powerful influences in the political dialogue and in the political resolution of social conflict. One is that the mass media do indeed influence political decisions—by giving or withholding publicity and sometimes endorsements, and by presenting editorials that help a small number of people make up their minds about issues. Another reason is quite simply that political decision makers often *think* they are important. If enough people whose collective influence is great think that the *New York Times* editorials are important, or that the CBS and NBC public affairs "specials" are powerful expressions of concern and popular value judgments, then these media presentations do become influential.

In part, this escalation of the mass media's importance occurs because there are so few ostensibly impartial indicators of what people think about public policy. Special-interest pleading there is aplenty; but the attentive decision maker has few ways of finding out "what the people *really* think." Political actors tend to believe that the mass media have insight into the "public mind" (an illusion carefully nurtured by the press). Bernard Cohen notes this overreliance on the newspapers:

> Lacking any other *daily* link to the outside, any other *daily* measure of how people are reacting to the ebb and flow of foreign-policy developments, the policy maker reaches for the newspaper as an important source of public opinion, as the instrument of "feedback." In fact, many officials treat the press and public opinion as synonymous, either explicitly equating them or using them interchangeably.[4]

Despite their giant-killing reputation among politicians, the mass media are not powerful and merciless defenders or destroyers of the good society. Their influence is, in most cases, less than overwhelming, never monolithic (an important point, to which we will return in a later chapter), and often inconsequential.

---

4. Bernard C. Cohen, *The Press and Foreign Policy* (Princeton: Princeton University Press, 1963), pp. 233–234; italics in original.

## 15.11 Most mass media are not very political

To keep a proper perspective on the political significance of the mass media, we should bear in mind that they are, to a large degree, apolitical—if not antipolitical.

Why do newspapers, TV and radio stations, movies, journals, and mass-circulation books exist? For one thing, they make money for their owners and producers—another matter to which we shall return. From the perspective of the consumer, however, the mass media serve three main functions: they provide (a) entertainment; (b) guidance and orientation for daily living; and (c) information and opinion about public events. It is undeniable that the third is least important for the majority of media consumers. Much of the intellectuals' criticism of the mass media misses this point: *most mass-media consumers neither want nor appreciate the subtleties of political discourse.* Moreover, for those who are politically aware and active, the mass media provide only a part of the environment of influence.

Working journalists in the news departments of daily papers and television stations believe they should emphasize political coverage and energetic reporting of national and international news. Table 15–1 summarizes what a large representative study found. The journalists of that sample seem to have felt that the first and fifth functions were then (in 1971) being quite well performed; 39 percent said there were "about the right number of crusaders and social reformers in the news media," while 35 percent said there were not enough and 22 percent said there were too many.[5]

## 15.12 Some media are more political than others

Despite what professional newspeople themselves believe, great differences exist in the way the general managers of the media interpret their public responsibilities. The history and traditions of the medium tend to shape its practitioners' image of its social function. Newspapers were historically very political but have become progressively less so in this century (see Chapter 17). At the other extreme, motion picture producers are fond of telling critics that Hollywood's job is to entertain people, not to teach them civic virtues or political philosophy. The great Sam Goldwyn himself is supposed to have said to an idealistic young screenwriter: "If you want to send messages, use Western Union." And the well-known Motion Picture Production Code straightforwardly says that "theatrical motion pictures...are primarily to be regarded as entertainment." Jack Valenti, head of the Motion Pictures Association, said in 1966 that moviemakers were addressing themselves "to a new era of leisure that is descending upon us,

5. John W. C. Johnstone, Edward J. Slawski, and William W. Bowman, *The News People: A Sociological Portrait of American Journalists and Their Work* (Urbana: University of Illinois Press, 1976), p. 231.

**Table 15-1** Journalists' views of media functions (percent)

| Function | Extremely important | Quite important | Somewhat important | Not really important | No opinion |
|---|---|---|---|---|---|
| Investigate claims and statements of government ............... | 75.8% | 19.1% | 3.5% | 0.9% | 0.6% |
| Provide analysis and interpretation of complex problems .......... | 61.0 | 25.2 | 10.9 | 2.5 | 0.4 |
| Discuss national policy while it is still being developed ........... | 55.2 | 26.8 | 12.1 | 4.6 | 1.4 |
| Concentrate on news of interest to the widest possible public ...... | 38.7 | 31.5 | 20.8 | 7.9 | 1.1 |
| Develop intellectual and cultural interests of the public ......... | 30.3 | 35.1 | 25.7 | 8.1 | 0.9 |
| Provide entertainment and relaxation .................. | 16.6 | 28.1 | 41.5 | 13.3 | 0.5 |

Adapted from *The News People: A Sociological Portrait of American Journalists and Their Work,* by J. W. C. Johnstone, E. J. Slawski, and W. W. Bowman. Copyright © 1976 by the University of Illinois Press. Reprinted by permission.

with its opportunity to open up a new horizon of entertainment and education, with its great potential for a cultural renaissance in our country."[6] Movies, in short, should deal with entertainment and culture but not politics.

Movie, television, and radio people have traditionally viewed their media in much the same apolitical way. But the history and therefore the traditions of public accountability in radio and TV are somewhat different from those of the movies. Movies are not limited, as TV and radio are, by a scientific fact that from the very beginning made regulation of the airwaves a matter of public necessity. The materials for making and showing movies are widely distributed and practically unlimited; but only a small number of radio transmission bands exist, and their rational use required early and continued governmental regulation at the national and international levels. Yet radio and TV—regulated by government because they were, as Chief Justice Morrison Waite said of railroads, "affected by a public interest"—resisted political involvement. TV and radio stations do relatively little editorializing, for example, even though they have been free to do so since 1949.

Leo Bogart makes the point that TV audiences do not fully understand that that medium uses many of its entertainment traditions and techniques in presenting news, and that the supposed objectivity of its newscasts is thus seriously compromised by the extent to which news is "staged," is presented out of context, and is unrepresentative in its importance, its violence, and its novelty.[7] These matters are taken up in greater detail in Chapter 18.

---

6. Jack Valenti, "Motion Picture Code and the New American Culture," *PTA Magazine,* December 1966, p. 19.

7. Leo Bogart, "Television News as Entertainment," in *The Entertainment Function of Television,* ed. Percy H. Tannenbaum (Hillsdale, N.J.: Erlbaum, 1980), pp. 209–249.

## 15.13  Audiences do not want the media to be very political

Audiences, too, resist the "public service" programming required of TV and radio stations. As television became accessible to more and more families from 1947 to 1957, it gradually replaced radio and the movies as the major source of entertainment for almost all categories of Americans. By the end of 1957, three-fourths of a national sample declared television to be their main source of entertainment. The electronic media are seen as part of the "fun" of the ordinary day—like the comic strips of the newspaper and the lunchtime chatter of bench- or office mates.

> It appears that television and, to a declining extent, radio are accepted as part of the daily routine, a reward of pleasure built into daily cycles of work and relaxation. At the end of a day's labor, most citizens seek entertainment, not the additional work involved in absorbing new information and ideas.[8]

About 85 percent of the content of commercial TV and radio stations consists of entertainment or of advertising related to entertainment programs. In view of the propensities of Americans, and in view of the fingertip availability of TV entertainment, it is not surprising that those who are heavy users of TV seem to be conventional in attitudes and in social and political opinions.[9]

## 15.2  THE COMMON DENOMINATOR IN MASS-MEDIA PROGRAMMING

Although the mass media generally do not regard themselves as political instruments—and although audiences do not want them to be or to become politicized—political leaders (for reasons we have hinted at and will soon develop further) *think* the mass media are (a) highly political and (b) politically very important. These perceptions are for our purposes the most significant things about the mass media.

Some characteristics of the media, however, do have significance for the opinion-policy process. Some have to do with the fact that the audiences of the mass media are unknown, in the most complete meaning of the word *unknown*— they are without personality. They are nonpersons, except in a statistical sense.[10]

---

8. Alfred O. Hero, *Mass Media and World Affairs* (Boston: World Peace Foundation, 1959), p. 110.

9. For references to earlier studies and for evidence that "involvement with television is associated with a syndrome of conventionality," see Russell H. Weigel and Richard Jessor, "Television and Adolescent Conventionality: An Exploratory Study," *Public Opinion Quarterly* 37 (1973): 76–90.

10. An appreciation of the nature of this anonymity in the mass media will help us understand why statistics and qualification generally have become so important to the economic well-being, the nature of "research," and the self-images of the mass media. With an audience necessarily consisting of "unpersons" (in the stark language of Aldous Huxley's *Brave New World*), "success" is measured by numbers of listeners, readers, or viewers (sometimes broken down by statistical subsets to show that program X reaches, for example, more families with greater purchasing power than program Y, and "research" consists primarily of counting noses in the field or (as a congressional committee discovered in 1963) of making arbitrary guesses in an office—see *New York Times,* March 13, 1963.

To counter this disability, the media try to "personalize" their content, using colloquialisms, first-person addresses, and ego associations with fictional characters who are indeed typical in their thought processes but unusual in their dialogue, since they appear clever beyond all commonness. The most successful TV commentators of the intimate genre, the night-show people, build up large followings of viewers who sense that these actors, though still actors and still commercial, in some way and to some degree cut across the common denominator. Such talents, however, have not often been used with avowedly political intentions. It is doubtful that even the most winningly personalized approach would make television useful for the direct shaping of the political opinions of persons who are generally indifferent to public issues. Perhaps discussions between disc jockeys and listeners on radio talk shows, increasingly popular since the early 1960s, have some influence on apolitical listeners who happen to tune in for the arguments that sometimes develop. It is hard to know whether these shows really do constitute a "media kindergarten" for politics, or whether the telephone callers who engage in "spontaneous" on-the-air conversations are citizens who are already politicized, and who also use other means to further the public policies they support.[11]

Because of the increase in the technical and commercial feasibility of appealing to what Nieburg calls "segmented" audiences, the variety of TV and radio programming has been increased since the 1960s. Twenty years ago TV programs could not focus beyond the most general interests—that is, beyond the average audience member's tolerance for either specificity or abstraction. Now, while "situation comedy" is still the most popular TV fare, there is evidence that specialized media systems (educational and noncommercial radio stations, private postal services, suburban newspapers, and computer networks) are growing faster than the conventional mass media. It may be as Richard Maisel contends, that "the mass media will—contrary to past expectations—play a less important role in the future, and the focus of scientific attention should be shifted to specialized media."[12]

## 15.3 MASS MEDIA AND THE FUNNEL OF CAUSALITY

It may be helpful to place the ideas discussed in this chapter in the model of

---

11. There has been little investigation of live conversation between listeners and broadcasters, and that is surprising inasmuch as the call-in shows constitute the only new public affairs programming to be developed in radio since the advent of TV. After an appearance on a TV call-in show in Nashville, Tom Wicker wrote: "One thing seems sure: the American people are an opinionated breed, and not hesitant to tell the airwaves what they think.... There is something else too...a listener in the glassy studios can sense in their words a note of desperation, an urge to communicate, to be in touch, to be heard, to register some statement amid the babble of voices" *(New York Times,* June 15, 1973).

12. Richard Maisel, "The Decline of Mass Media," *Public Opinion Quarterly* 37 (1973): 159. The general reader can profit much from the overview of new communication possibilities in Ithiel de Sola Pool, *Technologies of Freedom* (Cambridge: Harvard University Press, 1983).

opinion formation decribed in Chapter 7. The model compared the progressive focusing of interests and narrowing of opinions in each individual with a funnel. Into the large end of the funnel come various stimuli relevant to the developing opinion. They are played on by other stimuli within the funnel as time passes and as thinking and opinion formation proceed. The consequence is an opinion on an issue—as well formulated as is necessary to meet the level of articulation demanded of the individual by his own conception of the issue or by others with whom he interacts.

In the funnel of opinion causality (represented in Figure 15–1), A is a moment when an issue becomes significant for an individual, Ms. X. Suppose the issue is the building of a new school for which her tax money will be used or which her children will attend. There may be many stimuli of relevance to this issue, but for illustrative purposes we can put them in three clusters: *cultural predispositions* or preexisting attitudes; *personal influence* or leadership–followership relations; and *knowledge* (facts and impersonal opinions). Directly from the mass media, Ms. X may receive knowledge relevant to the question of the new school. Indirectly from the mass media—say, through her personal acquaintances—she may receive additional stimuli that help her form an opinion. The mass media will not influence the preexisting attitudes except in the broadest and most indirect ways. These and other stimuli, in which the mass media play some part, will mix over a period of time and may come down to an opinion that is acted on—in a bond referendum, for instance. But perhaps when the opinion has been formed, at point B, new stimuli of relevance will be experienced by Ms. X. To the extent warranted by the new stimuli, or to the extent that the new stimuli reopen earlier uncertainties, the funnel of causality is widened again, as Figure 15–1 indicates, and the resolution process is carried again to an opinion—the same or a different one.

## 15.4 CULTURAL PREDISPOSITIONS AND THE MASS MEDIA

In Chapter 9 we considered the effects of culture on opinions and noted that opinions are limited by the generally accepted standards of good taste, fairness, and the humanistic traditions of Western culture. We also observed that industrialized societies tend to be characterized by a great diversity of values and behavior standards and that the cultural restrictions of the United States in the 1980s, in contrast to those of premodern societies, are small indeed. Except for the myths that relate to nationalism and patriotism, almost all cultural commands and injunctions can be safely questioned; the range of potential opinion is great; and the limits of public opinion are not to be found so much in cultural prescriptions or proscriptions as in the deficiencies of imagination and in the ego needs that make conformity attractive and nonconformity painful.

Nevertheless, some cultural proclivities of twentieth-century America have relevance for the mass media. Herbert Gans found that media elites share six

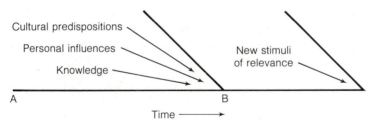

**Figure 15–1.** *Funnel of opinion causality: Elements that may be influenced by the mass media*

basic preconceptions and orientations; he calls them "enduring values." They are (1) ethnocentrism (concentration on our own ideals and superiorities); (2) altruistic democracy (the ideal that the "public interest" should always take precedence over self-interest and partisanship); (3) responsible capitalism; (4) small-town pastoralism (rural and non-industrial places and ways are to be preferred); (5) individualism; and (6) moderatism (extremism and excess in any form are to be discouraged).[13] All of these values have political implications, of course, but they are not specifically political in content.

Among nonelites there is a lingering belief that the citizen *ought* to have an opinion on all matters of public policy. The ideal of the omnicompetent citizen has filtered deeply and widely throughout American society. The evidence is found in the answers of survey respondents who say "yes" or "no" when they should say "I don't know." It is also seen in the deep contradictions of the New Haven workingmen interviewed by Lane, who were very badly informed but who refused either to blame others for their ignorance or to turn to others for advice. This phenomenon, which Robert Lane called "the parthenogenesis of knowledge," was observed by Tocqueville in the 1830s and is related to fears of being influenced as well as to the idea of the "rational man" that is so pervasive in American culture.[14]

Persons who believe—yet not too strongly—that they *ought* to have opinions tend to look to the mass media for help. But because the motivation for most people's opinions on public issues is weak, as the ease with which they order and assess relevant facts also is weak, the help sought from the mass media is in the nature of clues that make public events simple and consistent with preexisting values and a conventional world view. The mass media are consequently obliged to simplify, dramatize, and emotionalize the reporting of events at the same time that they cater to the need for personalization. Readers have their cake and eat it too when they read a headline telling them (without the intervention of another person, friend or stranger) that a public event or issue may be thought of in the

---

13. Herbert J. Gans, *Deciding What's News: A Study of CBS Evening News, NBC Nightly News, Newsweek, and Time* (New York: Pantheon, 1979), pp. 42–52.

14. See Robert E. Lane, *Political Ideology: Why the Common Man Believes What He Does* (New York: Free Press, 1962), pp. 373–377.

context of an already existing opinion or set of opinions. Eunice Cooper and Marie Jahoda found that persons introduced to ideas contrary to their existing attitudes adopted a number of compensatory and rationalizing devices to make the new data compatible with or irrelevant to those attitudes.[15]

Important differences in degree of influence exist between media the audience distrusts and those it considers more objective. A message may be widely accepted when it appears in a source thought to be trustworthy. The same message may be rejected when it is printed in a periodical thought to be untrustworthy.[16]

People generally give greater credence to the electronic media than to the printed word. Greater authority somehow attaches to facts or opinions expressed by TV and radio (see Table 15–2). Why the electronic media are considered more reliable and more fair than the print media may be partly a matter of individual psychological processes, but probably much of the difference can be attributed to the histories of the two kinds of media. In the Anglo-American tradition, newspapers and magazines have always been contentious, if not downright cantankerous, in their expressions of political opinion. At least since the seventeenth century, political controversies have been carried on by means of printed propaganda. The newspapers of the American Revolutionary period and the early years of our republic were unashamedly partisan, engaging in diatribe and invective that today would be considered extremely ill-mannered if not libelous. Newspapers still sometimes express their editorial views with conviction unmatched in any other media. By comparison, television and radio handling of public issues is dull, standardized, dryly descriptive, and nonpartisan. This difference is known or is sensed by the consumers of the media.

The print media are relatively unregulated by the U.S. government and are jealous of their freedom from regulation. The electronic media have a different

**Table 15-2**   Percentage of respondents expressing trust in various media, 1959–1978 "If you get conflicting or different reports of the same news story from radio, TV, magazines, and the newspapers, which one are you inclined to believe?"

| Mass medium | 1959 | 1963 | 1966 | 1971 | 1976 | 1978 |
|---|---|---|---|---|---|---|
| TV ..................... | 29% | 36% | 41% | 49% | 51% | 47% |
| Newspapers ................ | 32 | 24 | 24 | 20 | 22 | 23 |
| Radio .................... | 12 | 12 | 7 | 10 | 7 | 9 |
| Magazines ................. | 10 | 10 | 8 | 9 | 9 | 9 |
| DK/NA .................. | 17 | 18 | 20 | 12 | 11 | 12 |

Source: Roper Organization, for Television Information Office.

15. Eunice Cooper and Marie Jahoda, "The Evasion of Propaganda: How Prejudiced People Respond to Anti-Prejudice Propaganda," *Journal of Psychology* 23 (1947): 15–25.

16. For some experimental findings on this point, see Carl I. Hovland and Walter Weiss, "The Influence of Source Credibility on Communication Effectiveness," *Public Opinion Quarterly* 15 (1952): 635–650. And for a review of the recent literature see Brian Sternthal et al., "The Persuasive Effect of Source Credibility: A Situation Analysis," ibid. 42 (Fall 1978): 285–314.

history and posture in relation to the government; they are subject to close technical regulation by the FCC. It is popularly presumed that their content is also regulated, although there is in fact very little regulation of content. But because the users of the media believe the national government monitors the fairness and objectivity of TV and radio, they apparently feel more sure about those media.

A number of investigators have studied the effects of mass media on the political behavior of Americans. Lane's summary is still accurate:

> Exposure to the media increases political discussion, and political discussion increases exposure to the media.
>
> The reinforcement effect of the media is greater than the conversion effect.
>
> While reading, listening, and viewing political material in the media are sometimes substitutes for civic or political action (narcotizing dysfunction), usually they are preliminary to such action.
>
> While the media occasionally discourage political action by featuring the complexity of social problems, more frequently they oversimplify them, giving a (false) impression that the members of the public can devise their own solutions.
>
> The media present more news and comment on public affairs than most of the public demand, thus politicizing rather than apathizing the public.
>
> While the news sections of the media tend to give prominence to political figures, and, in this sense, confer status upon them and upon political activity, the fiction in the media fails to cast its heroes in governmental or political roles.
>
> Fictional presentations in the media attribute evil and suffering to personal, not social or political...problems presented, thus distracting attention from the gains to be achieved through political participation.
>
> Emphasis upon citizen duty in the media (to the extent that it is emphasized) serves to bring the widely recognized but private "do-nothing morality" closer to the official morality of the democratic dogma.
>
> The tendency of media owners, advertisers, and segments of the media audiences to dislike references to the roots of social conflict (class or ethnic) weakens the resonance of the media with the problems of the time and, hence, weakens the power to stimulate political response.
>
> On balance, however, exposure to the media is associated with: (a) interest in politics, (b) higher turnout, (c) joining community organizations, (d) superior information, (e) stronger views, (f) closeness to the party position, (g) strong candidate preferences.[17]

---

17. Robert E. Lane, *Political Life: Why People Get Involved in Politics* (New York: Free Press, 1959), chap. 19, "Mass Media and Mass Politics," pp. 275–298; quotation from pp. 288–289. Copyright 1959. Reprinted by permission of The Macmillian Company.

## 15.5 THE MASS MEDIA AS POLITICAL
##          AGENDA SETTERS

Not everything that happens in the world that *might be* of political significance can be reported by the media. It is apparent, then, that journalists, publishers, and producers must sift through the mass of available material and select items to print and to broadcast. That is the grossest sense in which the media decision makers become "gatekeepers" (another term, no longer as popular as *agenda setters,* for persons who perform the agenda-setting function).

Since the early 1970s, investigation of agenda setting by the media has taken diverse directions through three time periods. The first reaction was one of alarm and exposure, as if some new evil and threat to democracy had suddenly been revealed. Some of the concern and alarm was expressed in sophisticated and abstract speculations about sociopolitical elites who kept status-quo-threatening issues off the public agenda by monopolizing the institutions of government and the mass media.[18] Some commentators charged overt conspiracy, in consonance with the belief that regional or national power elites (discussed in Chapter 2) intimidated and/or patronized the mass-media managers in order to promote elite interests only. Some of these viewers-with-alarm employed the jargon of pop sociology and pop psychology.[19] And some, lamenting the lost dream of popular democracy, asserted that the people can never know the "truth" or "reality" of what goes on in the world because the powerful mass-media managers have political or commercial interests of their own that they promote as the only important issues of the moment.[20]

The second phase, in the middle and late 1970s, was given to more balanced and less alarmist examination of the dynamics of agenda setting. Who were the active participants in the events and pseudo-events that competed for attention from the mass media? What were the criteria and the processes of actual selection from print and electronic journalists? And what were the consequences of media selection of what-to-think-about for both mass and elite audiences?

In the third and current phase, as of this writing, the alarm of fifteen years ago has been much reduced, though not wholly eliminated. Few social scientists believe that the American democratic experiment is doomed to fail because of the machinations or the unwitting censorship of unorthodox views by a few media

18. See Peter Bachrach and Morton S. Baratz, "Two Faces of Power," *American Political Science Review* 56 (1962): 947–952, and, by the same authors, "Decisions and Nondecisions: An Analytical Framework," ibid. 57 (1963): 632–642.

19. See Alvin Tofler, *Future Shock* (New York: Random House, 1970), and two books by Vance D. Packard, *The Hidden Persuaders* (New York: David McKay Co., 1957) and *The People Shapers* (Boston: Little Brown, 1977).

20. G. Ray Funkhouser, "The Issues of the Sixties: An Exploratory Study in the Dynamics of Public Opinion," *Public Opinion Quarterly* 37 (1973): 62–75.

manipulators. The more thoroughly thought-out interpretations arrived at in the second phase of investigation are now being tested and refined.

By way of summary, here is what we now think we know about agenda setting:

1. Except for deliberate withholding and/or falsification at the request or with the connivance of governmental officials (dealt with in Chapter 17), very few concerns of even handsful of people are kept off the public agenda by mass-media censorship and/or neglect.

Occasionally, to be sure, the media fail to see the true significance of some events. It was almost certainly not a wish to protect President Nixon and his administration that initially kept the major papers and networks from challenging his contention that the Watergate break-in of June 1972 was merely a "second-rate burglary." That such an interpretation persisted for many months—even as Democratic candidate George McGovern labelled it "dirty politics" and a "cover-up"—is probably due more to journalistic laziness and cynicism about political charges than to a calculated misreporting of the significance of the break-in. Still, seen in retrospect, it was of great significance and, to use a cliché, just the tip of the iceberg of malfeasance, illegality, and obstruction of justice that characterized the Nixon reelection campaign of 1972.

The reasons that few significant events are neglected may be found in the great number and variety of reporting agencies in the United States. Long-term, chronic problems and inadequacies of American society and politics do not, in our opinion, get enough emphasis in the American mass media. The danger of nuclear war and the related dangers of nuclear power and waste management, the pervasive incivility and disinterest of public bureaucrats, our grossly unfair patterns of taxation and subsidies, and the manipulation of nationalistic images by president, State Department, and Pentagon (as by the Soviet Union and all nation-states) are dangers that the media, in the best of all worlds (according to our values), would emphasize, analyze, and help readers/viewers to understand in all their short- and long-term illiberal and antihuman implications. So we can agree with W. Lance Bennett that superficial, formalized, uncritical news stories, which constitute the overwhelming bulk of media news, are of little help to people who would like to develop what he calls "independent news judgment" through rich historical knowledge, understanding of the psychological and sociopolitical motives of elites, and a resistance to the journalistic ploys of personalization and superficiality. But Bennett asks newspapers and TV networks to be something other than mass institutions and to tailor their products to, in his words, the "tiny fraction of the public [that] has an understanding of American history of news politics, and [the] 10 percent of the public [that] can be called ideologues." [21] The danger he fears is not the media's agenda-setting role,

---

21. W. Lance Bennett, *News: The Politics of Illusion* (New York: Longman, 1983), especially pp. 100–102 and 148–152.

but the superficial and uncritical content of what journalists and political elites put on the agenda.

2. The meanings seen in agenda items by readers/viewers, rather than the existence of the items themselves, seem to determine what readers/viewers think about the items politically, and perhaps how they act with respect to those items. A message must be perceived as political and as having some personal meaning before it can influence any individual reader's or viewer's opinion—an important matter discussed earlier in connection with the funnel of causality. Lutz Erbring, Edie N. Goldenberg, and Arthur H. Miller make the point: "Estimates of media impact may become diluted beyond all usefulness if they merely represent average effects across a heterogeneous audience, only some of whose members are sensitive to the particular issue in question."[22]

For nonelites the mass media provide, for the most part, snippets of information, most of which is not seen as either political or personal. Repeated and reinforcing news, labeled as political, of the sort that occurs during major election campaigns, will be recognized as political by nonelites, and *may* have an effect on voting if it is economic in nature and related to the viewer/reader's own material well-being, or if it is perceived as symbolically related to national goodness and strength or to idealized qualities of a candidate or party. Doris Graber's conclusion seems generally applicable:

> Over time, the media do turn out to be effective providers of most of the information people need, given their desire to learn. Our panelists had learned specific details about the most prominent current news stories and had at least hazy recollections of the rest. They also had general notions about trends and broad patterns of politics, even though the media rarely supplied such analytical information explicitly.... What they knew, and the deductions and inferences that sprang from that knowledge, evidently was not limited to what the media supplied. The media are powerful, but not omnipotent, agenda-setters.[23]

For elites, the 10 to 20 percent of the adult population associated with long-term political interests, activities, and ideological underpinnings, the mass media provide details, last-minute information, and a few more or less sophisticated analyses. But such stimuli are supplementary to knowledge and convictions that are already in these people's funnels of causality. Some media stimuli conflict with and some reinforce stimuli received from conversations with primary-group peers and with those received through organizational channels

22. Lutz Erbring, Edie N. Goldenberg, and Arthur H. Miller, "Front-Page News and Real-World Cues: A New Look at Agenda-Setting by the Media," *American Journal of Political Science* 24 (1980): 19.

23. Doris A. Graber, *Processing the News: How People Tame the Information Tide* (New York: Longman, 1984), p. 78.

(interest groups and political parties, mainly). Thus the mass media alone do not set the agenda for political elites; they share that function with voluntary political and/or politicized groups that are made up, in large part, of those same political elites themselves.[24]

---

24. A major early statement of these phenomena may be found in Philip E. Converse, "Information Flow and the Stability of Partisan Attitudes," *Public Opinion Quarterly* 26 (1962): 578–599; a more recent confirming review of the literature may be found in Michael B. MacKuen, "Social Communication and the Mass Policy Agenda," in Michael B. MacKuen and Steven L. Coombs (eds.), *More than News: Media Power in Public Affairs* (Beverly Hills, Calif.: Sage, 1981), pp. 17–144. See also Michael B. MacKuen, "Exposure to Information, Belief Integration, and Individual Responsiveness to Agenda Change," *American Political Science Review* 78 (1984): 372–391; and a case study, Fay Lomax Cook et al., "Media and Agenda Setting: Effects on the Public, Interest Group Leaders, Policy Makers, and Policy," *Public Opinion Quarterly* 47 (1983): 16–35.

## Chapter 16

# Television and Radio

It is difficult to overemphasize the place of the electronic media in American lives. There are more than twice as many working radios in America as there are Americans. Virtually all Americans have at least one working television set in their living places. The average person spends six to seven hours a day watching TV or listening to radio.

It appears that a great deal of this watching and listening is not very attentive; it goes on passively and indifferently, often while people engage in conversation or in other activities. Still, the media pervade the waking hours of both children and adults. TV's entertainment figures, both real and fictional, and its news commentators are among our best-known celebrities; Johnny Carson, J. R. Ewing, and Dan Rather are recognized by more people than anyone except the incumbent president and the pope.

## 16.1 THE PERVASIVE REACH OF TELEVISION: VIOLENCE, HIGH CULTURE, AND POLITICS

It is not surprising that there is much controversy over the social and political effects of the electronic media. For the past sixty years, beginning with the proliferation of home radio receivers and local broadcasting stations, various reformers (with preachers and professors leading the pack) have indicted the radio and television industries for everything from indifference to modern art to the destruction of children's personalities.

The social charges can be summed up in three ideas: (a) the media have failed to reflect the rich and abundant culture of the United States and the world; (b) they have wasted the opportunity to instruct and uplift the masses through programs of substance; and (c) they encourage antisocial behavior in children.

Intense research has focused on TV violence and the behavior of children. Hundreds of studies, using both experimental and survey techniques, have investigated the hypothesis that violent TV programs increase aggressiveness and antisocial acts of children. The most comprehensive and expensive (nearly $2 million) investigations were done in 1969–1971 by the U.S. Surgeon General's Scientific Advisory Committee on Television and Social Behavior. Its five-volume report, plus Senate hearings, were published by the Government Printing Office in 1972, and interested readers are directed to those works. According to Leo Bogart, "The overwhelming weight of evidence from this research supports the thesis that exposure to filmed or television violence tends to lead young children to a state of heightened excitability and to an increase in subsequent displays of aggression."[1] Despite these findings, the broadcast industry insisted that the evidence was not conclusive. Its view was put in perspective by Douglass Cater: "Television executives angrily denounced these findings while steadfastly assuring their advertisers that the 30-second commercial can have a proved impact on the viewing audience's behavior."[2]

Since the mid-1970s there have been two noteworthy developments in the matter of TV and violence. The first is, in one sense, a nondevelopment because, despite the flurry of demands for governmental regulation of TV programming immediately after the Surgeon General's Report, neither Congress nor the Federal Communications Commission (FCC) took any significant action. Leo Bogart thought in 1980 that TV managers had voluntarily reduced somewhat the level of violence in the late 1970s, but had increased the level of sexually suggestive or explicit material; he concluded that the report had had an effect, "primarily because of the changed position of key advertisers, who no longer wished to be associated with violent programs."[3] Maybe. At about the same time that Bogart wrote those words, a group of critics and reformers reported finding an average of almost seven violent acts per hour during prime time,[4] and the *New York Times* TV critic, John J. O'Connor, estimated that on the average "by age 16 a youngster would have witnessed 18,000 murders on television programming."[5]

The second development with respect to TV and its possible antisocial effects was the linkage of technological improvements and free-market theory to justify

---

1. Bogart's excellent review deserves the attention of students of social science and public policy: "Warning: The Surgeon General Has Determined that TV Violence is Moderately Dangerous to Your Child's Mental Health," *Public Opinion Quarterly* 36 (1972–73): 491–521; quotations at 494, 521.

2. Douglass Cater, "Television: 'Opium of the People,'" *New York Times,* December 27, 1983.

3. Leo Bogart, "After the Surgeon General's Report: Another Look Backward," in *Television and Social Behavior: Beyond Violence and Children,* eds. Stephen B. Withey and Ronald P. Abeles (Hillsdale, N.J.: Erlbaum, 1980), p. 131.

4. National Coalition on Television Violence, *NCTV News* 2 (July–August 1981): 1.

5. John J. O'Conner, "TV: Youth-Oriented Violence in America," *New York Times,* September 3, 1981.

deregulation in place of further regulation. As new UHF channels became available for both commercial and noncommercial TV stations and as cable TV capabilities expanded, it was argued that specialized programming, some violent or sexually explicit to suit "adult" tastes and some more "family oriented," would give parents options in their efforts to protect children and adolescents. In the climate of general support for market solutions to social dilemmas that characterized the first Reagan administration, the FCC greatly relaxed its regulations on public affairs programming and advertising for radio broadcasters. In 1983, following a negotiated settlement of an antitrust suit brought against the National Association of Broadcasters, the NAB abandoned its voluntary, self-regulating "Radio and Television Codes of Good Practice," allowing "each broadcaster and network to set its own internal guidelines."[6] In related moves Congress in early 1984 was considering a bill that would repeal some special TV and radio requirements on fairness and equal time and another that would repeal the requirement that licences must be renewed every five years.[7] While these deregulation moves are not specifically directed at violence in programming (since there is no regulation of violence per se), they illustrate the pervasive tendencies to avoid the hard constitutional and administrative problems that are associated with the regulation of communications content in a democratic polity. "Public anxieties about television continued to support demands for some form of political oversight, but in an era of new technologies and strong deregulatory pressure, the fiduciary principle [that the government should uphold the public interest by protecting TV audiences from antisocial programming] was tending to give way to the rhetoric of increased competition and marketplace solutions."[8]

Beyond the matters of violence and sex, some of the criticisms of the electronic media have to do with the functions that they perform—or, as the complaints are ordinarily phrased, that they do *not* perform—in the opinion-policy process. Many people feel that the media have a responsibility to search out the facts on important issues; to make these facts available quickly and thoroughly to the public; to provide a forum for the discussion and consideration of these facts (and of all the opinions that might be relevant to the facts, or to the problems to which the facts are germane); and to subordinate to such programming (a) the commercial interests that finance it and (b) the desire for fame or affluence that motivates the individuals involved in the media.

Some people say that the mass media, especially television, encourage bad

---

6. "Broadcasters Dropping Their Code," Associated Press story in *San Francisco Chronicle,* January 6, 1983.

7. David Burnham, "Congress Is Considering New TV Licensing Law," *New York Times,* November 7, 1983, and "Broadcast Regulation Backed," ibid., February 2, 1984.

8. Willard D. Rowland, Jr., *The Politics of TV Violence: Policy Uses of Communication Research* (Beverly Hills, Calif.: Sage, 1983), p. 299. See also the related observations in Thomas D. Cook et al., "The Implicit Assumptions of Television Research: An Analysis of the 1982 NIMH Report on *Television and Behavior," Public Opinion Quarterly* 47 (1983): 161–201.

taste, pander to mediocrity, and do not take advantage of their many opportunities to educate the public. What the critics fail to recognize is that mass audiences in all places and at all recorded times have had bad taste (according to the critics' standards), have been mediocre, have delighted in violence and crime, and have rejected education. So before we adopt wholeheartedly the reformers' view that popular culture is morally or aesthetically inferior to "high" culture, we might reflect on arts critic Terrence O'Flaherty's warning that not all our attention should be focused on "wife-beaters, homicidal maniacs and other brigands adored by the violence-prone Nielsen ratings families,...neglecting the most bloodthirsty audience of all—grand opera lovers, the folks who find cussedness more acceptable in costume."[9]

In further explanation, if not in defense, of TV mediocrity, it must be pointed out that great art (violent or not) simply cannot be produced in large enough quantity to fill an eighteen- to twenty-hour broadcast day for three major networks and several hundred individual stations. There is not that much artistic talent in America, and there is no general evidence, despite some clear individual cases, that mediocrity, pressures, and discrimination keep people of excellence out of the television industry and its productions.

Even the most extreme critics acknowledge that some excellent television programs are aired. But they want more of what they consider excellent and less of what they consider bad or mediocre. They fail to acknowledge that (a) there is a great deal of choice (and, more important, public-service choice) in television; (b) a program-production system based on private, profit-taking enterprise cannot afford to "elevate" its audience's taste at the cost of losing viewers; and (c) when offered a choice between what the critics consider "high-taste" and "low-taste" programs, the public will usually (though not always) choose the "low-taste."

The critics admit that American TV programming has some variety and, if they are willing to turn the dial and shop around the channels, they can be informed and uplifted to some extent. The charge is that there are not enough good programs, and that what is available tends to be concentrated in Sunday-afternoon and early-morning oases in "the wasteland." The industry argues that, under conditions of private enterprise the good, small-audience programs are made possible only by the large-audience mediocrity to which the critics object.

We are interested in politics and in opinions of importance to the political processes in the United States. Except indirectly, through basic values and educational levels, the social criticism of television and radio is less relevant to our interests than are its political responsibilities and problems.

---

9. Terrence O'Flaherty, "Never Bury Your Mother in a Pasture," *San Francisco Chronicle,* September 28, 1983. More scholarly works on these matters include Herbert Gans, *Popular Culture and High Culture* (New York: Basic Books, 1974), and W. Russell Neuman, "Television and American Culture: The Mass Medium and the Pluralist Audience," *Public Opinion Quarterly* 46 (1982): 471–487.

## 16.2 TELEVISION AS POLITICAL SOCIALIZATION AGENT

Television, as we have seen, is a major influence in the lives of Americans, young and old. Its profound political effects, both direct and indirect, are obvious and are considered throughout this chapter. Here we shall do no more than comment on television as an agent in setting, reinforcing, or changing the political attitudes and opinions of children and adolescents.

There seems to be no general relationship between political interest, knowledge, and opinions, on the one hand, and, on the other hand, the viewing of entertainment, sports, or other nonpolitical TV programs. There is a strong relationship, however, between political interest, knowledge, and opinions and the viewing of TV public affairs and news programs. Margaret Conway, Jay Stevens, and Robert Smith found, for example, that among fourth-, fifth-, and sixth-graders in Michigan, regardless of partisanship, those who watched TV news had fuller and more sophisticated perceptions of party differences, lawmaking, and the political roles of various public officials than those who did not.[10]

This pattern is clearly to be expected, and is found among adults as well: people who watch more news and public affairs programming know more about politics, express higher levels of interest in politics, and have more opinions about political issues.

Conway and her colleagues also found that newspapers were a more effective source of political knowledge for children than was TV news. This finding, too, is consistent with that of other research showing that among adults the reading of newspapers is much more likely to be associated with knowledge and discriminating perceptions about politics than is reliance on TV news and public affairs programs.[11]

These investigations led to the provisional conclusion that television in general is not very directly important as a *motivator* of political interest or of political attitudes. Other agents—family, formal education, and peers—seem to be the basic determinants of political interest and activity in children and young adults. If they are, then TV serves as an important source of day-to-day political knowledge, but is perhaps not so important as printed sources such as newspapers and magazines.[12]

In a larger and indirect sense, however, television may profoundly influence

10. M. Margaret Conway, A. Jay Stevens, and Robert Smith, "The Relation between Media Use and Children's Civic Awareness," *Journalism Quarterly* 52 (1975): 531–538. See also Steven Chaffee et al., "Mass Communication and Political Socialization," ibid. 47 (1971): 647–659, and Charles K. Atkin and Walter Gantz, "Television News and Political Socialization," *Public Opinion Quarterly* 42 (1978): 183–198.

11. Peter Clarke and Eric Fredin, "Newspapers, Television, and Political Reasoning," *Public Opinion Quarterly* 42 (1978): 143–160.

12. M. Margaret Conway et al., "The News Media in Children's Political Socialization," *Public Opinion Quarterly* 45 (1981): 164–178.

the political learning of young and old. Statistical studies of heavy viewers versus light viewers will not reveal these indirect influences. Michael Hughes summarizes the more global possibilities of TV influence on American life, including political attitudes and opinions:

> [T]elevision in American society may be related to the diffusion of culture and to alterations in social structure, both of which affect the behavior of virtually all persons in the society regardless of how much television they watch. For example, persons who watch television may be carriers of cultural innovations, ways of conceptualizing the world, and variations in lifestyles which, through social interaction in the real world, are diffused to persons who had little, if any, contact with the original messages. Furthermore, television structures the markets for consumer goods of all kinds, and therefore is in large part responsible for the way consumers are tied into the economy and the way producers develop products and organize marketing activities .... Similarly, television has changed the structure of political campaigns, and modified the way persons view the political system and their personal relationship to it. In short, if the effects of television on American society are as pervasive as these limited examples suggest, then trying to uncover the effect of television by comparing heavy and light watchers is bound to result in inconsistent and largely uninterpretable findings.[13]

## 16.3 THE POLITICAL REGULATION OF TELEVISION AND RADIO

From 1934, when the Federal Communications Commission was established, until 1981, it was generally assumed that the scarcity of usable bands in the spectrum of radio waves (and, later, of television frequencies) required close national regulation of broadcasting licenses. Frequencies assigned, power of transmission, and hours of operation were, and still are, rigidly supervised by the FCC.

Beyond technical regulation it was held that broadcasters had some obligation to provide broad "public service" programming, since they were given the right to monopolize a public resource for private gain. But directing *what* someone may or must say—even a private broadcaster using public property—raises difficult First Amendment questions about free speech. And so it was not until the late 1940s that common-law traditions, statutes, court precedents, and policy deliberations came together to produce a more or less coherent body of rules governing the political uses of TV and radio. These regulatory policies and practices can be

---

13. Michael Hughes, "The Fruits of Cultivation Analysis: A Reexamination of Some Effects of Television Watching," *Public Opinion Quarterly* 44 (1980): 301. Reprinted by permission.

summarized under three headings: "fairness," "reasonable access," and "equal time."

## 16.31 The fairness doctrine

In 1949 the FCC authorized editorializing by radio and television stations. The commission at that time established two general requirements: that stations "devote a reasonable portion of broadcast time to the discussion and consideration of controversial issues of public importance...[and] make the facilities available for the expression of contrasting viewpoints when controversial issues are presented." In the application of these general requirements, station managers were to exercise their "best judgment and good sense."[14]

Nearly thirty years after the doctrine was promulgated, one observer believed that "the first part of the Fairness Doctrine—the obligation to cover important issues—has generally been left entirely to the discretion of broadcasters. ...[But] the second part of the Fairness Doctrine—the obligation, once an issue has been raised, to be balanced in presenting contrasting views—has led to much more significant official interference with programming."[15]

What *is* the fairness doctrine? In the early 1970s, station managers, advertisers, and political leaders asked the FCC to be more specific about which programming might be "fair" and which "unfair." The FCC held a five-day-long review. To its credit, the commission refused to issue detailed regulations or guidelines on what constitutes fairness. It said that the "genius" of the fairness doctrine lay in the leeway it allowed station managers to contribute to an informed electorate, and that more detailed regulation might inhibit those contributions. The commission continues to referee the matter by taking cases involving the application of the doctrine in specific circumstances. Through that process, the commission and its staff have in recent years provided some direction, case by case, with regard to:

**1.** Editorial advertising—that is, *selling* time to people who want to support or oppose a public policy. The rule seems to be that a station cannot flatly refuse to take such advertising, but presumably libelous or unreasonable editorial advertising may be refused.

**2.** Countercommercials—that is, free public service announcements specifically pointing out the dangers or deceptiveness of commercially advertised products (example: The American Cancer Society's antismoking ads). The commission has been reluctant to require station managers to accept countercommercials. In a case involving allegedly fraudulent toy ads, it said the fairness

---

14. Federal Communications Commission, *Thirty-Eighth Annual Report, Fiscal Year 1972* (Washington, D.C.: Government Printing Office, 1973), p. 32.
15. Benno C. Schmidt, Jr., "Pluralistic Programming and Regulation of Mass Communication Media," in *Communication for Tomorrow: Policy Perspectives for the 1980s,* ed. Glen O. Robinson (New York: Praeger, 1978), p. 200.

doctrine should not be applied to claims regarding the "efficacy or social utility" of general product advertising.

**3.** Response time—that is, free opportunity of reply by groups claiming they have been damaged by programs broadcast. The generalization here is that stations must provide time for rebuttals by organizations that have some representative quality, but single individuals do not necessarily have the right to request response time. Response time is appropriate only in cases of "controversial issues"—a matter of interpretation. Judicial reform, for example, appears to be a controversial issue to the FCC, while military recruiting is not.

**4.** Personal attack—that is, an individual specifically singled out for criticism by a station must be so notified, furnished with a script or tape of the criticism, and given a reasonable and timely opportunity to respond.

## 16.32 Reasonable access rule

In 1972 the Communications Act was amended to prohibit arbitrary refusal to broadcast campaign advertising by candidates for Congress or the presidency. The law says that "candidates for federal office" must have "an affirmative right of reasonable access to the use of broadcast facilities," that broadcasters cannot make blanket policies denying such access, and that all requests must be considered individually on the facts. The FCC's interpretation of the rule, affirmed by the Supreme Court, is that the requests must be timely and that the rule refers to *purchased* time only (free time being regulated by the equal time rule).

## 16.33 Equal time

Section 315 of the Communications Act requires that when free air time is offered to one candidate, all other candidates for the same office must be offered equal time. The commission and the courts have consistently observed both the spirit and the letter of this requirement, with consequences that would be merely ludicrous were they not damaging to the political process. If every publicity-seeking minor candidate must be offered time equal to that given major candidates, TV and radio stations will offer no one free time.

There is one general exception to the equal time requirement. When a bona fide news program carries a report or film clip of, or a brief statement by, a candidate, other candidates do not have to be given precisely equal time or treatment. As would be expected, much of the controversy over the application of the equal time rule comes on the point of what is and what is not a "bona fide news program." The national and local news summaries, aired at the dinner hour and again later in the evening, are clearly "bona fide" and exempt from the equal time requirement. Recent rulings have distinguished between "bona fide" news interview programs," such as "Meet the Press" and "Face the Nation," which are exempt from the equal time requirement, and such talk shows as "Donahue," which are not exempt.

For twenty-odd years, every study of campaign financing and regulation has recommended revision or abolition of the equal time provision. In a spurt of experimental energy, Congress exempted the 1960 presidential race from the equal time requirement, but it has not done even that in the last six presidential campaigns. There are two main reasons why the equal time provision is not amended or abolished. One is that the rule gives an advantage to incumbents who are running for reelection. They get more exposure on bona fide news programs and are usually better known generally than their major opponents. They need public service—that is free—television and radio time less than their major challengers do. And since incumbent members of Congress are the very ones who would have to revise a rule that benefits them, it must be clear why revisions have not yet been made.

The second reason for the failure, so far, to amend the equal time provision of Section 315 is that there are indeed serious questions of fairness to all candidates who might be affected. Should TV and radio managers be given complete freedom to select some candidates for free time and ignore other candidates for the same office? Should the law give free time only to the Democratic and Republican parties' candidates? Or should the FCC itself be authorized to choose in each race each election year which candidates are important enough to receive free time and which are not?

In a major 1981 policy announcement, the FCC adopted a legislative program that, in its words, "favored market forces over regulation." Specifically, the commission sought the "deletion of access rights for political candidates,...repeal of the equal time provisions, [and] repeal of the Fairness Doctrine"[16] The intention of the Reagan administration of the early and mid-1980s was to extend to electronic communication the deregulation policies begun earlier by the Ford and Carter administrations with respect to banking, airline travel, and interstate trucking. As of 1984, bills were pending in both houses of Congress to eliminate or drastically reduce the effects of the fairness, reasonable access, and equal time doctrines. Despite support from some Democrats as well as from Republicans, no changes had been made through the election campaigns of 1984.

### 16.34  Some suggestions for free and reduced-rate time

Speculation by critics and reformers often ends in agreement that the law should require some substantial free time for major candidates (say, a total of three or four hours of network time for a presidential candidate), with proportionately less time for other candidates who qualify for the same office. Thus in a U.S. Senate race, for example, the Democratic and Republican parties' candidates might be given one prime-time hour each (not necessarily all at once), and the

---

16. Federal Communications Commission, *Forty-Eighth Annual Report, Fiscal Year 1982* (Washington, D.C.: Government Printing Office, 1983), p. 14.

candidates of the other parties fifteen minutes each. Such formulas for allocation of free time would rest on the presumption that candidates who have no popular support would not be on the ballot (since state laws ordinarily require a substantial number of voters' signatures for a person to qualify as a minor or third-party candidate). And the allocations would give exposure to the more important races and candidates without making the media spend more resources than they can justify, or more time than their audiences want, on marginal and often irrelevant candidacies. The British for years have allocated free campaign broadcast time proportionately on the basis of votes the various parties obtained in the previous election. Such allocations would be more complex in the United States but not unworkable.

The television and radio industries, networks and individual stations alike, should be expected (and required by the FCC, if necessary) to provide additional special opportunities for candidates during campaigns. To avoid hardship to the broadcasters and to keep within the tolerance level of the apolitical portion of mass audiences, free or reduced-rate political time should be limited to a short period (say, thirty days) before the election. The current practice is for some free time to be given to candidates, either directly or through the airing of bipartisan panels and forums sponsored by such citizen groups as the League of Women Voters. Little such free time is available, however.

A guaranteed minimum amount of free time, or of combined free and reduced-rate time, should be made available in a general election to all candidates running in an electoral district that is larger than some minimum geographical size. The law (or FCC ruling) might say, for example, that stations must give thirty minutes of free time to each general-election candidate in all electoral districts that cover half or more of the broadcast area. Limiting the free-time period to general elections would avoid the intricacies of defining candidacy and the burden of providing time for large numbers of primary aspirants in some areas. It would also have the salutary effect of encouraging the minority party to field candidates, and thus speed the development of two-partyism.

In addition to free time for the major general-election candidates, reduced-rate time might be required for other candidates within the broadcast area. It is not desirable, of course, that *all* candidates be given reduced-rate time. A sound policy would discourage rather than encourage political broadcasts over a large area of which the candidate's district is only a small fraction. The citizens of twenty-four wards of a city should not be required to suffer the compulsory loss of a TV channel so that the candidate of the twenty-fifth ward can appeal to one twenty-fifth of the potential viewers. Obviously, any requirement of free or reduced-rate time must be sensible in its coverage and applied with good judgment.

Besides providing free campaigning time, television and radio stations ought to take positions on issues and candidates. Since 1949, individual stations have been free to editorialize, but few have taken advantage of the opportunity. Indeed, it was not until October 27, 1960, that an American radio station endorsed a candidate for president of the United States. On that evening, at 10:35 P.M., WMCA/New York came out for John F. Kennedy and declared that it would take its "public responsibility seriously, even when it means running risks of being ahead of the times." That WMCA was ahead of the times is not to be doubted, for less than one-third of American stations seem to be editorializing at all, and only a very few support candidates by name. There is as yet no evidence that the stations that editorialize have been harmed by the practice.

## 16.4 TELEVISION AND RADIO IN THE OPINION-POLICY PROCESS

### 16.41 Public service programming

Since the 1961–1962 campaign of Chairman Newton Minow of the FCC (who lost his fight in Congress for greater regulatory authority and resigned his office in early 1963), television has been not quite the vast wasteland he found it to be, and the networks have strengthened their public service programming. Public service news coverage of international events, space launchings, and presidential politics is more than adequate, is technically superb, and attracts large audiences. Smaller audiences are found for such discussion and issues programs as "Face the Nation," "Meet the Press," and the network "specials."

In September 1963, *New York Times* TV critic Jack Gould declared that he had seen "a turning point in TV's journalistic evolution."[17] His extravagant statement was elicited by a three-hour prime time NBC special, "The American Revolution of '63," depicting the black struggle for full civil rights. Never before had so much of the most heavily watched time been given to a public service program. The regular sponsors for NBC documentaries did not underwrite the program, fearing adverse economic consequences. As a result, the network lost an estimated half-million dollars by its decision to show "a balanced, thoughtful, and penetrating treatment of what is unquestionably the most important and most controversial domestic problem of our time."[18]

Since September 1963, a large number of special-events programs—many of them politically controversial and critical of powerful interests in the United States—have been seen by TV audiences. Programs on the exploitation of migrant workers, on hunger and malnutrition, on black extremism, on lobbying by the military, on industrial damage to the environment, and dozens of programs critical of U.S. foreign policies have added immeasurably to the vigor and quality of our dialogue on the public business. It appears that public affairs TV programming is watched by a smaller audience than regular entertainment

17. *New York Times,* September 3, 1963.
18. Richard Elden, "TV Nets Pick Up Some Big Costs," *Chicago Sun-Times,* September 3, 1963.

programming, but the audience is older, wealthier, and better educated.[19] Because of smaller audiences, sponsorship is harder to come by. Controversy still scares sponsors, too, and the losses the networks often take on public affairs programming have to be made up by profits from mass-appeal shows.

Commenting on TV's ability to get behind the sham and showmanship to the realities of sports events but its apparent unwillingness to do the same in political coverage, *New York Times* editor James Reston recently wrote: "Most of the time the networks are patsies for politicians and give them time to put their baloney on the screen. But when television puts its mind to a documentary, it is a powerful educational force. The trouble is that. . .it doesn't put on many documentaries because they don't get good popular ratings, which are the name of the television game."[20]

In the best of all worlds there should be, no doubt, more public service programming. But with present market demands, the electronic mass media offer American viewers and voters more pertinent facts and opinions than they are ever likely to need in discharging their civic responsibilities. The record of recent years seems to be that commercial TV is offering much that is insipid and banal and also much that is enlightening and politically controversial. Much television programming is mere chaff, but much of it is good wheat for the mills of the opinion-policy process.

## 16.42  Biases and pressures in electronic journalism

In recent years, television and radio have been about as good in variety and coverage of public service programming as the industry's economics and the audience's tastes will allow. Nevertheless, television especially is so important as a source of information and as one of the main agenda-setters for the mass public—and thus indirectly for political elites—that many additional matters need to be dealt with in this chapter.

One is the question of ideological and/or commercial pressures that may be brought to bear on news and public affairs broadcasts and so may compromise the integrity of TV journalists. Many critics, inside and outside of the broadcasting industry, have charged over the years that sponsors and advertising agencies have censored the political content of programming. It has also sometimes been charged that the networks unduly influence and dominate their affiliated stations.

Pressures toward conformity and the avoidance of controversy continue to be one of the hazards of TV programming. One may assume that the reported instances of pressure brought to bear by networks, sponsors, or advertising

---

19. See a study of documentaries on developing countries during the period 1963–1967: Gerald M. Jaffe, "Emerging Nations: What the Public Watches," *Television Quarterly* 7 (1968): 84–92.

20. James Reston, "Why Political Coverage on Television is Different," *Merced* (Calif.) *Sun-Star,* June 23, 1984.

agencies are only a small fraction of the total. Pressure from the networks or stations on individual commentators or actors is frequently reported, and scripts are often changed. Sometimes programs are "killed" outright. The hardiest and most independent commentators sometimes resign—occasionally with fanfare and drama—rather than suffer the subtle censorship or the threat of censorship that is, in Eric Sevareid's words, like "being bitten to death by ducks."

A reprehensible case was the 1972 boycott of CBS by Castle and Cooke Co., producers of Bumble Bee seafoods. Castle and Cooke executives objected to the way CBS News treated Senate hearings on water pollution in 1970. In August 1971 the company's agent wrote CBS asking that "in the future, when presenting news, you will more objectively present both sides of an issue." In January 1972 the same agent advised time buyers that "it is our clients' current policy not to advertise on CBS-TV affiliates." Richard Salant, head of CBS News, commented, "I do not recall ever having been faced before with so blatant an attempt by advertisers to influence news handling and to punish a news organization." This remark underscored the *Times* writer's observation that "sponsor pressure on commercial TV programming has been a center of debate since television's, and radio's, infancy."[21]

Herbert Gans's study of the NBC and CBS news departments found very little overt pressure for selection or deletion of stories or for preferential treatment of sponsors' interests. He reported that "the evening news programs and the news-magazines are virtually free of [advertiser's pressure]." Pressure may be felt, however, on the longer news documentaries. "Sponsors' lack of enthusiasm for news documentaries generally, and those on controversial topics specifically, can discourage their production."

In the relations between networks and their affiliated stations, pressures run both ways. At the local level, broadcasters may have to tailor their offerings to local tastes, and at times exercise selectivity, if not censorship, to avoid outraging community standards. The local stations can generate reverse pressure on network officials in New York, from the bottom up, as it were. Summing up that kind of pressure, Gans says: "While affiliates do not seem to effect censorship or self-censorship, they have been able to bring about, or hasten, the removal of individual on-air reporters." He cites as examples the 1950s radio firings of Martin Agronsky, Elmer Davis, and Raymond Gram Swing; the shifting of Dan Rather out of regular reporting when he was criticized by the Nixon administration; and the 1976 firing of Daniel Schorr for leaking a secret congressional document. It should be noted here, however, that though Gans reports these as affiliate pressures on networks, they are essentially *political* and not economic, and they do not seem to be related to sponsors' influence.[22]

On the other side, network national decision makers have the power to

---

21. John J. O'Connor, "Why You Won't See Bumble Bee Ads on CBS-TV," *New York Times,* March 7, 1972.

22. Herbert J. Gans, *Deciding What's News: A Study of CBS Evening News, NBC Nightly News, Newsweek, and Time* (New York: Pantheon, 1979), pp. 253, 256, 259.

intimidate, if they choose, both member stations and independent stations by threatening to buy or sell them or their competitors, by requiring packaged deals, and by preempting time for certain network shows. Network pressure can also run backward, in the course of program development, to the producers of the programs. One Hollywood producer of TV shows complained that the national networks "had more power than the seven members of the Federal Communications Commission" and that the three network presidents had "virtually complete control over the airwaves."[23]

## 16.43 Bias in TV campaign reporting

Whether the American mass media are politically biased is an old, interesting, and important question. Mostly it has been asked about the print media—especially newspapers—and here the answer is clearly yes. For historical and socioeconomic reasons already discussed, radio and TV have been relatively free from the charge of partisan or ideological distortion of the news. Edith Efron's *News Twisters* charged, however, that TV network news had a consistently liberal bias in the 1968 presidential election, airing ten times as much anti-Nixon as pro-Nixon comment.[24] A number of scholars criticized her methodology and polemical tendencies, but the large degree of unfairness she reported led to other evaluations of possible bias in TV political coverage.

The most ambitious of the studies of TV coverage of the 1972 presidential campaign distinguished between "structural bias" and "political bias." *Structural bias* was defined as advantage that might accrue to a candidate because of "factors associated with the medium itself," such as "the need to maintain an audience by dramatization of stories" or the rigid time constraints on TV news reporting. *Political bias* is deliberate favoritism on the part of "individual news personnel or executives." A total of 4,349 stories were examined as they appeared on all three networks between July 10 and November 6, 1972. Overall, the "analysis did establish substantial and consistent differences in the way . . . candidates, parties, and issues were covered." For example, the Democrats received both more coverage in more stories and more air time; but Nixon as a person and the Nixon campaign organization received more favorable coverage than did McGovern and his campaign organization. Thus there was some structural bias, but the balance of advantages and disadvantages seemed not to favor either candidate. And there was no pattern of political bias in the networks' news coverage of the 1972 campaign.[25]

Ideologues of both the Right and the Left criticize TV coverage of campaigns.

---

23. *New York Times,* July 29, 1961. See also FCC Network Inquiry Special Staff, *An Analysis of the Network–Affiliate Relationship in Television* (Washington, D.C.: Government Printing Office, October 1979).

24. Edith Efron, *The News Twisters* (Los Angeles: Nash, 1971).

25. C. Richard Hofstetter, *Bias in the News: Network Television of the 1972 Election Campaign* (Columbus: Ohio State University Press, 1976), pp. 197–203.

The Left ideologues claim there is structural bias because the networks and independent stations are part of the capitalist and anti-social-welfare establishment. We dealt with these charges earlier, and do again, passingly, in Chapter 17.

The criticisms of the ideological Right are different. They claim that the national "journalism establishment," so to speak, is disproportionately liberal and favors secular rather than religious values, nonmarket and pro-big-government economic policies, and too lenient attitudes toward internationalism and deviant moral and/or sexual lifestyles.

There is evidence that the *national* press corps in the United States is more liberal than the mass public. From 42 to 52 percent of samples of American journalists have described themselves as left of center in recent years (see Table 16–1), compared with 26 percent of combined national adult samples in 1980, 1982, and 1983.

In a series of articles in the early 1980s, Stanley Rothman and Robert and Linda Lichter documented the civil liberties, internationalist, anti-big-business, and pro-environmental biases of national television and print journalists, movie producers, and the prestigious mouthpiece for "advocacy journalism," the *Columbia Journalism Review*. Their overall conclusions were that the national media elite are "cosmopolitan in their origins, liberal in their outlooks, [and] aware and protective of their collective influence"; some people hail them "as the public's tribunes against the powerful...[while] others decry them for allegiance to an adversary culture that is chiseling away at traditional values."[26]

Gans's conclusion about the national media elite is balanced and accurate, we think. "Journalists," he says, "generally describe themselves as liberals, but liberalism is a synonym for being independent, open-minded, or both." Journalists are, "on the whole, more liberal than their superiors and their colleagues in the business departments, as well as their sponsors and advertisers. Journalists are more liberal than their vocal audience, inasmuch as the people who write letters of criticism are predominantly conservatives..., which helps explain why journalists are frequently under attack."[27]

Edwin Diamond reported in 1984 that "despite all the charges about liberal bias in the network newscasts, the best serious studies of ABC, CBS, and NBC—by Michael Robinson at George Washington University, James David Barber and colleagues for the Social Science Research Council and [the] News Study Group at MIT—detected no ideological slanting of the news." Diamond confirmed, however, other findings of *structural* bias, that is, systematic differen-

---

26. S. Robert Lichter and Stanley Rothman, "Media and Business Elites," *Public Opinion* 4 (October/November 1981): 42–46; Stanley Rothman and S. Robert Lichter, "The Nuclear Energy Debate: Scientists, the Media, and the Public," ibid. 5 (August/September 1982): 47–52; Linda S. Lichter, S. Robert Lichter, and Stanley Rothman, "How Show Business Shows Business," ibid. 5 (October/November 1982): 10–12; and Stanley Rothman, Linda S. Lichter, and S. Robert Lichter, "Watching the Media Watchdog," ibid. 7 (April/May 1984): 19–20; quotation from "Media and Business Elites," p. 60.

27. Gans, *Deciding What's News,* pp. 211, 212.

**Table 16-1** Political Journalists' Ideologies, 1971–1979

| Samples | Liberal | | Conservative | |
|---|---|---|---|---|
| Johnstone et al.[1] | "Pretty far to the left" 12% | "A little to the left" 40% | "Middle of the road" 30% | "A little, or pretty far to the right" 17% |
| Barton[2] | Giving liberal answers on civil liberties questions | | *Journalists* 70% | *Whole elite sample* 45% |
| | Giving "dovish" answers on foreign policy | | 77 | 62 |
| | Giving liberal answers on social welfare | | 81 | 72 |
| Hess[3] | "Liberal" 42% | "Middle of the Road" 39% | | "Conservative" 19% |
| National Adult Samples, 1980–1983[4] | "Liberal" 26% | "Moderate" 41% | | "Conservative" 33% |

Sources:

[1] Self-described. J. W. Johnstone, et al., *The News People: A Sociological Portrait of American Journalists and Their Work* (Urbana, Ill.: University of Illinois Press, 1976), pp. 93 and 226.

[2] Inferred from questions. Allen H. Barton, "Consensus and Conflict Among American Leaders," *Public Opinion Quarterly, 38* (1974–1975): 507–30.

[3] Self-described. Stephen Hess, *The Washington Reporters* (Washington: The Brookings Institution, 1981), p. 87.

[4] *Public Opinion,* April/May 1984, p. 25.

ces in treatment of political figures because of the traditions and/or assumed necessities of the medium itself. These structural biases produce a disproportionate emphasis on official governmental stories and perspectives, especially on the president and his office, as distinguished from stories discovered by journalists themselves or promoted by political interest groups. Other structural biases favor "the visual over the abstract, the anecdotal over the analytical and, above all, a preference for the steady standards of what I call 'olds' rather than news."[28] Diamond's "olds" are, for example, conflict between White House and Congress, California lifestyles, midwestern tornadoes, and endangered species. Politicians who are most adept at interpreting real events or staging pseudo-events that are visual, anecdotal, and easily presentable by TV nightly news formulas will be beneficiaries of these structural biases.

## 16.44 Campaign debates and confrontations

Since the so-called Great Debates of 1960 there has been a growing expectation that presidential candidates and other aspirants to major offices, such as governor and U.S. senator, should meet in televised debates. The presidential debate

---

28. Edwin Diamond, "New Wrinkles on the Permanent Press," *Public Opinion* 7 (April/May 1984): 4.

has become a tradition, at least in the sense that there is such an expectation, and the candidate who is perceived as ducking such a debate pays a cost in popularity. There were no presidential debates in 1964, 1968, or 1972, but since 1976 there have been many TV debates during the preconvention period in the out-party and several between the parties' nominees during the fall campaigns.

The controversies over televised debates have had to do with the tactics and strategies of the contenders in agreeing to or resisting the debates, the sponsorship and formats of the debates, and whether the quality of the presidential selection process is improved by the debates. The first matter is of great importance to the office seekers and their campaign organizations, and becomes itself a source of much media attention; but it is of less importance to us.

Format and sponsorship questions are more pertinent for us, in view of the FCC's equal time requirement and the networks' central role in determining the contexts as well as the explicit and implied meanings of political messages. Three kinds of sponsorship have been tried: (a) nonpartisan public-interest organizations, such as the League of Women Voters; (b) media organizations (the networks and major newspapers); and (c) the political parties and/or the candidate organizations themselves. Sponsorship by a public-interest organization has the advantage of seeming objectivity and independence, and may make candidates less reluctant to risk debating. Sponsorship by media organizations recommends itself as being professional and as making available the financial and technical resources of a wealthy industry. Sponsorship by the parties in general elections—though not yet widely practiced—would have the advantage of strengthening the parties and tying candidates more closely to the platform issues that had emerged in coalition building before and at the national conventions.

The evaluative question of the goodness or badness of debate may be left until we inquire whether the debates make a difference in public perceptions, opinions, and votes. The short answer is that the debates do seem to be significant. They make a difference in that they seem to change or confirm the impressions, opinions, and presumable votes of a small number of persons. And in tightly contested elections small numbers of persons determine the winner. In 1980—not a close election, perhaps in part because of the debates between Reagan and Anderson and between Reagan and Carter—the Republican challenger was thought to have been the more impressive. A poll conducted by the Michigan Center for Political Studies revealed that "Reagan's gamble paid off. He was judged by the voters who watched the debate to have been the better man, and this judgment appears to have been translated into votes."[29]

Historian Henry Steele Commager argued that TV debates "do not fulfill the

29. Paul R. Abramson, John H. Aldrich, and David W. Rohde, *Change and Continuity in the 1980 Elections* (Washington, D.C.: Congressional Quarterly Press, 1982), p. 46. See also Albert R. Hunt, "The Campaign and the Issues," in *The American Elections of 1980,* ed. Austin Ranney (Washington, D.C.: American Enterprise Institute, 1981), pp. 166–171.

Source: Drawing by Levin; ©1982 *The New Yorker* Magazine, Inc.

*"I found the old format much more exciting."*

most elementary political purpose of permitting the candidates to explore and clarify the vital issues." Worse, he said, they are more conducive to questions and responses "guaranteed to produce headlines" and "to provide sensations." And worse still, they are

> not designed to discover in candidates those qualities really needed for the conduct of the Presidential office...patience, prudence, humility, sagacity, judiciousness, magnanimity.... What we want in a President is the ability to think deeply about a few matters of great importance; what television questions encourage is the trick of talking glibly about a great many matters of no particular importance.[30]

Stanley Kelley made a careful and plausible answer to Commager's charge that televised debates result in a superficial treatment of issues. The 1960 debates, he said, required the candidates to admit that they were in agreement about most of the basic goals of public policy and prevented them from adopting the pretense, so common in solo performances, that they alone have concern for the problems and needs of society: "Thus debates may help to identify for the voter those issues on which rival candidates do not disagree, making it easier for him to center his attention on those issues on which they do." Moreover, "both candidates specified their program intentions in the debates on a greater number of issues than

---

30. Henry Steele Commager, "Washington Would Have Lost a TV Debate," *New York Times Magazine,* October 30, 1960.

they did in their televised speeches. . . . Thus the debates seem to have had some tendency to overcome the inclination—often remarked—of campaigners to say little about method and much about goals." Kelley also found that "the debates brought out the other side of a number of issues that remained one-sided in the speeches." Finally, Kelley's analysis of the total presidential-campaign coverage in 1960 convinced him that the debates were superior, in pertinency and the airing of differences, to the interviews and panel programs presented by the networks.[31]

John W. Ellsworth, following Kelley, compared the 1960 debates with two single speeches by each of the candidates. His research "indicates that the most important variable in the debate situation is the effect which imminent rebuttal has upon the candidates' statements." The overall consequence of the debate format, according to Ellsworth, is beneficial to the public dialogue in a democracy: "In debate they [the candidates] tended to devote more time to giving statements of position, offering evidence for their positions, and giving reasoned arguments to support them."[32]

Since 1960 the presidential debates have varied somewhat in format and rules. They seem to be well regarded by candidates, newspeople, and the public. A careful study of the 1976 Carter–Ford debates reached this optimistic conclusion:

> [The] presidential debates produced a better informed electorate than would have been the case without them. Watching the debates increased the level of manifest information that all citizens had about the candidates regardless of their education, political involvement, or general information-seeking habits. . . . Those individuals who watched the debates exhibited a heightened awareness at exactly the time when political information is crucial—shortly before an election.[33]

In 1980 the "big" debate just a week before the election focused the candidates', the media's, and the public's attention for several days before the event and for the six days to election. Analyses of who won and why nearly crowded out the "hard" news of the campaign and what was going on in the world outside American presidential politics. They nicely illustrated Evron Kirkpatrick's belief that it is

---

31. Stanley Kelley, Jr., "Campaign Debates: Some Facts and Issues," *Public Opinion Quarterly* 26 (1962): 360–362.

32. John W. Ellsworth, "Rationality and Campaigning: A Content Analysis of the 1960 Presidential Campaign Debates," *Western Political Quarterly* 18 (1965): 802.

33. Arthur H. Miller and Michael MacKuen, "Learning About the Candidates: The 1976 Presidential Debates," *Public Opinion Quarterly* 43 (Fall 1979): 344. See also Kenneth D. Wald and Michael B. Lupfer, "The Presidential Debate as a Civics Lesson," ibid. 42 (Fall 1978): 342–353; and Douglas D. Rose, "Citizen Users of the Ford–Carter Debates," *Journal of Politics* 41 (February 1979): 214–221.

impossible to separate entirely the impact of televised debates on the parties and the political system from the larger subject: the general impact of television on politics. The presidential debates are simply the most important single type of televised campaign event; they command the largest audience and the most attention from other media. Some of the effects of the debates are effects of the media. Some are shaped by the format in which the debates are cast; still others from the views of media commentators about these encounters. The debates become especially important because so many influential persons say they are especially important, and also because the notion of a "contest" or "confrontation" in public view between two men, one of whom is about to be chosen president, stimulates interest beyond that aroused by the appearance of a single candidate.[34]

## 16.5 TELEVISION AND POLITICS: A TENTATIVE SUMMING UP

It is not easy to arrive at a balanced judgment of TV's influence in politics. One evaluation says it has not had much of an impact. In 1962 Angus Campbell, of the University of Michigan's Survey Research Center, summarized TV's importance:

> [It] has succeeded in making a sizable part of the electorate direct witnesses to episodes in recent political history. . . . It has greatly extended the purely visual dimension of political communication; the public no doubt finds it easier to form an image of its political leaders. . . . But it seems neither to have elevated the general level of political interest nor to have broadened the total range of political information. . . . People who follow the election campaigns most closely on television are precisely the same ones who read about them in the newspapers and magazines. . . . Rather than adding an important new dimension to the total flow of information to the public, [television] seems largely to have taken over the role of radio.[35]

Campbell's view in 1962 was that TV had not generally changed the nature of American politics. That conclusion has been disputed. Some research by Philip Converse, also published in 1962, suggests that the party loyalty of apolitical Americans is weakened when they are exposed to new political stimuli on TV (or in any other medium); for people already interested in politics, new TV informa-

---

34. Evron M. Kirkpatrick, "Presidential Candidate 'Debates': What Can We Learn from 1960?" in *The Past and Future of Presidential Debates,* ed. Austin Ranney (Washington, D.C.: American Enterprise Institute, 1980), pp. 37–38. Reprinted by permission of American Enterprise Institute.

35. Angus Campbell, "Has Television Reshaped Politics? *Columbia Journalism Review,* Fall 1962, pp. 10–13.

tion is irrelevant to or may actually strengthen party loyalty.[36] Edward Dreyer's 1971 research, updating Converse's data base, did not find that less informed and less motivated Americans were more influenced by media exposure than were politically active persons.[37] It is therefore not clear that television has special influence on the political attitudes of our least interested citizens—though we know they are most likely to get political cues from TV (if they get any at all) and they have fewer competing sources of cues.

Gary Jacobson reviewed campaign expenditures for TV and radio in more than 2,200 general and primary election races in 1970 and 1972 (plus about 100 in 1956). His conclusion is that

> the impact of broadcast campaigning on electoral outcomes varies a good deal depending on the office and type of election, but. . .it is, in some instances, very substantial. It appears to be greater in campaigns for offices other than U.S. President and particularly in the primary elections for nominations to these offices. The findings do not support claims that extensive use of radio and television is the sole key to electoral success; many other factors, most notably incumbency, are also important. But they surely bring into question the common contention that mass media campaigning is normally ineffectual.[38]

At the individual level, any mass-communication medium will influence behavior if certain conditions are present—that is, if the individual (1) pays attention to the messages of that medium; (2) believes in the credibility of the messages; (3) is able to apply the messages to her own situation; and (4) finds the messages reinforced by stimuli from other primary or secondary sources. We accept this "transactional model" of communication influence as being most useful especially for evaluating the impact of TV on the political behavior of Americans.[39] We know that TV is used more than any other medium for entertainment and information, that TV is perceived as more honest and trustworthy than other sources of public affairs information, and that, to the extent that political messages penetrate the (normally apolitical) perception screens of Americans, those messages tend to be reinforced by friends and neighbors exposed to the same TV programming.

TV news programming, especially, appears to have a profound, pervasive, and long-term impact on the attitudes and behaviors of Americans. TV news injects a

36. Philip E. Converse, "Information Flow and the Stability of Partisan Attitudes," *Public Opinion Quarterly* 26 (1962): 578–599.

37. Edward C. Dreyer, "Media Use and Electoral Choices: Some Political Consequences of Information Exposure," *Public Opinion Quarterly* 35 (1971–72): 544–553.

38. Gary C. Jacobson, "The Impact of Broadcast Campaigning on Electoral Outcomes," *Journal of Politics* 37 (August 1975): 792. Reprinted by permission of the *Journal of Politics*.

39. For discussions of the transactional model, see Sidney Kraus and Dennis Davis, *The Effects of Mass Communication on Political Behavior* (University Park: Pennsylvania State University Press, 1976), especially pp. 131–145, 287–290, and their appropriate references.

continuous flow of potent symbols into the political environment. Viewers get political cues without seeking them—and from a trusted source. *Perceptions* of the world are changed, and changed perceptions often bring about attitude changes later. Field experiments in 1980 and 1981 tended to confirm that TV news programs "exert persisting effects on the judgments the public makes regarding the country's most important problems," and that this "is especially so among the politically naive, who seem unable to challenge the pictures and narrations that appear on their television sets."[40]

And even if mass attitudes do not change, or change very slowly, do not repeated TV news emphases allow political elites more scope for change?

> How much sooner did a large segment of the political elite shift to a position against the Vietnam war because of TV news reports? ...And how much more rapidly have ecological efforts snowballed and the issue become popular with both parties because of TV coverage of the subject? Perhaps these questions cannot be answered in the current state of social science, but more likely we have not devoted sufficient ingenuity to the quest.[41]

Besides the long-term impact of vivid TV news programming, some attention has been drawn to a particular characteristic of TV news. Paul Weaver argues that TV nightly news requires a *theme*—that is, an interpretive focus that is consistent throughout the reporting of each story. Newspaper tradition, by contrast, puts *the facts*—the familiar who, what, where, when, and how—into the first paragraph, with the rest trailing off in supposedly less important detail-filling and embellishment. The newspapers thus report "the facts," leaving readers with information but without an explicit interpretation or meaning. But TV's insistence on a story line from beginning to end allows—even requires— that TV newscasters tell viewers what to think about an event. TV news is in this way very different from newspaper news.[42]

Along the same lines are the comments of John William Ward about "the values implicit in the technology of television as a mode of communication": TV generates passivity in its viewers, it simplifies its subjects, it conveys immediacy, and it generates emotional intensity. Are these qualities, Ward asks, appropriate to a vigorous democracy? "If our sense of democratic politics requires that modern man have some tolerance for ambiguity, some understanding of the complexity of modern life, then television is not the medium by which to educate him to it."[43]

---

40. Shanto Iyengar, Mark D. Peters, and Donald R. Kinder, "Experimental Demonstrations of the 'Not-So-Minimal' Consequences of Television News Programs," *American Political Science Review* 76 (1982): 855. But see also an insightful critique of this article in ibid. 78 (1984): 201–202.

41. Gary L. Wamsley and Richard A. Pride, "Television Network News: Rethinking the Iceberg Problem," *Western Political Quarterly* 25 (1972): 434–450; quotation at 448.

42. Paul H. Weaver, "Is Television News Biased?" *Public Interest* 26 (Winter 1972): 57–74.

43. Martin Linsky, ed., *Television and the Presidential Elections: Self-Interest and the Public Interest* (Lexington, Mass.: D. C. Heath, 1983), pp. 11–12.

According to Weaver, network anchors, for example, report the New Hampshire presidential primary every four years as "establishing a front runner." Or the facts of a Watergate break-in are dismissed as a "second-rate burglary." The next evening, in order to appear correct or at least not inconsistent, all the network reporters adopt the anchor's version. Within hours, political leaders reassess their tactics in accordance with the TV news's interpretation of "reality"; opinion polls then show the effects and the self-fulfilling theme becomes self-fulfilled.

Michael Robinson elaborates on the implications of Weaver's argument. Like Kurt and Gladys Lang in 1968,[44] Robinson finds TV news themes to be systematically distorting, with potentially profound public consequences:

> The television news story is inherently interpretive because it is inherently thematic. And, given the special and the traditional exigencies of network television, the interpretive TV story is more likely to be negativistic, contentious, or anti-institutional (or some combination of the three) than is the same "story" told in print. It is also more likely to be overdone.[45]

Whether the fears of Weaver, the Langs, and Robinson are warranted, or whether the more sanguine interpretations of Gans are nearer the mark,[46] most analysts have abandoned the view, expressed by Campbell twenty years ago, that TV has no important effects on political behavior. Television has strong immediate influence on elite political behavior, probably moderate direct influence on mass opinions, and possibly a cumulative and indirect influence whose importance is as yet only poorly understood.

---

44. Kurt Lang and Gladys Lang, *Politics and Television* (Chicago: Quadrangle Books, 1968).

45. Michael J. Robinson, "Public Affairs Television and the Growth of Political Malaise: The Case of 'The Selling of the Pentagon,'" *American Political Science Review* 70 (June 1976): 428.

46. Gans, *Deciding What's News,* pp. 296–297.

## Chapter 17

# The Press and the Opinion-Policy Process

The short history of American newspapers is that of eighteenth-century publications that depended on politics and how they became twentieth-century publications on which politics depends. This statement, like all epigrams, exaggerates its message: newspapers were never wholly political, and only in a few places in this century can we say that politics depends on newspaper influence. Yet the general historical change in American newspapers is clear: they were once thoroughly political, but their political interests are now vague, occasional, and of no great importance to their own economic life. Although newspapers remain the most consciously political of the mass media—reflecting both their traditions and the expectations of their readers—the pervasiveness of politics characteristic of early newspapers has generally given way both to moderation in tone and to a physical separation of news from political advice (that is, from *editorializing*).

In our early national period, newspapers were weapons in the fight between Federalists and Republicans. The contest between John Fenno's *Gazette of the United States,* subsidized by Alexander Hamilton and the Federalists, and Philip Freneau's *National Gazette,* supported by Thomas Jefferson and the anti-Federalists, was marked by the bitter "no-quarter" style typical of the early American press. The editors delighted in trading such epithets as "fawning parasite," "blackguard," "crackbrain," jackal of mobocracy," and salamander."[1]

Culver Smith underscores the importance of these early political newspapers:

> One conclusion is indisputable. Both Hamilton and Jefferson (as well as Madison) believed in the value of a partisan newspaper, and each

---

[1]. See Samuel E. Forman, "The Political Activities of Philip Freneau," *Johns Hopkins University Studies in Historical and Political Science,* ser. 20, nos. 9–10 (September–October 1902), pp. 473–569. Forman says that "in the [*National*] *Gazette,* Jefferson's opinions were reflected as in a mirror" (pp. 529–530).

in his own way established, encouraged, and maintained a journalistic organ. Both papers circulated throughout the Union—thanks partly to cheap postage—finding their way to the political leaders in the states and the printers of other newspapers, giving the form for partisan writing and thinking.[2]

The first of the large-circulation, inexpensive newspapers of the 1830s and 1840s, the *New York Sun,* the *New York Herald,* the *Philadelphia Public Ledger,* and the *Baltimore Sun,* were not direct organs of partisan rabble-rousing; the *New York Sun,* established in 1833, emphasized police reporting, crime, sex, and disreputable advertising. But, as Frank Luther Mott says, whatever one thinks of the enterprise and success of the penny press—and however important its part may have been in the news revolution—the fact remains that up to the time of the Civil War, it was not the independent penny press but the partisan political press that dominated American journalism.[3] Newspapermen of the middle and late nineteenth century were often colorful propagandists, outspoken individualists, and capable of great passion. Henry Adams said that in 1866

> the press was still the last resource of the educated poor who could not be artists and would not be tutors. Any man who was fit for nothing else could write an editorial or a criticism. The enormous mass of misinformation accumulated in ten years of nomad life could always be worked off on a helpless public, in diluted doses, if one could but secure a table in the corner of a newspaper office. The press was an inferior pulpit; an anonymous schoolmaster; a cheap boarding school.[4]

Most American newspapers are still political to the extent that in editorials, and occasionally in their selection of news to report, they support or attack public figures and public policies. But the age of moderation, gentility, and the "soft sell" has come to newspapers, and only rarely does one encounter highly emotional or *ad hominem* political journalism—except for a few syndicated columns written by people whose stock in trade is extremism.

There are many differences between the older style of political journalism, as practiced by Horace Greeley, Charles Dana, Joseph Pulitzer, and William Randolph Hearst in the nineteenth century, and modern political journalism. That of the last century was personal; in this century it is institutional. Editorial pages are increasingly the products of groups, editors, and managers, who do not make the policy of the paper. The late Colonel Robert R. McCormick was probably the last of the great owner-publisher-editors who could say on the editorial page what he damn well pleased, because the policy of the *Chicago*

---

2. Culver H. Smith, *The Press, Politics, and Patronage: The American Government's Use of Newspapers, 1789–1875* (Athens: University of Georgia Press, 1977), p. 19.

3. Frank Luther Mott, *American Journalism,* rev. ed. (New York: Macmillan, 1962), p. 253.

4. *The Education of Henry Adams,* Modern Library ed. (New York: Random House, 1931), p. 211.

*Tribune* was what Colonel McCormick damn well pleased. There are still, perhaps, a few other such papers, smaller but of some local fame. But the fate of the large dailies has been almost uniformly either that of the *New York Times's* successful metamorphosis from the personal journalism of founder-publisher-editor Henry J. Raymond (1851–1869) to a stable though still family-dominated corporation; or that of the 173-year history of mergers by sixteen New York newspapers, which ended in 1966 with the *World Journal Tribune*—a merger that died within months of the economic arteriosclerosis currently afflicting all big-city news publishing.

It should not be thought that the large American newspapers are worse for their change from personalism to institutionalism. They are unquestionably better in their service to the balance, judiciousness, and moderation that, in any well-ordered society, must be central to the opinion-policy process. Not only are their editorials joint endeavors—which, like all products of committees, must respect the law of the lowest common denominator—but what passion remains is syndicated, nationalized, and mailed in. Thus William Buckley writes his national column from the New York office of his national magazine, and Jack Anderson writes his political gossip from Washington. Their indignation is muffled by the time lag between the writing and the reading in a hundred local dailies and by the requirement that a national audience must be fed commentary on national (and thus, for most people, less interesting) events.

Sheer size, too, has contributed to the increased blandness of editorial pages. A mass-circulation paper cannot support extreme political journalism—the model newspaper reader is not an extremist. A highly partisan paper may please those who are highly partisan, but such readers are too few to support large papers. When the 125-year-old *Boston Herald Traveler* folded in the spring of 1972, it sold its "name, good will, and physical assets" to the Hearst chain's *Record American*. The *Herald Traveler,* it was said, had been "for decades the voice of Boston's Republican establishment."[5] To keep those old *Herald Traveler* readers, the *Record American* must to some extent absorb also the politics of the defunct paper. Thus mass circulation begets accommodation and moderation.

Finally, the politics of moderation has a clear benefit not found in the extreme partisanship of earlier papers. Moderate papers will air controversy and opposing views within the limits of the moderate middle. The *Los Angeles Times* drew attention to these evolving characteristics of big papers:

> By the turn of the century a more comprehensive paper was emerging. It sought a wider audience than the audience afforded by party or faction.... This trend toward the comprehensive newspaper has continued to the present day.... With the development toward fewer and larger metropolitan newspapers came both a decline in partisanship and an increased effort by newspapers to look behind the daily

---

5. *New York Times,* May 18, 1972.

flow of surface events to examine their causes and consequences. This attempt to put events into context is more useful to the readers than a mere account of daily events—in fact it is essential—but it is also much more difficult to do well. It requires professionalism and good judgment and above all a sense of fairness.[6]

Ben Bagdikian surveyed "factors that help determine which of the twenty-five major domestic public affairs columnists and which of the twenty-five lesser but still nationally syndicated ones will be selected" by editors and publishers. He found a "dramatic" shift to a more even conservative–liberal balance, especially among the big-city dailies. The percentage of conservative columns in twenty-one big-city dailies went from 70 to 52 in the six years from 1959 to 1965. Bagdikian also found that editors

> seem ambivalent about colorful writing and strong opinion. They want stimulating material and often speak contemptuously of colum-nists who straddle issues. At the same time they frequently tone down columns, occasionally through fear of libel but more often because they don't wish the paper to appear biased or unfair.[7]

Most of us, unless we are of the small minorities at the radical or reactionary ends of the political continuum, can find both agreement and disagreement on the editorial pages of our major papers. Mass circulation may bring moderation, but mass circulation plus a sense of responsibility will also bring (at least to our better newspapers) a pertinence of materials and a reasonable exchange and confrontation of varied opinion. To find the right balance of conflict and consensus on the issues that really count is no easy task. It is a task that is not always undertaken and hardly ever achieved. But it is at least a possible objective for political journalism in the 1980s.

## 17.1 BIASES OF THE AMERICAN PRESS

American newspapers are generally conservative, jealous of their independence from governmental regulation, and presumptuous; but they are probably our most important safeguard against the manifold evils to which any large public may fall prey.

The characteristic biases of the American press are all displayed at the annual meetings of the American Newspaper Publishers Association. In April of each year that group meets to review and report on itself. Its committees invariably denounce governments for overzealous regulation of the media and for favoring

---

6. "Some Changes in the Editorial Pages," *Los Angeles Times,* September 23, 1973.
7. Ben H. Bagdikian, "How Editors Pick Columnists," *Columbia Journalism Review* 5 (1966): 41, 45.

unions in labor–management disputes. Taxes on advertising and on circulation are especially noxious to the ANPA, as is any attempt by the Postal Service to raise the second-class mail rates that have for decades subsidized the newspaper industry. The ANPA continues its practice of "accrediting" journalism schools and departments; about fifty schools have been blessed with the seal of approval of this self-interested private group. At the 1983 meeting the ANPA board of directors decided to aid television broadcasters in their efforts to repeal the FCC's equal time and fairness doctrines. This new policy was put in perspective by the *New York Times*'s Jonathan Friendly: "Historically, newspapers have been at economic odds with broadcasters, but most of the major newspaper companies now also own television and cable television systems that must adhere to the Federal broadcast rules."[8]

The presumptuousness especially of newspapers need hardly be documented: it is apparent at all times. The usual American newspaper coverage of prisoners charged with lurid crimes is so prejudicial to their right to due process of law as to be unacceptable to even the most minimal standards of fair play. Such coverage is illegal in countries that follow the British practice. A central part is played by the press in the public condemnations, prejudgments, vilifications, and horror (real and pretended) of alleged murderers and rapists. Celebrated cases of journalistic judging include those of Lee Harvey Oswald, the alleged assassin of President Kennedy who was exterminated by a media-inflamed citizen, and of mass murderers Richard Speck, Juan Corona, and Charles Manson.

The trial of John De Lorean on drug-trafficking charges was a notorious example of trial by publicity. Both defense and prosecution lawyers released information selectively, gave "backgrounders" (meetings with reporters with the understanding that everything said would be treated anonymously), and even held daily press conferences. The beleaguered judge at one point issued an order sealing all documents until he could review them but, on the appeal of media organizations, that order was struck down by the U.S. Ninth Circuit Court of Appeals.[9]

John Hohenberg, distinguished newspaperman and teacher, expressed alarm that reporters were being barred from some hearings or trials of notorious defendants. Hohenberg seems not to recognize the difference between sensational and detailed coverage of individual violence and sadism, which has no importance for public policy; and the grave issues of *official* corruption and malfeasance, which the media do have the responsibility to report fully and widely. He laments the unanimous 1976 Supreme Court decision to uphold "an order that limited the state's [Nebraska's] news media in their coverage of a mass murder." Though he quotes Justice Tom Clark's statement that "trials are not like elections.... Due process requires that the accused receive a trial by an

8. Jonathan Friendly, "Moynihan Warns Press on Freedom," *New York Times,* April 26, 1983.

9. Judith Cummings, "Publicity Issue Coloring De Lorean Trial," *New York Times,* May 14, 1984.

impartial jury free from outside influence," he seems not to have understood Clark's point.[10]

Anthony Lewis understands the distinctions between a single criminal proceeding and a general issue of public policy—that in the former, the defendant's right to a fair trial prevails over the press's right to get all the detailed charges and testimony; and that in the latter, the press's (and public's) right prevails over anyone's claim to secrecy. He notes that the Supreme Court in 1979 (by a 5–4 vote) "allowed a pre-trial hearing in a criminal case to be closed to the press and the public," but in 1980 (by a 7–1 vote) forbade the closing of trials themselves to press and public. Even this, Lewis admits, is not an absolute right. Referring to prisons and other public facilities as well as courts, Lewis observes: "Whatever the nature of the closed institution, the Court will plainly weigh the public interest in access to it against any convincingly articulated reasons for the closure.... A courtroom might be closed if there were real needs related to a fair trial; access to a prison might be limited for security reasons."[11]

Now and then the presumptuousness of some newspapers is exposed by one of their own. Thus when Carl Rowan, a long-time correspondent for the *Minneapolis Tribune,* became a public affairs officer in the U.S. Department of State in 1961, he was nettled by "the pious assumption that the only people in this country who really care about the public's right to know are the newspaper and magazine people." He added that "a great deal of this so-called concern about the public's right to know is really concern about the fourth estate's right to make a buck."[12] James Reston has also been refreshingly frank: "Some of the old newspaper traditions, of course, we maintain. Our self-righteousness, I can assure you, is undiminished. Our capacity to criticize everybody and our imperviousness to criticism ourselves, are still, I believe, unmatched by novelists, poets, or anybody else."[13]

That American newspapers have a high and exaggerated notion of their own importance is beyond doubt. But it is also beyond doubt that newspapers are indispensable elements in the public discussion and criticism that are fundamental to self-government. The foregoing critical comments do not mean that journalists should give any lesser weight to their responsibilities and their importance, but only that they should be aware of the fallibility of their judgments, and of those tendencies (which we all share) to mistake their own interests for the general interest.

The biases of the American press have historic, economic, and political roots.

---

10. John Hohenberg, *A Crisis for the American Press* (New York: Columbia University Press, 1978), pp. 197, 198.

11. Anthony Lewis, "A Right to Be Informed," *New York Times,* July 3, 1980.

12. "Outspoken Ex-Newsman," *New York Times,* January 22, 1964.

13. *Columbia Journalism Review* 5 (1966): 65. A. H. Raskin says, "Of all the institutions in our inordinately complacent society, none is so addicted as the press to self-righteousness, self-satisfaction and self-congratulation" ("What's Wrong with American Newspapers?" *New York Times Magazine,* June 11, 1967, p. 28).

The best journalists are acutely aware of the tradition of free inquiry in Western civilization and of the importance of printing in the history of intellectual controversy. We cannot overestimate the value of the printing press in the development of modern democratic societies. It is hardly debatable that Martin Luther, who was born fifteen years after Johann Gutenberg's death, was greatly advantaged in his reform efforts by the printing press; just as Luther's precursor John Wycliffe, who died fourteen years before Gutenberg's birth, was disadvantaged by the lack of the printing press. The most able present-day American newspaper people have a deep commitment to the arguments of John Milton's *Areopagitica* and a deep sense of participation in the honored profession of Peter Zenger and William Lloyd Garrison.

Sometimes freedom of the press means having the guts to resist intimidation and imprisonment, as did Jay Near, the Twin Cities editor whose outspoken attacks on public officials led to the Supreme Court's determination that the national government would guarantee newspapers against censorship by state and local authorities (Near v. Minnesota, 238 U.S. 697 [1931]).

Sometimes freedom of the press means confrontations by major institutions of our society—as when the *New York Times* defied the Nixon administration's claim that "national security" (as it alone defined that term) took precedence over the First Amendment (New York Times Co. v. U.S., 403 U.S. 713 [1971]).

Sometimes freedom of the press is asserted more informally, with a light touch—as when Georgia's governor Lester Maddox called the *Atlanta Constitution*'s editors "lying devils and dirty dogs" and threatened personally to picket their offices. The *Constitution* on that occasion editorially reminded its readers that it had been picketed by the Ku Klux Klan, the antifluoridationists, the women's liberationists, and the Committee to Stamp Out the Fire Ant. "So welcome, Governor... You won't bother us. We are used to characters carrying signs."[14]

It used to be thought that the conservative bias of the American press was maintained by a small and selfish group of wealthy investors and capitalists who prevented liberal reporters and "the common people" from expressing liberal or radical sentiments. Nowadays the conservative bias of the American newspapers is ordinarily attributed to more subtle factors, related to the nature of the industry. A major daily newspaper is a large business enterprise. It usually has a corporate form, a large and expensive plant, and a management separated from its ownership—although some newspapers retain a "family-corporate" flavor, like those of the Hearst, Chandler, Cox, and Cowles interests. Gerald W. Johnson calls this separation of management and ownership the "quandary of the editors."

> How can the editor of a big-city newspaper be at once politically liberal and financially honest? Consider his position. He is practically never the owner of the property he controls, but he is its custodian.

---

14. *Atlanta Constitution,* May 3, 1970.

> The paper usually represents an investment of many millions of other people's money, and a conscientious agent is not going to take chances with other people's money, even in circumstances under which he might gamble his own.
>
> To put an honest man in charge of $10 million or $20 million of highly perishable property belonging to other people and then expect him to lash out boldly in defense of what is right but unpopular is to subject human nature to an unbearable strain.[15]

The conservatism of large newspapers' economic and political views may be due in part to the natural conservatism of big and middle-sized businesses in America. It is hardly necessary to seek an explanation for it in Marxist and other anticapitalist ideologies. To understand why newspapers so often unheroically support the status quo, one need only observe that, while newspapers may have been "started by men who had something to say, they are carried on by men who have something to sell."[16]

Another variant of left-wing criticism used to be that newspaper owners and editors were intimidated by their large advertisers, and in turn pressured their reporters to slant the news in a conservative direction. This argument seems to have little present validity. There are, no doubt, examples of advertisers' pressures on newspapers, but most of the documented cases occurred many years ago. Economic reprisals by advertisers against editorial policies appear to be less common now than in former times (if only because papers are larger, on the average, and larger papers are harder to destroy). Such reprisals as are attempted are more apt to be related to labor or racial conflict than to a newspaper's overall policy.

Governments and political groups may exert more economic pressure on newspapers than commercial advertisers do. The *Atlanta Constitution's* experiences of being picketed by various "cause" groups, cited above, has been shared by other newspapers whose views and/or news coverage have led groups to boycott as well as picket them. The effect of such "direct action" on the advertising income of papers is unknown but probably slight. Governments, on the other hand, and more quietly, can give or withhold legal advertising according to the partisan or policy stands the papers take. Many small and middle-sized newspapers get an important part of their advertising revenue from legal notices that public agencies must place in "organs of general circulation." The Albany (New York) county executive, for example, in early 1984 canceled $60,000 a year in public notices that used to appear in the *Albany Times-Union* because that paper had published articles critical of the Democratic party's patronage activities.[17]

---

15. Gerald W. Johnson, "The Superficial Aspect," *New Republic,* May 2, 1955, p. 6.

16. William L. Rivers, *The Opinion Makers: The Washington Press Corps* (Boston: Beacon, 1965), p. 200, quoting Alan Barth.

17. Jonathan Friendly, "Albany Paper Irks Official, Loses Ads," *New York Times,* February 16, 1984.

Such political-economic pressure, direct and implied, is probably more common nowadays than pure economic pressure from business advertisers.

Some reporters may feel that managerial pressures limit their freedom to report objectively, but recent studies indicate that pressures toward conservatism and biased reporting are much diminished or too subtle to be noticed. Of 273 Washington correspondents queried in 1962, only 7.3 percent said that their stories had been "played down, cut, or killed for 'policy' reasons," whereas more than 55 percent of a 1937 sample of Washington reporters had had such experiences. When asked if they had experienced subtle pressures, 60 percent of the 1937 sample but only 9.5 percent of the 1962 sample answered yes.[18] Stephen Hess found that in 1978 no member of the Washington press corps complained of pressure by editor or publisher for policy or political reasons. Citing the earlier 1937 and 1962 studies, he said: "By 1978, writing to fit the editorial positions of publishers had simply disappeared as an issue for contention."[19]

The major antidotes to bias and falsification are (a) economic competition and (b) governmental regulation. Governmental regulation, the less favored remedy in the United States, has been resorted to only in flagrant cases, such as publication of libelous and grossly misleading, subversive, or inflammatory material.

As an inhibitor of press bias, economic competition is, first, a matter of alternative sources of news and opinion for the citizenry and, second, a matter of what the employees of the paper and its readers will tolerate. It goes almost without saying that monopoly control of the dissemination of news and opinion gives the monopolist an opportunity for unlimited bias and distortion of truth. The rulers of a totalitarian society, by definition, have such a monopoly. It seems unlikely that such control has ever existed in the United States—even in the smallest and most isolated company-owned mining town in the West.

It is often said that the monopolies enjoyed in one-newspaper towns encourage or at least increase the likelihood of distortion, slanting of the news, irresponsible exercise of editorial power, and so on. Such charges need to be examined. First, to be sure, there are fewer daily newspapers in the United States now than there were eighty-odd years ago. In 1900 there were about 2,500 dailies. In the thirties and forties many failures and mergers occurred. Since the mid-1950s, however, the number of dailies has remained steady at about 1,750. This overall stability masks important changes in locations, functions, and sizes of dailies, and says nothing about the changes in weeklies, biweeklies, and triweeklies.

Another development of the past twenty years is a weakening of metropolitan afternoon dailies. From 1965 to 1981 more than 50 of 1,444 afternoon dailies disappeared, and afternoon circulation dropped from 36 million to less than 33

18. William L. Rivers, "The Correspondents after 25 Years," *Columbia Journalism Review* 1 (1962): 5. Rivers compared his findings with those reported in Leo C. Rosten, *The Washington Correspondents* (New York: Harcourt, Brace, 1937).

19. Stephen Hess, *The Washington Reporters* (Washington, D.C.: Brookings Institution, 1981), p. 5.

million.[20] In the next two years more than 100 additional afternoon dailies disappeared and the total afternoon readership of dailies declined below morning readership for the first time in this century.[21]

The big pattern seems to be one of the closing or merging of the weaker central-city dailies, the expansion (in content and circulation) of the surviving central-city papers, and the selective increase of suburban dailies (some new, but more often former weeklies upgraded to dailies). Meanwhile, new weeklies and bi- or triweeklies also emerge in suburbs. Anthony Smith describes the Northern California example:

> At the center of the Bay Area newspaper region sits the *San Francisco Chronicle-Examiner*, a pair of newspapers...under rival ownership but...merging their production, circulation, and advertising collection. In the central area of the city this twin newspaper circulates very densely, thinning progressively in the surrounding area that covers almost all of northern California. This represents layer one of the regional newspaper system.
>
> The second layer consists of the newspapers whose centers are the satellite cities of Oakland (the *Tribune*)...and San Jose (the *Mercury News*). These papers, like the *Chronicle-Examiner,* circulate most thickly at their respective city centers and do not overlap with one another....
>
> The third layer consists of sixteen suburban papers...whose circulation areas are small (in relation to the satellite city papers) and do not overlap. There is a fourth layer of weekly, twice- and thrice-weekly papers, shopping papers and free papers, which are distributed at their densest in those areas farthest away from the circulation centers of the three previous layers.[22]

There is, of course, a great deal of literal monopoly: Oakland has a population of 400,000 and only one newspaper; San Jose, 700,000 in population, also has only one newspaper. But in the last five years two old newspapers have "gone national"—the *New York Times* and the *Wall Street Journal*—and a new national newspaper, *USA Today,* has appeared. Thus in the Northern California Bay Area, most residents can have up to six dailies delivered to their doors before noon.

A further monopoly danger to the press is found in the structure of the wire services. Most newspapers get their stories from monopoly news-gathering agencies—one or the other of the two great wire services in the United States. The argument is that the wire services may distort or selectively report the news,

---

20. Jonathan Friendly, "Requiem for a View," *New York Times,* July 24, 1981.

21. "The Press: Good News for Front Pages,"*Economist,* May 14, 1983, p. 38.

22. Excerpted from *Goodbye Gutenberg: The Newspaper Revolution of the 1980s,* by Anthony Smith, p. 58. Copyright © 1980 by Oxford University Press, Inc. Used by permission of the author and the publisher.

which then may be further distorted or biased by local judgment as to what to print. Monopoly, it is charged, shows its ugly power in the news-gathering agency when only one is subscribed to and also at the local editor's desk in one-newspaper communities. What little evidence is available indicates that the stories printed by small one-wire-service dailies do in fact follow a pattern much like that of the stories sent to them on the wire-service ticker. It is unclear whether the critical judgment of local editors just happens to coincide with the critical judgment of wire-service editors on what kinds of news to disseminate or, as seems more probable, whether wire-service judgments are uncritically accepted by editors of small-town dailies. Charges of bias in one-newspaper towns are heard most often from liberals and reformers, because they most consciously feel the general conservatism of American newspapers.

An imaginative study of two similar middle-sized urban areas, one with a media monopoly and the other with a competitive media pattern, was conducted in 1970. Representative samples of adults in York, Pennsylvania (population 101,000), and Zanesville, Ohio (population 82,000), were interviewed twice, in April and in June. An elite panel was also drawn for York. The contrast in media patterns was remarkable. In 1970, York was the only city of its size with all newspaper and broadcast media under separate and economically unrelated ownership. There were two daily papers, two TV stations, and six AM or FM radio outlets, all independent of one another. Zanesville, by contrast, was a thorough media monopoly: one newspaper, one TV station, and one radio station with both AM and FM facilities, all owned and operated by the Zanesville Publishing Company, Mr. Clay Littick, president. On tests of knowledgeability of places-things-names in the news, York residents scored significantly higher; this superiority was confirmed in subtests of carefully matched individual respondents. Although the citizens of Zanesville have equal opportunity to get news and opinions from outside their community, the researchers discovered that they are "substantially more dependent upon local media than are the people of York.... Thus, those who operate the media in Zanesville are in better positions to influence the political and other attitudes of the public than are those who operate the media in York."[23] Local media monopolies, this research seems to demonstrate, are detrimental to the electoral politics of democracies because the lack of an organized dialogue *delays* the crystallization of opinions about national and state candidates and may even *prevent* the full exposure of information about local candidates. "There is," this report concludes, "no question but that a media monopoly does have an adverse influence on the knowledgeability and political flexibility of the local audiences it serves."[24]

It may be that in some cities none but narrow and biased papers are published. But people in such cities may purchase out-of-town papers and newsmagazines

23. *Media Monopoly and Politics* (Washington D.C.: American Institute for Political Communication, 1973), p. 29.
24. Ibid., p. 167.

and may receive increasingly thorough television coverage of state and national news. Weekly papers and the publicity organs of community groups help redress the balance, too. A large city that cannot support a fair and responsible paper may ultimately be judged to be a city that does not deserve a fair and responsible paper. The possibility for variety, fairness, and comprehensiveness of news reporting is as great as the readers' desire for variety, fairness, and comprehensiveness.

If the American press is, on the whole, mediocre and intellectually unchallenging (and it is), it is not because of monopoly or fewer daily papers. The fact is that most producers and consumers of newspapers prefer mediocrity to intellectual challenge. There is a dearth of talent in American newspapers—a dearth of talented writers and a dearth of talented readers. It is, as Leo Rosten put it,

> a woeful fact that despite several generations of free education, our land has produced relatively few first-rate minds; and of those first-rate brains, fewer have imagination; of those with brains and imagination, fewer still possess judgment. If we ask, in addition, for the special skills and experience involved in the art of communicating, the total amount of talent available to the media is not impressive.[25]

In sum, the general social and political biases of American newspapers are what one would expect, given the large-business and corporate perspectives of their policy makers,[26] the imperatives of competition for recency and sensation—for the titillation of audiences consisting mainly of persons uninterested in public issues—and the endemic lack of journalistic talent to write and edit their millions of daily lines.

## 17.2 NEWSPAPERS AND PARTISANSHIP

As one would also expect, in view of the conservatism of the American press, most newspapers support Republican party policies and Republican candidates. At least such is the big generalization, which, like most big generalizations, does not take us far on the road to understanding. The pro-Republican tendencies of newspapers are by no means simple or direct; we must have some information on

---

25. "The Intellectual and the Mass Media: Some Rigorously Random Remarks," *Daedalus* 89 (1960): 335–336.

26. No statistical information could be expected on newspapers whose managers intend to be biased in their news coverage or advertising policy, simply because newspeople will not admit to such intent. Data on disproportionately great or favorable coverage must be more inferentially obtained—from content analysis, participant observation, or educated guesswork. Lewis Donohew found, for example, that the coverage of the Medicare issue by 17 Kentucky dailies was strongly influenced by the publishers' personal attitudes toward the subject, but hardly at all by the publishers' understanding of what their communities' opinions were or by the objective conditions of community need for Medicare ("Newspaper Gatekeepers and Forces in the News Channel," *Public Opinion Quarterly* 31 [1967]: 61–68).

three subtopics in order to know whether, or to what extent, a pro-Republican bias in newspapers is a matter of importance to the opinion-policy process. We need to know (a) how self-consciously pro-Republican American newspapers are (that is, how many newspapers intend to be pro-Republican in their editorial policy); (b) how the biases are shown generally and at critical junctures in the governing process (for example, in election campaigns and votes on public issues); and (c) how newspaper favoritism affects the outcome of electoral decisions.

Most newspapers adopt an official stance of nonpartisanship or political independence. The rhetoric of the free press places a high value on the word *independence,* so that even papers as notoriously pro-Republican as the *Columbus* (Ohio) *Dispatch* or the New Hampshire *Union-Leader* declare themselves to be independents. The *Chicago Tribune* claims to be "Independent-Republican," and the *New York Post* says it is "Independent-Democratic."

Among papers that, for historical reasons related to the papers themselves or to the sections of the country in which they are published, declare themselves to be either Democratic or Republican, the partisan balance may be about even. There has been a steep increase in the number of self-styled politically independent newspapers since 1944. Mott found 47.9 percent of his sample of dailies to be independent in 1944. In 1960, a somewhat smaller sample ("principal daily newspapers" only) yielded 61.0 percent independent, and in 1972, another increase to 68.3 percent. The number of partisan dailies decreased reciprocally. Because of differences in sample size and bases of reporting, the rate of change to a nominal independence may be exaggerated, but the long-run trend is clearly away from partisan self-identification, as Table 17–1 indicates.

The probable decrease in the numbers of self-identified partisan papers seems to be a result of several factors. The many mergers among newspapers in the past few decades have increased the circulation and geographical coverage of the remaining papers, making readerships more heterogeneous and less likely to welcome partisanship in their papers.[27] Moreover, there may be a general long-run increase in independent voting among the population at large, and the historic one-party areas (the Democratic South, the Republican New England and North Central states) seem to be moving in the direction of two-partyism. In a 1926 count of partisan dailies, and again in the 1960 and 1972 counts, there was "a more positive tendency for states of unusually heavy Republican or Democratic majorities to have the bulk of their newspaper circulation listed as of the same respective party affiliation."[28] Newspaper publishers and editors may be trimming their overt partisanship to the changing winds of two-party registration in their circulation areas.

---

27. There is some evidence, for example, that the *Los Angeles Times* became more liberal when the *Mirror* and old *Examiner* (both of which had had more Democratic readers) folded. See Jack Lyle, "Audience Impact of a Double Newspaper Merger," *Journalism Quarterly* 39 (1962): 151.

28. George A. Lundberg, "The Newspaper and Public Opinion," *Social Forces* 4 (1926): 714.

**Table 17-1**　Endorsement of presidential candidates by daily newspapers, 1956–1984

| Year | Republican candidate endorsed | | Democratic candidate endorsed | | Total papers endorsing |
|------|------|------|------|------|------|
| | N | % | N | % | N |
| 1956 ................. | 740 | 80 | 189 | 20 | 929 |
| 1960 ................. | 731 | 78 | 208 | 22 | 939 |
| 1964 ................. | 349 | 45 | 440 | 55 | 789 |
| 1968* ................. | 634 | 80 | 146 | 18 | 892 |
| 1972 ................. | 753 | 93 | 56 | 7 | 809 |
| 1976 ................. | 411 | 84 | 80 | 16 | 491 |
| 1980+ ................. | 443 | 73 | 126 | 21 | 609 |
| 1984 ................. | 381 | 86 | 62 | 14 | 443 |

Source: *Editor and Publisher,* issues from the first week in November of indicated years.
*Twelve papers (2%) endorsed American Independent party candidate George Wallace.
+Forty papers (6%) endorsed independent candidate John Anderson.

Two comments on Table 17–1 are in order. First, the numbers of endorsing papers are not so important as the *numbers of readers* who see the endorsements. An attempt was made to measure newspaper readers' exposure to presidential endorsements in 1976. A total of 202 newspapers were read by respondents of SRC's national sample that year. From the reports in *Editor and Publisher* and from telephone calls, the endorsements of 189 of those 202 were determined. Extrapolating from those data, and taking into account the larger average circulation of the pro-Carter papers, Roger Gafke and David Leuthold show that crediting Ford in 1976 with 84 percent of the endorsing newspapers, as Table 17–1 does, is misleading. They conclude, properly and helpfully, "that about half the newspapers being sold contained a Ford endorsement, about one-quarter contained a Carter endorsement, and about one-quarter contained no endorsement."[29] In 1984, although only 14 percent of the endorsing daily papers supported Democratic candidate Mondale and 86 percent supported Republican candidate Reagan, the pro-Democratic papers reached 29 percent of the total circulation of endorsing dailies. These data reinforce Gafke and Leuthold's point that in presidential races the pro-Democratic papers tend to have larger average circulations than the pro-Republican papers.

Second, fewer daily newspapers seem to be endorsing presidential candidates. It may be that fewer newspapers are endorsing any candidates for public office; if this is the case, it is further evidence of the withdrawal of newspapers from partisanship. There was a gradual decline in numbers of endorsing papers (right-hand column, Table 17–1) during the 1960s and a sharp reduction after 1972. The *Newark Star-Ledger* announced in 1973 that it would no longer endorse any candidates. *Newsday,* a highly regarded daily on Long Island, adopted the same policy in 1972. The *Los Angeles Times* in 1973 decided to end

29. Roger Gafke and David Leuthold, "A Caveat on E&P Poll on Newspaper Endorsements," *Journalism Quarterly,* Summer 1979, p. 386.

endorsements in presidential, gubernatorial, and U.S. Senate races. One estimate is that as many as one out of seven U.S. dailies have a policy or a tradition against ever endorsing candidates by name.[30]

Newspaper endorsements of state and local candidates have received very little study. It is probably safe to assume that papers endorse more Republicans than Democrats, judging from the distribution of presidential-candidate endorsements and from the findings of the few state and local studies. In one analysis of statewide campaigns in Connecticut and Wisconsin, four of the eleven dailies chosen in Wisconsin supported the Republican candidates, two supported the Democratic candidates, and four were neutral; in Connecticut, none of the nine dailies supported the Democrats. (Unfortunately, the authors do not indicate how many of the nine papers were pro-Republican and how many were neutral.)[31] In another study of newspaper treatment of partisan candidates and campaigning—this one in Pennsylvania—nine of twenty-six papers endorsed the two Republican candidates for governor and U.S. senator, three supported the two Democrats, four divided their endorsements, and ten remained neutral.[32]

In a careful study of editorial endorsements by California newspapers, James E. Gregg found that "80% are Republican in orientation, 10% are Democratic in orientation and 10% are either truly independent or are papers which do not make political endorsements."[33] Gregg suggests that the claim by 75 percent of California's newspapers (in 1963) that they were politically independent was a "sham."

Aside from self-admitted partisanship and from the endorsement of their partisan candidates, do American newspapers show partisan favoritism in their treatment of news? If the newspapers have a genuinely conservative bias as a result of their owners' and managers' general identification with big business, might they not expose this bias in giving preferential treatment to conservative candidates generally and especially to Republican candidates? To argue that this is likely to be the case is not necessarily to ascribe conscious favoritism to the newspaper managers—though conscious favoritism is consistent with at least one tradition of American journalism. Such favoritism may result from an accumulation of small advantages of news slanting or selection or placement in favor of the approved candidates. For information bearing on intended and unintended bias, we must turn to content analyses of newspapers during cam-

30. Steven L. Coombs, "Editorial Endorsements and Electoral Outcomes," in Michael B. MacKuen and Steven L. Coombs (eds.), *More than News: Media Power in Public Affairs* (Beverly Hills, Calif.: Sage, 1981), p. 187.

31. LeRoy C. Ferguson and Ralph H. Smuckler, *Politics in the Press: An Analysis of Press Content in 1952 Senatorial Campaigns* (East Lansing: Governmental Research Bureau, Michigan State College, 1954), pp. 65–71.

32. James W. Markham, "Press Treatment of the 1958 State Elections in Pennsylvania," *Western Political Quarterly* 14 (1961): 921.

33. James E. Gregg, "Newspaper Editorial Endorsements and California Elections, 1948–62," *Journalism Quarterly* 42 (1965): 533.

paigns. The author of one national study of thirty-five daily papers concluded:

> There was slanting in the news columns during the 1952 election, but it was not as widespread as some critics have maintained. A majority of the newspapers in this study—eighteen—met the highest standards of fair news presentation, and a large number of newspapers—eleven—showed no significant degree of partiality that would warrant a charge of unfairness. The six newspapers found to have demonstrated partiality in their news columns constitute a minority.
>
> It also is evident that newspapers which supported the Republican presidential candidate performed, on the whole, at a higher level than did the pro-Democratic newspapers.[34]

Studies of fifteen major American dailies' treatment of the 1960 and 1964 presidential campaigns concluded that there was such good balance and equal coverage, quantitatively, editors must have made a conscious effort to give 50–50 treatment.[35]

In 1968 and 1972 Doris Graber did content analyses of the presidential election coverage of twenty major papers "selected to be representative of the American press." In 1968, ten newspapers endorsed Democrat Hubert Humphrey and ten endorsed Republican Richard Nixon; in 1972, fourteen endorsed incumbent President Nixon and six Democrat George McGovern. Graber reported that "endorsements did not affect coverage patterns in either year." Summarizing the "slants" of 3,163 stories in 1968 and 4,826 stories in 1972, she found that "remarks made about Nixon were predominantly negative.... The slant of comments about Humphrey was slightly favorable in 1968.... For McGovern the picture was mixed [but] fifty-eight percent of all press commentary was unfavorable in 1972." She found that, generally, "the incidence of explicit and veiled criticism in news stories was slight in both elections," and that "the media in recent elections have succeeded in keeping statements about their own dislikes and preferences out of general news stories."[36]

To this point, our look at the partisanship of American newspapers reveals that most papers describe themselves as independent, and that of those admitting a partisan preference, the Democratic–Republican split is about even. As measured by endorsement of candidates, however, the newspapers as a whole seem to be significantly Republican, by 60 to 80 percent of the endorsements given in national, state, and local elections. Measurements of partisan bias in newspapers indicate that, overall, Republicans get more favorable treatment than Democrats. But this finding seems to apply significantly less to the larger and more influential dailies. On the whole, the claims of some Democrats that the United

---

34. Nathan B. Blumberg, *One-Party Press?* (Lincoln: University of Nebraska Press, 1954), pp. 44–45.

35. Guido H. Stempel III, "The Prestige Press in Two Presidential Elections," *Journalism Quarterly* 42 (1965): 15–21.

36. Doris A. Graber, "Press and TV as Opinion Resources in Presidential Campaigns," *Public Opinion Quarterly* 40 (Fall 1976): 286, 294–295.

States has a "one-party press" seem greatly exaggerated, although with a kernel of truth.

A different but equally important question is whether partisan support by newspapers actually helps the favored candidate. Here again most of our knowledge is about presidential elections. The best historical study, a review of two-party presidential campaigns since 1800, reported no evidence that newspapers unduly affect presidential races:

> In half of our comparable elections, candidates have won without the support of a majority of the newspapers, and losers have failed despite majority press support. There seems to be no correlation, positive or negative, between the support of a majority of newspapers during a campaign and success at the polls.[37]

However, more recent studies, using survey research and/or carefully controlled county-level data, indicated that newspaper endorsements do have an impact on presidential elections. Robert Erikson reviewed 1964 data in 223 northern U.S. counties where local newspapers had a near monopoly of circulation. He found an association of endorsements and voting far beyond chance possibility and concluded that "a Democratic endorsement from the local newspaper added about five percentage points to the 1960–1964 Democratic gain." After repeating this research on a smaller scale in the 1968 and 1972 elections, he concluded that

> a newspaper effect similar to that of 1964 was also present in the 1972 election, but probably not in 1968. Thus, a possible generalization is that newspapers may be more powerful forces in highly ideological contests, such as 1964 and 1972, than in more "normal" elections, such as 1968.[38]

John P. Robinson's analyses of SRC national poll data also find newspaper endorsements to be important in presidential elections. He believes newspaper endorsement may have been decisive in the 1968 election: "Once other possible influences were screened out, the pro-Nixon newspapers seem to have swayed about 3 percent of the total vote toward Nixon." And Robinson supports Erikson's suggestion that the newspaper effect may vary depending on the nature of the election: "In close elections (1960 and 1968), newspapers are associated with a shift in the votes only of independent voters. In landslide elections (1956, 1964, and 1972), newspaper endorsements appear to have even wider influence, affecting the votes of...the losing party as well."[39]

Most elections in the United States, however, involve thousands of more

---

37. Frank Luther Mott, "Newspapers in Presidential Campaigns," *Public Opinion Quarterly* 8 (1944): 358.

38. Robert S. Erikson, "The Influence of Newspaper Endorsements in Presidential Elections: The Case of 1964," *American Journal of Political Science* 20 (May 1976): 207, 220.

39. "Newspapers Play Important Role in Recent Elections: Help Nixon in '68 and '72," *Newsletter,* Winter 1974, Institute for Social Research, University of Michigan, p. 4.

obscure state and local candidates, often in jurisdictions where only a few communication channels exist. Are newspapers, in such circumstances, not more influential on election outcomes? The answer seems to be yes, although the evidence is too scanty to be conclusive.

Gregg's examination of California papers from 1948 through 1962 reveals that endorsements for local offices are more efficacious than those for state or national office. In the fourteen years of candidate endorsements, eleven papers with 40 percent of total state circulation had an average of 84.1 percent of winners in local elections, compared with averages of 63.3 to 73.8 percent for a variety of districtwide and statewide elections. Gregg also found, as he had hypothesized, that newspaper endorsements of referendum measures were even more effective than endorsements of candidates.[40]

A striking example of the importance of newspaper endorsements occurred in the 1969 Los Angeles County race for seven nonpartisan seats in a newly created junior college district. None of the 133 candidates who filed had the advantage of incumbency or party support. In that bewildering situation, voters apparently turned to newspaper endorsements as cues for voting. An analysis of the results showed that candidates endorsed by the *Los Angeles Times* got "an extra 24,000 votes and the *Herald-Examiner* candidates gained some 9,000."[41]

A somewhat more impressionistic but probably reliable report stems from the experience of the *Toledo Blade*. A former editorial writer of the *Blade* declares that it "has a notable long-run record of supporting local candidates who turn out to be winners." "Generally speaking," he says, "strong editorial support of a candidate is believed by experienced Toledo politicians to be worth three or four thousand votes out of a total city vote of around seventy thousand to ninety thousand." The reasons for this influence conform to common sense and to the scattered observations of knowledgeable students of local politics:

> While some political veterans can undoubtedly win without *Blade* support, more obscure political figures, including younger men trying to get a foothold on the city's political ladder, are critically dependent of the *Blade's* favor. An editorial or two lambasting or lauding a relatively unknown man can affect his fortunes crucially.... As for judicial candidates running on a non-partisan ballot, the *Blade's* verdict carries its heaviest punch in these contests.[42]

In 1972–1974 the University of Michigan's Center for Political Studies conducted some painstaking research on a sample of respondents in its 1972 election

---

40. Gregg, "Newspaper Editorial Endorsements," pp. 534–536.

41. John E. Mueller, "Choosing among 133 Candidates," *Public Opinion Quarterly* 34 (1970): 400.

42. Reo M. Christenson, "The Power of the Press: The Case of the *Toledo Blade*," *Midwest Journal of Political Science* 3 (1959): 235. For an excellent summary of what is known and knowledgeably inferred about the power of the press in urban political life, see Edward D. Banfield and James Q. Wilson (eds.), *City Politics* (Cambridge: Harvard University Press, 1963), chap. 21, "The Press," pp. 313–325.

studies to measure the impact of editorial endorsements. The researchers were able to link vote decisions, specific newspapers read by 226 respondents, and endorsements for president, governor, and U.S. senator in seventy-nine newspapers. Depending on the assumptions made in their research strategies, they concluded that in state races (for governor and U.S. senator) from 16 to 20 percent of voters will defect from their normal partisan vote when the newspapers they read support the candidate of the other major party. That finding, if true, means that "newspaper editorial endorsements are a major contributor to individual voting decisions."[43]

Finally, there is some evidence aside from endorsements that readers' overall perceptions of how their daily newspaper leans in an election (perceptions gained from editorials, news, and other cues) will influence them in the same direction. From the Michigan Survey Research Center's 1968 data, Robinson concludes that "with other variables controlled, it was estimated that a newspaper's perceived support of one candidate rather than another was associated with about a 6 percent edge in vote for the endorsed candidate over his opponent."[44] Perhaps 6 percent of the readers (or an even larger minority) are able to find voting clues in their paper, but apparently most do not. Graber investigated the images of presidential candidates held by American voters in 1968. At the same time, she reviewed the contents of twenty major national and regional newspapers to see what images of the candidates they were publishing: "The stress on personal image qualities...of the average American is, indeed, paralleled by a heavy emphasis on personal qualities in the press." But the press also laid before its readers a vast amount of information about the candidates, most of which was neutral and offered few evaluative clues (the newspapers' biases, in her judgment, were restricted mainly to editorials). She concluded that in the "torrent" of information, "people may have settled for the easy solution of ignoring all but the most readily absorbed human traits, or relying largely on party labels."[45]

## 17.3 THE PRESS, GOVERNMENT, AND THE FREE SOCIETY

The mass media are vitally important to the maintenance of democracy in the modern world. No system of face-to-face communication could possibly provide a network for the exchange of information sufficient for a society larger than the Greek city-state or the historic New England town. We depend on the mass media for the survival of self-government in the twentieth century.

---

43. Coombs, "Editorial Endorsements," pp. 210, 219; quotation at 194.

44. John P. Robinson, "Perceived Media Bias and the 1968 Vote: Can the Media Affect Behavior After All?" *Journalism Quarterly* 49 (1972): 245.

45. Doris A. Graber, "Personal Qualities in Presidential Images: The Contribution of the Press," *Midwest Journal of Political Science* 16 (1972): 71–72.

There is an inevitable symbiosis between public policy makers and the press. Bernard Cohen describes it in systems terminology:

> The mechanism involved here is a feedback loop, in the sense that foreign policy officials dominate the public discussion of a policy, which they (and Congressmen also) then monitor and on the basis of which they draw conclusions about their freedom to take the next steps. The loop may not even go any further or deeper than the media of communication; the public relations activity results in press coverage, which is then interpreted as significant public opinion.[46]

Thus "public opinion" on foreign policy often becomes the jelling of the views of officials and media opinion leaders, and few if any other individuals or groups are part of the process. No doubt the evolution of domestic policy involves wider participation, but this symbiosis of officialdom and media (especially the press) is a constant factor in decision making and is fundamental to the media's importance.

Our judgment of how well the mass media are performing their indispensable function will depend on whether we expect them to lead their readers' tastes or merely to satisfy them, or to be teachers as well as transmitters of news and opinions. If we cannot ask the media to be better than the communities they serve, then we must conclude that they are now performing well. An astounding range of material is made available to the American public by the print and electronic media. There is hardly a hamlet left where a person cannot get both the soaps and a Shakespearean drama in the same week on television, cannot watch both Oral Roberts and the top American political figures on the same Sunday, cannot buy at the local newsstand or receive at subsidized rates through the U.S. mail either the *National Enquirer* or the *New York Times,* cannot obtain *Playboy* or the *Atlantic.*

One can, however, ask the media to be better (in terms of one's own standards) than the communities they serve, and thus to be even better than they now are. One likes to believe—indeed, the evidence supports the belief—that the media promulgate less trash, bigotry, selfishness, parochialism, and mediocrity than they once did. Yet even greater responsibility and responsiveness can be expected. For those who feel that the media should be instruments of *information and instruction,* one rule of thumb may be whether the media have as much instructional content as the traffic will bear. The owners and managers of the media may not fairly be asked to relinquish the support of their mass audiences to satisfy the more demanding tastes of their critics. But are they attempting to meet the tastes of their critics (and acting as their own critics) at the same time that they retain their mass base of support? Mark Ethridge, former publisher of the *Louisville Courier-Journal,* makes the point well:

---

46. Bernard C. Cohen, *The Public's Impact on Foreign Policy* (Boston: Little, Brown, 1973), p. 178. See also J. W. Fulbright, *The Pentagon Propaganda Machine* (New York: Liveright, 1970).

> There are certain features you've got to have; the public kills you if
> you don't have them. One of them is a medical column; every Ameri-
> can is a hypochondriac to some extent. Ann Lander's column on
> dating and marriage is another very popular feature here. . . . And
> you are still not able to do away with comic strips. . . . We do carry a
> minimum of entertainment-type material. [Also] you've got to have
> the instant journalism, but you've got to have the elaboration of what
> happens. . . . In our "Passing Show" section we ask, "What does the
> news mean?" We have articles by our science reporters and political
> writers and men versed in international affairs.[47]

Beyond the canons of accuracy and the separation of news from editorial
comment, there are improvements to be made in the mass media. The media
often seem to let human laziness and archaic techniques stand in the way of their
reportorial functions. Much of the controversy over "managed news" in
Washington relates less to the willingness of bureaucratic press officers to hand
out the news in amounts of their choice with prepackaged interpretations than
with the willingness of Washington and hometown journalists to accept what
they are given. Bureaucrats are apt to use the weaknesses of others to further their
own interests. Journalists have a responsibility to go beyond the press release and
the press officer—though we do not dismiss the managed-news problem and
shall return to it.

Modern journalism suffers from the stultifying conventions that have to do
with "newspaper style" and the demand for immediacy. The archaic rules of
newspaper style require that a "good story" tell only what happened since the last
issue of the paper and that the essential features of the story be summarized in a
few crisp sentences in the first paragraph. This requirement, of course, is absurd.
Most of the important news of any day is not new at all, but a development of
yesterday's news, as that news was a development of the news of the day before.
The pretense that public events are discontinuous not merely distorts the facts
but exaggerates the ordinary citizen's tendency to envision the impersonal world
of public affairs as episodic snippets of reality rather than as a flow of interrelated
events. The best news media try to place the events of the day in perspective, but
there is still too much effort to isolate, concentrate, and capsulate the news in
"flashes."

Other conventions, especially some having to do with political reporting, are
equally senseless and equally misleading. One is the use of anonymous attribu-
tion. Consider the following examples from the first few lines of a *New York
Times* story (with our brackets):

> North Korean forces have been redeployed toward South Korea "in a
> major way" over the last few months, according to a Pentagon

---

47. *The Press,* interviews by Donald McDonald with Mark Ethridge and C. D. Jackson (Santa
Barbara: Center for the Study of Democratic Institutions, 1961), p. 13.

> official. [Who? In 1974 there were several thousand "Pentagon offi-
> cials."] That official and others interviewed [What others? Inter-
> viewed by whom? When?] said they were not predicting that North
> Korea was about to attack South Korea....
>
>    As described by the Pentagon official and confirmed by ranking
> State Department officials [A "ranking" State Department official is
> what?]...[48]

Leslie Gelb, the *Times* writer, and his editors have been faithful to the canons
of their craft: they have attributed their information to a source and used direct
quotes whenever possible. But close examination reveals that there is no attribu-
tion to real persons, and the quotes were all put in the mouths of unidentified
"officials" or "ranking officials." In short, it was a report without any verified
factual basis put out by a Defense Department flak, slightly rewritten to include
"attributions." A better—or at least equally good and certainly more honest—
story could have been written straightforwardly, telling what Mr. Gelb knew or
thought was going on in the Koreas.

We know very little about newspaper coverage of local politics. We suspect
there is a great deal of "sweetheart" interaction between officials and journalists,
the former wanting "a good press" and the latter finding that providing "a good
press" is the easiest path to regular paychecks, minimal friction with their editors,
and free gin and hors d'oeuvres at receptions and campaign rallies. An enterpris-
ing reporter of the *San Francisco Chronicle* in 1972 did an investigative exposé of
the Reverend Jim Jones, leader of the 1978 mass cult suicides and murders in
Guyana. Jones then had strong ties with San Francisco political leaders. The
*Chronicle* killed the story. *New West* magazine subsequently printed an investigation of Jones, written by the same author. But the *Chronicle's* timidity in 1972
stands, at the very least, as a retreat from journalistic ideals and perhaps as a lost
opportunity to prevent cult madness.[49]

David Paletz and his collaborators suggested that the professional conventions of journalism produce stories that are uncritically supportive of local
government officials. They investigated the activities of the Durham, North
Carolina, City Council and the way those activities were reported in the only
paper that regularly covered the council.

> The media do not increase and may diminish public interest in
> institutions and individuals vested with local authority...by not
> covering those who hold such authority, or by reporting their activi-
> ties in ways supportive of their authority. One result is often to
> insulate city councils from informed public scrutiny.[50]

48. Leslie H. Gelb, "Pentagon Official Reports Big North Korean Step-Up," *New York Times,*
February 23, 1974.

49. "Comment," *Columbia Journalism Review* 18 (March/April 1979): 18.

50. David L. Paletz, Peggy Reichert, and Barbara McIntyre, "How the Media Support Local
Governmental Authority," *Public Opinion Quarterly* 35 (1971): 92.

In their treatment of domestic public affairs, the mass media, especially the newspapers, may make a particular contribution to the administration of justice, to the maintenance of high ethical standards for public officials, and to the efficacy of the electoral process. Police brutality and denial of due process to indigent and minority defendants are all too common in the United States. Constant surveillance by local reporters and city editors over the administration of criminal justice is a service of great importance that any local newspaper can perform for its community—a service for which there is celebrated precedent in the history of journalism. Newspapers can also watch over the ever more complex ethical problems of conflict of interest among public officials, from governors to traffic officers. In the courts, in the legislative bodies, and in the administrative agencies, favoritism and the temptations to favoritism are so common—and so destructive of the public confidence on which democracy is based—that the alert reporter has no difficulty finding dragons to slay.

The press's right to criticize public officials was given support in 1964 by the Supreme Court's decision in *New York Times* and *Abernathy* v. *Sullivan*. A unanimous Court held that a public official cannot collect damages for published statements critical of his official conduct, even if such statements are false and defamatory, unless he proves actual malice. The mass media, and especially the newspapers as the political medium par excellence, can take new confidence from the Court's declaration that the United States has "a profound national commitment to the principle that debate on public issues should be uninhibited, robust, and wide open, and that it may well include vehement, caustic, and sometimes unpleasantly sharp attacks on government and public officials."[51] The Sullivan decision is still the "lodestar" case regarding the libeling of public officials by the media. It was called that by Irving R. Kaufman, chief judge of the U.S. Court of Appeals for the Second Circuit, at a 1984 conference marking the twentieth anniversary of the case. But other conferees noted that a more conservative U.S. Supreme Court in the 1970s and 1980s had "substantially narrowed the definition of a public official, . . . and has encouraged judges to let more cases go to trial instead of dismissing them on First Amendment grounds."[52] Thus the tension between freedom of the press and the protection of individuals' privacy and reputations, like all such clashes of rights, is never definitively resolved.

Citizens could ask of newspapers that firmer editorial stands be taken and defended with regard to candidates. James Reston's comments are much to the point:

> The newspapers themselves can do something about the Congress
> . . . if they will look at the . . . primary elections and tell the truth
> about the many dubs and incompetents who represent their states

51. *New York Times,* March 10, 1964.

52. Jonathan Friendly, "20 Years after Key Libel Ruling, Debate Goes On," *New York Times,* March 9, 1984.

and districts on Capitol Hill . . . the majority of men and women in the House and Senate are able and industrious public servants, but as the editors know, there is a minority of numbskulls in the Congress whom no self-respecting editor would trust to cover the local City Hall.

It would be difficult to overestimate the damage done to the quality of Congress by the amiable goodfellowship of newspaper editors and owners. Usually they know their senators and congressmen very well, and often go on backing them long after age or sickness has impaired their usefulness. Lacking any lead from the papers, the voters do the same.[53]

Alert journalists can usually find ways to discover the facts about local, state, and national news. Acting as the agents of "the people's right to know," a role in which they like to cast themselves, they can ordinarily ferret out all the facts that the people need to know about domestic public policy, even when information is withheld by government officials who feel threatened by such exposures. Reporters may not always be able to get the facts from one source, but with the help of officials in other branches or levels of government (members of Congress, state legislators, or attorneys general), the energetic press can well perform its responsibilities as critic and scrutinizer of the public's business.[54]

The task of obtaining facts is not so easy, however, with regard to foreign and defense policy. The problems of unfamiliarity, complexity, geographical distance, and espionage (real and imagined) are so great in foreign and military affairs that even a minimum public consideration of national policy in these areas demands the closest cooperation and understanding between governmental officials and the news media. There are three difficulties: secrecy, news "management," and cooptation of press by government in the name of some supposed higher good—usually "national interest."

Regarding secrecy, no nation under present or foreseeable international conditions is prepared to tell all it knows, and no country is totalitarian enough to successfully manipulate *all* information. What is practical, however, even in a nation with strong traditions of an open and free press, is a policy that employs selective openness and closedness regarding what the media are told by government officials. Public officials, like other human beings, prefer to have their work and their organizations well thought of. When government officials have convinced themselves that the "national interest" requires it, they have been known

---

53. James Reston, "The Press and the Congress and the Nation," *New York Times,* January 17, 1964.

54. Reston says, on this point: "Congressmen are different. Unlike officials of the Executive, they live most of the time in the open. They think the good opinion of the press is important to their reelection, which interests them, so they see us and some of them even read us. Also, they are always making speeches and, like reporters, looking for mistakes to correct or criticize, especially if they are in the opposition. So the reporter and the Congressman are often natural allies" *(Sketches in the Sand* [New York: Knopf, 1967], p. 192).

to withhold from the public some or all of the news about events, or some or all of the explanations about policy. The historic complaint of reporters (and members of Congress) is that the administrative agencies do not tell all they know. In some cases, no information may be given about an event or policy; in other cases, selectively misleading or inadequate information may be given.

The Reagan administration made a concerted effort to withhold information from the press and the public. Officially, the president and his assistants attributed the clampdown to efforts to cut government costs, to meet statutory requirements ignored by earlier liberal administrations, to improve national security, and to reduce what they regarded as inappropriate promotional activities by the national government.[55] Concurrently, the administration took stern measures and sought legislation against "leaks," that is, unauthorized disclosure of information by insiders. Pentagon officials began a policy of giving lie-detector examinations to selected military and civilian employees, and press reports indicated that 15,000 to 20,000 persons might be so examined.[56] The Intelligence Identities Protection Act, passed in 1982, made it a crime to expose the name of any American covert agent "with reason to believe that disclosure would impair or impede the foreign intelligence activities of the United States," making, for example, the exposure of illegal activity by named agents illegal itself.[57] An executive order of March 11, 1983, required more than 100,000 bureaucrats to agree to submit to government censors anything they wrote for publication for the rest of their lives. When asked for examples of harm done by leaks, the Justice Department person in charge of this clampdown is reported to have replied: "Examples of this are classified themselves."[58]

Something more than mere withholding is implied by the notion of governmental "management" of the news. News management involves the deliberate creation of partial truths or outright falsehoods in the furtherance of a governmental policy. An attempt at news management (in this case, unsuccessful) is illustrated by the official versions of the May 1960 flight of Francis Gary Powers over the Soviet Union in his U-2 reconnaissance plane. When it became apparent that Powers had been downed in Soviet territory, as the Soviet government claimed, both the State Department and the National Aeronautics and Space Administration gave out false (and different!) official stories—which both were forced to retract when the truth of the flights could no longer be suppressed. That news management is practiced by Democratic as well as Republican administrations is attested by the bold-faced statements of Assistant Secretary of Defense

---

55. David Burnham, "Government Restricting Flow of Information to the Public," *New York Times*, November 15, 1982.

56. Richard Halloran, "Pentagon Denies Polygraph Policy Is Move to Curb Press Disclosures," *New York Times*, December 10, 1982.

57. Floyd Abrams, "Naming Covert Agents," *New York Times*, June 11, 1982.

58. Stuart Taylor, Jr., " 'Necessary Secrets' vs. the Public's Right to Know," *New York Times*, October 25, 1983.

Arthur Sylvester in October 1962. In the crisis over Soviet missiles in Cuba, the U.S. agencies involved found it expedient to plant several lies in the American press to mislead Cuban and Soviet officials. Sylvester put the matter starkly: "It is inherent in government [to have] the right to lie to save itself when going toward a nuclear war. It's basic." The concept Sylvester laid bare is an old one, but he gave it a new name amidst some new frankness: "News as weaponry" means that "in the kind of world we live in, the generation of news by actions taken by the government becomes a weapon in a strained situation."[59]

It is apparent that high government officials of all administrations lie when selective withholding and interpretation fail, and when they think the chance of exposure is slight. Jody Powell, spokesman for the Carter administration, acknowledged after leaving office that he had lied about the attempt to rescue the Americans held hostages in Iran in 1980.[60] The implication is clear: on occasion a government administrator has a duty, as Sir Henry Wotton once said of diplomats, "to lie for his country."

Just as dangerous, and less understandable, is the acquiescence, even occasionally the connivance, of the press in official lies. Neal Houghton points out that before the Bay of Pigs invasion of 1961, American journalists knew they were being given false information but nevertheless published it. He quotes Reston's retrospective mea culpa in the *New York Times* of May 10, 1961: "The same press roared with indignation when Britain and France broke their treaty commitment [and] invade[d] Suez, but it had very little to say about the morality, legality, or practicality of the Cuban adventure, when there was still time to stop it."[61]

The long history of news manipulation, half-lies, and full lies that characterized our Indochina adventures from 1960 to 1972 was marked by press connivance in official deception. Withdrawal from Vietnam and post-Watergate purifications did not end such connivance. Anthony Lewis reported that in 1975 the press had information about American efforts to raise a sunken Soviet submarine but was persuaded by the CIA to suppress the story for thirty-nine days. He explained why the press is "easy to con":

When a defense or intelligence agency says that something must be

---

59. *New York Times,* November 1, 1962. See also Bernard C. Cohen, *The Press and Foreign Policy* (Princeton: Princeton University Press, 1963), pp. 198–202. Sylvester had Plato on his side, though he made no note of the fact: "Then if anyone at all is to have the privilege of lying, the rulers of the State should be the persons; and they, in their dealings either with enemies or with their own citizens, may be allowed to lie for the public good" *(The Republic* [Roslyn, N.Y.: Black, 1932], p. 65). Herbert G. Klein, President Nixon's press secretary, new at his job in early 1969, repudiated the Sylvester dictum, saying the government had no right to lie "even in situations involving national security" *(Washington Post,* February 29, 1969).

60. Jonathan Friendly, "Reporter's Notebook: The Editor's Critic," *New York Times,* April 25, 1981.

61. Neal D. Houghton, "The Cuban Invasion of 1961 and the U.S. Press, in Retrospect," *Journalism Quarterly* 42 (1965): 427. For a similar appraisal, see Victor Bernstein and Jesse Gordon, "The Press and the Bay of Pigs," *Columbia University Forum* 10 (1967): 4–13.

kept secret, it starts with a great advantage. The rest of us are likely to be unfamiliar with the subject, and we defer to the supposed experts. "National security" is a worrying phrase; who would want to risk that?

But bitter and recent experience teaches that "national security" is often a cover for a desire to avoid awkward questions. The most extravagant claims of risk turn out to be hollow.[62]

"Backgrounders" are a source of much news manipulation. Backgrounders have many ambiguities. A simple backgrounder requires reporters to use one of the standard circumlocutions employed in the Gelb story quoted above: "a White House official," "a senior official," "an administration source," and the like. A "deep backgrounder" seems to mean that the information "can be attributed only to 'sources,' or, worse, reported with such formulations as 'it was learned.'" And a "deep, deep backgrounder" is "so restrictive that writers must state the information on their own authority."[63] Bill Moyers, press assistant to President Johnson, believes that backgrounders often become "a primary instrument of policy, propaganda, and manipulation" that "cause harm and create an unbelieving and untrusting public." Sometimes such duplicity gets exposed. But, says Moyers,

> in the end very little will change. The Government will go on calling backgrounders as long as the Government wants to put its best face forward. Reporters will be there to report dutifully what isn't officially said by a source that can't be held officially accountable at an event that doesn't officially happen for a public that can't officially be told because it can't officially be trusted to know.[64]

Political scientist James David Barber, in the midst of the 1984 presidential campaign, wrote that the United States was "drifting into a mode of political thinking that is not only illusory but consciously, even proudly so." He reviewed a string of the Reagan administration's domestic and foreign policy assertions and interpretations that were based on drama, not reality, and quoted David Stockman's summary of White House strategy: "Every time one fantasy doesn't work they try another one."[65] Barber believes that "what we need from journalists...is a reality test," and suggests they ask political candidates to explain how they think "the real world works today, in this arena and that, and

---

62. Anthony Lewis, "The Secrecy Disease," *New York Times,* October 31, 1977.

63. Charles Mohr, "To Source or Not to Source: That Is the Question," *New York Times,* June 19, 1984.

64. Bill Moyers, "Read This, Please, but Don't Tell Anyone What It Says or Who Wrote It. If You Must Tell, Attribute It to a Former Government Aide Writing in a Large Metropolitan Daily," *New York Times,* January 6, 1972. For a recent general discussion of the ethics of political influence, including examples of news management, see Robert E. Goodin, *Manipulatory Politics* (New Haven: Yale University Press, 1980).

65. See also Mark Green and Gail MacColl, eds., *There He Goes Again: Ronald Reagan's Reign of Error* (New York: Pantheon, 1983).

how it worked yesterday, rather than in some hypothetical tomorrow." In that way, instead of hearing vague campaign rhetoric and promises, citizens might learn whether the candidates know any relevant, testable facts. "At the very least," he writes, "news stories carrying the answers would add refreshing innovation to the dreary formula pieces we labor through: stories of gaffes, half-day hype, dutiful recitations of freeze-dried remarks delivered in town after town after town."[66]

---

66. James David Barber, "Political Illusionism," *New York Times,* April 26, 1984.

# CHANGE AND THE OPINION-POLICY PROCESS

The first part of this book dealt with the nature of public opinion and the relationships between the opinions of publics and democratic governance. There we introduced the idea of the opinion-policy process, through which citizen interests, mediated by a variety of group and institutional interests, have influence on governmental policy and programs.

Part Two dealt with opinion measurement—everyday measurement, as engaged in by leaders and led, and the scientific measurement of survey research. It also surveyed the criticisms leveled against opinion research and its practitioners and dealt with the persistent problems of political polling.

Part Three dealt with the environment of public opinion—the cultural, social, and psychological forces that influence opinion formation, stability, and change. We considered both the intrapersonal or psychological aspects of opinion formation and the effects of social organization. We adopted the funnel of causality to represent (although with severe limitations) the opinion-forming process in the individual.

In Part Four we investigated opinion and communication networks, with primary-group relationships as the basic communication structures for the maintenance of psychological balance, ego identity, and cognitive meaning for the individual. Of course, many—probably most—of an individual's politically relevant opinions are neither original nor the outgrowth of small-group relations. Most have traveled through mass channels and are internalized because they happen to fit with the preestablished biases of the individual. Sometimes political opinions come about through conscious application of reason or logic. In Part Four we examined the characteristic modes of operation and biases of mass-communication media for what they may tell us about why publics think as they do about policy matters.

In this final section we will examine (a) the processes of opinion change and (b) the interrelations of opinion change with political behavior and policy change.

Underneath public opinion lies private opinion. The expression of points of view on issues by significant numbers of persons—what we have called *public opinion*—is possible only if many individuals have preferences (however formed) that they are able and willing to make public (when they volunteer or are asked to do so). Therefore, although public opinion is a phenomenon of aggregate human behavior, our analysis of it will be inadequate unless we have some understanding of how individuals make and remake their separate opinions. Daniel Katz has put the matter succinctly and clearly:

> The study of opinion formation and attitude change is basic to an understanding of the public opinion process even though it should not be equated with the process. The public opinion process is one phase of the influencing of collective decisions, and its investigation involves knowledge of channels of communication, of the power structures of a society, of the character of mass media, of the relation between elites, factions, and masses, of the role of formal and informal leaders, of the institutionalized access to officials. But the raw material out of which public opinion develops is to be found in the attitudes of individuals, whether they be followers or leaders and whether these attitudes be at the general level of tendencies to conform to legitimate authority or majority opinion or at the specific level of favoring or opposing the particular aspects of the issue under consideration. The nature of the organization of attitudes within the personality and the processes which account for attitude change are thus critical areas for the understanding of the collective product known as public opinion.*

All this is old stuff. It is repeated here because the relationship between private and public opinion is so fundamentally important. On this relationship depends the justification—indeed, the necessity—for our consideration of those processes in the individual that bring about new opinions and change old ones. But much more than understanding is involved, for the social fabric depends on individuals' ability to learn new attitudes, new opinions, and new behavior, and in the process to change and sometimes to give up old attitudes, opinions, and behavior. The susceptibility of attitudes, opinions, and behavior to change is a cardinal

---

* Daniel Katz, "The Functional Approach to the Study of Attitudes," *Public Opinion Quarterly* 29 (1960): 163. Reprinted by permission.

fact for parents and teachers concerned with the socialization of children, and for special pleaders concerned with the education or manipulation of individuals of every age.

Old opinions change, and new opinions are formed. But how? Under what circumstances, as a consequence of what forces, and with what political results? In the three chapters that follow, we raise some questions about how opinions change and about how these changes affect political life and public policy.

## Chapter 18

# Attitude and Opinion Change

In this chapter we will not make a distinction between *attitude* and *opinion*. Unless we indicate otherwise, each term may be substituted for the other. There are, of course, some dangers in this lack of discrimination. Opinions, we have agreed, are *sharpened attitudes* with more specific referents. As a rule, this is an important distinction, but in considering the psychological processes of attitude and opinion change, we may generally ignore it for simplicity's sake.

Milton Rokeach argues that it is misleading not to distinguish between opinion change and attitude change because unless they are differentiated, the researcher may take a compliant statement of opinion change to indicate a genuine attitude change.[1] Rokeach is right. "Sometimes," Freud is supposed to have said, "a cigar is a phallic symbol, and sometimes it's just a good smoke." Sometimes change in the expression of an opinion is only a change in the expression of an opinion, and sometimes it's an expression of change in an attitude. But, by and large, opinions and attitudes are consistent.

An individual may hold conflicting and even contradictory attitudes and opinions, or an opinion may be influenced by many (complementary or conflicting) attitudes. Furthermore, individuals may falsify their expression of attitudes or opinions or both. Despite these sources of confusion and misunderstanding, common sense tells us that a general consistency must be maintained between attitudes and opinions—and, as we shall see, there is experimental and empirical evidence of such consistency.

---

1. Milton Rokeach, *Beliefs, Attitudes, and Values: a Theory of Organization and Change* (San Francisco: Jossey-Bass, 1968), p. 139.

## 18.1 THE STUDY OF ATTITUDE AND OPINION CHANGE

Attitudes and the study of attitudes have been central to much of social psychology. In an historical survey, Gordon Allport says that *attitude*

> is probably the most distinctive and indispensable concept in contemporary American social psychology. No other term appears more frequently in experimental and theoretical literature. Its popularity is not difficult to explain. It has come into favor, first of all, because it is not the property of any one psychological school of thought, and therefore serves admirably the purposes of eclectic writers. Furthermore, it is a concept which escapes the controversy concerning the relative influence of heredity and environment. Since an attitude may combine both instinct and habit in any proportion, it avoids the extreme commitments of both the instinct theory and environmentalism. The term likewise is elastic enough to apply either to the dispositions of single, isolated individuals or to broad patterns of culture (common attitudes). Psychologists and sociologists therefore find in it a meeting point for discussion and research. This useful, one might almost say peaceful, concept has been so widely adopted that it has virtually established itself as the keystone in the edifice of American social psychology.[2]

Generally speaking, the study of experimental psychology, of neurophysiology, and of comparative psychology was well advanced before any systematic attention was given to attitude *change*. Not until Ivan Pavlov's work on conditioned responses and its popularization by John Watson and other early behaviorists was it clear that stimulus–response conceptualizations might be generalized to cover attitude change. If uniform stimuli produced more or less uniform responses, it might be possible to isolate causal factors in attitudes and opinions and to change attitudes and opinions by selective manipulation of stimuli. It was a long road by way of laboratory and professional journals from Pavlov's crude stimulus–response formulation to Hullian learning theory, but only a short jump of the imagination from Pavlov's dogs to the education of children in Huxley's *Brave New World*.

Plainly, if one could control all the stimuli received at the integrative center of the human brain, one could control the attitude structure, personality, and behavior of the individual. Or, in terms of explanation rather than control, if we could identify the kinds and degrees of stimuli associated with the measured responses of an individual in a given set of circumstances, we would be able to

---

2. Gordon W. Allport, "The Historical Background of Modern Social Psychology," in *Handbook of Social Psychology*, eds. Gardner Lindzey and Elliot Aronson, vol. 1 (Reading, Mass.: Addison-Wesley, 1954), p. 43. Reprinted by permission of Addison-Wesley Publishing Co., Inc.

explain behavior with a high degree of certainty. For prediction, we would have to have additional information based on patterns of usual behavior under similar circumstances.

Almost all study of attitude formation and change is based on *stimulus-response theory*. Stimulus-response theory (or *S-R*) is, as Leonard Doob says, "the magic formula of most modern psychology.... A stimulus is a change in the environment, including internal changes (like an accelerated heart beat), which affects the individual. A response is what the person actually does or does not perceive or do after being affected by the stimulus."[3]

The funnel-of-causality model, introduced in Chapter 7 and referred to several times later, is a simplistic device for demonstrating how opinions are formed over a period of time (short or long), during which varied stimuli reach an individual who is (at the moment the analysis starts) uniquely the product of physiological endowments and past experiences. At the moment taken for the beginning of the analysis, an individual has certain attitudes and opinions, each the product of an earlier funnel of causality and each more or less capable of being identified and measured. These are the *independent variables*—the factors that are given—and they may be described, in a shorthand that is often useful, as the *existing attitude structure*.

Our fictional Mr. Oblah may be said to have had, as a part of his attitude structure when we introduced him, the following characteristics: (a) distrust of the Democratic party, (b) a tendency to regard Republicans favorably, and (c) anti-Catholic feelings. Each of his attitudes may be thought of as a product of a funnel of causality that involved his earlier experiences and his personality needs. Each attitude is, in a sense, a long-lived response to various stimuli variously received, and his whole attitude structure is a *pattern* of his responses to various stimuli variously received.

Each attitude has two major aspects: (a) *cognitive* and (b) *affective*.[4] The cognitive aspects of an attitude have to do with the intellect—they are descriptive and reasoned. The affective part of an attitude has to do with feelings, emotions, and values. Amy's attitude toward dogs, for example, includes such cognitive elements as *animal, useful on farms, meat eaters,* and *capable of loud sounds;* but it also includes such affective elements as *rambunctious, overly friendly, servile,* and *source of filth in cities.* Cognitively, her attitude toward dogs squares pretty well with reality, insofar as reality is physical and testable; she knows what a dog is. Affectively, her attitude is filled with subjective judgments and value preferences; she does not like dogs.

---

3. Leonard W. Doob, *Public Opinion and Propaganda* (New York: Holt, Rinehart & Winston, 1948), p. 14.

4. Meanings, as given by *Webster's Third New International Dictionary,* unabridged: *Cognition:* the act or process of knowing in the broadest sense; specifically, an intellectual process by which knowledge is gained about perceptions or ideas—distinguished from *affection* and *conation. Affect:* the conscious subjective aspect of an emotion considered apart from bodily changes.

It is important to note here that the very qualities that make attitudes and systematic attitude patterns essential to human existence also act as deterrents to attitude change. Attitudes are generalizations and simplifications. Attitudes are learned and are necessarily based on yesterday's learning. Attitudes are patterned, and the pattern is necessarily a composite of yesterday's attitudes, which rest on yesterday's learning. Stability is thus built into each individual's sense of the world. Those indispensable ordering devices and time-savers called habits thus become possible.

But thus also the meanings of new stimuli are often distorted. We will have more to say about that later. It is clear not only that the *meanings* of new stimuli are impeded by the necessary conservatism of attitudes, but also that the very *perception* of new stimuli may be resisted or even rejected. *Selective perception,*[5] as the phenomenon is called, takes two forms. First, individuals avoid exposure to stimuli that may be inconsistent with existing attitudes. Second, even when such stimuli are encountered, they are less likely to be taken in. Thus we avoid—unconsciously, perhaps, more often than consciously—both the occasions and the acceptance of stimuli inconsistent with our existing attitudes.

## 18.2 MODELS OF OPINION AND ATTITUDE CHANGE

As with so much else in modern psychology, Freud and his followers seem to have been the first psychological investigators to consider the possibilities—and to some extent the dynamics—of attitude change. Earlier, the study of psychology tended to be static, descriptive, and concerned with the nature of such presumed "drives" as egoism, or with the pleasure–pain formulation. From the beginning, psychoanalysis had both the advantage and the disadvantage of being developed in the context of therapy and medicine. Freud's methodology, though unscientific in many ways, had an empirical base; he dealt with real people who had real psychological problems. More important for the point being made here, his objective was to produce changes in attitudes and attitude structures (and in even deeper levels of the personality).

Unfortunately, the Freudian concern for attitude change is too narrow to meet the demands for generalization made in this book. The very thing that moved the Freudians to focus on attitude change—namely, a desire to reduce neurotic

---

5. The "law of selective perception" has been subjected to rigorous testing and qualification. It appears that, at least in laboratory situations, individuals will often actively seek out communication discrepant with existing attitudes. The general principle, as described above, seems entirely valid, however. See William J. McGuire, "The Nature of Attitudes and Attitude Change," in *Handbook of Social Psychology,* eds. Lindzey and Aronson, vol. 3 (1969), pp. 218–224; also David O. Sears and Jonathan L. Freedman, "Selective Exposure to Information: A Critical Review," *Public Opinion Quarterly* 31 (1967): 194–213; and Drury R. Sherrod, "Selective Perception of Political Candidates," *Public Opinion Quarterly* 35 (1971–72): 554–562.

conflicts in the individual—now limits the usefulness of Freudian conceptualization for the general study of attitude change. The attitudes of interest to psychoanalysts come about through conflicts of drives and training—conflicts that are unresolved but that in some way distort or repress emotions and therefore prevent satisfactory personal relationships. The Freudian concern for attitude change is therapeutic, the question being: How are unsatisfactory (that is, dysfunctional) attitudes changed into satisfactory (functional) attitudes? For the study of political science, the lasting and valued contribution of psychoanalytic theory is that it demonstrates the direct policy implications of personality needs and identifies the psychological impediments to realizing the democratic processes. For an understanding of how conflict-based attitudes agitate the human mind, prevent satisfactory interpersonal relations, and impede the peaceful resolution of social issues, Freudian thought is extremely helpful.

But the Freudians do not tell us the psychological processes by which attitudes are changed, or even how such processes operate in psychoanalytic therapy. Clara Thompson's statement of attitude change is essentially a description of any problem-solving process: identification of problem, gathering of knowledge through trial and error, insight, and reintegration of meaning. "The test of the insight's validity," she says, "should be an effortless change of attitude."[6] This is all well and good—and helpful to the individual patients, if it works[7]—but it tells us nothing of general use about how attitudes change.

There are two other and more general approaches to the study of opinion change: (a) *balance theory* and (b) *functional theory*. We will briefly describe each, but the systematic statement of attitude change that follows the descriptions is in terms of a functional analysis incorporating balance mechanisms.

Balance theory[8] is based on the proposition that the human organism needs

---

6. Clara Thompson, *Psychoanalysis: Evolution and Development* (New York: Hermitage House, 1950), p. 240.

7. Although it is not at all certain that psychoanalysis works any better than other forms of psychotherapy, see Bernard Berelson and Gary A. Steiner, *Human Behavior: An Inventory of Scientific Findings* (New York: Harcourt, Brace & World, 1964), p. 289. Thoughtful opinion is divided on the question whether *any* kind of professional psychotherapy is better than letting nature take its course. The testimony of psychiatrists and clinical psychologists is suspect on the grounds of self-interest. For a brief review of evaluation efforts, concluding that 80% of more than 100 studies find positive results for psychotherapy, see Julian Meltzoff and Melvin Kornreich, "It Works," *Psychology Today* 5 (1971): 57–61.

8. We have adopted the term *balance* because we believe that the words *consistency* and *inconsistency* have some logical and evaluative connotations that social science should avoid as much as possible. We would use Leon Festinger's term *dissonance*, but do not find his formulation the most useful for students of public opinion and the opinion-policy process. Festinger's major statement pays inadequate attention to the affective elements of individual attitudes and to the nonrational capacities and devices to tolerate rational inconsistencies. See Leon Festinger, *A Theory of Cognitive Dissonance* (New York: Harper & Row, 1957). For a critical review of the work of Festinger and his students, see Natalia P. Chapanis and Alphonse Chapanis, "Cognitive Dissonance: Five Years Later." *Psychological Bulletin* 61 (1964): 1–22. See also Robert L. Abelson, "Whatever Became of Consistency Theory?" *Personality and Social Psychology Bulletin* 9 (1983): 37–54.

and seeks a total configuration of beliefs, attitudes, and behavior that (a) reflects internal consistency, (b) shows a general state of equilibrium, and (c) squares with the objective facts of the environment. Not all beliefs, attitudes, and behavior need to be regarded as rational, but rationality plays an important part in balance theory. The belief structure that is in equilibrium will reflect reason as well as irrational needs, the individual's state of knowledge or of ignorance, and a host of environmental factors of which cultural prescriptions and group pressures are among the most important.

If major inconsistencies are perceived to exist between the cognitive and affective aspects of an attitude, or between different attitudes, balance theory predicts some direct or indirect changes to bring the attitude or attitudes into greater consistency. For example, if Mr. Oblah finds himself in the presence of friendly, pleasant, likable Catholics, he may sense the inconsistency between (a) what he observes as the facts of the moment (his *cognitions*) and (b) his general dislike (negative affect) of Catholics. Balance theory tells us that Mr. Oblah's attitudes (either the cognitive or the affective elements or both) may well change under these conditions. It was, in fact, in studies of prejudice that some of the elements of balance theory were first brought to the attention of Leon Festinger and others. The basic, generalized proposition of the balance theory of attitude change has been stated as follows:

> When the affective and cognitive components of an attitude are mutually consistent, the attitude is in a stable state; when the affective and cognitive components are mutually inconsistent (to a degree that exceeds that individual's present tolerance for such inconsistency), the attitude is in an unstable state and will undergo spontaneous reorganizing activity until such activity eventuates in either (1) the attainment of affective-cognitive consistency or (2) the placing of an "irreconcilable" inconsistency beyond the range of active awareness.[9]

The third, most general, and most integrating approach to the study of attitude dynamics is the *functional approach*. As Daniel Katz explains, "the basic assumption...is that both attitude formation and attitude change must be understood in terms of the needs they serve and that as these motivational processes differ, so too will the conditions and techniques for attitude change."[10]

Katz has categorized the four major functions of attitudes as:

**1.** *The instrumental, adjustive, or utilitarian function:* "Essentially, this function is a recognition of the fact that people strive to maximize the rewards in their external environment and to minimize the penalties.... The dynamics of atti-

---

9. Milton J. Rosenberg, "An Analysis of Affective-Cognitive Consistency," in Rosenberg et al., *Attitude Organization and Change* (New Haven: Yale University Press, 1960), p. 22.

10. Daniel Katz, "The Functional Approach to the Study of Attitudes," *Public Opinion Quarterly* 24 (1960): 167. For much of what follows, we are indebted to this thoughtful and illuminating essay by Katz. Quotations reprinted by permission.

tude formation with respect to the adjustment function are dependent upon present or past perceptions of the utility of the attitudinal object for the individual."

**2.** *The knowledge function:* People, Katz says, "seek knowledge to give meaning to what would otherwise be an unorganized chaotic universe. People need standards or frames of reference for understanding their world, and attitudes help to supply such standards" by providing definiteness, distinction, consistency, and stability. William McGuire's understanding of the difference between the utilitarian and knowledge functions is that attitudes that serve the utilitarian function tell us what we need to believe to get along with the social world, while attitudes that serve the knowledge function tell us what is accurate or true about our environment. Thus the knowledge function is a special case of the utilitarian, with heavy (but not exclusive) emphasis on cognitive elements.[11]

**3.** *The value-expressive function:* Value-expressive attitudes give "positive expression to [the individual's] central values and to the type of person he conceives himself to be." Such attitudes are in a sense the reciprocal of the ego-defensive attitudes; ego-defensive attitudes are designed to prevent damage to the self-image, whereas value-expressive attitudes enhance the self-image.

**4.** *The ego-defensive function:* The individual "protects himself from acknowledging the basic truths about himself or the harsh realities in his external world." Devices by which the individual defends his ego (his self-image) include those designed to avoid the dissonant elements entirely—denial, misinterpretation—and those, less incapacitating, that distort the dissonant elements—rationalization, projection, displacement.[12]

Although a great deal (perhaps most) of the attention given to attitudes and attitude change has been directed at understanding the way attitudes contribute to the ego-defensive and value-expressive functions, it is likely that the utilitarian and knowledge functions are more important for the everyday life of the individual. This proposition doubtless holds especially for the *political* attitudes of the average American. The evidence is overwhelming that politics is not ego-related for most people—although we must bear in mind the relevance of *role* and *elite* factors. Most people do not construe public issues as capable of threatening or enhancing their self-image. The average citizen does not internalize political ideologies or controversies to the point where they matter at any but the most superficial level of consciousness. For political leaders, however, quite the reverse may be true; the ego-defensive and value-expressive functions may become so important that their satisfaction impedes the knowledge and utilitarian functions.

It should be clear from the general statement of the problems in understanding

---

11. McGuire, "Nature of Attitudes and Attitude Change," p. 159.
12. Katz, "Functional Approach," pp. 170–175.

opinion change, and from the examples given above, that the functional approach to the study of attitude and opinion change is directed primarily to the question of the uses the individual makes of attitudes and opinions, and of how change relates to those uses. The functional approach says, in effect, that attitudes serve needs of individuals, and that attitude change should be considered in terms of what change would mean for those needs. The several methods of balance theory deal with the presumed psychodynamics of opinion change, in both meaning (cognition) and emotion (affect). In highly oversimplified terms, functional theory is concerned with the *why* of opinion change and balance theory with the *how* of opinion change. They are not, therefore, alternate or interchangeable approaches. They are complementary, and they are applied in this chapter in a complementary way.

## 18.3 ATTITUDE/OPINION CHANGE: FICTIONAL CASE EXAMPLES

M. Brewster Smith, Jerome S. Bruner, and Robert W. White, using a research framework quite similar to Katz's, suggest that functional analysis may be very helpful for an understanding of attitude and opinion change. Attitudes and opinions, these authors maintain, serve the following functions: (a) *object appraisal,* which is reality testing and is analogous, in part, to Katz's "knowledge," "adjustment," and "value-expressive" functions; and (b) *externalization,* which includes part of Katz's "value-expressive" function and all of his "ego-defensive" function.[13] Smith, Bruner, and White relate changes in individual attitudes and opinions in regard to public issues in the following way. They say that attitudes change only when there is some dynamic interaction of reality appraisal, social factors, personal interests or values, and "the inner economy of personality." What people think about public issues will

> involve different weightings of the broadly realistic, social, and projective components, and these may differ on the same issue from one time to another....
>
> To the extent that object appraisal predominates, the person tends to react rationally, according to his lights and according to the information at his disposal. In terms of this function, his interests and values stand to be advanced by flexibility on his part in assimilating the implication of new facts....

---

13. See M. Brewster Smith, Jerome S. Bruner, and Robert W. White, *Opinions and Personality* (New York: Wiley, 1956), pp. 39–44. We use Katz's categories here because the fine distinctions he makes among the knowledge, utilitarian, and value-expressive functions seem more adaptable to political phenomena. But we agree with Smith, Bruner, and White that "definitions are matters of convenience, and they attain high status only in the advanced stages of a science. In time, greater precision will come. In the meantime, we think that little is served by quarreling about definition in the abstract" (p. 34).

> To the extent that a person's attitudes are primarily rooted in his social adjustments, he is less oriented toward the facts than toward what others think. Probably the effective strategy for changing opinions serving this function is that of the propagandist who relies on "prestige suggestion"—creating the "impression of universality," drawing on testimonials, and discrediting the group support of opposing views. This strategy is often effective, but not always. . . .
>
> To the extent that a person's attitudes serve to externalize inner problems, and are therefore imbedded in his defenses against obscure and unresolved tensions, we may expect them to be rigid and not particularly amenable either to reason and fact or to simple social manipulation. Anything that increases his anxiety and sense of threat may be expected to heighten their rigidity.[14]

It is clear from this statement of the process that opinion change will take place only if a number of conditions are met. Attitudes and opinions are remarkably stable—and necessarily so, for maintenance of the individual's mental health and for dependability in social interaction. Resistance to attitude change is ordinarily high; habit and stereotypical thinking satisfy most of the functional needs of most people; and messages may be quite easily distorted to fit existing attitudes, thus eliminating the need for change.

As an example, we may consider a fictional Harold Nawarski, Polish-American husband and father in Cleveland, Ohio, who has well-defined and strongly held attitudes about busing children to achieve racial integration in schools. Underlying his views is a stereotypical racist notion that black children are loud, lazy, rough, immoral, and probably not very clean. This racist thinking is of long standing, having been created by the uncontradicted influence of parents, white peers, and social institutions during Mr. Nawarski's childhood and youth in a Polish district of Buffalo, where he lived until he became manager of a Howard Johnson's restaurant in Cleveland.

One day Mr. Nawarski's neighbor tells him that the school board is considering busing some of the children in their neighborhood to a school six miles away that is 90 percent black. Whether this message has any meaning for his attitudes will depend on a number of factors; for example, the source and form of the message, how it is related to other attitudes or attitude structures, and what psychological devices he has for dealing with it.

Mr Nawarski's existing attitude structure is most easily protected if he does not believe the message that his children may be bused to a black school. If the source of the message (the person who told him) is regarded as untrustworthy, it is easier to ignore the message completely.[15] In the absence of later, confirming informa-

---

14. Ibid., pp. 276–278. Reprinted with permission of John Wiley & Sons, Inc.

15. See, on this point, Carl I. Hovland and Walter Weiss, "The Influence of Source Credibility on Communication Effectiveness," *Public Opinion Quarterly* 15 (1951): 635–650.

tion, he may simply not believe the message, and that will be the end of it—message disbelieved, no change.

But if Mr. Nawarski thinks his source is credible, or if he receives other messages supporting the initial one, he will no doubt believe that busing is being considered as a way to integrate the schools. This is not an important message, however—even if he believes it—unless it is related to attitudes that serve one or more of the knowledge, utilitarian, ego-defensive, or value-expressive functions. Since this particular message is, no doubt, easily related to one or more (perhaps all) of these functions, one would expect Mr. Nawarski to be in a state of attitudinal imbalance from the moment he receives it. He will probably relate the message to his knowledge of busing in other communities and of the courts' commitment to prevent extreme racial imbalance in the schools. He will see possible busing in utilitarian terms (it will change the children's daily schedules, and maybe his own). He will perhaps see it in ego-defensive terms and almost certainly in value-expressive terms (his children's manners and social status may be damaged by association with black children—and on the other hand he will almost certainly be under cross-pressures to try to project an image of tolerance and fairness as an American and a Christian).

How he perceives and internalizes the message about school busing, and with what consequences for his existing attitudes, will depend, as we have noted, on the source and form of the message and how he interprets it. His general personality needs are also important, as are his impressions of how the message is interpreted by persons whose judgment he respects and whose goodwill he wishes to gain or keep. If Mr. Nawarski demonstrates a general rigidity in his thinking, if he has little tolerance for ambiguity, or if he shows other traits of the authoritarian personality, the message will be especially difficult for him to deal with. Rigidity of thinking and intolerance of ambiguity are often associated with a low evaluation of one's own abilities and a compensating need to have one's opinions supported by experts or by a "gospel."[16] Thus the individual with a rigidly stereotypical mind-set will be disposed to harbor one-sided, simple, and unambiguous attitudes that resist change *unless* the source of the change-producing stimulus is thought to have special authority or competence. In short, the individual who holds certain attitudes because of deep-seated feelings of insecurity and ineffectiveness is likely (a) to hold these attitudes intensely and tenaciously; (b) to have attitudes that are simple and uncomplicated; (c) to regard contradictory or modifying messages as threatening; (d) to reject or distort the threatening messages, thus reducing the threat—unless (e) the source of the new

16. See Charles D. Farris, "Authoritarianism as a Political Behavior Variable," *Journal of Politics* 18 (1956): 61–82; Robert E. Agger, Marshall N. Goldstein, and Stanley A Pearl, "Political Cynicism: Measurement and Meaning," *Journal of Politics* 23 (1961): 477–506; and William J. McGuire, "Personality and Susceptibility to Social Influence," in *Handbook of Personality Theory and Research,* eds. Edgar F. Borgatta and William W. Lambert (Chicago: Rand McNally, 1968), pp. 1130–1187.

messages is regarded as authoritative, in which case attitude change will take place.

If, as is likely, Mr. Nawarski's attitudes toward blacks serve important ego-defensive and value-expressive functions, he probably holds simple but intensive attitudes that will be highly resistant to change. Given the social structure and opinion leadership he has experienced all his life, it is doubtful that Mr. Nawarski's attitudes toward blacks can be easily changed. Individuals and groups that are important to him and that serve to anchor his acceptance of attitudes and opinions that he considers authoritative are likely to have strong racist attitudes similar to his own.[17] Thus, under the conditions hypothesized here, attitudes would change (if at all) only in their intensity, and opinions only in their specificity in regard to the busing issue. The message creates imbalance, because (a) it arouses utilitarian and knowledge conflicts and (b) it threatens ego-defensive and value-expressive needs. The imbalance is reduced only when Mr Nawarski's antiblack attitudes are increased and when he holds an even stronger opinion against busing to achieve racial integration.

Let us suppose, however, that Mr. Nawarski was raised in Medford, Massachusetts, where he attended public schools and a college with a racially and ethnically mixed student body, then moved into a middle-income apartment house in New York City. He hears one day that a black family is moving into the apartment next door. Although he has associated with blacks since childhood, he has never known any as friends and neighbors, and he is apprehensive, because most of those he has known have been poor, living in slums and blighted areas. He likes privacy, quiet, decorum, and cleanliness, and his casual experience has reinforced the stereotype that blacks are noisy, indecorous, and untidy. So he would prefer to have white neighbors.

But this Mr. Nawarski has been exposed to a different set of psychological and social influences from those bearing on the first Mr. Nawarski. He believes that prejudice based on physical characteristics is immoral and destructive. Further, he knows that the law in New York (which he supports in a general way) makes it a crime to discriminate against blacks in a housing project supported or subsidized by state funds. Considering such cross-pressures, we may predict that Mr. Nawarski's attitude will be in a state of imbalance, but that he will acquiesce in the new circumstances. We may also predict that he will experience new stimuli of relevance to this situation, with the likelihood that his attitude will change. The second Mr. Nawarski's premessage attitude may have been positive toward blacks living in black districts, and also positive toward equality of opportunity. Now his attitude toward blacks living next door is negative; but toward equality

---

17. For an experimental study of the ways in which an individual's expressed attitude may be influenced by what he believes his friends think, see Raymond L. Gordon, "Interaction between Attitude and the Definition of the Situation in the Expression of Opinion," *American Sociological Review* 17 (1952): 50–58. For a more general statement, see H. H. Kelley, "Salience of Membership and Resistance to Change of Group-Anchored Attitudes," *Human Relations* 8 (1955): 275–289.

of opportunity he remains positive. His attitude structure is thus in an unbalanced state, and it can be balanced only by reduction of the inconsistency—which means either a change in attitude toward blacks living next door or a change in attitude toward equality of opportunity. Experimental and empirical field studies of racial bias indicate that reduction of antiblack prejudice usually (but not always) results from regular, day-to-day contact in a residential or work situation.[18]

Milton Rosenberg and Robert Abelson speculate that the process of reducing attitude-structure imbalance occurs somewhat in this order: (a) a *"search* for balance-appropriate material"; (b) a *"reality test* of such material (Does it 'make sense'? Is it appropriate and realistic in context?)"; and (c) an *"application* of the material (attending to it, 'rehearsing' it) if it satisfies the reality test."[19] Applying this microprocess to the first Mr. Nawarski, we may find that he considers the threat of busing to be one forced on the local community by a liberal and integrationist national government. To some degree he would be right, of course, since both the federal courts and the Department of Education are committed to school desegregation. Then Mr. Nawarski may believe that when a new, antibusing president and Congress are elected, the perceived threat will go away; thus, the imbalance in his attitude structure is reduced.

Similarly, the process may help to explain a possible reduction of imbalance in the attitude structure of the second Mr. Nawarski. He may believe that his new neighbor will be an educated, middle-class black (balance material); and if this turns out to be the case (reality test), that fact, when incorporated into the cognitive elements of his attitude structure, reduces the imbalance.

## 18.4 ATTITUDE CHANGE: THE GENERAL MODEL

Let us try to put all of the above points together. *The process of opinion change, from the point of view of functional analysis, appears to operate as follows.* The individual becomes aware of (perceives), ordinarily at the conscious level, a new stimulus (a message, in communication terms), then *if*:

---

18. For a review of such studies through the mid-1960s, see John Harding et al., "Prejudice and Ethnic Relations," in *Handbook of Social Psychology,* eds. Lindzey and Aronson, vol. 5 (1969), pp. 48–55.

19. Milton J. Rosenberg and Robert P. Abelson, "An Analysis of Cognitive Balancing," in *Attitude Organization and Change,* eds. Rosenberg et al. (New Haven: Yale University Press, 1960), p. 22. Hovland and Rosenberg appropriately ask whether experimental subjects, especially in a university setting, may not place a high value on rational consistency, whereas "in real life, people do not particularly value consistency...and...do not really strive to achieve or conserve it" ("Summary and Further Theoretical Issues," in ibid., p. 221). For an important review and summary of the research on ego involvement and social involvement in attitude change, especially as they relate to "threshold for response," see Carolyn W. Sherif, Muzafer Sherif, and Roger E. Nebergall, *Attitude and Attitude Change: The Social Judgement-Involvement Approach* (Philadelphia: Saunders, 1965).

a.   the stimulus is seen as related to attitudes serving one or more of the functions named above, and

b.   the stimulus is internalized (cognitively or affectively or both) in such a way that imbalance is created in an existing attitude or attitudes, and

c.   the imbalance is sufficiently disruptive; then

d.   cognitive or affective (or both) aspects of the existing attitude or attitudes will be changed until the dissonance is reduced.

These processes of change in an individual in a social context are shown schematically in Figure 18–1. The change-promoting stimulus or message may be any fact or opinion that is perceived by the individual as related to but inconsistent with existing attitudes or attitude structures. Any perception that is recognized as inconsistent with existing attitudes, regardless of the intensity of the perception, may be thought of as a change-promoting stimulus. The question of intensity will be dealt with in a moment; it is sufficient here to have the stimulus recognized, no matter how mildly.

For analytical purposes, the whole stimulus situation may be qualified in terms of form, source, personality factors, and environmental conditions. These intervening variables must be taken into account for any satisfactory understanding of the process of attitude or opinion change. Stimuli that come in threat- or fear-arousing form may produce one kind of response, and less threatening or fearful forms may produce another kind. Stimuli from trusted sources are more likely to change attitudes and opinions than are stimuli from distrusted sources. Personality variables are mainly those having to do with the ego-defensive and value-expressive functions of attitudes and opinions. Messages related to significant personality needs of individuals are often dealt with in dysfunctional ways (denial, projection, rationalization) and are often exceedingly difficult to adjust into healthier and more realistic balance. Finally, the social context in which the change-promoting stimulus appears is highly significant both for the subjective responses made by the individual and for the overt expression or behavior it occasions.

The concept of *threshold for response* is a necessary recognition that perceived change-promoting stimuli will not always produce responses. All persons are capable of withstanding some inconsistencies within attitudes and among related attitudes. Some people have very high tolerance for inconsistency. Attitudinal dissonance is a fact of life, a necessary part of realistic uncertainty, of trial-and-error living, of the scientific method, and, on the whole, of the adventure of human thought and feeling. "What is assumed [by balance theory] is that for any particular attitude as held by any particular person there is some limit to the degree of inconsistency that he will be able to tolerate. If this limit, which may be conceived as an 'intolerance for inconsistency threshold,' is exceeded, the attitude will then be rendered unstable."[20]

---

20. Katz, "Functional Approach," p. 199.

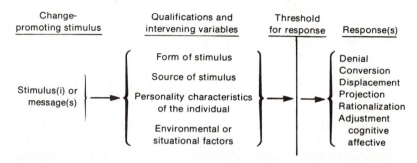

**Figure 18–1.**   *Stimulus–response formation for attitude and opinion change*

## 18.5 EFFECTS OF ATTITUDE CHANGE ON RELATED ATTITUDES

Consideration of the threshold for intolerance of inconsistency leads to a related question, that of the generalization of attitude change. A rational model of attitude change would lead one to expect that once changes take place in an attitude, related changes also take place in other attitudes. Theories of balance should (and do) suppose that the change or abandonment of one attitude will set up a chain of imbalance with other attitudes that are inconsistent with the change (or absence, or replacement) of the original attitude. Any change, in short, should not be confined solely to the changed attitude, but should bring about complementary changes in related beliefs and feelings.

Although, as Katz points out, "research evidence on the generalization of attitude change is meager...it is puzzling that attitude change seems to have slight generalization effects, when the evidence indicates considerable generalization in the organization of a person's beliefs and values." Katz suggests three possible reasons for the apparently small amount of generalization of attitude change:

**1.** The overall organization of a person's attitudes and values is highly differentiated, and "the many dimensions allow the individual to absorb change without major modification of his attitudes."

**2.** "The generalization of attitudes proceeds along lines of the individual's own psychological groupings more than along lines of conventional sociological categories." Therefore much of the generalization that exists escapes our analytical schemes and techniques.

**3.** "Generalization of attitude change is limited by the lack of systematic forces in the social environment to implement that change. Even when people are prepared to modify their behavior [and other attitudes] to a considerable extent they find themselves in situations which exert pressures to maintain old attitudes and habits."[21]

Herbert Kelman's distinctions among compliance, identification, and internalization as three processes (or levels) of attitude change are related to the first of Katz's reasons why attitude change is not more generalized. Kelman's distinctions may provide a framework for speculation and research on the generalization of attitude change. *Compliance,* Kelman says, occurs "when an individual accepts influence because he hopes to achieve a favorable reaction from another person or group." *Identification* takes place when the individual "accepts influence because he wants to establish or maintain a satisfying self-defining relationship to another person or a group." *Internalization* involves the acceptance of influence "because the content of the induced behavior—the ideas and actions of which it is composed—is intrinsically rewarding...[and] congruent with his value system."[22] Implied in this differentiation and in its elaboration—though not explicitly stated—is the notion that attitude generalization is least apt to accompany a response of compliance and most apt to accompany the internalization of attitude change. If, as Katz and others maintain, a person's belief structure is highly consistent and articulate, and if, as Kelman says, internalization of an attitude change involves the integration of the change into the whole belief system, then we would expect that the internalization of the change would have significant and perhaps far-reaching consequences for other attitudes anchored in the belief system. Such a widespread and interlocking change may take place, for example, in the cataclysmic reordering of attitudes and belief structures under conditions of religious or political conversion.

It might also be hypothesized that one's belief structure and the attitudes closely associated with it are necessarily so stable in the normal person that only minor attitude changes involving minimal repercussions will be internalized. In that case, the consistency defenses of the belief system must be regarded as so strong that no change would be admitted if significant generalization were necessary. This hypothesis, if true, may be a fourth explanation (added to the three offered by Katz, above) for the apparent resistance of attitude change to generalization.

Until such variables are more clearly understood, we can say only that, for whatever reasons, individuals show a remarkable ability to hold their attitudes and opinons discretely, tolerating a great deal of inconsistency and lack of integration. One cannot predict, on grounds of consistency, what the secondary effects of attitude change may be.

---

21. Ibid., pp. 200–201.
22. Herbert C. Kelman, "Compliance, Identification, and Internalization: Three Processes of Attitude Change," *Journal of Conflict Resolution* 2 (1958): 53.

## Chapter 19

# Opinion and Behavior: Consistency and Change

People do not always say what they think; nor do they always act as they believe. Difficult as it is to discover attitudes and opinions, it is at least as difficult to know when behavior reflects attitudes and opinions. We are not concerned now with the problems of sources, development, or measurement of attitudes, or even whether opinions are consistent with attitudes. Here our questions concern the possibility that attitudes and opinions, under some circumstances, may be quite inconsistent with behavior.

## 19.1 OPINION STABILITY AND RESISTANCE TO CHANGE

Aside from traumatic conversions of the religious variety—and perhaps not even so dramatically as is alleged in those cases—sudden changes in attitude and opinion are probably rare. It is probable, too, that the more intensely an opinion is held, the less likely it is to change quickly; and the more solidly an opinion is based on knowledge, facts, reason, and common sense, the less likely it is to change quickly or profoundly. Moreover, regardless of their factual or rational bases, opinions that are important to the holder's personality are resistant to change. Opinions are hard to change if they have been expressed publicly and are known by other persons who are important to the opinion holder. Finally, when change is required, there is a strong tendency to make the least change possible.[1]

1. Experimental evidence supports the above statements. For a useful summary of studies before 1954, see Carl I. Hovland, "Effects of the Mass Media of Communications," in *Handbook of Social Psychology,* eds. Gardner Lindzey and Elliot Aronson, vol. 1 (Reading, Mass.: Addison-Wesley, 1954), pp. 1062–1103, especially pp. 1086–1088. For summaries since 1954, see William J. McGuire, "The Nature of Attitudes and Attitude Change," in ibid., vol. 3 (1969), pp. 136–314; and Walter

It should not be thought that behavior changes follow chronologically, any more than logically, after opinion change. In many instances, opinions change, if at all, only *after* related behavior changes. As Bernard Berelson and Gary Steiner point out, "Behavior, being visible, is more responsive to extreme pressures and accommodations. OABs [opinions, attitudes, and beliefs], being private until expressed, can be maintained without even being subject to question or argument. And there is no necessary reason for OABs and behavior to be in harmony."[2] Opinion change tends to follow behavior change if the behavior is repeated, is approved by one's reference groups, and is generally sanctioned by social environment. Under extreme conditions of deprivation—psychological, physical, or both—when support for preexisting opinion is removed and contrary behavior is forced or strongly urged, large shifts in attitudes and opinions may occur. The identification of Jewish concentration-camp victims with their captors and the defection of American prisoners of war as a result of Communist brainwashing are examples of such extreme opinion shift following or concurrent with behavior change.[3]

## 19.2 OPINION CHANGE AMONG POLITICAL ELITES

Opinion leaders, more than opinion followers or "ordinary citizens," are apt to have attitudes and opinions that are stable and resistant to change. Political leaders are shown to care more intensely about the ends and means of public policy and to hold their opinions more firmly, with greater articulateness and self-consciousness, and with greater persistence.[4] Given these anchorages in

Weiss, "The Effects of the Mass Media of Communication," and David O. Sears, "Political Behavior," both in ibid., vol. 5 (1969), pp. 77–195, 315–458. Survey evidence is also abundant; see, for example, E. Jackson Baur, "Opinion Change in a Public Controversy," *Public Opinion Quarterly* 26 (1962): 212–226; Angus Campbell et al., *The American Voter* (New York: Wiley, 1960), pp. 256–265; and Philip E. Converse, "Information Flow and the Stability of Partisan Attitudes," *Public Opinion Quarterly* 26 (1962): 578–599.

2. Bernard Berelson and Gary A. Steiner, *Human Behavior: An Inventory of Scientific Findings* (New York: Harcourt, Brace & World, 1964), p. 576. For discussion of the interrelations and dynamics of behavioral change without related attitude change, see also Milton Rokeach, *Beliefs, Attitudes, and Values: A Theory of Organization and Change* (San Francisco: Jossey-Bass, 1968), pp. 142–147.

3. The Jews who identified with their Nazi guards and the prisoners of war who "confessed" and defected to the Communists were few and were extremely deviant cases. See Bruno Bettelheim, "Individual and Mass Behavior in Extreme Situations," in Eleanor E. Maccoby et al., *Readings in Social Psychology* (New York: Holt, Rinehart & Winston, 1958), pp. 300–310; Patricia Hearst's conversion to the views of her SLA captors in 1974 seems to have been an example of such opinion change under extraordinary environmental conditions.

4. Herbert McClosky, Paul J. Hoffman, and Rosemary O'Hara, "Issue Conflict and Consensus among Party Leaders and Followers," *American Political Science Review* 54 (1960): 406–427; Robert S. Hirschfield, Bert E. Swanson, and Blanche D. Blank, "A Profile of Political Activists in Manhattan," *Western Political Quarterly* 15 (1962): 489–506; Herbert McClosky, "Consensus and Ideology in American Politics," *American Political Science Review* 58 (1964): 361–382; and John H. Kessel, "Cognitive Dimensions and Political Activity," *Public Opinion Quarterly* 39 (1965): 377–389.

reality, and in their own personality and social needs, it is not surprising that the opinions of political leaders are least susceptible to whim and to the chance effects of random information or propaganda stimulation.

On the other hand, precisely because the views of opinion leaders are tied to reality and are more self-consciously held than those of their followers, significant changes in the environment of such leaders tend to be evaluated more accurately and quickly by them and may therefore lead to appropriate changes. Rationality is more characteristic of the opinion-change processes of opinion leaders. The collection and evaluation of relevant information, along with increased use of discussion and consultative devices, are likely to accompany opinion changes among social and political elites. Theoretical models that emphasize cognitive balance will be more useful in the explanation of elite opinion change than they will be in the explanation of nonelite change. In sum, among political leaders, opinion change will probably be less volatile than among nonleaders, more deliberate, more informed by social facts and trends, and more predictable—and at the same time (in a free society) more gradual and incremental in its pace and scope.[5]

Take, for example, the attitude-opinion-behavior changes in prominent elected leaders who switch from one major party to the other. Given the bedrock importance of party identification in American electoral politics, nothing could be more dramatic, and ostensibly more sudden, than the announcement of a switch to the other party. In the real world of day-to-day behavior, nothing is sudden about such changes except the announcement. The facts about such prominent party-switchers as Senators Wayne Morse of Washington, Donald Riegle of Michigan, Strom Thurmond of South Carolina, and Congressmen Phil Gramm of Texas, Eugene Atkinson of Pennsylvania, and Andy Ireland of Florida all testify to the gradualism of such opinion and behavior change. So incremental was Senator Morse's change from Republican to Democrat that he spent several years as a self-proclaimed "Independent"—perhaps thus demonstrating the falsity of the adage that you can't cross a ditch in two jumps. While opportunism might be suspected in a few cases of celebrated party-switching, the more common and important consideration is that the politicians' long-time personal opinions on issues are out of step with modal opinions of the party they leave and much more consistent with average opinions of the other party. Congressman Ireland's change from Democrat to Republican, the most recent as of this writing, is typical: his district is among the safest (he got 69 percent of the vote in 1980 and was unopposed, still as a Democrat, in 1982); his voting record was described by the authors of *The Almanac of American Politics, 1984,* as one

---

5. See Philip E. Converse, "The Nature of Belief Systems in Mass Publics," in *Ideology and Discontent,* ed. David Apter (New York: Free Press, 1965), pp. 206–261; Norman R. Luttbeg, "The Structure of Belief among Leaders and the Public," *Public Opinion Quarterly* 32 (1968): 398–409; David E. RePass, "Issue Salience and Party Choice," *American Political Science Review* 65 (1971): 389–400; and Norman Nie et al., *The Changing American Voter,* enl. ed. (Cambridge: Harvard University Press, 1979).

of the most conservative among Florida Democrats; on July 5, 1984, he announced that he was now a Republican but promised to remain " 'the same old Andy,' supporting the positions he has embraced in the past."[6]

Even in the most famous cases of elite opinion change on important single issues there is reason to believe that the change processes are longer in germination and less dramatic in scope than the publicity of announcement would suggest. On January 10, 1945, Michigan's senator Arthur H. Vandenberg, who was the most influential Republican foreign policy leader in the U.S. Senate, made a famous speech declaring his support for the United Nations and, in general, for active participation by the United States in world affairs. The speech was widely thought to mark a sudden break with Vandenberg's past views, which had been strongly noninterventionist, even isolationist. Yet Vandenberg himself did not regard his action as an about-face. His son and biographer said that the speech

> was generally (although mistakenly) regarded as a great turning point in the Senator's attitude. . . .
>
> He fully realized that he was going to make an important proposal, but he had little idea, as he admitted later, that he was "taking off" into a new era, or perhaps more correctly that this speech would be regarded as the point at which he definitely abandoned forever the last vestige of the isolationism with which the public still associated him.[7]

The senator's son (and then administrative aide) described his father's condition for many months before the January 1945 speech as one of "soul searching," and as that of a man who had come to an "acceptance of certain realities regarding foreign policy," and who gradually, between 1941 and 1944, "had fully accepted in his own mind the extensive future role of the United States in international affairs."[8]

Vandenberg's acceptance of internationalism, besides being less dramatic and sudden than it was said to be, illustrates the importance of rationality and reality for opinion leaders. The historic posture of nineteenth-century American aloofness from the affairs of Europe, Asia, and Africa was finally seen as inconsistent with the actual condition of the United States in 1944 and 1945. The dissonance between Vandenberg's perception of international reality and his former isolationist views was too great; change had to occur in his opinions.

The Vandenberg case illustrates another difference between elite and nonelites in regard to opinion change. The very fact of leadership position is both cause and consequence of the leaders' greater ability to sense the needs of themselves

---

6. Associated Press story in *San Francisco Chronicle,* July 6, 1984.

7. Arthur H. Vandenberg, Jr., ed., *The Private Papers of Senator Vandenberg* (Boston: Houghton Mifflin, 1952), p. 131.

8. Ibid., p. 125. "The whole world changed. . . with World War II, and I changed with them," Senator Vandenberg later wrote (p. 139).

and others and the social ramifications of their own behavior. The senator was very conscious of his role as a Republican leader. As he remarked in a letter written while he was working on his famous speech, he was worried that the Republican party would not change its policies to conform with the changing political world. His party, he said, had "to be far more realistic about the 'social revolution' which has swept the entire world (and to which we cannot expect to be immune) than we were when last we were in power." The forces that impelled him to change his opinion were thus not only his reality testing as an individual and the imbalance he found between his old image of the world and his new one, but also his notion of what was expected of him as a leader of his party. Afterward he wrote: "It seemed to me that it had to be a Republican voice from the then minority benches which had to undertake this assignment. This, in turn, narrowed the responsibility to a point where I felt it was a personal challenge to me."[9]

Finally, the Vandenberg example illustrates the point that minimum rather than maximum change occurs even in the most dramatic cases. His son points out that the senator "did not record much about the January 10th speech at the time, except to express his surprise at the reaction to it. 'I still don't understand what clicked so terrifically,' he wrote his wife late in January."[10] The public response may be considered not so much a reaction to Vandenberg's change, perhaps, as an indication that he had properly assessed his leadership role in articulating the latent or incompletely expressed attitude and opinion changes of many prewar isolationists during the war years. In any event, Vandenberg's opinion change was no more extensive than it needed to be. He remained a conservative, an American nationalist and patriot, and a staunch leader of the opposition party in all ways that were consistent with his new belief in a bipartisan foreign policy.[11]

## 19.3 NONELITE OPINION CHANGE

We have repeatedly pointed out that for most people political questions are not important. Politics and public issues play only small and episodic parts in the lives and thoughts of most individuals. This low salience has great significance for the consistency and inconsistency of opinions and behavior. If people have

---

9. Ibid., pp. 129, 130.

10. Ibid., p. 144.

11. Another, if less dramatic, illustration of elite opinion and behavior change may be found in Sen. Everett McKinley Dirksen's (R.–Ill.) championship of the civil rights bill of 1964. Before that year, Senator Dirksen's record was one of opposition to extensive federal intervention in civil rights matters. When questioned on his change of mind, he argued that social and political events (his reality testing) and his leadership responsibilities (his self-image) were responsible for his behavior change; quoting Victor Hugo, he declared that "nothing is more powerful than an idea whose time has come" (*New York Times,* May 18, 1964).

little motivation, little knowledge, and few occasions to experience relevant stimuli, they will display a great range of attitudes, opinions, and verbal behavior, often logically and politically inconsistent.

William McPhee, Bo Anderson, and Harry Milholland have described the way political opinions are held by nonelites and the way those opinions change under varying social conditions.[12] When ordinary people are asked for political opinions, what emerges is a hodgepodge (almost) of independent and often inconsistent statements of opinion:

> The person has an observable opinion only when he is prompted to react, for example, by a dinner party, interview, or whatever. Thereafter, "out of sight, out of mind," that is, he soon forgets these casual responses.... When some months later he is again prompted to respond on this topic, it is a *new* response independent of the first.... If another opinion on a related topic was also elicited at the first time, it is not only independent of the first opinion... but independent "of itself" when a new version of it is given at some second time a month or two later. No "dynamic interactions" could have gone on between the two topical opinions meanwhile, for neither really existed in the interim as a continuous entity. No more than, if we observe a man tipping his hat to a lady on two occasions a month apart, we assume he held his hat that way all month as one continuous response.[13]

The authors of this essay persuasively argue that two or more expressed opinions, given casually and in an offhand manner by a person who has little interest in the subject, probably will be independent of each other, and may be logically inconsistent. Such opinions may be related in a loose way to larger, more general attitudes; but unless these relationships become recognized by the individual, no inconsistencies will be felt and there will be no tendencies to bring the disparate opinions together for comparison or change to greater consistency. If, later, the same question is answered a different way, this does not mean that change has occurred, but merely that the earlier question and answer seemed unimportant and were not remembered. In such cases, analytical theories such as Festinger's notions of cognitive dissonance are inappropriate. Only when attitudes and opinions are important will the individual care whether they are consistent with one another.

When giving their opinions, people have both internal and external reasons for consistency or inconsistency. The reasons, as McPhee, Anderson, and Milholland point out, have to do with underlying dispositions and with the momentary importance attached to the matter at the time the opinion is given. The underly-

12. William N. McPhee, Bo Anderson, and Harry Milholland, "Attitude Consistency," in *Public Opinion and Congressional Elections,* eds. William N. McPhee and William A. Glaser (New York: Free Press, 1962), pp. 78–120.

13. Ibid., p. 91. Copyright 1962. Reprinted by permission of The Macmillan Company.

ing or "motivational" variables that these authors assumed to be significant for their study were (a) *partisanship* (the tendency to adopt or hold beliefs consistent with the general policy of the respondent's party) and (b) *environment* (community support for or against the party's general policy). The importance attached to the issue at the moment of response was measured by internal and external "attention" variables: (a) *interest* (the person's own ranking of interest from "a great deal" to "none") and (b) *salience* (the person's evaluation of how much the community cared about the issue). When a person has high internal motivation and high interest, opinions are most apt to be consistent and change is least apt to occur. This is the general case of the opinion elites. If, in addition to high internal motivation and interest, there is strong environmental support for consistent opinions, and if the community is seen to regard the issue as a matter of importance, consistency will be greatest and opinion will change least over time.

Conversely, when persons have little internal motivation and interest, and when the degree of interest or support from the environment is unknown, inconsistency will be greater and change most apparent over time. This is the general case of the apathetic person who, instead of saying honestly "I don't know" or "I don't care," gives casual answers to questions about public issues.

The probability of a person's having opinions consistent with one another and, at the same time, behavior consistent with the relevant opinion sets will then be a function of the person's interest and knowledge, as well as his estimation of how important the matter is to others with whom he identifies. Consequently, change toward greater internal consistency of opinion sets and opinion–behavior pairings will depend on increase in internal motivations (interest and knowledge) or increase in environmental motivations (perceptions of importance to others). Internal and environmental motivations are obviously tied together. Those most informed and interested are best able to judge the modal opinions of groups important to them (although even the best informed often seriously misjudge the opinions of others).[14]

Among the several practical applications of this way of conceptualizing opinion and behavior consistency is the meaning it gives to political campaigns. As McPhee, Anderson, and Milholland point out, campaigns increase the environmental motivations. They make issues and political opinions temporarily more salient. They allow persons whose opinions and behavior are idiosyncratically inconsistent to learn what the "party line" and what majority or peer-group sentiment may be, or to ponder the issues more carefully, thus increasing consistency, rationality, and predictable behavior. These authors' summary statement of the relations between consistency and motivation (internal and external)—a statement that has meaning for mass media and political leadership generally, as well as for campaigns—may be paraphrased as follows:

In the long run, the learning and holding of inconsistent opinions

---

14. Warren Breed and Thomas Ktsanes, "Pluralistic Ignorance in the Process of Opinon Formation," *Public Opinion Quarterly* 25 (1961): 382–392.

and inconsistent behavior patterns is reduced if the individual has strong internal motivations and is surrounded by others similarly motivated. In the short run, changes of opinion and behavior in the direction of greater consistency seem to be a result of increased attention to the topic.

In the absence of *public* attention to a matter, *private* opinions show a great range of scope and contradiction. When a matter commands great public attention, private opinions narrow in range and become less inconsistent. Inattentive people, when asked to give opinions, show large dispersions or much idiosyncratic response; attentive people show narrow dispersions and their responses are more environmentally oriented and more clearly based on the logical consistencies of social reality.[15]

This explanation of what happens psychologically in the ordinary not-very-interested citizen also makes clearer our earlier discussion (Chapter 15) of the agenda-setting function of the mass media during political campaigns. The TV and newspaper journalists give us "themes" and "meanings." *Themes* tell non-elites that something is happening out there in the political world and indicate the labels and importance that may be attached to those happenings. The meanings provide explicit and usually appropriately simple opinions that may be held without social embarrassment. That is, the media meanings are legitimated merely be being determined or repeated by the nightly news anchor or by the syndicated columnist. Thus, as recent research has demonstrated, "a candidate or other political actor need only repeat a message for it to be accepted as a matter requiring political attention," and citizens' views are shaped by "the mere volume of political appeals that is surely in the hands of political elites, [and] rulers may set the standards by which they are judged."[16] In this way closure is made: salience is increased, private (individual-level) opinions become more consistent, and public opinion as the campaign unfolds becomes more complete (fewer "don't knows") and more reliable (less variation from poll to poll).

## 19.4 THE FUNCTIONAL USES OF OPINION AND THE PROCESSES OF OPINION-BEHAVIOR CHANGE

In Chapter 18 we considered the various functions that attitudes and opinions serve for individuals. These may be categorized as the knowledge, utilitarian, value-expressive, and ego-defensive functions (listed roughly in order from the most superficial to the deepest levels of meaning for the personality). Consistency

---

15. McPhee et al., "Attitude Consistency," pp. 102–111. See also B. K. L. Genova and Bradley S. Greenberg, "Interests in News and the Knowledge Gap," *Public Opinion Quarterly* 43 (1979): 79–91.

16. Michael MacKuen, "Exposure to Information, Belief Integration, and Individual Responsiveness to Agenda Change," *American Political Science Review* 78 (1984): 386–387.

or inconsistency of opinions and behavior will depend in part on the functions opinions serve. If an opinion serves only a knowledge or utilitarian purpose, it will be more susceptible to the "drive to consistency" and will be more consistent with related or socially "appropriate" behavior than if it serves value-expressive or ego-defensive functions.

Katz suggests a number of conditions under which change can be expected in attitudes and opinions that serve one or more of these functions. His categories of change conditions may be integrated with a conceptualization of opinion change developed by Herbert C. Kelman. As we have seen, Kelman distinguishes three processes of opinion change: *compliance, identification,* and *internalization:*

> *Compliance* can be said to occur when an individual accepts influence from another person or from a group in order to achieve a favorable reaction from the other.
> *Identification* can be said to occur when an individual adopts behavior derived from another person or group, because this behavior is associated with a satisfying self-defining relationship to this person or group.
> *Internalization* can be said to occur when an individual accepts influence because the induced behavior is congruent with his value system.[17]

What happens in terms of functions and processes when individuals are under pressure to change their opinions or behavior—that is, when they perceive change-provoking stimuli? Whether such persons change will depend on why they hold the opinions they do, how important the existing opinions are to them, and what techniques are available to hold or change them. Opinions held for knowledge or utilitarian reasons are apt to be changed easily when the stimulations for change include increased or more accurate knowledge, or if adjustment (the utilitarian function) is facilitated by discarding the old and adopting the new opinions or behavior. Opinions held for value-expressive or ego-defensive reasons will not be changed so easily, despite any components of reason, knowledge, or utility that may accompany the arguments for change. In such situations, the familiar psychological processes of denial, conversion, and rationalization may occur.[18]

Using an example of elite behavior, let us suggest how these elements might appear in political life. In the 1980 debate over shipment of nuclear fuel to India, members of Congress were asked by the Carter administration to permit the

---

17. Herbert C. Kelman, "Processes of Opinion Change," *Public Opinion Quarterly* 25 (1961): 62–65.

18. Denial is a form of psychological evasion which, as the name implies, allows the individual to refuse to believe in the existence of the change-promoting stimulus. Conversion is the process by which a threatening stimulus is made into an unthreatening stimulus by distortion or complete change of character. Rationalization is the finding of acceptable explanations for opinions or behavior the individual believes he must justify. See Robert P. Abelson, "Modes of Resolution of Belief Dilemmas," *Journal of Conflict Resolution,* 3 (1959): 343–352.

shipment even though India had not agreed to the "peaceful use" rules that had been stiffened after the original contract was signed. Those who opposed the action did so for a variety of reasons: some from deep fears of nuclear proliferation, some because they thought the shipment would interfere with the pursuit of other international or domestic goals, and some simply in reaction against Indira Gandhi's tilt toward the Soviet Union.

In such a situation, a few members might be influenced to change their opinions (or at least to deliver their votes) by what Kelman describes as the process of *compliance*. Such a course might be expected from those who opposed the bill on utilitarian grounds but would be less likely if their opposition were based on value-expressive or ego-defensive needs. Some might be inclined to change their opinion on the bill as a result of the process Kelman calls *identification*. They might believe that loyalty to the administration, or to Democratic party leadership, required them to overcome their opposition to the bill. Here again, change through the identification process would occur more easily when the opposition opinions served knowledge or utilitarian functions rather than value-expressive or ego-defensive functions. Those who were antimilitary in principle, for reasons having to do with their self-image or ego needs, would not easily have their opinions or behavior changed by appeals to secondary-group ties such as party loyalty or leadership. The strategy of the administration and party, of course, was to strengthen their identification with reluctant members, but their chances of success were small with those whose personality needs were met in part by their views on this issue. Finally, opinion or behavior change through the process of *internalization* was not to be expected in those who opposed the bill. In short, the bill's opponents might come to support through the processes of compliance or identification, but probably only if their opposition was originally based on factors that did not involve their self-images or their egos.

Functional uses of opinions and change processes are summed up, in an admittedly impressionistic way, in Table 19–1, which is generalized to situations of administration attempts to change the opinions or behavior of members of Congress of the president's party.

**Table 19-1.** Hypothesized probabilities of change in members of Congress opposed to bill sponsored by own administration when under pressure from administration to vote for bill

| Functions served by existing opinion | Compliance | Processes of change<br>identification | Internalization* |
|---|---|---|---|
| Knowledge | High probability of change if administration arguments are informative and logical | High probability of change if administration's arguments show why members should accept its interpretation of the "facts of the case" | |
| Utilitarian | High probability of change if administration arguments indicate advantages to members (that is, logrolling and so on) | High probability of change if administration arguments show why a pro-administration vote will be beneficial to mutual interests (such as party) | |
| Value-expressive | Moderate probability of change if rationalizations made easier for members | Moderate to low probability of change depending on administration's demonstration that common values are best served by change of opinion or behavior | Low probability of change, depending on a fundamental reordering of belief structure (not likely to occur quickly through political argumentation) |
| Ego-defensive | Moderate to low probability of change if rationalizations are made easier | Moderate to low probability of change, depending on member's obtaining greater ego satisfaction from alliance with administration than from retaining existing opinions | Low probability of change, depending on its becoming more satisfying of ego needs than retention of existing opinion |

* If we understand Katz and Kelman correctly, value-expressive and ego-defensive functions, which depend on deep-lying personality needs, are internalized; but opinions held for knowledge and adjustment, being relatively superficial and unimportant to the personality, are not internalized. The concepts of value-expressive and ego-defensive functions and of internalization are heavily indebted to psychoanalytic theory; see, for example, Irving Sarnoff, "Psychoanalytic Theory and Social Attitudes," *Public Opinion Quarterly* 24 (1960): 251–279.

## Chapter 20

# Opinion Change and
# Policy Change

Opinions matter for policy. The reason is simple: opinions are usually reflected in votes; and, in a democracy, votes—if ever so indirectly—make policy.

Whatever science there is in government is the science of probabilities—of the probabilities that those who participate in government, however much or little, from the president to the once-in-a-lifetime voter, will behave in predictable ways. All analyses of political relationships rest on such probabilities. For policies and administrative ways that are long settled and to which the power network of the society is well adjusted, the probabilities of predictable behavior are very high. In the 1980s, support of the U.S. Social Security system is very high, and policy makers in Washington can rely on the routine compliance of 99 percent or more of those involved. In the mid-1930s, however, that was not the case; the opinions of those involved were then so sharply polarized that the probability of obtaining agreements was perhaps no greater than 60 percent.

Now, it may be objected that when a policy is at the legislative stage, as the Social Security system was in 1935, the probabilities of agreement will be smaller than they will be later, when the policy has been adopted and has proved successful. This is the difference between a policy when it is a *proposal* and a policy when it is a *program*. At one time in the history of the United States, it was literally unthinkable that the federal government should establish a nationwide system of pensions for workers in private industry. At least until the beginning of the twentieth century, this was an idea that could not have been seriously put forward in the political arena. The probability of agreement was nil, or close to it. From 1900 to 1935, the notion of a national old-age pension system grew from an idea to a proposal, and at length the proposal commanded enough attention in both governmental and nongovernmental circles so that it became a bill in Congress. Given such notice, the elite and mass opinions on the subject rapidly increased in number, intensity, and polarization. Then, at the time of decision, the legislators, with ears to the ground and to the White House and to their fellow legislators' words, testing probabilities and consciences as they deliberated their way to a vote, passed the measure. No one knows whether a majority of the people—or a majority of the *important* people (whoever they are)—favored the Social Security Act of 1935. In the nature of representative government, such knowledge is unattainable. We know that a large majority of the U.S. Congress favored the bill and must have believed that it was not only sound policy but policy that the American people, on the whole, would support. As it turned out, they were right—if that is what they thought. Considerable opposition remained for several years after passage of the act, but noncompliant behavior was quickly tested and discouraged, and American business found that it could live and prosper under the act's provisions. Support for the policy has grown, and though some political extremists would abolish the Social Security system, it seems likely that 90 percent or more of the American people favor it. In other words, the probability of support is extremely high.

## 20.1 IDEAS, OPINIONS, AND POLICIES

One can generalize the interdependence of opinions and the political process as public policies evolve from private thoughts. The description of the opinion-policy process presented in Chapter 2, based on the group theory of politics, was somewhat static in that it took no account of changes in the numbers, intensities, or salience of individual or group opinions. The scheme offered here has different components, although it interlocks with the earlier presentation in many ways.

Public policies evolve from governmental responses to human needs and desires. All public policies were once merely *private ideas*. Private ideas, when shared by large numbers of individuals, become *proposals*. Proposals, when they are adopted by governmental authorities, become *public policies*. So simplified, these three stages are clear. Nevertheless, it must be at once obvious that, while the distinction between a proposal and a public policy is marked by an official act (by an executive signature or a legislative engrossment) and by a point of time (the "effective date"), no such sharp distinction can be made between an idea and a proposal. Clues may be offered in an attempt to make the distinction more operational—percentage of people who know about or support the idea, or numbers and estimated political strength of groups that favor the idea—but the marginal cases, as in all such matters, must be left to individual judgment. The simplified trichotomy is thus:

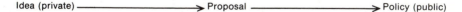

Idea (private) ⟶ Proposal ⟶ Policy (public)

Let us immediately elaborate, More extreme than ideas are unthinkable thoughts—which may be called *latent ideas*, but which are proscribed by the culture and will be given the name of *sacrilege* (though we mean, of course, to free the word from its narrow religious connotations). Beyond policy is *tradition*, which may be called *assimilated policies* and which is required by culture (just as sacrilege is forbidden by culture). As we noted in Chapter 9, on opinion and cultural patterns, in modern societies very little is forbidden to ideas; sacrilege is almost an extinct commodity in the Western world and is rapidly disappearing in nonwestern lands. On the other hand, considerable tradition, in its postpolicy or ultrapolicy form, exists. The English common law is perhaps the best example of the dynamic relationship between tradition and policy. The body of practices from which the common law is drawn (or which *is* the common law—a legal distinction, mainly semantic) is precisely a tradition about which there is so much agreement that conflict seldom arises. When conflict does arise over this tradition, a policy statement—that is, a judicial application of the common law— has to be made to settle it. But it can hardly be denied, if one accepts the common law system at all, that such a tradition is ordinarily beyond contention. With sacrilege and tradition added, the schema becomes:

(Sacrilege) ⟷ Idea (private) ⟶ Proposal ⟶ Policy (public) ⟷ (Tradition)

Let us add a simple representation of opinion, not to take account of the rich variety of views that flower in the attentive public at the proposal stage, but simply to represent the probability of agreement. Thus:

(Sacrilege) ⟷ Idea ⟶ Proposal ⟶ Policy ⟷ (Tradition)

0% ——————————————————————————————— 100%
                     Probability of agreement

Greater precision would require us to use the language of probabilities, to label the left end of the continuum "Approaching 0%" and the right end "Approaching 100%." But perhaps our readers will accept this as the rough creation that any such schema is in the social sciences.

Greater detail and concern for realism will move us to represent some of the characteristics of the proposal stage. Between idea and proposal come agitation, education, and diffusion of the idea. Organization and politicization follow or come about concurrently as the numbers of supporters (and probably opponents too) grow and as the intensity of opinions increases. At some point, public notice is taken of the *idea-become-proposal,* and governmental officials move for its transformation into policy. The proposal then takes the form of a motion, a resolution, a bill, or an executive order. Intensification of opinions and nongovernmental-organization efforts proceed rapidly at this stage. At some time a decision is made to stop the proposal (temporarily or permanently, as time will reveal) or to move it to the policy stage:

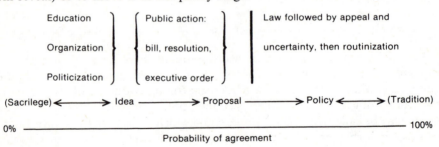

Education           Public action:        Law followed by appeal and

Organization        bill, resolution,     uncertainty, then routinization

Politicization      executive order

(Sacrilege) ⟷ Idea ⟶ Proposal ⟶ Policy ⟷ (Tradition)

0% ——————————————————————————————— 100%
                     Probability of agreement

One other element needs to be added: a representation of numbers and intensities of opinions. As the proposal stage moves to a climax, the general case will exhibit a maximization of involvement, both mass and elite, of intensity and notoriety. In short, more people will care more about the proposal (though even *more* people may not be a large percentage of the population). After the decision is made to end it at the proposal stage or to move it onto the policy stage, both intensity and notoriety fall off. If the proposal fails to become policy, its supporters lose some interest out of discouragement and rationalization, and its opponents withdraw somewhat from the battle. If the proposal becomes policy, its supporters tend to rest on their laurels, and its opponents suffer the fait accompli effect—the withdrawal of emotional attachment and a rationalization of the changed state of affairs. The size of the interested public and intensities of opinions may be represented by the shaded area in the completed schema below.[1]

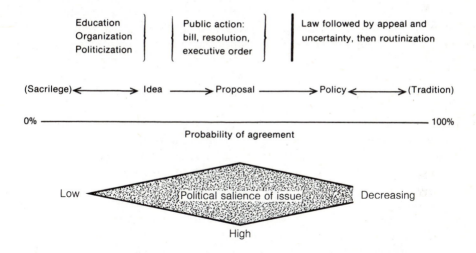

The political salience of an issue is the amount of political heat generated by the issue, a measure of its importance, and a composite of numbers and intensities of opinions.

Two points should be made about the schema. First, any given case history of policy development may be a great distortion of the model. The idea-proposal-policy stages may be completed before politicization and political salience are great enough to ensure a high probability of agreement.

This is what happened in the case of the hurried, unpopular, and unenforceable Eighteenth (Prohibition) Amendment. Conversely, the probability of agree-

1. For an overall view of the public policy-making process in the United States, see Charles O. Jones, *An Introduction to the Study of Public Policy,* 3rd ed. (North Scituate, Mass.: Duxbury Press, 1984).

ment on an issue may be very high but, because of a volatile and episodic political salience or because of institutional advantages enjoyed by minorities, the proposal may never become policy. Compulsory military training is a case in point. Perhaps a better example is the proposal for a conflict-of-interest law that would apply to Congress; such a law would command wide popular support, but it has been avoided by a Congress understandably reluctant to limit its own freedom.

The second point is that the schema has no necessary time schedule built into it. Many possible proposals never become actual proposals. Many ideas do not become politicized issues on which governmental leaders are asked to take a stand. The idea of a world government has never become a serious policy proposal in any nation. Decades, even centuries, may elapse in the evolution of a proposal from an idea. As we mentioned earlier, the idea of governmentally approved or subsidized old-age pensions in America was a proposal for forty years before it became policy. Recent research on opinions about alcoholic beverages indicates that they were socially approved in the eighteenth century in America, but gradually became sufficiently disapproved to be restricted in some states and finally to be prohibited nationally, though even then, it seems, prohibition's time had not yet come.[2] Sometimes the whole process may be quickly experienced, as was the case with the creation of a federal policy toward the production and use of nuclear energy.[3]

There may be an important general difference between domestic and foreign policy making. The accepted view among political analysts is that the president and the Washington elites in the executive departments have much greater freedom and policy choice in foreign than in domestic matters. There are two basic reasons for this difference. One is that the interests of *domestic* groups are regularized and particularized, while the interests of *foreign* groups are uncertain and poorly articulated. Bankers, realtors, the large labor unions, the professional welfare lobby—all of the major national political groups—have clearly defined perspectives on domestic proposals, and a president who wants to get a proposal enacted is constrained by the intersections of those views. The foreign policy interests of national or transnational groups are less clearly defined.

And there is a second reason why the opinion-policy process of foreign policy making differs from that of domestic policy making. That cloudy concept the "national interest" provides a lot of cover and legitimation for executive action. Mueller's Law is pertinent here: In perceived foreign crises, the president's popular support increases, no matter who he is or what he does.[4] The anaesthetizing power of patriotism is such that policy debate is shortened, weakened, and

2. Harry G. Levine, "Spirits in America: The Birth of Demon Rum," *Public Opinion* 4 (June/July 1981): 13–15.

3. See Harold P. Green and Alan Rosenthal, *Government of the Atom* (New York: Atherton, 1963), pp. 1–5.

4. See John E. Mueller, *War, Presidents, and Public Opinion* (New York: Wiley, 1973).

sometimes completely abandoned during the hours and days of international crises. Time and "cool heads," two elements indispensable to democratic policy making, are often not to be had in such moments.[5]

That opinion change influences policy change has been empirically demonstrated with respect to 357 instances of opinion change and related policy changes from 1935 to 1979. The authors of that research concluded:

> The findings of substantial congruence between opinion and policy (especially when opinion changes are large and sustained, and issues are salient), together with the evidence that opinon tends to move before policy more than vice versa, indicate that opinion changes are important causes of policy change. When Americans' policy preferences shift, it is likely that congruent changes in policy will follow.[6]

When the differences in type of policy making are borne in mind, the schema presented in this section should help further understanding of the opinion-policy process. And, finally, the schema illustrates why existing policy (the status quo) has the advantage over proposals. Once a policy has become widely accepted and its salience has decreased, the probability of agreement rises while the level of importance goes down. Real or imagined advantages may be found in the policy, and, as lives are adjusted to the demands and benefits of the policy, support for it increases. Or, at the very least, attention is reduced by the adoption of a better-the-devil-you-know perspective. At an even higher level of generalization, there is a presumption in favor of existing policy, a presumption compounded of the ease of habit, the majesty of the law, and the desire for social stability, which can be achieved only when there is much agreement on many governmental policies.

## 20.2 OPINION CHANGE AND THE OPINION-POLICY PROCESS

The conceptualization above is obviously incomplete as an explanation of the way an idea becomes public policy—a "natural history" involving the spread of the idea, mobilization of support, debate about alternatives, and legitimation of the idea as policy in governmental routines. Still missing is a generalization about the political process by which the proposal becomes law in the context of the official and unofficial machinery of a representative democracy. We have not shown how the dynamics of increased political salience and increased probability

---

5. For the suggestion that an enlarged foreign-policy public may be constraining presidential discretion since the late 1960s, see William L. Lunch and Peter W. Sperlich, "American Public Opinion and the War in Vietnam," *Western Political Quarterly* 32 (March 1979): 21–44.
6. Benjamin I. Page and Robert Y. Shapiro, "Effects of Public Opinion on Policy," *American Political Science Review* 77 (1983): 188–189.

of agreement are related to the institutional dynamics of policy change. We have not accounted for the role of governmental agencies (legislatures, executives, bureaucracies), or the roles of parties and pressure groups. To do so, even in a preliminary and inadequate way, we may recall our conceptualization of the opinion-policy process, first set forth in Chapter 2.

The original model of the opinion-policy process was limited to the interactions of expressed opinions, through group memberships and alignments, on legislative action. Majority, minority, and effective opinions were differentiated, and consideration was given to the way group memberships mediate the opinions of individuals so that the language of politics speaks of "carrying the farm vote," "alienating labor," or "losing favor in the business community." The model given in Chapter 2 frankly adopted the point of view that has become known as the *group theory of politics*—a point of view that, however inadequate it may be for the nuances of political explanation and prediction, represents what we regard as the most useful orientation for the study of American politics. Bearing that model in mind, let's see if we can describe (and show in Figure 20–1) how changes in individual opinions, changes in opinion distribution, and changes in levels of politicization operate through political groups and governmental institutions to bring about policy change.

Individual opinion change is related to governmental policy change by linkages that transmit new or revised opinions, usually through the mediation of groups, to policy makers in such form and intensity that the policy makers are moved to change policy. A representation of individual opinion-change processes, social policy-change processes, and their linkages through elections and groups is shown in Figure 20–1. It is unnecessary to repeat the details of the opinion-change processes at the individual level, as described in an earlier section of this book. Elites are distinguished from nonelites by levels of knowledge of, interest in, and participation in public affairs. The collective evidence from field and experimental studies indicates that opinion change for elites (as compared with nonelites) will involve (a) the more accurate perception of stimuli relevant to the issue about which the opinion has been or is to be formed; (b) more detailed cognitive structuring and interpretation of the source and form of the stimuli; (c) more complex and realistic manipulation of the stimuli's meanings in terms of personality and environmental factors; (d) greater recognition of the fact of change (that is, crossing the threshold for response) when and if it occurs; and (e) more complex and multiple use of the response factors (denial, conversion, displacement, projection, rationalization, and adjustment).

In Figure 20–1, the arrows connecting *elites* and *nonelites* are meant to represent two conditions. The first is that democracy supposes, and American society in large measure provides for, free and relatively easy transition from one status to the other. Simply by increasing their knowledge, interest, and participation in political affairs, persons may move from nonelite to elite (we bear in mind, of course, that such changes are not "simply" made, but are almost always aspects of complicated and fundamental changes in education, socioeconomic

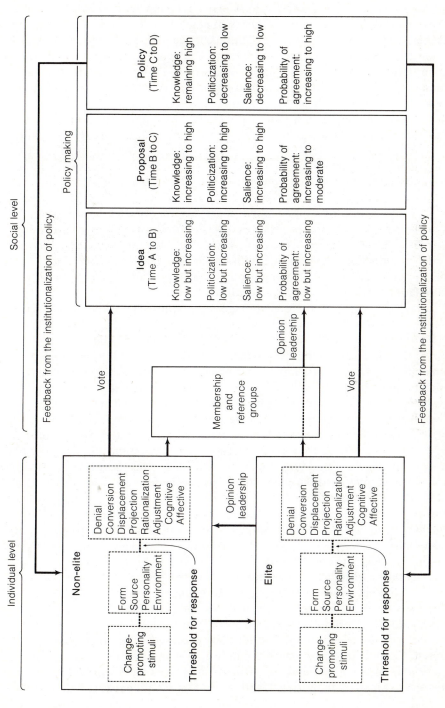

**Figure 20-1.** *Opinion change and policy change*

conditions, lifestyles, and personality). The second point actually has to do with the social rather than the individual level of analysis, but it could not be shown otherwise in the figure. It is that the opinion changes of each group influence the opinion-change processes of the other group. The nonelite acquiesce more easily in their own opinion changes if testimonials from the elite support their new opinions. The elite are strengthened in both their opinion changes and their general elite status if their opinions find ready acceptance among the nonelite.

Both elites and nonelites form, test, and revise their opinions in a dynamic and never-ending series of choices, mostly by referring to groups that are important. Reference groups—those that the individual regards as providing standards for the appropriateness and inappropriateness of opinions and attitudes—are more important than membership groups for the individual processes of opinion change. But—*and note this well*—in making the linkage from individual opinions to public policy, the policy maker must rely very heavily on the size and activity of membership groups. The reference group is a psychological fiction, a construct that helps us understand why people hold the attitudes and opinions they do, but it is not a concept or condition that can be aggregated directly for political purposes. The membership group, however, is ideally suited to policy manipulation, coalition building, and rationalization.

The obvious and immediate advantage for political life of the membership group over the reference group has two major consequences. First, it introduces considerable distortion of the true distribution of opinion. The policy maker assumes that individuals employ as reference groups those groups of which they are members. Of course, policy makers assume the existence of some idiosyncratic opinions, but they tend to believe that veterans' organizations can speak for veterans or medical societies for doctors (that is, that doctors use medical societies as reference groups on some issues). Such a presumption is undoubtedly, in a rough-and-ready way, valid for political analysis and strategy, but real opinions get distorted. The second consequence of the political importance of membership groups is that group officials and those who speak for the group become key communication channels between private individuals and policy makers. Opinion leadership becomes, then, a function not merely of elite criteria (knowledge, interest, participation) but also of position and status as recognized official or voice for a recognized group. The president of the National Education Association is elected for a one-year term. At the end of that term she is no longer the opinion leader she once was because she is no longer the chief articulator of group interests—although the pattern of reference-group attachments and real opinion of individual teachers has presumably changed little, if at all.

The lines labeled *Vote* running from elites and nonelites through groups to policy making are meant to represent more than the mere act of voting. They symbolize the linkages through the electoral processes that, on the one hand, represent the only *direct* influence the individual can have on choosing policy makers and, on the other hand, are strongly influenced and mediated by group attachments. One way of putting it is to say that opinions about candidates (and referendum issues), while formed like other opinions, internally and through reference to groups, have an additional and direct channel of expression via the ballot. It is the particular task of the political parties, as one kind of membership and reference group, to influence the vote. The political interest group (any group that seeks to serve as a reference group for individuals regarding opinions about the group's objectives) may also focus on the vote but will, more than political parties, diffuse its energies throughout all the processes shown in Figure 20-1 as it pursues its specialized policy objectives.

The large box labeled *Policy making* is a representation of the way opinions are funded, interpreted, and given meaning as policies are arrived at through legislation, executive action, and judicial action. It shows the relative changes expected in levels of knowledge, politicization, salience, and probability of agreement, as issues move from the idea stage to the proposal stage to the policy stage.

We assume that policy makers, as individuals, are subject to the same kinds of opinion-change processes as other members of the political elite, and that each individually interacts with other policy makers, as indicated in Figure 20-1. For the policy makers collectively we also assume an equilibrium model in which no change is expected unless the prochange pressures felt by the policy makers are greater (by some quantity we can call *system threshold for change*) than the antichange pressures they feel. The elements of pro- and antichange pressures are both internal and external. Internal pressures are policy makers' personal attitudes and opinions, reflecting their ideologies, personality needs, and knowledge about the issue. External pressures arise from the social institutions, group identifications, and communication networks that impinge on the policy makers and that they see as relevant to the issue under consideration.

In practice, internal and external pressures are systematically related. While the ideologies and personality needs of policy makers presumably change slowly, their opinions and votes on proposals may change suddenly with an increase in knowledge resulting from such external factors as interest-group activities or access to a communication channel previously closed. Moreover, the relationship between external and internal pressures is not one-way. The common conception of pluralistic politics is that interest groups put pressure on policy makers, but just as often policy makers actively seek the pressure of interest groups. They also place the interest groups under countervailing pressure and constraints. Policy makers look for interpretation and facts that will strengthen positions they intend to support for reasons of their own.

Finally, the arrows from *Policy making* back to the individuals represent the effect on individuals of the establishment of new or revised policy and the institutionalization of that policy in programs and bureaucratic procedures. As field programs and central bureaucratization implement new or changed policy, various individuals and groups will feel differential effects on taxation and/or service levels. These changes may then be perceived as new change-producing stimuli, bringing about new imbalance and resulting in further individual responses (adjustment, denial, and so on) and revisions of individual–group and group–group relations.

In response to changes in the opinion environment, policy makers will adjust their own thinking and behavior. Some adjustments will be of a regularized and bureaucratic nature. Change-promoting forces may have to follow prescribed forms of petition, bill drafting, and orderly progression from district to central officials; change-resisting forces will have the same or other channels of institutionalized access or influence.

Beyond the general constraints of bureaucracy, other sets of variables have significance for the processes that translate opinions into public policy. First, the influence of opinion in policy making will vary with the specific organizational context within which the decision makers operate. If the governmental agencies have elaborate and specialized services for collecting and processing information about public opinion, they are likely to pay more attention to the distribution of popular and group views on the issues at stake. Governmental agencies obviously vary in their ability and willingness to provide facilities for collecting and analyzing opinion distributions. Historically among U.S. federal agencies, the State Department and the Agriculture Department have provided more of such services for policy makers than have Interior and Defense. Most governmental agencies at state and local levels make little or no effort to provide decision makers with systematic intelligence on the distribution of opinion.[7]

Second, the time demands of the decision situation will have consequences for the opinion-policy process. If the situation is regarded as one of crisis, there will be little time to measure and weigh the distributions of opinion on the matter at hand. A crisis situation is one in which there is a short period of time to respond to a basic threat that the decision makers did not anticipate. Under such circumstances, public opinion will be less important in the decision. The development of U.S. atomic-energy policy in 1945–1946 is a case in point. The 1961 decision to block Soviet expansion in Cuba is another case in which public opinion was less influential than it was in, say, the 1948 decision to provide massive aid to European countries through the Marshall Plan.

Finally, the impact of opinions will vary with the personalities of the decision makers. Some political leaders are inclined to attach less importance to public opinion—or, if they grant its importance in policy-making processes, to show great confidence in their ability to judge it for themselves. Woodrow Wilson was not disposed to accept advice on either the importance or the status of popular or group opinions on the issues with which he was confronted as president. Presidents in more recent years, on the other hand, have seemed more inclined to pay

7. For the points made in this and the next two paragraphs we are indebted to James A. Robinson; see his statement of them in James A. Robinson and Richard C. Snyder, "Decision-Making in International Politics," in *International Behavior: A Social Psychological Analysis,* ed. Herbert C. Kelman (New York: Holt, Rinehart & Winston, 1965), pp. 435–463, especially pp. 456–458.

attention to polls, newspaper reports, and professionals who are reputed to have their "ears to the ground."

Thus these factors internal to the official government—generalized bureaucratic routinization, specialized services for reporting and assessing public opinion, crisis level of the decision situation, and personality differences of decision makers—must all be considered in the elaborated model of the opinion-policy process.

Political parties enter the opinion-policy process in two ways: first, in their efforts to determine who the officeholders will be in the official government; and second, in their efforts to mediate and resolve the conflicts among interest groups. American political parties are primarily interested in winning public office. To win public office under two-party conditions, a candidate must normally receive a clear majority of the vote. To win a clear majority of the vote, a candidate must attract from individuals and groups greater support than the opposing candidate attracts. The art of politics consists, then, in gaining and keeping a coalition of support greater then an opponent's coalition of support. Politicians and political parties are thus the policy brokers of the American democracy—softening, mediating, and reconciling the intergroup conflict, and at the same time peopling the government with legislators, executives, judges, and administrators, whose function it is to make and carry out policies that are tolerable for most groups, if perfect for none.

The above description of the function of parties is familiar to all. To represent it in Figure 20–1 is difficult, however, because the political party embraces all the elements shown there. The parties bind individuals and groups together with the official government; the party apparatuses within the government provide organization and procedures by which proposals become transformed into policy; and the parties, through their mass organizations and the communications media, provide a vital element in the feedback channels that are so important for the stability and change of opinions. The parties—to use an organic analogy—are like the lymphatic system of the human body: not separable and discrete like the lungs or heart but spread throughout the whole organism. Like the lymphatic system, the parties inform and sustain the body politic, sometimes highlighting differences but more often compromising conflict, searching out and supporting leaders who are representative, and providing channels for all who care about the continuation of the democratic dialogue.

In the end, even this more elaborate representation of the opinion-policy process, including the overlay of the party system, like all such schemas, is much too simple and anemic to catch the richness of complex human and governmental processes. For any adequate understanding of the dynamics of opinion and policy change, one must envision the varied involvement of thousands of groups and potential groups, and of tens or hundreds of thousands of individuals, some caring a lot and others not much, some with skills and resources at their command and others meagerly endowed—all initiating, responding, evaluating, calculating, and projecting their strategies toward the reduction of their grievances and the enhancement of their happiness. Such is the process of government where individuals are free to form, hold, and revise their opinions, where their opinions may be openly expressed and related to behavior, and where social institutions encourage opinion-holding individuals to participate—as their inclinations and abilities permit—in the public enterprise.

# NAME INDEX